Semper Fi, Mac

Semper Fi, Mac

LIVING MEMORIES OF THE U.S. MARINES IN WORLD WAR II

Henry Berry

QUILL
William Morrow
New York

It is the policy of William Morrow and Company, Inc., and its imprints and
affiliates, recognizing the importance of preserving what has been written, to print
the books we publish on acid-free paper, and we exert our best efforts to that end.

Library of Congress Cataloging-in-Publication Data

Berry, Henry.
    Semper fi, Mac : living memories of the U.S. Marines in World War
II / Henry Berry.
      p.   cm.
    Originally published : New York : Arbor House, © 1982.
    Includes index.
    ISBN 0-688-14956-1 (alk. paper)
    1. World War, 1939–1945—Campaigns—Pacific Ocean. 2. World War,
1939–1945—Personal narratives, American. 3. United States. Marine
Corps—Biography. I. Title.
D767.B48   1996
940.54'26—dc20   96-32779
                                                     CIP

Printed in the United States of America

First Quill Edition

8   9   10

Dedication

This book is dedicated to my mother, the late Jane Celina Berry, and to all the other mothers who received the dreaded telegram informing them that one of their sons would not return home from World War II. It left a scar on their hearts that only the grave could erase. For these mothers the war never ended.

Acknowledgments

It goes without saying that *Semper Fi, Mac* could never have been produced without the World War II Marines who freely shared their memories with me.

The following is the Henry Berry Roll of Honor:

Thomas Barry; Hank Bauer; Richard Bennett; William Berlanger; Harry Bills; George Booz; Bing Bromfield; Norris Byron; Louis Caporale; William Colligan; Vaughn Collins; Frank Cooper; Kenneth Cosbey; Joseph Crousen; Carl Dearborn; Edward DeMayo; Edward DeMar; William Donovan; James Doyle; Edward Driscoll; Louis Dubuque; Lawrence Eckwell; Don Ellis; Stan Ellis; Joseph Fater; Charles Ferree; Ben Finney; Arliss Franklin; Orville Freeman; William Getz; Samuel Griffith; Paul Guttman; Edward Harris; William Hawkins; Joseph Hendley; Joseph Horgan; William Johnson; John Keener; Keith Renstrom; Edward Landry; Augie Lepore; John L'Estrange; John Lindeman; Frank Loomis; A.W. Martin; Francis McGrath; Herbert Milke; Spencer Mosely; Richard Murtaugh; Carl Nichols; Brooke Nihart; John Nuyianes; Stan Oblachinski; Ted Pafko; Sam Petriello; Warner Pyne; Irving Reynolds; Irving Schechter; William Sellers; John Siroka; William Soren; Richard Spooner; Prate Stack; Charles Stein; Robert Stewart; Robert Stiles; Raymond Stramel; Fred Sturges; John Thompson; George Tremblay; Richard Washburn; Richard Wheeler; Robert White; William Wiggins; William Woolman; Duane Wright.

I would also like to thank many friends who aided me in locating the Marines who were so essential to my book. I owe an especially strong salute to Colonel Brooke Nihart USMC (Ret.), the Deputy Director Museums, who came through like a real tiger when it was time to secure the butts.

Anyone interested in Marine Corps history owes himself a trip to the Corps Museum at the Washington, D.C. Navy Yard. Colonel Nihart, Brigadier General Edwin Simmons, the Museum director, and the whole staff do a tremendous job.

I would also like to thank my editor, Arnold Ehrlich, for believing in *Semper Fi, Mac.* He is a nice guy, especially for a "doggie."

Above all, I owe once again a debt of gratitude to my wife for her tireless typing. It is time for her to do her own book.

Contents

About the Title

"Of course I remember Semper Fi," recalls Duane Wright, a one-time member of the 17th Engineers. "On the surface it meant, 'Pull up the ladder, I'm on board' or 'Hooray for me and you know what you.'

"But you know what it really meant was, 'Look, pal, you got to take care of yourself out here.' You might ask another Marine for a cigarette and he'd tell you, 'Semper Fi, Mac.' Then the chances are he'll give you one, but what he means is for you to try and get your own the next time. It was no picnic in the Pacific and you had to take care of yourself."

This former sergeant of Engineers is right on target. If a Marine did not take care of himself in the Pacific, he was in trouble.

Actually, there were slight variations of the expression. If you were in the 2nd Marine Division, you would probably say, "Semper Fi, Cobber"—Cobber meaning buddy in New Zealand, where the 2nd spent considerable time.

And, of course, it could also be "Semper Fi, Buddy" or "Semper Fi, Bill, George" or any other name. The point is that Marines did say "Semper Fi," and they said it from one end of the Pacific to the other.

At the Slop Chute

There is a song that tells of the Halls of Montezuma and the Shores of Tripoli. To many of those who know this song it is called the Marine Corps Hymn. But this is not actually the name of the song. The correct title is "The Marines Hymn."

And so it is with this book. It is not about the Marine Corps, not as such anyway. It is a book about Marines. The difference between the two may be a fine one, but it is there.

In reality, *Semper Fi, Mac* is an oral history based on some seventy-five personal interviews with men who have two common denominators. They all served as Marines during World War II and they all went to the Asiatic-Pacific Theater of Operations. Most of these interviews took place at that spot forever enshrined by Marines, the slop chute.

While originally there was no set pattern concerning units or battles in these interviews, it turned out that eventually I visited with at least one man who participated in each of the divisional actions in which Marines fought once the counteroffensive started at Guadalcanal on August 7, 1942. With the exception of Tarawa, where I did actually pursue a member of the 8th Marines who fought at that bloody spot, the pattern just evolved that way.

Locating the men with whom I talked was not difficult. I had done a book a few years ago in which I interviewed World War I doughboys. Here the age factor frequently made tracking down veterans a more onerous task. However, the average age of the World War II Marine—late fifties—was a plus. These veterans are not only plentiful but are normally very willing to discuss their memories of the days when they wore green skivvies.

It was not always this way. Time and time again I heard:

"Jeez, it's a funny thing, but for years I didn't want to discuss this at all. I was really pissed off about the whole thing. You know, I'd have bad dreams and all that. But now I can relax, particularly over a beer or two, and it all comes back."

I was greatly aided by the divisional reunions. I attended the reunions of the 1st, 4th and 6th Marine Divisions. These meetings accounted for about a third of my interviews.

The reunions also allowed me to obtain group interviews on two of the many especially desperate happenings of the war—King Company of the 1st Marines on the Point at Peleliu and the 2nd Battalion, 22nd Marines at Sugar Loaf Hill on Okinawa. *Semper Fi, Mac* is not necessarily about combat. After all, actual battle takes up a very small part of military service. But I believe the accounts of both the Point and Sugar Loaf Hill accurately reflect the three prevailing memories of most men in combat: confusion, thoughts of survival and that little slice of hell surrounding each man.

As my interviewing progressed, I realized that I would have to make one change in my format. Originally I had intended to include the Marine Air Corps in my book. After all, men who served in the aviation end of the Corps are certainly Marines just as much as the men who carried rifles. But after interviewing two Marine pilots, Bill Donovan and one-time All American football player Spence Moseley, I realized that the air war was a different operation altogether. They should have their own book.

But as far as the ground war is concerned, I did have good fortune in the diversification of my interviews. Riflemen, mortarmen, machine gunners and their officers, second lieutenant through captain, make up the bulk of my interviews. However, I also talked to engineers, members of artillery regiments and defense battalions, communications men, a map maker and even a Marine, Ed DeMayo, whose job was the disposal of unexploded bombs.

My interviews did not, however, cover men who performed every single function that made up a Marine operation, nor was it my intention to do so.

The one unit that I did not cover, where I am certain coverage would have added substantially to *Semper Fi, Mac*, was the Paramarines. While these men never did jump in combat, they served extensively in a role similar to that of the Raider battalions. They were disbanded halfway through the war, many of these jumpers going into the 4th Marines, while others joined the 5th Division.

And, by the way, I should point out the difference between Marines and divisions. If one means the 5th Division, he says 5th Division. If he means the 5th Regiment, he says 5th Marines. This can get somewhat confusing to one who was not a Marine. The 5th Marines were not in the 5th Division. The term Marines refers to the regiment, not the division.

As for these divisions, I talked with at least five men who served in each of the six divisions of the Corps during the war. Purely by chance my interviews with men of the 1st Marine Division greatly outnumbered my visits with men of other divisions. This was not intentional; it just happened that way.

The age mix of the Marines with whom I worked started at fifty-four (in 1981) and went through age eighty-two. But only two of these men were over seventy when I visited them. The mean age was fifty-seven, which is low for World War II veterans. But a tremendous number of Marines went into the Corps between the ages of seventeen and eighteen. Two of the men I talked with acknowledged that they entered the Marines before their seventeenth birthday.

I did hope to contact Marines who represented every section of the United States and in this I succeeded. The men I interviewed were raised in twenty-six of the then forty-eight states of the Union.

In their postwar careers, these Marines also covered a rather diversified spectrum. I talked with bankers, taxi drivers, company presidents, policemen, advertising executives, salesmen, carpenters, restauranteurs, construction workers, machinists and, of course, six men who were USMC (ret.).

One of the most interesting aspects of these conversations were the constant references to growing up during the Depression, the days when a Big Little Book cost a dime and movies, not television, were the big things. My last interview occurred on the day after a seventy-one-year-old actress named Virginia Bruce had died. Mog-Mog Martin, the man I was interviewing at the time, and I both agreed that while Virginia may not have been a Sarah Bernhardt, she truly was beautiful. Apparently, we both had experienced teenage fantasies about Miss Bruce in the 1930s.

Mr. Martin could also recite the lineup of the Newark Bears in 1937. This well might have been the greatest minor league baseball team ever assembled. Mog-Mog had seen them play whenever he could scrape up the price of a bleacher seat.

For those who enjoy studying the personalities of men, almost all of these Marines were interested in sports, with baseball and football the most popular. Many of them also showed an interest in professional boxing, but the period they were interested in was when the previous week's major bout was part of the newsreel at the local theater. Very little interest was shown in today's fight scene.

A real insight into this interest in sports is the fact that twenty-four of these men listened to a professional football game on December 7, 1941; two of them were actually attending such a game when they heard about the Japanese attack.

But in each of my interviews, the conversation would always get back to the Pacific and the brutal, dehumanizing thing the Marines' war had actually been. The Bushido code of the Japanese does not recognize surrender. On many occasions men told me of witnessing a cornered Japanese soldier who would calmly pull out a hand grenade and blow himself to kingdom come. When a Marine division assaulted a Japanese island that was garrisoned by 10,000 hostile troops, most of these Japanese would be dead when the battle was over. The rest would be hiding out somewhere in the brush. The mop-up of the enemy could sometimes be as nasty as the battle itself.

One of the things of which I became acutely aware as my interviews progressed was the repetition. Naval shelling was always worse than an aerial attack; the food situation on Guadalcanal was abominable; everywhere in the Solomons harbored malaria-carrying mosquitoes; it rained constantly on New Britain, Bougainville and around Naha on Okinawa; Iwo Jima was a nightmare where the big hope was for a "Hollywood" wound that could get one out of that hellhole.

Then there were the cases of seasickness. There were always men who would vomit on the transports. But the worst cases were on the assault crafts going in. These boats would frequently cruise around the transports for hours before going in to shore. Half the Marines would be so sick by the time they hit the beach that they would storm Hades to get off those boats.

Above all, these men talked about their buddies. Some of their friends made it and some did not. Whatever, they are all remembered. The memories of men dead almost forty years will be fresh as long as their friends who came home are alive.

My greatest concern was how to handle the U.S. Army. Many Marines talk with great respect about such outfits as the 164th Infantry and the 77th, 81st, and 96th Army Divisions. There are other Army outfits these Marines do not think too highly of. And, of course, in all probability the U.S. Army feels the same about the various Marine divisions.

The fact remains that of the nine major Marine battles there were only two (Tarawa and Iwo Jima) where Army divisions did not fight alongside the Marines.

Semper Fi, Mac does not state the Marines won the Pacific War. But it is a book about Marines, not a history of that war. This book does not then dwell long on the part played in the Pacific by the other services.

My biggest regret is that I could not employ the material I was given by many of the Marines I interviewed. It was extremely difficult to decide which interviews would turn into major sections. In several cases it practically got down to the flip of a coin. One could write another book using material that does not appear in *Semper Fi, Mac*.

The following short synopsis of what the Marines did in the Pacific will probably be of help to many readers as they continue into the heart of the book, the interviews with the men who were there.

The Marines' War

Over four decades have gone by since the Japanese attack on Pearl Harbor catapulted the United States into World War II and precipitated the war the Marine Corps had been waiting for since its inception in 1775. The awesome expanse of the Pacific Ocean with its multitude of Japanese-held islands called overwhelmingly for amphibious landings, a battle tactic that has always been a Corps specialty.

As a matter of fact, in the early Twenties a brilliant Marine officer, Lieutenant Colonel Earl (Pete) Ellis, drew up a plan specifying what the United States would be forced to do in order to defeat the Japanese empire in a war that Ellis was convinced was coming.

According to Marine Corps historians this plan was uncanny in its accuracy. Parts of it were actually used by the Corps twenty years later in the war that Ellis had predicted but had not lived to see. In 1923 he tried to inspect some of the once German-controlled islands that had been mandated to the Japanese after World War I. One of the stipulations of the mandate was that Japan could not fortify the islands, something that they went right ahead and did anyway.

It would appear that Ellis found out about these fortifications, as he died suddenly on his inspection trip and was cremated by the Japanese. Whatever the cause of Pete's death, both the Marine Corps and the United States in general owe Colonel Ellis a debt of gratitude.

During the Thirties, it became more and more apparent that the U.S. and Japan were on a collision course. There was not much money available at this time for military spending, but the Marine Corps managed to continue to practice assault landings. It took Colonel Ellis's plan very seriously, even if the U.S. Navy did not.

The part of Ellis's plan that apparently the Navy ridiculed the most was the one predicting a sneak Japanese aerial attack on the Americans' Pacific Fleet. It was, of course, just such an attack that started the Pacific war.

Marines fought at Pearl Harbor, on Wake Island and a small detachment was captured on Guam. The 4th Marines, the regiment of the old China hands, was moved from China to the Philippines in

November 1941. After Corregidor fell in May 1942, the Marines burned their regimental colors. Their colonel, Sam Howard, lamented, "My God, I'm the first Marine officer to surrender a regiment." One hopes that someone told the good colonel that you really don't use the word "surrender" when you have nothing left to fight with.

But while the old-line regulars were fighting for their lives in the Philippines, the Marine Corps was gearing up in the United States. The heroic stand on Wake Island introduced the Marine Corps to a generation of Americans who flocked to the recruiting offices as never before in Corps history.

Then there was a film titled *To the Shores of Tripoli*. Its plot was rather routine. It was the old conflict between the young, rich know-it-all and the stalwart drill instructor. But it painted a picture of the Corps that appealed to young Americans, many of whom heard "The Marines Hymn" for the first time when they saw the film. *To the Shores of Tripoli* would never win an Oscar, but it deserves accolades for its timeliness in producing a tremendous shot in the arm for Marine Corps recruitment.

Whatever the reasons, the Marine boot camps at Parris Island and San Diego were loaded to the brim. The two understrength Marine divisions, the 1st on the East Coast and the 2nd on the West Coast, were quickly filling up. For the first time in its history, the Corps was getting ready to go into combat in divisional strength.

The goal, of course, was to get as many of these men to the Pacific as quickly as possible. The Japanese movements into areas like Burma could not be stopped by the Americans nor could anything be done for the struggling troops in the Philippines. But the Pacific area is a huge mass of ocean, loaded with islands, atolls, archipelagoes and even a subcontinent. The more island areas that could be denied the Japanese, the easier it would be to start the inevitable Allied counteroffensive.

So the Marines started to leave the United States for the Pacific. First it was detachments, headed for defense battalions whose job was to be ready in case the Japanese attempted to swallow up more places like Wake Island.

Then came the single regiment movements and, finally, in May of 1942 the 1st Marine Division, minus its 7th Marines who were already in Samoa, left for New Zealand, where they were slated for several months of extensive training before assaulting one of the Japanese-held islands.

They never did get that extensive training. There is a great story about Franklin Knox, the Secretary of the Navy, having breakfast with a high-ranking admiral, who informed Knox that the Japanese were building an airfield on an island called Guadalcanal at the southern end of the Solomon Islands.

"Great!" Knox is supposed to have exclaimed. "Let them build it and we'll move in and take it." Or so the story goes anyway.

At any rate, Major General Alexander Archer Vandegrift was informed that in July 1942 his 1st Division, reinforced by Marine Raiders, Paramarines and the 2nd Marines, were to invade Guadalcanal and some neighboring smaller islands.

Vandegrift was aghast. A large part of his division was still on the high seas. His pleas of unreadiness earned him a short reprieve until August 7 but no longer. The Marine part of the Allied counteroffensive was to start with a division whose commanding officer was convinced that in no way was it ready for a major assault.

Then, good luck entered the picture. The Japanese were not expecting such an attack. When the Marines stormed ashore on what was soon to be called the Canal or just the Island, they were unopposed. A perimeter of some five miles long and three miles wide, including a partially built airstrip, was quickly established. In spite of having what their general considered insufficient training and carrying a good deal of World War I equipment, the Marines had landed and, as it were, the situation was well in hand.

But then, as several Marine veterans told me, the stuff hit the fan. The Japanese Navy, Air Force and Army made their appearance and one of the truly decisive battles of World War II was joined. Before it was over, the 1st Division's 7th Marines would come to the Canal from Samoa and all three infantry regiments of the 2nd Marine Division, the 2nd, 6th and 8th Marines, would see action, as would thousands of American soldiers.

And the battle would not be waged only on the Canal; the naval actions in the surrounding waters would be many and constant. The Navy experienced more surface-to-surface action there than in the rest of the war put together. In a sea war that was basically dominated by carrier-based planes, the actions off the Canal produced what will undoubtedly remain as the last large-scale surface–sea battles of military history.

In any case, when the shooting at Guadalcanal was over, the scene was set for the Marines to start their island-hopping campaign that would end on the island of Okinawa three hundred or so miles off Japan.

After Guadalcanal a Marine division did not go into action until November 1, 1943, when the 3rd Division went ashore on Bougainville on the opposite end of the Solomon Islands from Guadalcanal. Marine Raider battalions had seen action in the central islands of the Solomons, but not divisions.

From Bougainville on, however, the Marine divisional assaults occurred constantly.

On November 21, 1943, the 2nd Division, united as a divisional force after Guadalcanal, suffered its short but horrible bloodbath at tiny Betio, a Tarawa atoll of the Gilbert Islands.

A little over a month later the 1st Division, after a long rest in Australia, went ashore at Cape Gloucester on New Britain Island. During this campaign the 1st fought under the control of Douglas MacArthur. The Navy had a hell of a time getting the Marines back after their part in the battle was over.

At the beginning of 1944 a new Marine division, the 4th, appeared on the scene. Starting with the Marshall Islands it would fight in three campaigns (Saipan-Tinian is counted as one action) and suffer casualties second only to the 1st Division as listed in the Marine Corps Roll of Honor.

In contrast to the 1st and 2nd Divisions, and to a lesser extent the 3rd, the 4th Division would have a noticeably smaller percentage of pre-Pearl Harbor Marines in its ranks.

After the Marshalls the 4th would set up its base on Maui in the Hawaiian Islands. It would team up with the 2nd Division which, much to their tearful regret, had not returned to their original camp on New Zealand after Tarawa. For the first time in Marine Corps history, two full Marine divisions would go into combat side by side. The place they assaulted on June 15, 1944, was Saipan, an island in the Marianas.

Another novel experience awaited the Marine Corps on Saipan. This island had a sizable Japanese civilian population, something the Marines had not previously encountered.

But the island also had many thousands of crack Japanese troops. The well-known, and frequently maligned, Marine Corps public relations crews never could properly get this fact across to the American public, which was more concerned with the progress of the Allied troops who had landed on Normandy nine days before the assault on Saipan. Along with Peleliu, which came three months later, the bloody victory on Saipan never received its just due from the American media.

When things started to quiet down some on Saipan, both the 2nd and 4th Divisions figured they were due for a rest, but it didn't turn out that way. These men were quickly sent to the island of Tinian, a few miles off Saipan.

Now, Tinian is frequently called the perfect campaign. Not only did things seem to fall in place as they should but the casualty list was small. Perhaps so. But four of the seventy-five men I interviewed were wounded on Tinian. Whenever Marines had to kill Japanese soldiers, the Corps would suffer casualties.

While the action was occurring on Saipan, the 3rd Marine Division was having a miserable time aboard ship while they were held in reserve.

Along with the 3rd Division, in this unenvied position of waiting to go into action, was a new outfit, the 1st Provisional Brigade.

While this brigade was indeed brand new, its two regiments were not. One, the 22nd, had arrived on Samoa in September of 1942 in time to relieve the 7th Marines so that outfit could join the 1st Division on Guadalcanal. The 22nd had experienced its baptism in combat with the 4th Division in the Marshall Island campaign. It probably also suffered the highest rate of filariasis (mu-mu) of any regiment in the Corps.

The other regiment in the brigade was the resurrected 4th Marines, who had burned their colors on Corregidor. Made up primarily of one-time Raiders—the Raiders were disbanded early in 1944—the 4th was loaded with combat veterans.

The 3rd Division and the brigade invaded the former American possession of Guam on July 21, 1944. Once again, the Marines were forced to kill thousands of Japanese in order to take over an island, but now it was a little different. There was great gratification in recapturing an island whose inhabitants were American citizens.

It was also the last island where the Marines witnessed a senseless banzai charge. While the accusations that these charges were performed by Japanese heavily fortified with alcohol were usually exaggerated, there can be little doubt that the Japs who charged on Guam did include a great many drunken soldiers. Whatever, Guam would be the last place where the enemy would waste its strength in suicidal charges.

The defeats suffered by the Japanese in the Marianas and the accompanying Japanese naval losses, including the famous "Turkey Shoot," sealed any possible hopes of a Japanese victory. Tojo's government fell in Tokyo as the enemy attempted any move that could stave off total Japanese destruction. But for the Marine Corps, three more islands remained, islands whose grim toll of casualties would outnumber the Corps's losses to date in the war.

The first of these would be the island of Peleliu, six miles long and two miles wide, in the Palau group. The 1st Division assaulted the island on September 15, 1944. The cost in Marine blood in taking Peleliu was so staggering that controversy will always surround this campaign.

First, why was only one Marine division assigned to this battle? Peleliu offered an incredible obstacle to even such a crack unit as the 1st Division.

Then comes the challenge that will always accompany a fight quite as horrifying as Peleliu. Did the island really have to be invaded at all? The reason given for the assault was that an enemy-held Peleliu would constitute a direct threat to MacArthur's coming invasion of the Philippines, a statement that in itself is open to question.

Necessary or not, Peleliu was invaded and taken but not without yoeman's service from the 81st (Wildcat) Division of the U.S. Army. Trying to find a rifleman from the original assault group of the 1st, 5th and 7th Marines who was not wounded on Peleliu is a difficult task.

By January 1, 1945, the Marine part in the final defeat of Japan has been mapped out.

First would come the capture of a volcanic island which was six hundred or so miles southeast of Japan proper. It was named Iwo Jima. The Navy's boast of shelling this "evil, little island" into nothingness had been said about so many other places that it begs description to think it would be believed. But then again, one is inclined to believe what he wants to believe and obviously assault troops want to believe that they face an easy campaign.

At any rate, it is difficult to imagine anything that could produce more raw terror than the four weeks spent by the 5th Marine Amphibious Corps on Iwo Jima. There is no need for me to elaborate on what actually happened here. Men who fought on Iwo are heard from in this book. There is only to say that the Corps suffered more casualties on Iwo than in any other battle in Marine Corps history.

There were some 23,000 Japanese soldiers on Iwo Jima; over 22,000 of them were killed. The Marine units that first went ashore on February 19 were the 4th and 5th Divisions. Iwo was the only fight the 5th Division fought and the saddest part may be the fact that the 5th's three infantry regiments, the 26th, 27th and 28th Marines, were loaded with men on their second tour of duty in the Pacific.

Two infantry regiments of the 3rd Division, the 9th and 21st Marines, also went ashore on Iwo. Their losses are right in line with those suffered by the 4th and 5th Marine Divisions. There was no place to hide on Iwo.

Immediately following the action on Iwo, the 3rd Marine Amphibious Corps assaulted the island of Okinawa. Now the Americans were only 300 miles from Japan itself.

The 3rd Corps consisted of the veteran 1st and 2nd Divisions and the newly formed 6th Division. The 6th had been made up of the two regiments of the 1st Provisional Brigade, the 4th and 22nd Marines and the 29th Marines.

The role of the 2nd Division in the battle of Okinawa will always remain a mystery. Perhaps the Corps realized that the three divisions from Iwo Jima needed a rest and regrouping before they would be fit for further action; and with the 1st and 6th Divisions already committed on Okinawa, they wanted to keep a division ready for instant action.

At any rate, only the 8th Marines of the 2nd Division went into Okinawa and they did not land until June 15.

However, the 1st and 6th Divisions did go ashore on April Fools' Day, 1945. At first the campaign was a lark. Then they moved south. What followed was the equal of many of the other incredibly ferocious battles experienced by the Corps during the war. Once again, I'll let the men who fought on Okinawa describe the campaigns themselves.

I should point out one more thing about this final campaign. Okinawa was the closest thing to a land mass battle in which Marine divisions participated. The Japanese force on Okinawa numbered roughly, 100,000 men, the large majority of whom were on the southern end of the island.

Four Army divisions also fought and suffered tremendously on Okinawa. It was the largest joint Marine and Army campaign of the war, but like everything else in the Pacific War, it would have been dwarfed by the third campaign that was being planned. This, of course, was Olympic, the invasion of Japan itself. Fortunately, its designated date, November 1945, found Marine troops already on occupational duty in both Japan and China. Atomic might was unleashed against Japan. The war that had started on a Sunday morning nearly four years before on the island of Oahu was over.

Now—

"READY ON THE RIGHT,
READY ON THE LEFT,
READY ON THE FIRING LINE,
COMMENCE FIRING!"

The Old Breed

Joseph Crousen
Francis McGrath

Did Dan Daly truly say to a company of Marines at Belleau Wood:
"Come on, you sons of bitches, do you want to live forever?"

Did Lou Diamond really put a mortar shell down the stack of a
Japanese destroyer off Guadalcanal?

In reality, who cares? The importance of these two legends is not
their validity—it's the part they play in the mystique of the Marine
Corps, something that has been with the Corps since its inception at
Tun Tavern, Philadelphia, in 1775.

The mystique is passed on from generation to generation by the
small group of Marines known as the professionals, the Captain
Flaggs and Sergeant Quirks of the Corps. These are the men who are
always used as the foundation for a greatly expanded Marine Corps
made up of civilians who turn into wartime Marines.

While attending a reunion of the 1st Marine Division at Kansas
City, Missouri, I had the good fortune to visit with two of these old
salts.

One of them was a former Marine warrant officer by the name of
Joe Crousen. He had left Woodson, Texas, to enlist in the Corps in
1925. He comes right to the point when asked why he enlisted.

"Ah'll tell you why ah signed up," recalls Joe. "By Gawd, ah was
hungry, that's why! Someone had told me Marine food was pretty
damn good. Ah must have liked it, ah ate it for twenty-five years."

Joe's buddy, Sergeant Major (ret.) Francis McGrath, originally from
Worcester, Massachusetts, joined up for a similar reason.

"My mother," said McGrath, "God rest her soul, died in that goddamn flu epidemic of 1918. She had come from Ireland. Dad did his
best to raise our family on twenty-five dollars a week, but it was rough
as hell, even in those days.

"I knew a man then named Dan Malloy," Mac continued, "who
had been in France with the 6th Marines during what we used to call

the Great War. Dan told me all about how outstanding the Marine Corps was.

"Well, I reached age eighteen in 1927. There was no Social Security or anything like it back in those days. I decided to go into the Marine Corps and stay there until I retired. That way, I'd never be a burden to anybody and I'd always have a damn roof over my head."

Francis stayed in the Corps for thirty-two years.

During their period on active duty, these two men saw their beloved Corps climb from a complement of fifteen thousand to a World War II figure of half a million. But the change in the Corps was a great deal more than just numbers.

"When I joined up," says McGrath, "it was something like a club. Hell, if you stayed in long enough, you eventually seemed to get to know all the other career men."

And that is what my meeting with Joe and Mac was all about. I wanted them to tell me about that period between the wars when the Corps was something like a club, with special emphasis on the men they served with.

Today, tremendous advancements in technology and sweeping changes in America's foreign policy have changed the roles played by Marines like Joe Crousen and Francis McGrath. But the old campaigner types are still there. Without them it wouldn't be the same Marine Corps.

WARRANT OFFICER JOSEPH CROUSEN
SERGEANT MAJOR FRANCIS MCGRATH

"Hell, you think this is something, you should have been in the old Corps!"

—Traditional Marine saying

Mac: Let me tell you one thing—the Marine Corps didn't get all their brains out of Annapolis. Plenty of the old-line sergeants were as smart as any commissioned officers. They were the ones who ran the Corps. And plenty of our officers came up through the ranks anyway.

Joe: Oh, we sure had some smart ole boys in the ranks, no doubt about that. Why, take Bill Whaling—he was the 1st Marines' colonel at Cape Gloucester—he came up through the ranks.

Mac: I think he did at that. And I don't think Gerry Thomas went to Annapolis. Most of us felt Thomas was Vandegrift's brains on Guadalcanal.

Joe: Of course, all the enlisted men weren't no geniuses. We had a PFC by the name of Deacon Jones and so help me Gawd, the ole

Deacon had twenty-eight years in the Corps and he was still a PFC. Can you beat that? You remember the Deacon, don't you, Francis?

Mac: Oh, Christ, the Deacon! You could put Jones in the Sahara Desert and he'd find some booze before the night was over.

Joe: That was his problem. When he'd make corporal, he'd go out and get a snootful. Then he'd tell all the officers to go to the devil—he'd lose that second stripe every time.

Mac: God, no one could tell off the officers like the Deacon. Tell us how he gave the word to Sam Gould.

Joe: Well, that was down in Nicaragua back around '26 or so. We were chasing them Sandinistas. Lieutenant Walter, who is dead now, was in charge and we had another officer by the name of Samuel Gould.

Anyway, we run into an ambush. Then, ole Deacon—he was hell in a fight—he just took over. Did everything right. There was never no messing around with the Deacon when them bullets started to fly. Hell, I don't think we had a single casualty, thanks to Jones.

That evening we camped over near a town called Jicaro. Lieutenant Gould, he figured he better give us a pep talk, so he gathered us all around him.

"Men, I'm damn proud of you," he said. "First time under fire for many of you and you done real good. And the Deacon here, why he's a real tiger. Going to make you a corporal in the morning, Deacon. And, goddamn it, keep the second stripes this time. Don't get falling-down drunk and make an ass out of yourself."

Why, hell, we was just about bedded down for the night when Gould gave us his little pep talk, but somehow Jones got ahold of some of that fermented sugar cane juice they had down there. Think they called it Guiro. Hell, you could blow stumps with it!

So, old Deacon, he got all lit up and he staggers into Gould's tent.

"Lieutenant," he roars, "you're a good Marine, but you're a god-damn officer and there's no getting away from it!"

Well, that was the end of his being corporal. And that was the way of it with the Deacon.

Mac: And that's the way it was in Nicaragua. They had to stop selling bay rum and Aqua Velva. Some of those old-timers would drink it and get in a hell of a mess. Remember, we had a lot to do down there other than go blind drinking a bunch of crap.

Joe: Yeah, we was suppose to be chasing that ole devil, César Sandino.

Mac: And we did. But, you know that guy Sandino, he got all the PR, but I think the man calling the shots was that old bandito, Pedro Altamiro—he was the head honcho.

Sandino, you see, he'd been to the States for an education. He was a smoothie. But Altamiro, he was the real power. He'd been living off the countryside for thirty years. He'd just as soon stick you in an anthill as look at you. He was real bad news.

Joe: Yeah, but no one remembers old Pedro, just Sandino.

Mac: But there is one thing *I* can remember. I can remember almost every officer I served under, some good, some not so good. Remember H. H. Hanneken—we used to call him Hot-Headed Hanneken. He ended up with the 7th Marines on Peleliu. He was a typical example of an enlisted Marine who got himself a commission in one of those constabularies—I think Hot-Headed got his in Haiti—and then got a regular Marine Corps commission. Lewie Puller did the same thing. A great many of our top officers in the Pacific served somewhere south of the border between wars.

Joe: That's true, but many of them officers we had in the Twenties and Thirties were too old for World War II. Remember all them captains in their fifties. Gawd Almighty, it was nothing to see an officer retire at sixty or so as a major or even a captain. Some of those old boys should have been on crutches.

Mac: Well, there was just no money floating around the Corps then. Hell, we only had two or three brigadier generals or above at the same time.

Joe: That's right. Now, you called Hanneken old Hot-Headed. Them nicknames was something! Once you got one, it stayed with you.

Mac: You're damn right. Remember Haircut Charlie Lyman?

Joe: Hell yes, C. H. Lyman. We turned around his first two initials and came up with Haircut Charlie. This was 'cause he'd walk around with a rule and measure your hair. If it was too long, why, he was 'bout to run your ass up.

And if he caught you with your hands in your pocket, he just might make you sew up those pockets. Oh, he was a lulu!

Mac: Then there was Hair Trigger Hollingsworth and Dirty Neck Roselle. Hair Trigger, he'd blow his top in a second and Dirty Neck, he figured if you had a dirty neck, you were a lousy Marine.

Joe: Now, that Roselle was something! One night when he was in command of the Marines at the Portsmouth Navy Yard, he and his ole lady was walking their dog, Pomp-Pomp. This sentry, he had a bottle on his hip and been nipping on it.

So he yells out:

"Who goes there?"

"Colonel and Mrs. Roselle, walking their dog."

Then the sentry says:

"Colonel Roselle, advance and be recognized."

Then, it's:

"Mrs. Roselle, advance and be recognized."

Finally:

"Pomp-Pomp, advance and be recognized."

That story sure spread throughout the Corps. Ah always figured that little old Pomp-Pomp probably saluted. After all, it was ole Dirty Neck's dog.

Mac: Don't forget Major Taylor. We knew him in China. T. T. Taylor. Naturally we called him Tough Titty Taylor.

Joe: Naturally.

Mac: And that's what it was if you got nailed by Taylor for anything —Tough Titty.

Joe: Oh, that China station, that was really great duty. Ah had two tours out there. Well, they had a kinda German combination delicatessen-saloon in Peking with a meat counter at the front and a restaurant in the back. It was run by an ole German named Pa Hempel.

Mac: Oh yeah, what a spot, over on Hatamen Street. You could buy the best meat in China there. They had a big red pig sign hanging near the door and 'neath it they had written: *You can't beat Hempel's meat on Hatamen Street.* The boys got a huge laugh out of that one.

Joe: That backroom, that's where we used to go and drink our beer, or something else if we was flush.

They had this long table that became famous all over the Corps. If you became a regular customer, you was apt to become a member of their Knights of the Round Table, but you had to drink down this huge ole stein of beer without stoppin'—

Mac: Wait a minute, what about the dance?

Joe: Right. Yuh had to strip down to your skivvies and do a hoochie-koochie dance on the table. By the time you did this, you was so full of beer you didn't care what all yuh did.

Mac: Once you were in the club, they'd put a silver-plated tag with your name on it in the table. When you died, they'd change it to a gold-plated tag. They used to get the *Leatherneck* magazine every month so they could keep track of which men had left us.

Joe: We was always having Marines passing in and out of Peking and most of 'em would come over and check the table. If they saw a new gold-plated tag, they'd usually give a sigh.

"Well, poor ole so-and-so has gone west; let's drink him a toast," they'd say.

After the first toast, there'd be another and another. Didn't make no difference if they figured the dead guy was a SOB or not, they'd toast him anyway.

Mac: One of the men who used to come in there was a character named Muscle Belly Christner. He had this big gut you could hit with all your might but it wouldn't bother old Muscle Belly.

He had a habit we used to laugh like hell at. You see, he'd come into Hempel's and eat all the goldfish they used to have swimming in this big bowl. So, everytime they spotted Christner coming, someone would pass the word:

"Here comes Muscle Belly; hide the goldfish."

It got so he'd try and sneak in, but it would be hard not to spot that gut of his.

Joe: Don't forget ole Chicken Bone.

Mac: Jeez, the guy who got the chicken bone caught in his rear end. He stayed in China after he got out of the Corps. He used to go to Hempel's a lot and drink that good beer.

Well, everyone lost track of Chicken Bone after the war started. Then, after the Nips surrendered and the Marines went back to China, who comes out of the woodwork but Chicken Bone. A bunch of old-timers took him out to dinner and what does he ask for but a dozen fresh eggs.

Joe: That sounds like Chicken Bone. He'd never eat any of the caviar there at Hempel's, even though it cost so little. Said he liked chicken eggs better.

Mac: That's right. He used to say the only good eggs came out of a chicken.

Joe: Ah'll tell you one officer I remember from China because he was such a straight shooter. Old John Thomason, the writer—wrote that great book *Fix Bayonets*.

Mac: No, he wrote *Salt Winds and Gobi Desert*.

Joe: No, goddamn it—he wrote *Fix Bayonets*. [Author's note: I pointed out to the old salts that Thomason had written both these excellent books.]

Joe: Well, Thomason, he was my captain then, called me in one day.

"Crousen," he says, "you've been over here too long. If you stay much longer, your eyes will start to slant—hell, you'll look like a Chinaman. Ah'm going to send you back to the States."

"Oh hell, captain, don't do that. Ah'm next on the list to make sergeant. You see, if ah went to another lashup back in the States, I'd have to go to the bottom of the list for making sergeant."

"All right, all right," he says. "We're going to make a sergeant next month—you'll get it. But after you get that extra stripe, goddamn it, you pack your sea bag—you're going home!"

And that's how I made buck sergeant. I think it was in '38. I guess I was just about the youngest sergeant in the Corps.

Mac: That's probably right. In '31, when I came back to the Brooklyn Navy Yard, we had a buck sergeant named Charley Dowd. He'd made sergeant in 1909—can you believe that—a buck sergeant in 1909 and *still* one in 1931?

Joe: Yeah, well, money was real scarce in them days. Why the only time I was run up for office hours was for stealing coal—I mean for stealing coal from one barracks to heat another barracks. Hell, it was all the same Marine Corps, wasn't it? Thank Gawd we had this great first sergeant, old Red Hale, or I might have gone to the brig.

This happened down at Quantico. Being still a private then, I had the fire patrol. We had these ole pot belly stoves to keep us warm and I had to see it kept goin'. Well, we ran out of coal this night, so I went to Sergeant Hale.

"Sergeant," I said, "we ain't got no coal left and it's colder than Alaska."

"All right, Crousen," he answered, "go over to the next barracks' coal bin and git some."

Well, blazes, I does what he says and I'm shoveling the coal into this coal bucket and this sentry comes over and sticks his '03 in my face.

"Stealing coal, huh," he snarls. "I'm running your ass up."

So I goes up in front of old Colonel Gulick.

Mac: Gulick, he had a son, Lieutenant Ray Gulick, used to stutter. I served under him in China—used to say ah-t-t-t-t-tention!

Joe: Don't remember the son, but I was real scared of ole Colonel Gulick. First Sergeant Hale showed up and told my side of the case. I guess they all thought it was funny, but not me. They didn't do nuthin' to me about it though, 'cept tell me not to steal any more coal.

Mac: You were lucky they didn't fine you a month's pay. We were hardly making any money to speak of as it was. Look how small the pots were in most of the poker games. Yet, a private could be broke for weeks if he had a streak of bad luck.

Small as those pots were, though, the men played for keeps. I can remember one of the games that Tony the Greek used to talk about when they caught a guy cheating. He had hidden a card in a sandwich he was supposed to be eating—don't know where the hell he got the sandwich. Anyway, they really kicked the shit out of the guy.

Joe: Tony the Greek. Wasn't he the Marine who retired after thirty years and went back to Greece for a long visit?

Mac: That's right. His real name was Anthony Marcus, but everywhere he went in the Corps they called him Tony the Greek.

Then he goes over to Greece and everyone thinks he's a rich American. *Mr.* Marcus, *Mr.* Marcus, that's what they called him in Greece. Tony began to think he was a big wheel.

Then he returned to the States and stopped over to the Brooklyn Navy Yard to say hello. Naturally, it started all over again.

"Tony the Greek, Tony the Greek," that's what everyone says to him. It took the wind out of poor Tony's sails all right.

Joe: Tony was something, all right! But the character I really recall was the Medal of Honor man, Louie Cukela. Hell, he could hardly speak English. I heard he actually joined up in Europe. I know he was born over there anyway. I could hardly understand him; he had such a thick accent.

"If Louie vant ze damn fool go fer ze mail, he go hisself," he used to say.

Mac: Oh, I could understand the old SOB. He was our, whatyoucallit, supply sergeant in Quantico. I walked in on him one day when he was tearing pages out of the *Marine Corps Manual*.

"No need zis page," he would say, and rip it out. "It not Louie's vay to do zis."

He didn't do things any way but Louie's way.

Joe: Yeah, but he sure was one hell of a Marine. He got himself the Medal of Honor by cleaning out some German machine gun nests with just a bayonet—think it was at Belleau Wood.

Mac: Then there was old Gimlet Eye, Major General Smedley Butler, a truly great Marine and one hell of a character.

Joe: He was that.

One night in that big recreation hall at Quantico, Smedley made a speech to a packed hall—some of the men even had their wives there.

"Now, ah'm a-going to talk to my men tonight. Any of you ladies don't want to hear Marine talk, you better git the hell out!"

Not a one left.

Then he started pickin' at his nose and scratchin' his rear end.

Mac: Oh, I'm sure about that; Smedley couldn't make a speech without scratchin'.

Tell me, Joe, you made platoon sergeant at Quantico in '40—right?

Joe: Yes, I had thirteen years in at the time. I remember walkin' into the NCO club there and seein' all these buck-ass sergeants with hash marks up and down their sleeves. Plenty of 'em had lots of time on me. I had to git the hell outa there—thought they was going to whip the hell outa me.

Mac: Oh, you were a boot to some of those men. Well, I made buck sergeant at the same time. You had to have that third stripe to have a car on the base. So, I dashed over to Stratford, Virginia, and bought me a brand new Plymouth for $842.

Christ, I thought I was really something! So, I drove the Plymouth over to the NCO club to have a couple of drinks.

Now, Joe, do you remember Shorty Smallwood at Quantico?

Joe: Why hell yes, Shorty and his ole lady lived next to us there.

Mac: Well, while I was in the club, Shorty's wife drove her car into the side of my new Plymouth, tore one of my fenders right off. Was she upset!

"Oh my, oh my," she was saying and sobbing at the same time. "Who owns the new car I just hit?"

"I do," I told her.

"Thank God, it's yours, Francis," she said. "At least we know you!"

All of which didn't do my car any good. Anyway, I got it fixed and started sporting it around the base.

Now, Joe, do you remember Lou Diamond?

Joe: Why that sly ole devil, of course I do.

Mac: Well, every time Lou saw me driving by, he'd grunt out: "Quantico's playboy—Quantico's playboy—big *deal!*"

He had that real deep voice, you know. But, Christ, could he drink that beer. Wow!

Lou's long dead now—came from Cleveland, Ohio. And what a bird! He used to go to Washington, D.C., and keep drinking beer until he couldn't move. They'd lock him up, then send him back to Quantico.

Joe: Well, goddamn it, you know Lou was a mortar man and I was a machine gunner. When Lou and me was in H Company, I was running the Company, not Lou. But I don't think he knew it. Hell, we didn't have any officers knew machine guns like I did. I would have stayed on machine guns 'cept the war came along.

After the Japs hit Pearl Harbor, this gunner, name of Dusty Hughes, he was a tank man, got ahold of us.

"Joe," he said, "you come over to the tanks. We ain't got no one who knows beans about machine guns on the tanks."

So, I went over to the tanks and spent the whole war on 'em.

Mac: That's right. You were with tanks on the Canal. I was with the 1st Marines there. But war or no war, we kept bumping into the old-timers.

For instance, Al Pollock. He had the 2nd Battalion of the 1st Marines there on Guadalcanal when the Japs hit us on the Tenaru River. It was Al's battalion that did such a great job, particularly the machine gunners like Al Schmidt, during that fight.

Well, hell, I first served under Pollock when I had sea duty on the *S.S. Salt Lake City,* the queen of the seas, back in the Thirties.

Then I drew duty at the Mare Island Naval Prison and so did Pollock—he was a captain then and one hell of a fine officer.

Our major there was old Tough Titty Taylor, who I'd known in China. I remember that Taylor sometimes thought Pollock was a little too salty.

"Don't get too chesty, captain," he'd say. "Don't get too chesty."

"Chesty," you see, was an old Marine expression meaning cocky. That's how Lewis Puller got the nickname "Chesty," even though most of the old timers always called him Lewie.

Anyway, Al Pollock ended up a general so I guess he knew what he was doing.

Joe: Well, Francis, I guess we're what you'd call the Old Breed. Our time has long come and gone. But damn it, there's plenty of career men on active duty right now, probably a generation or so younger than we are. And if this country gets into real hot water again, I bet they'd do as good a job as we did in turning a bunch of kids into Marines. There ain't nothin' ever going to change the Corps. No sir.

Mac: Joe, you're probably right. But where in the hell did the time go to? How would you like to turn the clock back fifty years and once again be sitting around the table at Hempel's joint on Hatamen Street—maybe just one more stein of beer there. What would you say to that?

Joe: Amen, Sergeant Major, Amen!

Marine Lingo

The Marines used a number of expressions constantly during World War II. Some of them, such as gung ho, have become part of the American language. Others, such as earbanger and slop chute, still remain peculiar only to Marines.

Then there are the nautical terms like scuttlebutt and the terms used in all the services . . . such as "the Eagle shits."

Whatever, the following words and expressions were first heard by this author while on active duty in the Corps. They are used by men throughout *Semper Fi, Mac.*

ASIATIC: A Marine who served in the Pacific too long. He would usually be pointed out to newcomers as someone who ate raw fish.

BOONDOCKERS: Marine field shoes.

BOONDOCKS: Rough terrain; wild country. Also called the Boonies.

COLD COCK: Lower the boom on someone; knock him flying.

COBBER: New Zealand word for buddy. Commonly used in the 2nd Division.

CRUISE: One tour of duty; an enlistment period.

DOGFACE (also doggie): Any soldier, no matter what branch. Marines also called army pilots doggies.

EARBANGER: One who fawns on another for personal gain. An asskisser; brownnoser.

DITTY BAG: Small bag for carrying toilet articles.

DING HAO: Chinese for very good. Ding Boo Hao meant not so very good.

GEAR: Marine equipment.

GUNG HO: Originally borrowed from the Chinese by Colonel Carlson of the Raiders. It means "to work together." Later changed to describe an overly zealous person.

HORSE COCK: Cold cuts.

THE ISLAND: One of several places but most likely Guadalcanal.

K-BAR: Marine fighting knife. Great for opening cans. Also excellent for infighting. Used in this capacity more often in sea stories than in actual combat.

HEAD: Any form of toilet.

JUNK ON THE GUNK: Marine gear is laid out on a sack for inspection.

GE-DUNK SHOP: Naval term for PX aboard ship. Frequently used by Marines ashore.

POGEY BAIT: Candy. Old naval term.

LASHUP: Outfit, unit. "Hey, Mac, what's your lashup?"

PX: Post Exchange.

MAGGIE'S DRAWERS: Zero. A complete miss on the rifle range.

THE MAN: The officer in charge. Also, skipper. The one who passes out the word. "If you don't shape up, I'll run your ass up to the man."

PIECE: Weapon. Only word interchangeable with rifle.

MUSTANG: An enlisted man who wins a commission.

REAR ECHELON PULL: Anyone who is behind you in battle. For instance, mortar men were usually behind riflemen, sometimes by only a matter of yards. The mortar men would jokingly be called "Rear Echelon Pull" by the riflemen.

QUEER TOAST: French toast.

SACK: Where Marines sleep. Also called rack; sometimes bunk.

SCUTTLEBUTT: Rumors; also drinking fountain. Rumors frequently started at the drinking fountain. Thus, scuttlebutt started at the scuttlebutt.

782 GEAR: Marines' equipment. It had better be in top shape for inspection.

SALTY: Time in the Corps. All Marines try to look salty.

SLOP CHUTE: Any place that serves alcohol, especially beer. Usually Post Exchange (PX) but could even be "21" Club in New York City.

SHITBIRD: Feather merchant. A nothing person. But on Parris Island any boot (recruit).

SOS: Shit on shingle. Dried beef on toast. Quite good.

SURVEY: Turning in used equipment for new gear. Also, surveyed out of the Corps, usually under strained conditions.

TOP or TOP SOLDIER: First Sergeant. *Very* important rating.

SEA BAG: Marine khaki barracks bag.

SWAB JOCKEY: Also swabby. Any sailor, from Admiral Halsey on down.

THE EAGLE SHITS: Payday.

Captain William Hawkins

Born in Bridgeport, Connecticut, Bill was at Tufts College when he enlisted in the Marine Corps Reserve to attend the first platoon leader's class that the Corps offered. He was called to active duty late in 1940.

Bill's tour of overseas duty fits into two different categories.

First, as captain of Company B, 5th Marines, he was the first Marine to land on Guadalcanal. He spent the next ten weeks on that island.

Then, without the customary trip home, he became a seagoing Marine, serving on transports in the South Pacific. He was forced to abandon ship three times, which must put him close to a Marine record.

Amazingly, during his ten weeks as an infantry officer on the Canal, plus the three times he was forced to go over the side while on the transports, he did not receive a scratch.

The bulk of Bill's postwar business career was spent as the chief executive officer of the Bridgeport Chamber of Commerce, a position from which he retired in 1980. That fall he started law school, which is quite a trick when you are sixty-five years of age.

Colonel William Hawkins (USMCR-ret.) has a personality best summed up at a meeting about ten years back with a journeyman ballplayer named Cedric Durst. The now deceased Mr. Durst's chief claim to fame is that the Boston Red Sox traded pitching great Red Ruffing to the New York Yankees for outfielder Durst. It turned out to be a memorable disaster for the Red Sox.

"I was walking down a street in San Diego," recalls Bill, "when I saw a sign that read, 'Cedric Durst's Fish Market.' I had been raised in Boston where my dad was New England sales manager for the Bridgeport Brass Company and was a real devotee of Fenway Park.

"Well, I walked into the market to find out if this was the same Cedric Durst who had played with the Red Sox. I asked the lad behind the counter if this was true.

" 'I guess so,' he shrugged, 'Cedric says he played ball; he's out back cleaning fish. I'll get him.'

"You know, it was *the* Cedric Durst," recalls Hawkins. "So, I really laid it on thick. You'd have thought he was Babe Ruth when I got through. And I talked loud enough for everybody in the market to hear me. You should have seen the smile on Durst's face when I left the market!"

CAPTAIN WILLIAM HAWKINS
1st Battalion, 5th Marines

"Captain Hawkins, I found, had achieved the honor of being the first American invader to set foot on Guadalcanal."
—Richard Tregaskis, *Guadalcanal Diary*

My connection with the Marine Corps goes back to my freshman year at Tufts College (1935) when I first heard about their Reserve Unit. Actually, I say Marine Reserve Unit—hell, I'm not even sure they had one; I think this was the beginning of it. The whole Corps wasn't any larger than fourteen or fifteen thousand men at the time.

Anyway, they sent a major around to various colleges telling the students about a platoon leader's class they were going to start at Quantico, Virginia.

"Come on down next summer," he said, "it will be sensational. Plenty of time for tennis and golf. And we'll teach you something about the Marine Corps. If you come for three summers, we'll make you a second lieutenant in our new Reserve Unit."

This sounded great. So the next summer I boarded a train in Boston, headed for Quantico. By the time we reached Virginia, we'd picked up students from Yale, Princeton, Pennsylvania—all the colleges on the Eastern seaboard. We were having a ball.

Then came the shock. When we arrived at Quantico, this big sergeant gave us a Marine Corps greeting. I can still picture him today, hash marks and campaign ribbons, the whole bit. He took one look at us and let out a roar.

"What the hell do you think this is, Palm Beach? You're here to become Marines, not playboys!"

Then he started putting a size thirteen shoe through every tennis racquet he could grab and throwing golf clubs in every direction. The honeymoon was over before it started. From right off the top of the barrel there was no tennis, no golf, *no nothing* but Marine Corps.

This was the introduction to my Marine Corps career and the start of the platoon leader's class, a program we still have. And what a different Marine Corps that was from the one that developed during the war.

Remember, back in the mid-thirties the Corps was clannish as hell. I don't think it had more than eight hundred officers. Everyone

seemed to know everyone else, regardless of rank. I can remember
once being stretched out on the firing line when this officer came by
and started to move my legs.

"Here, young fellow," he advised me, "change into this position;
you have better balance this way."

I looked up and who was it but Tom Holcomb. He was either
commandant of the Corps, or about to become such. You can bet
your life that he didn't spend much time showing young officer
candidates how to fire their rifles after Pearl Harbor.

Another Marine officer I got to know at Quantico was Clifton
Cates. He was then the major in charge of our group, but he was just
jolly old Cliff to us, really one of the boys. Naturally, Cates and most
of the other regular officers we met down there ballooned in rank
after the war started. Cates was the colonel in charge of the 1st
Marines on Guadalcanal and major general commanding the 4th
Division on Saipan and Iwo. Eventually he became commandant
right after Vandegrift.

Well, I went to Quantico those three summers and I do think we
learned what the Corps was all about. And we did learn who the
regular officers were. No matter where I went later on, I was always
bumping into someone I had met at Quantico.

I received my commission when I graduated Tufts in 1937. Shortly
after this I went to work teaching Latin and English at the Milford
Academy, located between Bridgeport and New Haven in Connecticut. This was the period when Hitler was trying to grab everything
that wasn't nailed down. By the time he reached Poland, Great
Britain and France said no more and, bang, we had World War II.
I knew it was just a matter of time before they'd start calling up the
reserves and I was right. My turn came in December 1940, one year
before the Pearl Harbor attack.

The funny thing about this period was that none of us thought
about fighting the Japanese. Nazi Germany—that was the big menace. We'd been told all about Belleau Wood, Soissons, Mont Blanc,
all those big fights from World War I. Most of us just didn't think
about Japan.

At any rate, the Corps was trying to expand and naturally we had
a lot of growing pains. Someone was always coming up with a bright
new idea, all of which were thrown out the window once war started.

One of those brainstorms had us putting one hundred or so Marines on destroyers to practice night landings up and down the East
Coast.

What a fiasco!

You just can't land troops from destroyers, particularly at night. I
had been made a first lieutenant and put in command of one of these

detachments on a World War I tin can called the *McKeen*. Nothing ever went right, but it took us about six months to realize that the destroyer method was for the birds—it just didn't make any sense.

While we were going through those absurd landings, I encountered one of the old-time tigers—a real Marine Corps legend. It was one searing experience.

We had finished loading the *McKeen* down in Norfolk. I was sitting down, leaning against a shed, and my men were more or less hanging around. All of a sudden I heard this yell from three or four hundred feet away.

"What in *the* hell is going on here—*who* is in charge of your *people?*"

Jeez, it was Holland M. Smith, old "Howling Mad" himself.

He then read me off from asshole to appetite—making sure, I might add, that the men couldn't hear any of it. A good officer *never* reads off another officer in front of the men.

Now, you don't see many men like that anymore; they're usually ruled off the track. But there is a certain tribal force about them. Lewie Puller was another one. So was George Patton. And they weren't all in the military. Fiorello LaGuardia was another and so was Jasper McLevy, who was mayor of Bridgeport for so many years. I guess we'd call them dinosaurs today. You could like them or dislike them, but you sure as hell couldn't ignore them.

Let me say one more thing about Smith. Without the good general, we would have never had our landing boats for Guadalcanal.

Smith, you see, had become friendly with this creative thinker type down in New Orleans named Andrew Jackson Higgins, the developer of the Higgins boat. Higgins had tried to sell his boat to the Navy, but they wanted no part of it. So Smith got into the act. He knew the future of the Marine Corps would center around amphibious landings and he wanted that boat. He went straight to Ernie King (Admiral King) and sold him the idea of buying Higgins's boat. It didn't have a landing ramp, you'd disembark over the sides, but without it, I don't know how we would have gone ashore on the Canal.

Well, after we had given up on those destroyer landings, most of us were sent over near New River, North Carolina, to build a new Marine Corps base, starting from scratch. We succeeded in setting up what we called Tent City to house the fast-growing 1st Marine Division.

This new lashup had come as somewhat of a surprise to most of us. We'd constantly been hearing how General Marshall didn't want the Marines to have a division. The Army brass had felt the same way in World War I. It seems that most of them didn't trust a Marine officer in an open field with more than fifty men, but by the time World War II started, we had the 1st Division on the East Coast and the 2nd Division out in California.

The big day, of course, was December 7, 1941, the well-remembered quiet Sunday. Along with a buddy of mine, First Lieutenant Paul Barton, I had gone over to Raleigh, North Carolina. We were sitting in a bar, accompanied by a couple of young beauties whose names are best forgotten, when the news of the Japanese attack came over the radio. Barton and I were shocked.

After we regained our composure, Barton started to whine.

"Oh hell, Bill, there goes a great Sunday afternoon." So we dashed back to Tent City. What a laugh! There really was nothing for us to do Sunday night. We should have stayed with the young ladies.

Things did certainly liven up the next day though. Our general was a man named Phillip Torrey and he started working like the devil to fill up the 1st Division, particularly the 1st, 5th and 7th infantry regiments and the 11th Marines. The latter was our artillery regiment under the command of Colonel Pedro del Valley, later commander of the 1st Division on Okinawa, a real interesting gentleman.

Del Valley came from an aristocratic Puerto Rican family. As a matter of fact, he might have been the first Puerto Rican to graduate from the Naval Academy. He had been sent over to Africa as an observer with Mussolini's troops when the Italians had invaded Africa. That's what we'd been told, anyway.

From then on del Valley had stood to the right of Attila the Hun and he wasn't very shy about it. He was always blasting FDR and, as he called it, Roosevelt's policy of leading us into war.

Now, shortly before Pearl Harbor, General Torrey sent out invitations to the division's officers for a large Sunday afternoon picnic. Naturally, most of us did not want to spend our free time at a damn picnic. A great many of the young officers weren't married and we wanted to leave the camp on Sundays. The result was very few officers showed up at the Torrey shindig.

Well, sir, there was hell to pay. Torrey really blew his stack. He sent out the following order to all officers:

"There *will* be an officers' picnic next Sunday. All hands will attend! All hands *will* have a good time!—By order of Major General Phillip Torrey, USMC."

Not long after Torrey's "Papal Bull," a congressional committee came down from Washington to investigate just what was going on. We were at war by this time and the word was that Washington wanted to find out just how serious Colonel del Valley was about what he had been saying. They started interrogating many of the junior officers with such questions as:

"Have you heard Colonel del Valley making derogatory remarks against the government of the United States or against the Commander-in-Chief of the Armed Forces?"

"Hell no!" we'd answer even though we knew he had. You know how the Corps takes care of its own. Then the committee started perusing the divisional orders. They came across Torrey's order on the picnic. So, it's Torrey they ended up lowering the boom on. I guess they figured anyone who'd send an order out like the one on the picnic was a little off the wall. Archey Vandegrift ended up taking over the 1st Division and did a magnificent job with it.

As for Pedro, he kept his 11th Marines and also did a truly outstanding job. I think he eventually retired a lieutenant general.

At any rate, we continued to build up the division. I had been made captain of Company B in the 5th Marines. The Japs were smashing up everything in their way and many people were beginning to look at them as supermen. We all knew we'd be headed for the Pacific and we felt the sooner the better. Then they hit Vandegrift right where he lived, by taking away the 7th Marines and a battalion of artillery. These men were then rushed to the island of Samoa.

Oh, how our general roared! How in hell could he build his division if they took part of it away? Besides, as our departing men were going overseas, they would naturally take our best equipment. Vandegrift was really teed off.

We didn't have long to stew about it though. Our own turn came soon enough. Toward the end of May we received our marching orders. The rest of the division was to load up and head for New Zealand. The 1st and 11th Marines took a troop train to San Francisco for embarkation, while my outfit, the 5th Marines, boarded ship in Norfolk. I was on a transport called the *American Legion*.

Our convoy sailed down the east coast headed for Panama and it was there that we unintentionally set the morale of the enlisted men back a hundred years. One of our captains pointed out that we had made no arrangements for an officers' club in New Zealand. We all chipped in—I think we ended up with about three thousand dollars —so we could buy some liquor while passing through the Panama Canal.

When we reached the canal, three of us, including myself, went ashore, running like hell to see if we could find a package store. We finally found one and quickly entered the shop.

"We want three thousand dollars worth of liquor, and in a hurry!" I told this startled Panamanian.

"Si, si, amigo," he answered. God was he happy! He started jumping all over his shop, grabbing some of this and some of that, jabbering away in Spanish for someone to go get a truck, pronto.

As you can well imagine, a forage like this was something that you couldn't keep secret. You know how news travels on a transport. When our truck pulled up alongside the *American Legion,* there are all these troops lining the railing of the ship, glaring at us.

God, if looks could kill! Naturally, the men are thinking that all the officers will be drinking themselves silly, while the troops are doing all the work. It was a mistake for us to get the liquor all right, but live and learn, I guess.

After we cleared the canal, we headed straight for New Zealand. Other than the constant sighting of enemy submarines that weren't there, the trip was uneventful. We pulled into Wellington around the middle of June. Here we were supposed to train for a combat landing against the Japanese sometime toward the end of '42, or at least so we had been told.

Right away we were in trouble. I don't recall if the unions were on strike or what have you, but we couldn't get our ships unloaded. Vandegrift moved fast. The orders came through for the division to turn to and unload the gear ourselves. Naturally this caused some problems with the local unions, but we heard that Peter Frazer took Vandegrift aside and thanked him:

"I may be Labor Prime Minister of New Zealand," he is alleged to have said, "but bully for you, General!"

As for the New Zealand people themselves, they treated us like knights in shining armor. Most of their young men were in Africa with the Australia-New Zealand Army Corps fighting Rommel, and they felt that their island was ripe picking for the Japanese. By and large our men also conducted themselves wonderfully, but every now and then you'd hear some asshole calling the islanders gooks. This hurt, but you know the old Marine expression: "There's one in every outfit."

We soon settled down to some real combat training, but not for long before a shocking bit of news came through. Our orders had been changed. We were now slated to hit the Japanese in August. It seems that Frank Knox (Secretary of the Navy) or some other big wheel found out that the Japs had landed at a place called Guadalcanal in the Solomon Islands and were building an airfield. They wanted the 1st Marine Division to make an assault landing on Guadalcanal and a couple of small islands (Tulagi and Gavutu) adjacent to the Canal. As we were still shy part of our division, the 2nd Marines and Edson's Raiders were going to reinforce us.

We didn't know this right away, but we did know that we'd be going into combat much sooner than we thought, and this was one time the scuttlebutt was right on target. We left New Zealand toward the end of July, ostensibly headed for extended maneuvers in the Fiji

Islands. In reality, we were to make two dry runs at the Fijis, then head for the Solomons. I think our first rehearsal took place on July 28. It was a complete bust.

Not only were many of the boats' engines defective, but we didn't realize to what extent the coral reef would knock the hell out of the propellers. We got ashore but just barely. Thank God those Fijis weren't in Japanese hands. If they had been, we would have been slaughtered.

There was also a sad personal note connected with the foul-up at the Fijis, a perfect example of the problems facing this country when we try and put a military force together in a hurry.

There were three young privates in my company who decided they'd spend the night on the island where we landed. I don't know why, maybe they'd seen too many of those Dorothy Lamour films. Anyhow, they wanted to look the place over. They knew we were scheduled to come back the next day, so I guess they figured, what the hell, no harm done, they'd join us when we came ashore.

The problem was that after the coral damage to our ships during the first landing, our orders for the second day were changed. We would climb down the nets and get into the Higgins boats but then just make a pass at the island, turn around, and come back to the ship.

You can imagine what happened. When our boats made their pass, then started to turn around, these poor guys came running out of the bush, yelling their lungs out for us to come back. But their luck had run out. They weren't picked up for several months. I assume they were court-martialed, but I never heard how it turned out.

The tragic part was they weren't bad Marines. They just didn't realize the seriousness of the whole operation. We weren't playing war any longer and they had to pay for their stupidity.

After that second day in the Fijis we headed for Guadalcanal where we were to go ashore around eight o'clock or so on the morning of August 7, 1942. It was to be the beginning of a counteroffensive against the Japanese Empire that was to end three years later on the decks of the *U.S.S. Missouri.*

The landing itself was perfection. Our intelligence reports were way off base on the number of Japs originally on the island. There were nowhere near as many of them there as we originally thought. Our real combat was to come from reinforcements the enemy sent to the Canal.

My company was part of the first assault group, and the boat I was in was the first to unload. I guess I was the first Marine ashore on the Canal. Thank God we met no resistance; every Jap in the area would have been firing at my head.

We later found out that the unexpected bombardment from our

warships had really caught the enemy with their pants down. They'd hightailed it back into the jungle. Fortunately, they'd abandoned a tremendous amount of stores, particularly food, which was to be a lifesaver for us in the weeks to come.

Our job was to hit Red Beach and move inland. Then the 1st Marines were to go through us, heading for the airfield. This was to be our modus operandi anyway.

The reality of the situation was a little different. The dope we had was poor. Our maps showed this huge ditch, maybe six feet deep and ten feet wide. The night before the landing we'd spent hours putting together these grappling hooks. When we got to the damn ditch, it was nothing at all. You could spit across it. So we started to heave the hooks into the jungle, following the time-honored tradition of all armies when it comes to surplus equipment.

While we were at it, I figured it was a good time for me to toss my ridiculous Reising submachine gun. What a lemon—a real .45 caliber hunk of junk. I think before long every officer who had one had dumped it. I wonder who hung that beauty on Uncle Sam. Later on I got hold of a Thompson, a *real* submachine gun.

After we'd gone the three or four hundred yards we were supposed to, we got the word to go into the jungle at an angle. For the next two or three hours we moved into that swill. It was just a putrefying nightmare. And did it stink! You could hardly see more than a few feet in front of you in broad daylight. Then orders came for us to return to our original position, so back we went.

The amazing thing is, we found out later, command was disappointed because they thought the 5th had only gone four hundred yards the first day. What a lark!

The next day we saw our first Japs—some four or five unarmed prisoners who had been flushed out of the jungle. Our interpreter, First Lieutenant Corey (later killed in the Goettge Patrol*), found out they were part of a labor battalion. They looked like skinny Munchkins out of *The Wizard of Oz!* They seemed so puny and appeared to be scared out of their wits. They kneeled down in front of us with their heads bowed. Corey told us they expected to be shot, having been told that the Marines took no prisoners. I can remember one of my men starting to giggle.

"Christ," he snorted, "if they represent the Japanese supermen, this should be a breeze!"

We would soon find out how wrong he was.

In the meantime something had been fouled up with the unloading of the transports. Most of the troops were ashore, but a hell of a

*See page 74.

lot of our equipment was still on the ships. We didn't realize what a disaster this was going to be.

Our real trouble started that second evening when all hell broke loose out on Savo Straits. It looked like the Fourth of July. Naval guns were firing everywhere. You could see the flashes for miles. Naturally we all thought our Navy was knocking the Japs galley west. We'd seen too many Hollywood versions of the U.S. Navy. No one could lick our fleet.

What a shock we later received! My kid brother, Bob, a Marine lieutenant, was an artillery spotter for the *U.S.S. Vincennes,* one of the cruisers out in the bay. He'd come ashore on the 8th to set up coordination between the guns of his ships and the people on the Canal. He told me that in a surface-to-surface sea battle, no planes involved, the Japanese had kicked the hell out of us. His ship, two other American cruisers, the *Quincy* and the *Astoria,* plus an Australian cruiser, *H.M.A.S. Canberra,* had gone to the bottom. Not a single Japanese ship was lost.

The next thing we knew the Marines were orphans. After the cruisers went down, the Navy pulled the transports out. Hell, I don't think they were half unloaded. Before long we were on one meal a day. This is where those Japanese stores we had captured came in handy. The rice wasn't bad, but I never cottoned to the raw fish heads. It always seemed to me the damn fish was looking at you.

Of course our men then became expert scroungers. One of their tricks was to throw a hand grenade into the nearest river. The concussion would always kill some fish which would come to the surface.

The only problem with this was, as we began to have more fire fights, Japanese bodies would frequently end up in these rivers. It didn't seem to bother the men though. They cooked the fish to a crisp, but it was a meal that just didn't appeal to me.

Lousy diet or not, we had our job to do. The first objective of the operation was to secure the airfield on Guadalcanal, or, as we soon started to call it, the Island. The 1st Marines had quickly done this without any serious opposition. We named it Henderson Field after Major Loften Henderson, a Marine flyer who had been killed at Midway.

The 5th Marines command post had been set up east of Henderson, near the Matanikau River. This was the area where most of the fighting was to occur over the next ten weeks. It was also where we were constantly shelled by the Japanese Navy.

The enemy had a cruiser-scout airplane we nicknamed Louie the Louse. Its job was to relay Marine positions to both the Japanese ships and airplanes. Louie had this droning sound that you couldn't miss. When we heard it, we knew what was coming.

As far as I was concerned, the naval bombardments were worse than the aerial. The night bombings would keep you awake, but I don't remember that they did much damage. The Japanese vessels were different. After the Savo disaster their navy could move at will. They were experts at night attacks and it got so we could expect them practically every evening. They occasionally even brought a battleship into the area we called "the slot." They would sit offshore and fire away. All you could do was lie in your hole and hope.

I later found out that the newspapers back home were full of our early "victories" on the Island, but in truth our perimeter was only about three miles deep and five miles wide. Those Jap ships had plenty of targets. Naval shelling can be fearsome, particularly if you have nowhere to go. Add to their shelling the fact that the malarial mosquitoes were appearing in droves and so was the jungle crud, and you can imagine what our nights were like.

Our side of the airport, however, was not where all the action occurred. As a matter of fact, the first big fight happened on the east side, over on the Tenaru River. At least that's what we called it. I guess it was really the Ilu. So, like the historical mixup between Bunker Hill and Breed's Hill, the battle of the Tenaru was really fought on the Ilu.

In any event, a Japanese colonel named Ichiki landed about thirty or so miles east of the airport with a thousand or more troops. Cliff Cates, the 1st Marines colonel, soon found out about the landing. He immediately started to fortify the west bank of the Tenaru, and here's where good luck played a big part.

It seems that Cates had gotten hold of some barbed wire but not nearly enough to set up a proper defense. He strung up what he had in a sandbar area not far from the ocean. When the attack came (early in the morning of August 21), its major thrust was exactly where Cates had strung the wire. Can you beat that for luck?

My company had been moved over from the Matanikau to act in reserve. Initially we didn't know how many men the Japs had, so we didn't know what the hell was going to happen. As it turned out, they didn't have nearly enough to break through unless the Marines broke and ran. That was not going to happen.

They started coming early in the morning of August 21. You could hear their Nambus and mortars blasting away along with their yells of banzai.

The Marines answered them with everything we had. My God, it was butchery. We stacked them up like cordwood. They tried it two or three times, but each time their casualties were enormous. A few of them reached our lines and some nasty hand-to-hand stuff went on, but none of the Nips came near my company's position. I don't think my unit fired a shot.

The next day the 1st Marines went to work on what was left of Ichiki's men. Some of the Japanese even tried to swim out to sea, but the Marines riddled them. I'll be damned if I know where they thought they were headed—maybe they planned on swimming to Japan.

Later that day I took a walk out toward the sandbar and, from then on, I knew I was at war. Christ Almighty, what a sight! The Japanese are truly much shorter than we are as it is, and dead men always appear smaller than they really are. They looked like contorted rag dolls. With that brutally fierce sun, they'd already started to puff and swell. The stench was beginning to sweep the whole area. My God, what a gruesome sight!

We later heard that close to nine hundred of them had been killed and that Ichiki had burned his colors and committed hara-kiri. We lost forty-three Marines. As tragic as those forty-three deaths were to the families of these Marines, the hard, cruel mathematics of war call that a very successful ratio.

However, I think there was something more important about the fight than the fact we had annihilated a Japanese command. Seeing all those corpses, and realizing how stupid the attack really was, knocked the aura of the Japanese superman into a cocked hat. Unfortunately, there was a lot of dying to be done on both sides before we could convince the Japs they weren't invincible, but at least we now knew it. None of us questioned their bravery or their willingness to die—it was extraordinary—but courage, combined with stupidity, does not make a successful soldier.

After that debacle on the Tenaru (Ilu), we moved back to the Matanikau area. Here we were either bored to death or out on patrol. It got so we'd even welcome the chance to look for the Nips—it beat the hell out of trying to shoot coconuts out of trees. One of these sweeps gave me the surprise of my life.

This happened when LeRoy Hunt, the colonel of the 5th Marines —one of the many World War I heroes I served under—decided to send us out in strength. Along with my B Company, he sent L Company under Lyman Spurlock and I Company, which I believe was led by a captain named Hardy.

My job was to keep B on the flank near the ocean with I in the middle and Spurlock's group on the other flank. We ran into tremendous machine gun fire and couldn't move. As hot as the fire was on B Company, it was Spurlock's company that was really shot up.

After a short, but very tense action, I started moving B back toward our command post. As my company, hugging close to the water, moved around a point, I was literally thunderstruck. Right in front of us was a Japanese cruiser. A couple of the Nip sailors actually waved. My immediate thoughts were how in the hell did it get in so far and how damn big its guns were. I was in a trance but only for a second. We took off for the jungle as fast as we could. Thank God they didn't fire a shot, but seeing that cruiser as if it had come out of nowhere was something I'll never forget.

On another occasion I saw an unbelievably heroic deed that ended up in one of those tragic ironies of war. We had been taken by Higgins boats up the coast of the Island. We were to sweep the area clean as we came back. We'd returned about halfway when the Japs hit us. We all jumped for cover, but several of the men were hit. You couldn't see the Nips, so we began firing in the direction from which their fire had come.

Then this runner of mine named Wesley Simmonds started to yell: "Christ, there's Bernie Fetchko, lying out in the open. He's still alive!"

It would have been suicidal to go after him, but he was a good buddy of Wes's and that's all there was to it.

He said, "I can't leave him out there to die. The hell with those bastards!" And with that, he took off.

We gave him all the covering fire we could. He got to Fetchko, threw him over his shoulder and started back. It all looked like a picture out of a Civil War book I'd had when I was a kid. This picture showed a big Union soldier carrying a wounded buddy in. The caption read, "Saving a Buddy Under Fire."

Anyway, I'm sorry to say that Wes got about halfway back when he went down.

After a while the firing stopped. I guess the Japanese just took off. We went over to where Simmonds and Fetchko were lying. Fetchko was dead, but Wes was still alive. He'd been badly hit, but it looked like he would make it. We got him back to our area as soon as possible.

This happened sometime late in September. Plenty of our planes were using Henderson by this time, so one of our hospital ships had pulled in to pick up our sick and wounded. We immediately rushed Wes out to the ship.

Then they did a baffling thing. They put Simmonds in an upper rack and didn't strap him in. That night he started to thrash around and finally fell out of his sack onto the deck. We heard he was killed instantly.

I'd lost six men in that action, and several others at various times, but it's Wes's death that has haunted me. He was an outstanding

Marine, but not necessarily one that you would pick to commit such a selfless act. Yet, for one short moment, he went as far as one can above and beyond the well-known call of duty. Then, to have him die like he did was very sad. We never knew if he would have died anyway—his wound was certainly serious enough—but I sure as hell wish it hadn't happened the way it did.

Well, that was pretty much what the fighting on the Canal was like for me, constant patrol action, usually around the Matanikau River. Sometimes the fight would break off suddenly, like the one where we lost Wes, and other times we'd run into too many Japs to handle. Then we'd break off the action, which is exactly what happened on one of these fights when I came very close to becoming a battlefield statistic—the fire we received on this occasion was just too over-whelming.

I had to make a snap decision. I decided to haul my men out of there pronto and return to our perimeter. The next thing I knew, General Vandegrift called me into his command post.

"Hawkins," he said, "I understand you have reported that you were pinned down by tremendous fire. Just what the hell does that mean?"

"Well, sir," I told him, "this is what I mean by being pinned down." Then I showed him where Jap machine gun bullets had creased both sides of my helmet. To make sure he knew what I meant, I also showed him where another bullet had taken off part of my Tommy gun's stock.

Vandegrift looked at me for a minute or so.

"Captain, that's being pinned down!"

In the meantime we had started to get some cargo and troop transports through to the Canal. The general felt many of the large transports should have a Marine officer aboard. I ended up being one of these officers. Around the middle of October, about ten weeks after I'd landed on the Canal, I left for Noumea, New Caledonia, and a new Marine Career as a transport officer.

Hawkins of the *"Wacky Mac"* recalls:

They didn't waste any time with me in Noumea. I went aboard an AKA called the *Alchiba* that was loaded to the gunnels with supplies for Guadalcanal. They actually tied a barge to our ship that we were to tow along to the Canal. We were connected to this barge by a cable stretching out about one hundred and fifty yards. This is a little more complicated than hauling your old Chevy down to the repair shop, believe me.

Well, we pulled into the bay between Savo Island and the Canal.

They called this Iron Bottom Bay because there are supposed to be some 120 ships on the bottom there. It's about seven miles from Savo Island across the straits to Guadalcanal. If you were a giant, you could walk across that bay, stepping on a different sunken ship with each step.

We no sooner got into the bay than we spotted one of those two-man Jap submarines. Everyone starts yelling orders on how to get the midget sub; naturally all eyes are on her.

In the meantime, a full-size Jap sub is coming in on the other side of the *Alchiba,* but no one knows this.

Wham! we take a torpedo on the other side of our ship—the side no one is paying any attention to.

Now we were in real trouble. It looks like all our supplies are going to end up on the bottom of the bay.

Then our captain, Jim Freeman, from Alabama, had a brainchild.

"Head her for the shore!" he yelled. "Maybe we can beach her and not lose the cargo. The men ashore really need this gear."

So we headed for the beach, the very spot where I had landed on August 7. Now it became a race between the *Alchiba* and the bay. We won, but not by much—the water was close to our gunwales when we beached her. She hit the bottom and plowed about fifty yards into the sand. Captain Freeman got on the loudspeaker.

"Abandon ship!" he yelled.

Jeez, this was great. Everybody went over the side with no problems whatsoever. We thought we were heroes. We'd survived the Japanese and saved the supplies. But, as it turned out, the Nips had not finished with us, and the second time they hit us we were *really* lucky.

You see, the most important thing we had on board was the aviation gas and the aerial bombs. A few days after the abandon ship order we started to unload that precious cargo. We had taken all the gasoline off the ship and had just finished unloading the last one-hundred-pound bomb when another two-man submarine showed up and stuck a torpedo into our ship. It hit exactly where the bombs and gas had been stowed. If it had hit us an hour or so earlier, we would have all gone to kingdom come.

What a mess! I can vividly remember seeing a sailor go flying into the air and into the bay. He had been sunning himself on a hatchway exactly where the torpedo hit. He never knew what hit him.

Once again we got the word to abandon ship, and once again we went over the side. It was getting to be a habit.

We may have saved the gas and the bombs, but one part of the cargo we lost was hundreds of cartons of candy bars. You could see Baby Ruth and OHenry wrappers floating all over the bay for weeks

—a situation that really pissed off the men on the Island.

Believe it or not, when living conditions are as primitive as they were on Guadalcanal, a small thing like a candy bar can become a luxury; it sure beat the hell out of maggot-laden rice.

Well, that second abandon ship meant the end of the *Alchiba* for me. I received orders to report to Noumea, where I was to board the *U.S.S. McCawley,* one of the most famous transports in the fleet.

I really mean it. Ask any Marine who was in the Solomon Islands between August '42 and July '43 and the chances are he was either carried by the *Mac* or at least saw her. She was named after a one-time Marine Corps commandant (Charles McCawley—Commandant, 1876–1891) and had somehow gained the nickname "Wacky Mac." Actually, she was a great ship that met an unfortunate end.

It was on the *McCawley* that I found out what transports were all about and how important the type of captain the ship had was to the troops being carried.

Remember, most naval officers wanted to run a real spic-and-span ship. When many of them ended up running a transport with maybe a thousand or so Marines aboard, they'd blow their stack.

"I can't have these troops above decks during the day," they'd say. "It just doesn't look shipshape. All they do is lie around and sweat all over the place. Most of them don't shower enough and they smell. We can't have this on a United States Navy ship. Keep them below decks and batten down the hatches."

Naturally this kind of thinking would drive the troops up the wall. I mean, what the hell were they—animals? They did the best they could to keep clean—after all, hygiene had been drilled into them at boot camp—but it wasn't easy. You know how crowded those ships became and those salt water showers were scarce and in great demand.

Anyway, we had what you'd call a "Marine's skipper" on the *McCawley.* His name was Bill Rodgers and he was a peach. I think he was from Long Island. I believe he's dead now, but my memories of him are not.

"Sure, let these men go topside anytime they want to," he'd say. "What the hell, many of them are going to get their heads blown off. We should do anything we can for them."

As for landing the troops, Rodgers would take our ship in as close to shore as possible.

"The shorter the run they have in toward shore," he'd tell us, "the less chance their Higgins boats have of getting hit."

Anytime a Marine or, indeed, a GI hears the name Captain William Rodgers, they should salute. Rodgers really cared.

Well, I stayed on the *Mac* until she went down on June 30, '43. Our job was to move men and equipment up from Noumea to the Russell-Solomon Islands area. Along with Captain Rodgers we had Rear Admiral Richard Kelly Turner aboard—the *McCawley* was his flagship.

The admiral was a strict old-line Navy man. But, to his everlasting credit, he never interfered with the way Rodgers ran his ship. That can be an awkward situation for the captain when the admiral had his flag aboard a captain's ship, but it worked perfectly well on the *McCawley*.

We normally managed to have some free time when we'd pull into Noumea and as Rodgers did have quite a reputation throughout the fleet as a playboy, he'd try and come up with an interesting idea. On one of our layovers he decided to have a party. He called me and our chaplain into his cabin.

"Look, men," he said, "I know it's hard as hell to get any nurses aboard ship, but if you two go ashore and do a selling job, I'll bet you can convince some of our Florence Nightingales that they should come to a party I want to give. They're certainly going to believe our chaplain, and you, Hawkins, are the most innocent-looking officer aboard. Give it a try."

So the chaplain and I took off for the nurses' quarters in New Caledonia, where I ran into a very fine-looking nurse who I would say was about thirty-five. She was a Naval lieutenant, a rank on a par with my Marine captaincy. I put on my most angelic face and delivered the invitation.

"Captain Hawkins," she answered, "we don't usually do things like that, but you two seem like perfect gentlemen and the invitation is quite attractive. I'm in charge of these nurses. I'll see if I can get ten of them who don't have the duty tomorrow night and we'll come over to the *McCawley*. But, remember, I'll tolerate *no* monkey business."

Oh, this was great! The next evening at about 5:30 I took a launch in toward the dock. The lieutenant and ten of her nurses were waiting for me. As she boarded the launch she pointed a finger in my face.

"Captain," she warned me, "remember, no hanky-panky with my girls."

It was obvious she wasn't kidding.

Well, we all boarded the "Wacky Mac" and headed for a wardroom we had decked out for the shindig. There was a phonograph going full blast and plenty of liquor. All our officers were in their dress uniforms and looked like a million dollars. Everyone was soon having a ball, including the head nurse—hell, she seemed to be having the best time of all.

Then, to my utter amazement, the lady lieutenant and one of our senior officers headed topside. It was obvious he was taking the head nurse to his cabin, which was right above the wardroom.

About a half hour later we heard a loud crash, shortly after which the head nurse reappeared with the wrath of God glaring from her eyes.

"Ladies!" she ordered. "Stand by, we are leaving this ship at once! And by the way, captain," she continued, "you will find your friend in his cabin. He does not know how to treat a lady."

Oh, we found our friend topside, all right—out like a light. He'd apparently tried to get the head nurse into his cabin and she'd lowered the boom on him. Jeez, she'd clobbered the poor guy with a lamp. He quickly recovered, but we never let him forget what happened.

Okay. Enough of the laughs, let's get back to action. If your ship kept on that route between New Caledonia and the Solomons, you were bound to run into trouble and we were no exception. The *McCawley's* problems happened at the end of June '43. We were taking General Hester's 43rd Army Division into Rendova at the time. Not only did we lose our ship but Captain Rodgers lost his brand new jeep that I had broken my hump securing for him.

You see, the captain was PO'd about not having a jeep. He was always on my butt to "procure" one for him.

"For Christ's sake, Hawkins," he'd rant, "I'm the only captain in the fleet without a jeep. The next time you can get your hands on one, get it aboard. I'll take care of it from then on."

Well, when we loaded up for the Rendova invasion, we had an inventory of thirteen jeeps, but fourteen were on the dock. The extra one belonged to the Army division's paymaster, but through some real fast footwork, I got my hands on it.

We no sooner had the jeep aboard, when a crew of swabbies went to work on it with blow torches. Hell, they took that khaki color and its serial numbers off that jeep as fast as one of today's stolen car rings could do the job. Then they painted it navy blue, gave it a phony number and stuck Captain Rodgers's name on it—presto, Rodgers had his jeep. Then we took off for the invasion of Rendova.

Now, if there was one thing Rodgers was an expert at, it was unloading his ship. He was a real tiger!

"Get them in as fast as possible," he'd say, "and that includes their equipment. Then get our ass out of there. We'll save lives that way, both the troops and ours."

One of the things he'd do was get within a thousand yards of the beach before he'd start to unload. The books call for two miles offshore before disembarking, but Rodgers always claimed his way allowed twice as many trips in and out within the same time as if you were two miles out. He was right.

We started to unload early in the morning of June 30. The operation was part of the overall New Georgia campaign. We landed our troops at Rendova, which is only seven miles from the all-important Munda airstrip.

Then we started to pour in the equipment. I remember watching what looked like a two-holer being hoisted up. Kelly Turner, the admiral, also saw it.

"What in the hell is that?" he yelled.

The sailors started to laugh.

"It's General Hester's own personal shithouse," one of them answered.

"Well, toss it in the Pacific!" Turner bellowed. "We unload only men, bullets and beans. The hell with his Chic Sale."

So into the water went the general's outhouse. But we unloaded those bullets and beans in record time.

And it's a good thing we did because around noon the Nips hit us hard. Submarines, Mitsubishis and dive bombers came at our transports. We took a torpedo early and Admiral Turner quickly transferred his flag to a destroyer.

For the next six hours our ships were under attack. The *Mac* was in real trouble, but we kept our .50 caliber machine guns firing at their planes. Normally, it's quite a feat to hit a plane with a machine gun, but there were so many of them up there that if you kept firing, you had a good chance of hitting one.

In the meantime it became obvious the *McCawley* had a good chance of going under. Our captain had ordered most of our men off. I was manning one of our guns and had the satisfacation of seeing one of my targets go down. All in all, the *McCawley*'s guns were credited with knocking down three Jap planes.

Finally, Captain Rodgers gave up.

"My God," he said, "my ship is going to sink! We better get the hell off her."

We signaled the *McCalla*, a nearby destroyer, to come over and get us. After we were safely aboard the tin can, Rodgers started to whine.

"Christ," he said, "look at my beautiful *McCawley,* just sitting there dead in the water. Let's go back and save her."

He then asked the captain of the *McCalla* to get us back to the "Wacky Mac." This startled the tin can's skipper.

"What are you doing, going bananas?" he said to Rodgers. "It's almost dark; we've got to get the hell out of here!"

But Rodgers was one smooth talker. Finally he convinced the destroyer's captain we should chance it. So six of us, including Captain Rodgers, got in a launch and headed back toward the transport. We were going to try and attach the *McCawley* to the *McCalla*.

We got to within one hundred yards of the *McCawley* when we were rocked by an explosion. It was the *Mac* all right and now she was definitely finished. We sadly headed back to the *McCalla*, which then took us to Guadalcanal.

A day after we landed, one of the Marine officers on the Canal came over to me.

"Bill," he said, "did you know the *McCawley* has been sunk?"

"Bad news sure travels fast," I answered. "Of course I do, I was *on* her!"

"Oh, do you know who sunk you?"

"Yeah, a Jap submarine."

"Bullshit! It was an American PT boat. It was getting dark and the PT boat's captain had been given some bum dope. He'd been told that any ships in the area would be Japanese—reinforcements for New Georgia. So, he put a torpedo in the *McCawley*. Then the clown put in for a medal for sinking her. Can you believe that?"

What the officer had told me became a persistent rumor. The word was that Admiral Turner knew all about it. He wanted to give the PT captain a kick in the rear end, not a medal, but he figured it might upset the people back home if they thought American ships were sinking each other in the Pacific. So, the blunder was hushed up. While we did lose fifteen men on the *McCawley*, they had been killed long before the PT boat showed up. I guess Turner felt the *McCawley* was going under anyway so there was no harm done.

Well, I was given the Silver Star and sent back home. It was the summer of '43 and there weren't many combat men back in the States then. I was ordered down to the Naval Office at 90 Church Street in Manhattan for a large press conference. All the newspapers wanted to hear about the Canal and the two ships I had been on that were sunk.

I did get a kick out of all this, but I especially enjoyed the Navy brass at 90 Church who were fighting the Battle of the Stork Club. Do you remember that little ditty that someone wrote for a magazine at the time? It went like this:

> *Twinkle, twinkle, little star,*
> *How I wonder what you are?*
> *Do your feet withstand a warship's lurch,*
> *Or do you hang out at 90 Church?*

After a few months of this fat duty, I was sent to the West Coast to help train both Marine and Army troops for the Pacific. I spent well over a year doing this. Then, at the beginning of 1945, I left for the Pacific again. This time I was a major on the staff of the 3rd Division. We turned to, working on the big one, the coming invasion of Japan.

Then came the A-bomb and our work became academic. Did you ever think how many lives were saved by *not* invading Japan?

Well, I came home and raised a family. I stayed in the Marine Corps Reserve and retired a colonel a few years ago.

But you know, those Marine Corps days still pop up. About ten years ago I was in San Francisco for a business convention. I met this fellow at a bar and we got talking about the war. Then he really threw one at me.

"Oh," he said, "I was in the Pacific all right, but I'm afraid I didn't have a distinguished record. I was on a PT boat that sank an American ship."

I was in a state of shock.

"Wait a minute," I answered, "you don't mean your ship sank the *McCawley?*"

"That's right. Do you know about it? I was a lieutenant JG at the time. Thank God there was no one aboard her. I think it was pretty much hushed up."

"Well, you SOB," I laughed, "you sank *my* ship!"

Then we both had another drink.

Savo Bay

" 'Haul Ass' Fletcher, that's what we used to call him. Why, that was his best maneuver. He could break all records getting away from something he didn't like.

"But I'll tell you, don't be too hard on him. There wasn't much left of old 'Haul Ass' when Sam Morrison got through with him. You should read Morrison on the subject of that naval action around Guadalcanal. Sam was a beautiful writer.

"And Fletcher did have a point. We just couldn't lose our carriers but, damn it, how the Marines suffered!"

The above remarks were made by Brigadier General Samuel Griffith (USMC-ret.) in a taped interview at his summer place in Maine. Sam was referring to the decision made by Rear Admiral

Frank Fletcher to move his aircraft carriers out of the Guadalcanal area on August 8, 1942. Fletcher claimed that his fuel supply was almost gone and that the Japanese had air power superior to what he had on his carriers. Both these statements, according to Griffith in his splendid book, *The Fight for Guadalcanal*, were later shown to be highly questionable.

Admiral Fletcher's decision to remove the air coverage was devastating to Major General Vandegrift, commander of the Marines already ashore on Guadalcanal, Tulagi, Gavutu and Tanambogo, and to Rear Admiral Kelly Turner, who had command of the partially unloaded transports off Guadalcanal.

As frightening as this news was to Vandegrift and Turner, the worst was yet to come. For in the early hours of August 9, 1942, the Japanese were going to inflict on the United States Navy what was to be the most crushing defeat in the history of the fleet.

At the same time that Vandegrift received word of Fletcher's withdrawal, the brilliant Japanese Admiral Gunicki Mikawa was moving toward Savo Bay with a Japanese cruiser task force. If Fletcher had remained, it is possible that his carriers' planes would have spotted these Japanese.

As it turned out, Mikawa's fleet succeeded in completely surprising the Allied force of cruisers off Guadalcanal. The Japanese lopsided victory was complete. There are somewhat conflicting reports on how long the actual battle took, but in approximately an hour and a half three American cruisers, *Vincennes, Astoria* and *Quincy*, were sunk, and a fourth, *Chicago*, was put out of action. The Australian cruiser, *Canberra*, was also sunk.

The Navy succeeded in connecting with only one telling shell. Probably fired by the main battery of the *Quincy*, it destroyed the operational room of the *Chokai*, Mikawa's flagship.

Now it was the Japanese admiral's turn to pull out. Not knowing that Fletcher's carriers were miles away, he felt that the dawn would make his ships easy pickings for the American airplanes. Realizing he had achieved a tremendous victory, Mikawa decided to head north with all due speed. If he had stayed, he would have easily sunk every one of the American transports.

The reasons for the American defeat are not a subject for this book. The fact that Turner, now helpless, immediately had to head south with the transports only partially unloaded is important. Now the Marines on Guadalcanal were truly orphans.

Of course, the troops did not immediately know their predicament. Thousands of them could see the brilliant flashes of the naval gunfire. Several veterans told me they actually cheered what they thought was an American victory.

"In the next day or so," remembers Warner Pyne, "we saw the recovery of hundreds of wounded Americans and the washing up on the island of our dead sailors. It was hard for these Marines to acknowledge the American disaster, but they did. In the oncoming weeks they would cling tenaciously to their small perimeter which would so frequently seem to be as fragile as a thread. Ill-equipped, sick and exhausted, they wrote one of the truly great chapters of American arms. It would be at least twelve grinding weeks before they knew for sure that the Japanese not going to push them off the Canal.

"Oh, and by the way, if you ever go to a reunion of the 1st Marine Division, don't pass the hat for a statue of Admiral Fletcher."

The 11th Marines Battler

Warner Pyne

Warner Pyne was one of the many seventeen-year-old Marines who had accomplished very little in school before enlisting in the Corps. After thirty months in the Pacific as a PFC, three battle stars, a Bronze Star, Purple Heart and several bouts with malaria he became convinced to take life a little more seriously.

"I figured if I didn't, I'd be an enlisted man the rest of my life," says Pyne.

After the war ended, Warner returned to his home town of Pelham Manor, New York, and resumed his education with a vengeance. He graduated from Columbia University, then decided the time had come to make some money. He became a manufacturer's representative in electronics.

Then came the kind of a break most businessmen dream of. A growing non-U.S. electronics firm wanted to develop a market in the United States and were looking for a representative. They set up an interview with Pyne.

"I was a little nervous about the meeting," Pyne recalls. "The last time I had seen any of these people it was bang, bang. You see, they were Japanese.

"That meeting turned into one of the great happenings of my life. Not only did we go into business together but it has turned into an immensely productive arrangement for all concerned. They make great products and, above all, they are as honorable as any businessmen on this planet. This arrangement has allowed me to have a happy marriage and comfortably raise six children. I am probably set for life and then some.

"And I'll tell you something else, a lasting friendship between our two countries, America and Japan, must remain one of the foundations for a peaceful world."

My interview with Warner Pyne took place at the Winged Foot

Country Club in Westchester County, which, as he points out, is a hell of a lot different from Guadalcanal.

PFC WARNER PYNE
11th Marines, 1st Division

I'll tell you one thing, the food they serve here is a lot different than the crap they gave us on the Canal. We ran out of chow early there, so they started giving us the rice we'd captured at the airfield after the Japanese had taken off for the boondocks. My God, it was awful, loaded with maggots. You'd do your best to separate those fetid creatures from the rice, but it was a losing fight. One of the jokes we Catholics had went like this:

"Hey, it's Friday, don't eat the maggots, they're meat."

Well, let's start with the fall of '41. I'd been canned from the Admiral Farragut Academy for fistfighting, the bane of my life when I was a kid. I was one of those feisty little nuts who was always ready to swing. My father had pointed out that since I wasn't very big, I'd better get the first shot in quickly or I'd be wiped out. He also told me I was a lunatic to get into so many fights.

Unfortunately, I did not agree with dad about being an idiot. To my total consternation fistfighting was a habit that was to cause me several courts martial during my service in the Corps. The worst of these offenses occurred when I slugged an Australian doctor. How stupid can you get?

Well, my father was an admiralty lawyer. During the first war he'd been with the judge advocate's office as a naval officer. He knew a lot of people in Washington, so after I'd been booted out of Farragut, he got me a job with a court reporter in the nation's capital. That's where I was on December 7, 1941. When I heard the big news, I went over to the White House to see what was going on. Just as I got there, the Japanese envoy was driving up in a limousine to deliver something.

And, my friend, the hatred being displayed toward that limousine was astounding. Some hotheads were even throwing stones at it. Can you remember how Americans felt toward Japan that Sunday? Wow!

At the time I'd already joined the Marine Corps and was waiting to be called up. I'd turned seventeen that September so both my parents had to sign my enlistment papers. Mother had agreed to sign because she was sure my father wouldn't, while dad had agreed simply because he was convinced mother would not. They were hardly pleased, but they both did sign and on December 13, 1941 I boarded a train for Parris Island, South Carolina.

Remember, this was just a week after war was declared. Our train kept picking up more Marine recruits as we moved south. One of these new arrivals had a bottle of bourbon, as did one or two of the civilians. Jeez, we were really living it up, until we reached Beaufort, South Carolina. Here we met the Marine Corps.

Our welcoming committee was a group of non-coms who herded us into trucks for the ride to Parris Island. The ride itself was a nightmare for me because I was feeling the first effects of ptomaine poisoning I had picked up on the train. If you have never had this vile malady, don't get it. Christ, was I sick! I ended up being put back several platoons and lost all my newly found friends from the train ride.

Now, any memories that most men have about those miserable weeks at boot camp revolve around that tyrannical figure known as the Drill Instructor. Mine was a crackerjack. Tough—hell, he was as tough as nails, but what a Marine! I can still see this big guy with that campaign hat, yelling, "Fall out!" and I mean we fell out. He was bound to shape us up and he did.

"On the double, on the double!" Everything he said was on the double. But I can't think of anything he did that wasn't directly aimed at making us Marines. He was the perfect example of the DI who could do a tremendous job without being a sadist. I wish I could remember his name; I'd like to thank him for the job he did.

There is one other thing I remember from Parris Island because it can still give me a laugh. We were making either seventeen or twenty-one dollars a month at the time, can't remember which. When we lined up for our first pay call—probably a month or so after we arrived—we were given the magnificent sum of one dollar and sixty cents each. This was not much money even in those days. First they took our insurance out, then there was the controversial pail of toilet articles.

You see, when we first arrived, they had presented us with these pails that were loaded with such items as toothpaste, shaving cream, stuff like that. We all thought they were general issue, nobody felt we had to pay for this gear, but we did. Hell, they may have even charged us for those baldy haircuts they gave us, for all I know. But one dollar and sixty cents! Could Uncle Sam really spare it?

Well, early in our training we had taken aptitude tests. I guess I did pretty well on mine because after boot camp I was sent to radio school at Quantico. After I arrived there, I quickly found out two things, something like those good news and bad news jokes of recent years.

First, the good news. It seemed that one of the first benefits about being a radio man was you did not have to go on mess duty. Hooray. I had hated that job my last week at boot camp.

Now, the bad news. When I had enlisted, I had been given this big song and dance about joining the regulars, not the reserves.

"Listen," they told me, "the regulars are always sent to the head of the line at mess call, pay call, sick call—everything. Join the regulars and always be first." So I joined the regulars.

Baloney! When you stood in line, you were a Marine, period. You took your regular spot no matter what you were, if you wanted to save your teeth. That's the way it was everywhere in the Corps.

My job at Quantico was to learn everything I could about field communications in a hurry. The Corps was growing as fast as possible because headquarters wanted to send a division overseas as quickly as they could. They needed radio men badly. The next thing I knew, I was ordered to report to the 11th Marines at New River, North Carolina. I don't think I was at New River long enough to unpack my sea bag before new orders came through. My outfit was to take a troop train to San Francisco where we would embark for the Pacific. I'd been in the Corps five months at this point. During this time I had been granted one lousy seventy-two hour pass to see my family. I wasn't to return to the States until November '44. How does that grab you, shipmate?

Our trip to the Pacific was a horror story in itself. We were headed for Wellington, New Zealand, which is a long cruise, especially under wartime conditions. During that entire voyage I don't think we had one decent meal.

You see, this was not a U.S. Navy ship, it was a merchant ship. The government was paying the ship owners per head to take us to the Pacific. Part of this allotment was to go for our food. Hell, someone must have gone south with that money. When they did feed us, it was slop. We used to line up at the ship's stores just to buy peanuts. Not much of a diet I'll grant you, but better than what we were getting from the ship.

And what a waste the whole deal was. Here the government had spent this money getting us in good physical shape and it all went out the window because someone was making a bundle. It was quite an eye-opener to a young kid to realize that someone was probably hosing a bunch of men on their way to combat. I heard there was a big investigation about the whole deal afterward, but I never found out how it turned out.

Well, New Zealand ended up being another one of those quick stopovers. Instead of a lengthy training period with our 105s—which we desperately needed—we found that we were about to take off again. This time we were to go aboard the *U.S.S. Hunter Liggett*. Our next port of call would be Guadalcanal.

By now our group had become P Battery, 5th Battalion, 11th Marines. Back in the States we had trained mainly with 155s, but now we had 105s. I guess they felt the smaller gun would be more practical in jungle fighting.

As for the *Liggett*, it was no luxury liner, but it was head and shoulders above the one we came over on.

One of our old-line sergeants told us that Hunter Liggett had been a leading Army general in World War I and had been a favorite of this sergeant. According to him, Pershing had originally wanted to send Liggett back to the States because he was so overweight, but Liggett had told Pershing that while he was overweight, he had no fat above his collar. I might add that our sergeant weighed in at about 230.

I can't remember how long we were on the *Liggett* or when we found out it was Guadalcanal we were to hit, but it really doesn't make any difference. None of us had ever heard of the Canal anyway. We had one guy from Brooklyn in the battery who kept calling it the Gowanus Canal.

Well, whatever we called the Island, it was surely deceptive looking. Hell, it would put you in mind of some kind of a tropical dream, at least where we were to land. You know, something like one of those travel posters or a scene out of a Dorothy Lamour film. From our vantage point we couldn't see what a putrefying shithole it really was.

We went ashore sometime during the morning of August 7, a really bright day out there. Then we waited around for our artillery and equipment. Our job was to set the guns up around what was to be called Henderson Field. This way we could cover the field from all directions.

All of a sudden we heard these planes overhead. I think they were bombers. I know they were Japanese. We weren't expecting this so the only thing we could think of doing was to blast away at them with our Springfields. Did we ever feel foolish when someone pointed out that the range of our rifles didn't begin to go far enough to reach the planes. It is really ridiculous when you look back and think of some of the stupid things we did out there.

I pulled another beauty one night after we'd set the guns up. We got the word—which by the way proved false—to expect the Japs to infiltrate our lines that evening. So we all sat in our holes and waited. In the hole nearest to mine was this roly-poly sergeant. Now, don't get me wrong. At a time like this everyone's scared unless he's squirrelly. But this guy was petrified. I mean, he was driving me crazy with his whimpering. Hell, the poor guy might have been balmy, but you don't think of something like that when you're fidgety yourself.

At any rate, I snuck over to his hole, grabbed his arm and whispered something in Japanese.

"Mother of God!" he yelled out and took off like a big-ass bird. I never told him I had been his evening caller because there was no way you were going to convince the fearless sergeant that he hadn't been accosted by Tojo himself.

Actually, fun and games aside, I had been a goddamn fool. There were plenty of Marines killed by our own people at night during the war. I'm lucky I didn't become one of them. I never did anything as stupid as that again.

It wasn't all laughs though, believe me. Our job was normally to fire in support of the infantry. My own job would vary. Sometimes I would be out phoning the grids back on the wire. Other times I would be at the command post or on the guns receiving the information. My real specialty was finding a wire break and repairing it. I think I became rather good at this, if I say so myself.

While our post was never overrun on the Canal, we did take casualties. Remember, the artillery battalions almost never suffer as much as the rifle companies, but we certainly did have some rough moments on the Canal. Ironically, our worst loss came not from the Japanese soldiers but from one of their warships.

Now, I say loss, but you could say devastation. It happened, I believe, one night around the middle of October. It seems that their ships could come in then and shell us almost at will. The night the disaster occurred I was originally sitting at our command post. When the shelling started, it sounded like the end of the world. We were later told that the enemy had a battleship throwing in fourteen-inchers that night.

Whatever, it was too much for one of our men. He completely broke down. His crackup was starting to get to me, so I hightailed it over to our guns. The lieutenant in charge of the battery, a man named Marshall Smith, didn't seem too happy to see me. I tried to explain what had happened, but he didn't really care.

"Oh hell, Pyne," he said, "shut up and get in a foxhole. This is going to be a rough night." He was right.

The command post itself had been located about a half mile from the guns, on the reverse side of a hill. It was just about as safe a spot as you could find.

Sir, do you know that night the command post took a direct hit after I had left it? It must have been caught by a fourteen-incher because there was nothing left. I mean, that's all she wrote, nothing! The nine men at the post were all blown out of town. The place where I had been was obliterated.

Later, on Cape Gloucester, a buddy of mine standing next to me had his face blown off. Then, on Peleliu, the wound I received could have easily killed me. But those were the rub of the green. The command post was different. It was almost ordained that I should leave there. Talk about the fickle finger of fate. Wow!

Okay. I would like to add something about Lieutenant (later Major) Marshall None Smith. The None was Marine Corps. Smith actually didn't have a middle name, but the Marine Corps said you had to have one, especially if your name was Smith. So, Smith told them to just put down None.

The morning after the shelling Smith had to pick out a detail to find what was left of the men at the command post. He knew that two of the dead men had been with me since boot camp. He realized it would be a living hell for me to look for their arms and legs. So, he deliberately left me *off* the detail.

Why was Smith this way? The answer is simple. He was one hell of a leader, the epitome of what an officer should be. Integrity, courage and, above all, a regard for his men. Smith had it all. I heard he went to work for the Hoffman Machinery Company after the war, but I don't know where he is now. He's one officer I'd like to have a drink with.

Well, thank God the command post shelling was real rare. The rest of our action against the enemy on the Canal never approached the devastation of that disaster. But we were constantly moving in and out of combat. After a while you get somewhat used to it. It does, however, prey on your mind, and you'd be surprised how deep your thinking can become.

Take one morning when I was on forward observation duty over on the Matanikau. I had reached the crest of a hill that gave me a commanding view of the whole area just as the dawning, as the poet says, was kissing the darkness good morning. The sight was magnificent beyond belief. A thinning mist was rising from the river. You could hear what seemed to be hundreds of birds chirping, along with any number of other sounds that came from a tropical jungle. I thought to myself, "My God, this is what the island must have looked like millions of years ago." I wondered what kind of creatures were living there then and did they also go around killing each other?

Then, Bang! A Japanese shell landed over on my right. They had brought me out of my trance in a hurry. I was in the same business and I knew the next shell would come a lot closer. I got lost as quickly as I could. But, I ask you, do you know anything more stupid than war? I don't.

Part of what we'd do could be the luck of the draw. For instance, I missed out on Edson's big fight on the ridge but a buddy of mine named Braddock didn't. When something big like that was coming up, they might not take the whole battery, just some fill-ins to make sure they had enough. Incidentally, he did quite a job over there; I think he ended up getting the Navy Cross. I lost track of him after the Canal. He's another guy I'd like to run into. It's funny, every now and then you'll think of someone who you once lived in such close proximity with. Then you realize, hell, you'll probably never see the guy again. I just might go to one of those reunions some day to see whom I can locate.

Well, around the middle of December they moved us off Guadalcanal. We'd been there for four months and we were beat. That constant strain of combat, the lousy diet and, above all, the goddamn malaria had turned us into scarecrows. We were a mess.

So they took us to Australia and then came an incredible blunder. We landed at a designated camp near Brisbane. And guess who was waiting for us? Our old friend, the malaria mosquito. These pests started arriving in the thousands. They'd bite the men who were still infected, then go to a Marine who'd gotten over the bug for their next meal. The first thing you knew our sick bays were overflowing.

Then General Vandegrift got into the act. He raised the roof with General MacArthur, pointing out that we were trying to rebuild the division, not decimate it further. MacArthur agreed, and as fast as they could they started moving us over near Melbourne. There was no malaria there, but I managed to get myself really in hot water anyway.

You see, as I was one of the men who was reinfected with malaria up near Brisbane, I had to turn into the hospital when we arrived at the new camp. Things were rather lax there so the first chance I got I went into town, figuring it would be great to sit in an Australian pub and knock down a few beers. This happens to be just what you should not do when you have malaria. I got sick as a dog. Hell, I don't even remember getting back to the hospital.

The next day the sisters—you called nurses sister in Australia, but they weren't nuns—were nice as pie about it. However, they did tell me I had been listed AWOL and that the Australian doctor was quite upset about it. He was a major in their army and I became quite concerned.

As it turned out, I should have been worried. The minute the doctor appeared, he started reading me the riot act. I could take this because I knew I had been wrong. But he wasn't going to stop with me. The next thing he jumped on was the Marine Corps. I asked him to please take it easy, which just seemed to infuriate him further.

"Besides,' he yelled, "not only are you Marines a bunch of tramps, but all Americans are worthless. I wish we could get you the hell out of Australia."

On and on he went in spite of my pleading. He hated all of us, from George Washington on.

Finally, I reverted to form. I jumped out of bed and gave him my best Sunday punch, right on the money. Jeez, he went sailing on his ass for about twenty feet. All the other Marines in the ward had heard the whole thing. Hell, you'd have thought I had won the war. Joe DiMaggio never had more cheers. And that's what saved my hide.

Originally they put me up for a general court martial. Then all these other Marines started to stick up for me. Our officers did not take it too kindly when they heard about the doctor's unbelievable tirade about everything American. I ended up with a summary court martial. Of course I was busted from PFC down to private and was also sentenced to a long stretch on bread and water, which turned into a joke. I was guarded by my own buddies who made sure I ate like a king.

Now, please don't let the major stand as typical of the Australian people. My God, they were the warmest, the friendliest, the most beautiful people in the world. I have a strong penchant to go back and see some of those generous people again. But not the major.

In turn, most of the time, we returned their kindness, but not always. Two of our men registered in a Melbourne hotel as PFC Chester Field and Corporal Philip Morris. They promptly stole all the sheets and pillow cases they could find and took off. We all thought this was rather crummy. However, no one gave any of the stuff back.

Our discipline in Australia hit its heights, or its depths, depending on how you look at it, when they read off the findings of another Marine's summary court martial in front of the whole battalion. Everything was very formal indeed until they got to the man's offense; this the captain read off very slowly, enunciating each syllable quite clearly.

"Ur—in—nat(e)—ing on The King's High—way."

We all broke up, including the captain. I always felt the whole thing was done as a gag, but who knows.

In the meantime, we were constantly receiving replacements to rebuild the division. When we were back in shape, we started the well known tough Marine Corps training. After several months of this we went to New Guinea for some advance work. We all felt it was back to the jungle for us and we were right.

This time it was a place called Cape Gloucester on the tip of New Britain Island. It was right off the eastern end of New Guinea. Once again we were going after an airfield. We boarded our LSTs on December 24, 1943—a hell of a way to celebrate Christmas Eve.

These LSTs would have been all right if they'd had about one-third as many troops aboard as they did. As it was, we could hardly move. I tried to sleep up on deck on a canvas between the ribs of an F.W. Dig truck. By the time we landed, December 26th, we were all punchy from lack of sleep and seasickness. Fortunately, like the Canal, the landing was unopposed. Strangely, while the casualties on Gloucester were the lowest our division was to have in any of its campaigns, it was the first time that our battery had real eyeball-to-eyeball action with the Japanese.

It isn't the action that stands out the most to me about Cape Gloucester though, it is the awful weather. Rain, rain, rain, every day and night. Someone said the brass had picked the rainy season to go in because they felt we would surprise the enemy. Maybe so, but the area we fought in became a goddamn masterful mudslide.

The 11th picked up a unit citation here because we did such a great job slugging the guns through the mud. You'd be trying to move through the jungle when you'd find yourself up to your knees, or deeper, in a mud pit. There was a joke floating around that went like this:

This captain is looking at one of those mud pies when a helmet appears moving through the mud. Then it comes up a little higher and the captain sees a head.

"Jeez," the captain says, "you must be in real deep."

"Real deep," the Marine replies. "Wait 'til you see the bulldozer I'm driving!"

As you can imagine, the damn diseases ran rampant. Malaria came back and so did dysentery—just think what happened to your bowels in weather like that. Even our ponchos began to disintegrate.

Then there was jungle rot. You couldn't possible keep your socks dry, much less your boondockers. This knocked the devil out of your feet. By the time we left New Britain many of our men could hardly walk.

Another menace was those big trees. They were rotten. The shelling and the lightning were always knocking them over. Our division actually had several men killed from either lightning or falling trees.

Remember that during all this we were trying to fight a war. I did a lot of forward observing with the 7th Marines and could actually see the Japanese during some of their charges. Call them fanatical if you like, but, my God, they were brave! Our artillery and automatic weapons cut them to ribbons, but they'd come at you until they'd drop. Sometimes they'd come at you until they were close enough to toss grenades, and sometimes we'd toss them back. That Jap grenade must have had much more of a delayed action than ours did. That's the way it seemed to us anyway.

Then there was their sniper fire. I was talking to a buddy when the left side of his helmet was hit by a bullet that came out the back side without touching the guy's head. That's about as close as you can come to the end of the ballgame. A day or two later another Marine I knew also took a slug in his helmet that came out the other end, but this time it took the poor guy's brain with it.

Well, we took our airfield, killed a lot of very brave Japanese soldiers and sometime in the early spring, they took us off New Britain. The division had suffered about fourteen hundred battle casualties and a great deal of sickness. Scuttlebutt had us going back to Australia, but we were in for quite a letdown. Instead of Australia we went to an abomination called Pavuvu in the Russell Islands. It was only sixty miles from Guadalcanal. Malaria, ringworm and all that jungle crap was there. It's a good thing we received a large number of replacements because what was left of the original division was fast becoming Asiatic. The morale of many of the old-timers was so low they didn't even engage in that time-honored Marine occupation known as gum-beating. And that, my friend, is truly a sad state of affairs. All good Marines bitch.

One of the few bright memories of that dump was the visit of Bob Hope and Jerry Colonna. Most of us had grown up listening to the Bob Hope radio show. If there was one person who could bring the States to the Solomons, it was Bob.

You know, Hope went everywhere—I'd like to get his opinion of Pavuvu. I'll bet it's also at the top of his shit list. However, as it turned out, the next place we were to hit—of course we were after a Jap airfield—was to make us wish we were back on Pavuvu.

The name of the island is Peleliu. It's part of a group named the Palau Islands, about six hundred miles west of Mindanao in the Philippines.

What I saw and went through during my short stay on that butcher shop so overshadows anything else that I can't even remember how we got there. It must have been either on an APA or an LST, but get there we did.

The initial landing took place on September 15, about a month before MacArthur went into the Philippines. I was not in the first wave—the artillery never is—but I wasn't far behind. I landed with our observation group because part of my job was to locate places where we could set up the guns as they arrived.

We could see from shipboard that the riflemen were having a brutal time, but we didn't realize how brutal it really was. Once we were in the LCIs, we were told to keep our heads down. We didn't actually know the whole story until we landed.

Oh, my God, what a sight! You could see Marines lying all over the place, some dead and other wounded, wrecked landing craft of all types, abandoned equipment everywhere—just a gruesome mess. It looked as if we were getting the hell knocked out of us and we were. But we were still there. You know, I think that was the only time the 1st Division landed under real heavy fire and it was one time too many. I'll never forget that sight.

Well, we landed and started inland. I don't think we'd gone more than two or three hundred yards when our captain, a man named Marvin Polen, gave us the word.

"Down, down, hit the deck!"

We all went down just as the bullets started going over us, but we really didn't know where the fire was coming from. So I stuck my head up to see what was going on. I spotted this emplacement about a hundred or so yards in front of us. It seemed to me it was a dug in pillbox. I figured if I crawled far enough to my left, I would be able to flank the damn thing without any Nips seeing me and drop a hand grenade into the hole where the gun was. Believe it or not, I was able to maneuver around just as I thought and found myself on top of the pillbox.

Then came the moment of truth. I hadn't brought any hand grenades with me. As a matter of fact, I didn't have a weapon of any kind. Did I ever feel like a horse's ass! But ask anyone who was in combat; you frequently act like that, you know, not thinking; you just act on an impulse.

Anyway, by this time a couple of my buddies are moving over on the pillbox's flank. I motion for them to toss me a grenade, which one of them does do. Fortunately, I caught the grenade and promptly dropped it into the pillbox. No more machine gun!

Then our captain, who knew how to tell the Japanese to surrender in their own language, yells into the pillbox. We stood back and waited. Pretty soon one of them came out with his hands over his head. He looked dazed but wasn't wounded.

Now, I'm ashamed to say this, but one of our men shot him down. Not only was this a vicious thing to do but it was asinine. You can bet your life that none of the others are now going to come out.

In the meantime, one of our tanks had come ashore. So the tanker stuck his 37 millimeter gun right into the pillbox and let go a couple of rounds.

Naturally, there is no one left alive in there, right? No—wrong! Wiseass Pyne looks into the damn place to find out what's happening. Out of nowhere a Japanese hand grenade makes its appearance. I was in a state of shock. Involuntarily I moved backward, bumping into the side of the trench the Japanese had dug round the pillbox. I missed the full blast, but several fragments tore into my chest, knocking me over. I looked at the front of my blouse. It was a bloody mess.

"Holy Christ," I thought, "I'm only nineteen years of age and I'm dying. What a lousy deal!"

Captain Polen came running over, looked at all the blood and bellowed, "Corpsman, corpsman!" I don't know how he did it but Polen had one of those pill pushers there in a jiffy. And speaking of corpsmen, they were our real unsung heroes. What a job they did! All in all, it took them about an hour to get me off the beach on to the hospital ship *Bountiful*.

Surprisingly enough, none of the grenade fragments had hit a vital organ. The wound was serious, but I was going to live. Can you imagine what it means to think you're dying and then being told you are going to make it? Hallelujah!

They sent me back to a staging area to recuperate to, of all places, Guadalcanal. "Jeez," I said to myself, "this is where I came in."

While I was on the mend, I received some bad news. Captain Polen had been killed a few days after I had left Peleliu. I can still remember his last words to me.

"Pyne," he said, "that was a real gutty thing you did. I'm putting you in for a Silver Star."

Somewhere along the line it was knocked down to a Bronze Star, but so what. I'd give up all the ribbons I have to sit down and have a drink with Marvin Polen. What a guy!

Once I was back on my feet, I thought they'd send me back to the 11th. But, the doctor just shook his head.

"Pyne," he chuckled, "you've been over here thirty months and gone through three campaigns. We really don't want to turn you into a basket case. You're going home."

"Doctor," I replied, "you'll get no argument from me!"

So I headed back to the States, which to me meant Pelham Manor, New York. Then, a funny thing happened.

It wasn't only that I was treated like a hero, which I figured I wasn't —hell, the heroes were all dead—but it was the fact that I just couldn't relate. You take a seventeen-year-old kid, send him out to the Pacific War for thirty months, and then drop him off in Westchester County, New York, and it's bound to baffle him.

When people started to fall all over me, I just couldn't handle it. Can you imagine describing the beach at Peleliu to your mother? The good woman would have been shocked beyond belief. Or taking a young beauty out that you are trying to score with and telling her about the men who had the shits in the rain on Cape Gloucester. It took me quite a while to get back into their world.

After a long stay at home, I reported to advance artillery training at Quantico, Virginia. Man, was this ever fat city! Great duty. Plenty of liberty and all that went with it. I knew eventually I'd be going back over, probably for the invasion of Japan. I tried not to think about it, but it was always lurking in the back of my mind.

Then came August 1945. Thank God! I felt a huge load had been lifted from my shoulders.

I really went after my education after the war, graduating from Columbia University in 1950. You know how fortunate I've been since, both with my family and in business. There are times, however, when I'll be dealing with my Japanese friends and I just can't imagine how we ended up fighting them. They're the salt of the earth, believe me.

The Goettge Patrol

THE KILLING WAR

"Well, hell," recalls Bill Hawkins, "I didn't even know that patrol was going out. I could have told them it was real dangerous territory.

"This bloodletting hit me particularly hard because Lieutenant Ralph Corey, our interpreter, had been a buddy of mine ever since I went on active duty back in 1940. He didn't come back from that patrol. Only three did out of the twenty-six who went out."

Hawkins is talking about a patrol that Colonel Frank Goettge, the 1st Division's intelligence officer, took out from the Marines' perimeter on Guadalcanal. It is hard to understand why Goettge did what he did, but I guess it can be attributed to the lack of knowledge the Americans possessed then about the Japanese soldier.

Whatever, on August 12, the colonel set out on what he believed was both a military and humanitarian mission. It seems that a Japanese prisoner had told of a starving group of soldiers in a native village just beyond the Matanikau River. He said he was sure the Japanese would be delighted to surrender providing they would be fed a square meal or two.

This was just what Goettge was looking for, the first sizable surrender of Japanese forces in the war.

To make the story even more attractive, a patrol on the previous day reported a white flag flying in a village they had encountered near the area the prisoner was talking about.

So Goettge rounded up twenty-four Marines and a Navy doctor, Lieutenant Commander Malcomb Pratt, and headed down the coast in Higgins boats for a quick landing.

When they went ashore, the colonel stuck a leash around the neck of the Nip prisoner and told him to lead on. They had just gone a short way when the alleged starving Japanese opened up with automatic weapons. The colonel and the prisoner were killed instantly. The rest of the patrol then tried to set up a defense but their position was hopeless.

One by one the Marines were hit by the enemy fire. Only three members of the patrol succeeded in returning to the perimeter. Proceeding partially by foot and partially by swimming, the men were lucky enough to reach the Marine area.

One of the survivors had a shocking tale to tell. The last member of the group to leave, he had jumped into the surf shortly before the position was overrun. As he took one last look at the beach, he could see the flash of Japanese bayonets as the enemy slaughtered the wounded Marines.

The report of Goettge's demise spread throughout the ranks of the Marines like wildfire, especially the part about the butchering of the wounded. The deaths of twenty-three men would not seem so drastic later on. But at this point, the Marines on Guadalcanal had seen very little action. They did not realize that when you fought the Japanese, you could not expect quarter. They gave none and expected none. The killing war had started.

The Scout and Sniper from the Bronx

Bob Stiles

Bob Stiles is seventy years of age. He is still a very successful paper salesman in New York City. Born and raised in the Bronx, he has lived in Glen Rock, New Jersey, for the past thirty years. To Bob, the country's change over the last four decades has been bewildering.

"The Bronx was a lot different when I was growing up," he tells you. "We lived on Ogden Avenue, then we moved over to Hull. I think you had much more of a community feeling in those days than you do now. You never said you came from New York; it was always the Bronx.

"And people don't have values built in them the way we had," he continues. "I'm in the office most mornings between 8:00 and 8:30. My boss, George Stone, another old-timer, will greet me.

" 'Bob,' he'll ask me, 'what the hell are you doing here at 8:15?'

" 'George,' " I'll answer, " 'may I reverse the question?' I guess we must be the last of the Mohicans.

"You see, when I went to work, I guess I believed in the old theory, work hard and you'll be a success. These efforts may be old-fashioned, but they've worked for me."

Indeed they have. He and his wife Vivian have raised three children, two sons and a daughter. One of his sons is a lawyer, and the other a doctor.

"My daughter," he says, "is a graduate of the University of Vermont. Once a fashion model, she is about to be married and get me some more grandchildren."

And Bob adds, "Not bad for a kid from the Bronx!"

PFC ROBERT STILES
1st Marines, 1st Division

"I'm a horse's ass from Yemassee,
The biggest ass you'll ever see."

—Parris Island Lament

In 1941 I was working for Marquardt and Company, a paper company in the Bronx. I was twenty-nine years of age and a bachelor. I joined the Corps in December and left for boot camp the following month. Shortly after I arrived at Parris Island, I received a letter from my boss, Ossie Marquardt. It went like this:

"Sorry I missed seeing you before you left. Get a Jap for me! I hope this covers incidentals."

Jeez, it was a check for two hundred dollars. That was a month's pay. What a great guy that Mr. Marquardt was! Of course, he's long gone now, but that shows you the way people thought forty years ago. There was no question who wore the white hats—we did.

Well, I'd been brought up in the Bronx, went to Roosevelt High School and was hooked on the Yankees—the Bronx Bombers. I first saw them in action when they still played in Manhattan at the Polo Grounds. Jake Ruppert, the beer guy, owned them.

Then they moved over to Yankee Stadium in the Bronx, and what teams they had there! That guy, Ruth, he didn't care; he could hit home runs out of Central Park. And Gehrig, what a gentleman! Then came DiMagg, King Kong Keller and those guys—the Yanks, all great players. Nothing could be better on a summer afternoon than going to the stadium, drinking some beer, and watching those guys play.

Well, the day after Pearl Harbor I went down to 90 Church Street to enlist in the Marine Corps. No one was going to do to Uncle Sam what the Japs did and get away with it. Remember, at twenty-nine years of age I was no kid, but I was in great shape and I knew I could stand Marine training. Above all, I wanted a crack at those Japs as soon as possible.

I did have one fear. I only weighed 140 pounds and as I looked around at all those big guys, I began to wonder if I could get in. Four policemen in uniform, each weighing over 200 pounds, real big guys, were standing in front of me. If this was what they wanted, I would be in trouble. The Marine sergeant quickly gave me the word.

"Don't worry," he said, "you'll be a smaller target than those birds. Besides, big guys like that frequently can't take the punishment a little guy can take."

That was it. They took us all and we were off for Parris Island. The train ride wasn't bad until we got to a town called Yemassee, South

Carolina; there we switched to old-fashioned trains that must have been used by General Custer. We kept making jokes about watching for Indian attacks.

Now, Parris Island at this time seemed to be in utter confusion. Boots were arriving by the thousands and they're throwing all this gear at them at the same time. I recall looking at my '03 rifle, all covered with cosmoline and wondering what the hell am I supposed to do with this? I was a city boy; I'd never fired a rifle in my life. Little did I realize how I was going to fall in love with that beauty. Remember? "This is my rifle; this is my life." Well, it turned out to be true with me.

The first thing they did was put us in tents. And do you know that's all I lived in, tents, I mean, until the summer of 1944 when I came home from Pavuvu. Thirty months in a tent and it wasn't all that bad, even for a Bronx boy.

I can't tell you how many recruits we had to each of these tents, but I do recall I was in with a lot of guys from the South and they wanted to be sure everyone knew it. Jeez, you'd have thought the Civil War was still going on. Back in the Bronx, we just didn't look at people as either Rebels or Yanks, but those southern boys sure did. Here it was, eighty or so years after General Lee surrendered, and these characters wouldn't admit it.

There was one other northerner in my tent. His name was Tony; I think he was from Philadelphia. The two of us became great pals. Later we both became members of the scouts and snipers. We lost Tony on Cape Gloucester; a Jap sniper got him in the head. I've never forgotten him though, and I never will.

So we were originally set to spend ten weeks in boot camp, but you can remember what February '42 was like. The Japs were moving fast and picking up everything that wasn't nailed down. They cut short our course on Parris Island to six weeks and hustled us over to Tent City near Jacksonville, North Carolina. When we got there, they gave us an advanced rush course in weapons.

Jeez, what an ordeal that was! The .45s, mortars, light and heavy machine guns, the Tommy submachine gun, everything you can think of.

Take the .45. We'd have to go into a tent where they'd blindfold you. Then you had to take the darn thing apart and put it back together again, naming each part as you put it into place. If you fouled up, good-bye weekend pass—not even any beer at the slop chute—you'd spend Sunday doing the whole thing over and over. We all thought this was chicken shit, but it came in handy later on.

Every now and then you'd have guys who just couldn't keep up the pace they were throwing at us and some of them would crack up.

One kid from Georgia—he'd said he was seventeen, but we all felt he was fifteen—just snapped. He shot his trigger finger off with his '03. Poor kid, he just couldn't take it. But, better that he did it in North Carolina than on Guadalcanal.

We did try to blow off steam on the weekends, but Jacksonville was hardly New York City. One of our guys was a local man and he would sometimes have a girl friend drive several of us over to Myrtle Beach which was a lot better liberty than Jacksonville—nowhere near as many servicemen.

Jeez, wait a minute, don't let me forget Mr. Love, the Jacksonville hustler. Every Saturday he'd run a couple of taxis up to the woods near the gate. He'd have a hooker in each cab ready for instant action. It was a little too gamy for me, but several of the boys didn't look at it that way. That creep, the pimp, he made a bundle. Can't remember any of the boys getting the clap, but I guess some of them must have.

Our next stop was San Francisco where we laid over for a while, waiting for a troopship. Our train ride across the U.S. wasn't bad but it kept dragging on and on. Christ, it must have taken ten days to reach the West Coast, but this was nothing compared to the time we spent on the troopship that took us to New Zealand; we must have been aboard her five weeks before we reached Wellington.

Anyway, by the time we reached New Zealand, we were all out of shape, particularly me. I've always hated heights, so naturally I ended up on the crossarms as a lookout. Everything went all right as long as I didn't have to look down at the deck. After my two-hour watch was over, I started to climb down. The minute I hit the deck, my stomach cracked—I puked all over the place. Everyone thought this was funny as hell.

Well, we finally went out on deck one morning and there were the green hills of New Zealand with the sheep grazing everywhere. But, damn it, we never got to see any of the place. The 5th Marines of our Division (the 1st) had arrived earlier than we did and had a chance to spend some time with the New Zealanders, but not my outfit (L Company, 3rd Battalion, 1st Marines). All we did in New Zealand was change our gear over to another ship and hang around the docks. The first thing we knew, we had taken off for Guadalcanal.

As each day passed, we realized our transport was taking us closer and closer to wherever it was we were going to meet the Japs. The men started to get real edgy. Remember, the large majority of us had never been in combat. We didn't know what to expect. All we knew was we were about to fight these guys who had been knocking the hell out of everybody else in the Pacific.

Then, at about 3 A.M. on August 7, we got the word.

"NOW HEAR THIS—NOW HEAR THIS!" came over the loudspeaker. "You are going to have steak sandwiches for breakfast. This will be your last meal before debarking. Good luck!"

So this was it. We all knew where to go. Everything had been worked out long ago. In a situation like this, nothing can be left to chance. After all, we didn't know what kind of reception to expect. Any kind of a foul-up can cost lives. We were to wait for the dawn and then move.

Oh, my God, when dawn did break, what a sight! All these ships had moved up during the night, battlewagons, cruisers, carriers, tin cans, you name it, it was there. It looked like the whole U.S. Navy was supporting us. We had company. It gave us all a comfortable feeling.

Then, wham! the wind blew and you know what flew. Those swabbies opened up on the island with a vengeance. We didn't realize it at the time, but it was almost a complete waste. The few Japs in the area had hauled ass back into the boonies the minute they saw us.

After the barrage stopped, we all got ready to go down the net into our designated Higgins boat. Some guy, you see, has a megaphone, like the one Rudy Vallee used to use, and he's calling out each boat number when that boat is to be loaded. We had no problem going over the side, but when we were safely aboard our Higgins boat, the trouble started.

We had to keep circling our mother ship waiting our turn to hit the beach and, hell, some of the guys started getting seasick. One guy would puke and he'd start a chain reaction. The combination of the rolling ship and the stink of that second-hand breakfast steak could get anyone going.

But believe me, it doesn't take long for you to stop feeling sorry for the sick ones. You are worried about yourself, you know—Semper Fi, Mac. So we start trying to keep all the pukers on one side of the boat, but it really didn't work. It was just a mess.

Thank God there weren't any Japs firing at us. I understand the water was even rougher over at Gavutu and when some of those Paramarines went in, they didn't care if the Japs hit them or not.

At any rate, orders were being given by the color and numbers of the flares being shot off. Our turn came and we landed. My buddy, Tony, and I moved inland as fast as we could to see what we could find. There were no Japs around but we found an uneaten breakfast near the airfield. Our bombardment had taken those Nips completely by surprise.

Now, you might wonder how a couple of city guys like Tony and I became scouts and snipers. I think it was because of the rifle. Both of us had shot expert at Tent City, so when they were asking for sniper volunteers, we applied and were accepted.

Also, we were both what they used to call "street smart" and we didn't have that much trouble adapting to the jungle. Survival is survival, be it the Bronx or a stinkhole in the Pacific.

Here's the way it worked. We remained part of L/3/1, but we were on constant readiness for assignments from battalion, regiment, or division. Most of our orders came from Lieutenant Colonel McKelvy, CO of our 3rd Battallion, and as the campaign dragged on, it seemed he had more and more for us to do.

Take the time I had come back from a three-day patrol in that cruddy jungle. I was beat down to my socks which, I may add, hadn't been washed in two weeks and smelled like skunk cabbage. McKelvy called me to his tent.

"Stiles, get ready for a big one," he said. "You're going out again."

"Holy Christ, colonel," I answered. "I can hardly walk!"

He just smiled. "What's the matter, Stiles, don't you want a Purple Heart?"

I mumbled something about what he could do with his Purple Heart. Bullshit with that nosie! But I went out. I was gone for three more days and got back without a scratch.

Now, don't get me wrong. McKelvy was 4.0, a great officer. When he wanted something done, he wanted it done. That's all there was to it.

Well, we first started going out on these patrols with regularity shortly after we landed. Most of the time I would either work alone or with one or two other guys. My favorite team would have me on one point and Tony on the other and a guy named Sergeant Saychek in the middle. But you could never count on always being with the same guy.

I once went out with a Marine who shall remain nameless. He wasn't a bad guy, but he was not the kind of guy for my type of work. Here's what happened.

McKelvy called me and this other guy to his tent.

"Tokyo Rose knows we're here all right," he said. "We just heard her broadcast. She's boasting that none of the Marine criminals is going to get off the island alive. The Imperial Japanese are going to fix our wagon. So, you two go out near the Tenaru River and see if you see any signs of the Nips."

Okay, so we went out and combed the bushes all day but saw nothing. We then headed back to McKelvy to give him the scoop, but he still was dubious.

"I know those sons of bitches are out there. I just want to know in what strength. Are they strong enough to mount an attack? Go back into the jungle. Go out about a thousand yards or so. Bring a signal telephone with you and report anything that stirs. You can take turns sleeping."

So we got a phone and wire, and headed out. After we're all set up in a foxhole, I turned to my companion.

"Look," I told him, "I'm a city boy. I never go to sleep 'til real late. I'll stay up as long as I can, while you sleep. If I reach a point where I really need to sleep, I'll let you know."

Well, I stayed up until I knew I better hit the pad myself. I woke up my foxhole mate and gave him the word. Then I conked out.

Jeez, it seemed I had no sooner fallen asleep when the clown's snoring woke me up. I gave him a big kick in the ass.

"Oh, God," he blurted out, "I'm sorry, I'm sorry."

As I said, he wasn't a bad guy at all. He just was no one to trust in a deal like this.

"Okay, okay," I answered, "this goes no further than right here. But don't *ever* ask to go out with me again. That was my life you were playing with."

You see, if there was one thing the Japs were good at, it was night infiltrating. They could cut your throat before you knew what they were doing. You can bet your life I didn't sleep again with that guy on guard.

We didn't see a thing that night, but when we reported in the next day, we were told to get back to the perimeter. A bunch of Japs had landed and our brass felt they'd hit us around the Tenaru the coming evening. They did.

When the attack came, I was checking to see if our telephone wires were set up right. And let me tell you, the wind really blew and the shit really flew. What a blast! We were throwing everything we had at them.

Many Japs in the first wave didn't even carry rifles. They had these big mats they'd throw on the barbed wire. This way the men behind them could get over the wire.

I was just behind our lines firing my '03 wherever I could line something up. The Marines with the .30 and .50 caliber machine guns were firing so fast they were burning out their barrels. They couldn't use short bursts because those Nips kept coming. The Marine fire was so heavy it actually cut down trees. Please don't say I said the Marines weren't scared. Most of us were, but we didn't break.

One of the guys I knew was a lad we called Little Chuck. He was so scared he set his rifle up on a bias with the bayonet at a forty-five degree angle. There was no way a charging Jap could get into Chuck's foxhole without going through that bayonet. Then Chuck lay back holding that rifle stock with all his might.

As the dawn came up, you could see that a Nip had tried; he had ended up impaled on the bayonet. Chuck had crawled over to the back part of his pretty good-sized hole and was staring at the dead Jap. I guess he was—whatyoucallit, transfixed.

When he saw me, he got embarrassed. Something really smelled and it wasn't all the dead Nip. You guessed it; Chuck had, to put it bluntly, crapped his pants. He got up, sighed, and cleaned himself up. You know, I never heard of Chuck being petrified again.

After that night, it seemed to me most of the ground action moved over to the Matanikau River and I hope you're ready for something that happened over there that's hard to believe. But it's true, so help me Hannah.

McKelvy got ahold of me for what seemed to be a routine mission. "Stiles," he said, "you know where company such and such is. Well, they're catching hell from a sniper no one can locate. Everytime a guy moves, he's fired on. No one has been killed yet, but they will be. Go get that bastard!"

So I moved over to where the company was and started moving through that damn konai grass and looking into the treetops. I was completely concealed by the konai yet I had a perfect view of those high trees.

Eventually I saw some movement in one of the trees. Pretty soon a head and then a rifle barrel came into view. I had my rifle sling nice and tight and my sight elevation was perfect. I let one go and, wham, out of the tree comes the Nip. I'm not bragging, but you asked me what I did on the Island and that was part of it.

Whenever one of us did hit a Jap sniper, we were supposed to search the corpse for any papers or unit identification.

My God, I started going through the dead Jap's blouse and I ran into breasts! Much to my utter amazement, the sniper was a woman. I don't know what the records say, but the Japanese had at least one female sniper on the Island. I know. I shot her.

Now, you might ask if the shooting of a woman bothered me, particularly as this happened in an age when women were more on a pedestal than they are now.

My answer is simple—not at all. The woman had already wounded two Marines. She was bound to kill one sooner or later. As I look back, the killing of anyone is horrifying, but once that Japanese woman went up into the tree with a rifle in her hand, she became fair game.

Okay, we are still on the Island. Here's another one for you—a time when I could have been killed by another Marine. Our password always began with an L because the Nips had trouble pronouncing Ls. This one night the word was Lilliputian. Where the hell they got that sweetheart, I'll never know.

Anyway, I'd been sent out on a mission. It was raining like the devil, so naturally I'm really pissed off. You know, the hell with the war. I want to keep dry. I'm moving through the brush when one of our sentries spots me.

"Halt, what's the password?" he asks. I can't see him very well, but I know he's got an '03 aimed at my gut.

Well, Jeez, I couldn't remember Lilliputian.

"Lillian, lollipop, Lazzeri. Hey, I'm Bob Stiles from the Bronx!"

Fortunately for me, the sentry knew something about the Yankees but he still wasn't sure.

"What is Gomez's nickname?" he asked.

"Lefty, Lefty," I answered, "there's another L for you."

It ended up all right, but if the guy had been a baseball hater, I would have been in trouble.

It's hard to pinpoint dates, but I think that password fiasco happened about the same time the western National Guard outfit (164th U.S. Infantry from the Dakotas) came to the Island. This was a great bunch of soldiers, but I feel they could have saved some of their men if they had listened more to those of us who had been there a while.

I was over in McKelvy's tent one day when he pointed out to their colonel that the Nips were tricky as hell.

"Oh, don't worry about that," the army colonel said, "I've got a bunch of rugged farm boys. They can handle the Japs."

He was partially right. His troops were superb soldiers, but there were so many things I wanted to tell them. For instance:

When one of the Japs fires at you from concealment, especially at night, don't have all your men open up on him. He may be a suicidal decoy. There are probably several other Japs watching and ready. They'll saturate the area where they see the return fire coming from.

Pay no attention to their yells of gas attack. They'll send over a smoke screen hoping you'll think it's gas. They know most of your men have thrown away their gas masks and the fear of a gas attack might panic your troops.

The wires. Those guys can set wires up in the jungle that can wipe out half a platoon.

Never go by a bunch of so-called dead ones without spraying the lot. There might be some of them playing possum who will open up on you when you've walked by.

And, above all, if they capture one of your men, write the poor guy off. They'll tie him to a tree and go to work on him. They're experts at this. They want your men to come running in to rescue the guy. They'll be waiting for you and not one of your men will survive.

I later heard—remember, I heard this, I didn't see it—they did try and rescue one of their men and got shot up pretty badly. They were brave men and good soldiers, but they had to learn some things the hard way.

Well, as the time went on, we became more and more efficient on our patrols. We were supposed to get information and we did.

There was one time when McKelvy wanted to check out reports about a large concentration of Japs some ten or so miles from our perimeter. Along with Tony and Saychek, my favorite team, I jumped into a Higgins boat that took us over to the spot McKelvy was anxious about. The three of us went ashore, while the Higgins boat waited to find out what the score was. Saychek and I stayed on the beach while Tony went into the bush to do some reconnoitering. A few minutes later, Tony came walking back to the beach.

"I can't see the bastards, but I can smell 'em, and lots of 'em at that. Let's drop our packs, the hell with 'em, and move toward the water as if we didn't know the Japs are here."

Okay, so we start to walk calmly toward the ocean, talking all the way. When we got to the water, we started to run through the surf toward the Higgins boat. When we got up to our hips, we began to swim. The minute we climbed aboard, the boat took off.

Jeez, we no sooner were under way when a slew of Japs came out of the jungle and opened up on us. If we hadn't taken off just when we did, we would have been goners. Those Nips asked no quarter and gave none. They were tough, brave guys, but that no quarter business could become pretty crummy. Normally, if we spotted several of them in the jungle, we'd backtrack. But if it was a matter of one or two of the Nips, and if it was an important mission, we had to kill them and not think twice about it.

I vividly remember going with Tony one time when we had this sergeant with us who could go through that jungle like a panther. I think our mission was to try and find out what kinda artillery the Japs were moving up. We found their camp all right, but they had a sentry out who was barring our way.

Christ, this sergeant crawled on his belly around the Nip so he could come on him from the rear. Then he put his hands over the Jap's mouth and stuck a knife in the guy's back so fast the poor SOB never knew what hit him. Oh, some of our guys were good, real good.

At any rate, sometime in December they moved us off the Island. We'd had four months of the worst kind of living you could imagine and we were used up. You've never seen a happier bunch of Raggedy Ass Marines than the 1st Division when they told us we were being sent to Australia.

Now, here's a crazy one for you. All that crap I went through on the Island—I never got malaria. Guys are getting it all around me, but not Stiles. But, when we first arrived in Australia, they sent us to Brisbane which also had those damn malaria bugs.

I not only got malaria but also yellow jaundice. I was sick as a dog.

They later told me I almost died which would have been ironic—I mean going through that whole mess on Guadalcanal and dying in Australia just wouldn't have been fair.

The malaria never comes back on me though. I think most of the men who did have the bug are long over it now. But not all of them. There is a guy from L Company named Cullen. I think he owns a bar in Boston. He told me he still goes into the VA hospital almost every month with that damn bug.

Well, they soon found out that Brisbane was not the place for a lashup already full of malaria, so they moved us to Melbourne. And what a reception they gave us there. They acted as if we were real heroes.

It must have been about four o'clock in the morning when our train pulled into the Melbourne station, yet there was still a big crowd of Aussies waving American flags. Remember, they didn't cheer us because we were Marines—hell, we could have been Girl Scouts—it was because we had stopped the Nips on the Island.

You see, in this summer of '42, the Australian Home Guard was made up of men over fifty and boys under seventeen. If the Japanese had invaded their country, the Aussies would have fought like hell; they always do, but they would have been in trouble. They felt our victory on the Island played a big part in keeping the Japs out of Australia. They wanted us to know they appreciated it, which was great because we sure appreciated them.

Besides, we hadn't been paid on the Island. Now all of a sudden we get paid a bundle. Jeez, you got PFCs taking a suite at the Hotel Australia. A girl wants to go to dinner—okay, honey, where to? These guys are taking the dolls to the best places in town. You never saw a Marine without a beauty on his arm, maybe two.

Now, don't get me wrong. Yes, there was plenty of hanky-panky going on—what do you expect?—but there were also plenty of lasting relationships formed. Many of the 1st Division Marines married Australian girls.

Anyway, we were really having a great time when, bang! came the explosion. Thousands of the ANZACs came home. Hell, they'd been away fighting the Germans for two or three years. What do they find —these bloody Yanks with their women.

What a battle! They had those big boots and we had our belt buckles. There were fist fights all over town. Many of us felt we should have been given a combat star for the battle of Melbourne.

Then the brass stepped in. Our generals decided to give a joint beer party for the Diggers at the cricket grounds. Thank God they didn't allow bottles, just keg beer. The public relations people sent out a glowing report that all was quiet and serene at the party. I say bullshit! I saw plenty of fights. But I will say things seemed to quiet down after the party.

But, you know, you really couldn't blame the Aussies. Think how we would have felt if we came home to the States and found all the girls going out with foreigners, even if they were our allies. Once again, the Australians were the salt of the earth. That whole scene between the troops was certainly to be expected.

In the meantime, we're getting back on our feet. There's plenty of war left and our next show is going to be Cape Gloucester on New Britain Island. This was a mudhole we were going to invade via a short stop on Goodenough Island off New Guinea. They should have given us submarine pay for Cape Gloucester; there was more water there than at Coney Island.

I think it was the day after Christmas when we went in and we weren't there more than an hour or so before I received one of the biggest shocks of my life. Tony and I, remember, we're scouts, have the point as we're moving up this road. We haven't seen a single Jap or taken any casualties.

Then, bang! one shot from a sniper in a tree and my pal Tony is gone. Oh, sweet God! We'd been together for two years. Liberty in the States, countless patrols on the Island and slop chutes in Australia, always the two of us. Can you imagine how close you can get to a guy in a situation like that?

I was stunned, but only for a minute. I really wanted to kill! I'd been trained to know what tree a shot had come from and I was pretty sure I had the sniper zeroed in.

This time I called for a BAR. I sprayed that fuckin' tree with a whole clip and down came the Nip. As I look back on it, what the hell, he was only doing his job, same as me, but I'm still glad I was the one who got him. All right, it was a vindictive act—so what!

Well, our job was to get the airfield and we did. From then on, most of my action was sporadic.

I do remember one case where the damn weather probably saved my life. I was standing in mud and water up to my kneecaps when a shell came in right next to me.

Now, get this, the area was so soft it didn't explode. It wasn't a dud; it just didn't explode. Can you believe that?

Another thing about Gloucester I can remember is one officer who was really yellow—and that's a word you never hear anymore. He was the only lousy officer I knew in the Corps. I'm not saying all the rest were bargains, but this guy was just plain rotten.

Now, you don't expect a general to be out front waving a sword, but you do expect the junior officers to be leading their men; that's their job. This clown I'm talking about just didn't believe it. Let me give you one perfect example of how bad he was.

It happened when we were moving on the airstrip. Our artillery had opened up on the Japs. The first thing I noticed some of our shells were falling behind us.

Well, come on, what the hell is going on? If I'm going to get killed, let the Japs do it, not my own people. So, I got into a foxhole with this runner who had a two-way radio. I asked him to radio back about the shells. He just laughed.

"SNAFU, buddy," he said. "This thing hasn't worked in an hour."

So we both started to crawl back. We had to get word to our artillery about the shells falling short. When we reached the nearest sergeant, I collared him.

"Where's your lieutenant?" I asked.

"Oh, that crum! He's way back—keeping his eye out for stragglers, he tells us."

Well, hell, his job is to be on the lines and relaying the position of the forward men to our artillery so they can lift their elevation on the guns. If someone isn't doing this, the men up forward have their ass out in the cold.

Well, they finally caught up with this lieutenant. Do you know what they did to him? Why hell, they sent him home. Every now and then I'd think of that guy, swaggering around the bars in the States, flashing his campaign ribbons. Big hero—baloney!

At any rate, we left New Britain sometime during the spring of '44 and headed for the Russell Islands. Our division was to get ready for its next fight which was to be Peleliu.

After we'd been on the Russells a month or two, they told what was left of the original Guadalcanal men to stand by. If enough replacements arrived, most of the old-timers were to go home.

Jeez, I got to tell you, I was on pins and needles. I'd already made two invasions. You know, three strikes and you're out. I wanted to go home. Each time some new men would come into our battalion, the old-timers would anxiously wait to see who was heading for the States. It was nerve-racking as hell.

Finally, it was my turn. I left for the States about three weeks before my outfit pulled out for Peleliu. I had no regrets.

When I got home, they gave me a thirty-day furlough, after which I did guard duty in Massachusetts, but for all intents and purposes, it was the end of the war for me. When the Japs surrendered, I was one of the first Marines discharged. I was way the hell over the points quota needed.

I went back into the paper business, this time as a salesman. Those days as a scout and a sniper are four decades behind me. I can't say it was any bed of roses, but if I could turn the clock back, I'd do it all over again. If being able to live your life in a country like this isn't worth going to war, what the hell is?

There is one thing that does still pop into my head. All the times Tony and I worked together as a team I didn't get a scratch. Why did Tony end up getting it and not Bob Stiles? Who can answer such a question?

Then, I'll wonder what would Tony's life have been like if he'd made it. Do any of the other Marines you've talked with say things like that about buddies who were killed?

[Author's note: Just about every one, Mr. Stiles, just about every one.]

Here and There—I

THE EXTRA JAP

"As a courier my job was to circulate throughout Iwo," remembers Ken Cosbey, "usually in a jeep. When I passed this one spot behind the lines, I noticed four dead Nips. When I drove back over the same route, I was surprised to see five Japs lying there. I thought, 'What the hell is going on?' So I called over a couple of Marines and gave them the word.

"They started to jab the bodies with bayonets and, sure enough, one of the 'dead' Nips jumped up and took off. He was undoubtedly waiting for nightfall when he had planned to raise hell behind our lines.

"And when I left that spot," continued Cosbey, "there were really five dead Japs."

THE MISSING PICTURES

There were two items that I tried unsuccessfully to locate for this book. One was an alleged photograph and the other was a privately drawn cartoon.

The photograph, probably doctored, was always popping up all over the Pacific. It allegedly depicted a smiling Samoan native male who obviously suffered from filariasis (mu-mu). He was holding a wheelbarrow and his tremendously swollen testicles were resting in it. I never could figure out what he was smiling about.

The cartoon showed an astonished Marine standing in front of a urinal. Standing in front of the urinal next to him was a woman Marine. She had her legs spread and her skirt pulled up. She was doing into the urinal what one is expected to do. The caption read: "What the hell are you staring at? I'm a Marine, ain't I?"

THE ADMIRAL AND THE COOK

General Vandegrift had an old line Marine as his cook named Butch Morgan. This old salt did his best during those early dark days on Guadalcanal to make sure the general had a halfway decent table. It wasn't easy.

On November 8, 1942, Admiral Halsey decided to pay a visit to the Canal to see for himself how things actually were. Now Butch had a real challenge. He was to prepare dinner for his general and an admiral. Morgan really turned to. Under the circumstances the dinner was superb.

After the meal was over, Halsey requested the presence of the cook.

"I'd like to thank that man for a wonderful job," he said to Vandegrift.

Butch showed up and as might be expected, all spic and span—clean skivvy shirt and pressed khaki trousers. His red mustache was trimmed to perfection. The admiral started to praise the cook and it went on and on. Morgan stood there getting more and more embarrassed. Finally, he could take it no longer.

"Oh bullshit, Admiral!" he said.

Naturally the officers broke into hysterics.

The next day, when Halsey was about to fly back to Noumea, he gave Vandegrift a parting smile.

"And, Vandegrift," he said, "don't you do a damn thing to that cook."

"Don't worry, Admiral," replied the general, "he's priceless."

THE FIRST JAP

Second Lieutenant David Curtin was one of the many products of the Marines' V-12 program who helped assault Okinawa on April

Fools' Day, 1945. Like any young man going into battle for the first time, Dave was both curious and apprehensive about the coming combat. He asked a fellow officer in his company what to expect.

"Look, Dave," he was told, "one thing to keep in mind is you rarely see those little bastards. After the fight is over I'll buy you a bottle of whiskey for every Jap you can definitely say you shot and a bottle of beer for every live Jap you've had a good look at."

Dave got to see a live Jap, and more than one, but it was that first Nip he remembered most.

"I was coming around a corner," said Dave, "and, wham, there he was, a Jap officer. He was as surprised as I was. We both took off in opposite directions without firing a shot.

"You know, I never did report that one to the other officer; can't understand why."

THEY WERE NEVER USED

During World War II several Marine barracks maintained a special throne in the head. Above this water closet was a sign that read "Venereal Disease." I even walked into a head that had an additional throne with a sign stating "Crabs." Many of the Marines I interviewed had the same experience.

We all agreed on one thing—we had never witnessed a Marine sitting on either throne.

And, by the way, the heads in question were for enlisted men. Perish the thought that such signs should exist in an officers' head.

THE COINCIDENCE

Throughout 1941 the newly formed 1st Marine Division practiced amphibious landings on the East Coast. One of their favorite landing spots was an island off the coast of Maryland. It was named Solomon Island.

THE WRONG DIRECTION

Bill Clear fought with the 8th Marines on Guadalcanal, Tarawa and Saipan. He was wounded on the latter two islands. Bill was in his late twenties while in the Pacific. His memories of Tarawa were mainly concerned with wading in to shore.

"Jeez," Bill would say, "the fire was heavy as hell as we went in.

I was scared to death. An eighteen-year-old Marine over on my right was not at all concerned.

" 'Christ, Bill,' he said, 'ain't we givin' those Japs hell!'

"I didn't have the heart to tell him most of that stuff was going the other way."

THE GOONEY BIRDS

Johnson Island is a speck in the Pacific. When flying over it, according to Colonel Brooke Nihart, it looks like a tiny cocktail olive with the island's airstrip playing the part of the toothpick. It was also one of the loneliest duty stations in the Pacific.

At first it hadn't been too tough for the Marine defense battalion stationed there. This was when the possibility of a Japanese invasion seemed quite strong. Then as it became obvious that the war would pass Johnson by, duty on the island became more and more tedious. The author remembers vividly talking to a PFC who spent some thirty months on Johnson. This conversation took place in 1945.

"It wasn't too bad at first," he said, "then it started to drag. We had a standing rule there. Anyone who had spent at least a year on Johnson was allowed to talk to the gooney birds.

"But," continued this Marine, "if the gooney birds started to talk back to you, they sent you home."

TOKYO ROSE

Ken Cosbey, 23rd Marines, 4th Division, on his way to Iwo Jima, listening to Tokyo Rose:

"Good morning, 4th Division," she said, "I understand you are headed for Iwo Jima. The week after you land you can hold your roll call in a phone booth." Unfortunately, for once the lady was not far off the mark.

Barry of the 1st Marines

Thomas Barry

Several years ago Tom Barry was attending a 1st Division reunion at the Sheraton Park Hotel in Washington, D.C. Several Marine generals addressed the group. It finally became time for the commanding general, David Shoup, to introduce the last speaker.

"Gentlemen," he announced, "I now present Chesty"—he never got the last name out. The place turned into bedlam.

Finally, Lieutenant General Lewis Puller faced the audience. After looking around the banquet hall, Chesty uttered one word: "MARINES."

Now the cheers were truly deafening. All the tremendous feeling that the veterans of the 1st Division had for their outfit seemed to explode.

Tom Barry is now sixty-one, a magazine executive who lives outside of Chicago. He is married to his wife of forty years and is the father of four grown children. He is, by any standard, a very successful man.

It is a rare treat to relax with him and listen as he recalls his memories of four decades ago when he wore the patch with the number "1" in it and the single word, "Guadalcanal."

CAPTAIN TOM BARRY
3rd Battalion, 1st Marines
Marine Detachment—*U.S.S. Randolph* (CV-15)

"If the 1st Division had a fault, it was that we began to feel we *were* the Marine Corps."

—Tom Barry

Do I remember that attack on Pearl Harbor? Of course I do! The night before, I had given my girl friend an engagement ring. The next day we were kinda lounging around her family's home in Winnetka, Illinois, reading the Sunday paper and listening to the Chicago

Bears football game on the radio. An announcer broke in with the shocking news of the attack. I just shook my head.

"Honey," I said, "stand by. I'll be gone in three weeks." I was right.

I was then a senior at Marquette University in my hometown of Milwaukee. I'd already spent two summers at the Marine platoon leaders' class at Quantico, Virginia, and was slated to get my commission at my June graduation.

Did things ever move fast! A week or so later they gave me some examinations that Mortimer Snerd could have passed, and bid me adieu. My formal graduation was held in June '42 at which time I was on my way to New Zealand, halfway around the world.

When I first reported for active duty, it was to the Philadelphia Navy Yard. Our commanding officer was Clifford B. Cates, a hard guy to figure out. He always looked as if he'd stepped out of a bandbox from his FDR type cigarette holder down to the spit shine on his shoes. But when push came to shove, there wasn't a better officer in the Corps.

Sam Puller was also down there as one of the instructors. He was a good Marine, but you always felt a little sorry for him. His brother, Chesty, was already a Corps legend and it seemed that Sam always tried to emulate him. There was no way he could help being overshadowed by his brother; he should have just been himself.

After we had been indoctrinated at Philadelphia, we went to Quantico for what I guess you could call a second lieutenant's boot camp. But officers or not, our boss was an old salt named Sergeant Bales. You know the type, the kind who'd sit under a tree and have you march around him.

"Don't do as I do!" he'd yell, "Do as I say!"

There was no appeal. He felt he was always right and ninety percent of the time he was. Later on, down at Tent City (New River), North Carolina, when I had a chance to pick my own platoon sergeant, I asked for Bales and got him. When I was made company commander, I promoted Bales to gunnery sergeant. My advice to a officer is to get a good sergeant. Hell, they really run the Corps, the nitty gritty part of it anyway.

Well, while at Tent City, I had been assigned to Company I, 3rd Battalion of the 1st Division. We trained as fast as we could, then boarded a troop train for San Francisco. Then we embarked for Wellington, New Zealand, aboard the *John Ericcson*. I think the trip took about thirty days.

As we pulled into the harbor at Wellington, I spotted a guy I knew standing on the dock. His name was Jim Donahue and he was from Chicago. Jim gave me a big wave.

"Don't unpack your sea bag!" he yelled.

"Why not?" I answered.

"Because we're reloading; we're going into the real war."

Jim was in the 5th Marines. They had arrived in New Zealand about four weeks ahead of us. By the time we got there, Vandegrift had received the word about Guadalcanal. There just wasn't any time for us to go into camp. We ended up spending a week or two at the docks moving our gear from the *Ericcson* to the *McCawley*, the ship that was going to take us to the Canal. Much to our regret, one of the things we moved over to the *McCawley* was our foot-lockers.

You see, we had been originally told we would be spending several months training in a mild climate. Naturally, we had packed our dress uniforms, our cordovan shoes, the Sam Browne belts we had in those days—the whole bit.

Hell, we didn't see all that gear until we'd spent a month or two on Guadalcanal. By this time the brutal tropical climate had ruined almost everything—you know what mildew can do. I can laugh about it now, but remember, an officer has to buy all that stuff. The gear in that foot locker represented a big expense in those days.

Besides, even if the uniforms hadn't been spoiled, where the hell were we going to wear them? Can you imagine patrolling along the Matanikau River with a spit shine on your cordovans?

Well, we shoved off for the Canal aboard the *McCawley* around July 25. Along with the 3rd Battalion, 1st Marines, we had the 1st Division headquarters people aboard. This turned out to be a tragic bit of fate for a good buddy of mine. As they say, luck is being in the right place at the right time. I guess being unlucky is being in the wrong place at the wrong time.

My friend's bad break came about around the 2nd or 3rd of August. Four of us were sitting in the wardroom, shooting the breeze. There was Charlie Barrett—his dad was a Marine general—a fellow named Ed Gilson, later killed on the Canal, and Jay Griffith from L Company. One of our headquarter colonels, Gerry Thomas, came over to us.

"Any of you young officers want to volunteer for airplane observing duty?" he asked.

Trying to show how salty I was, I made some crack about the number one Marine Corps rule, "Never Volunteer!"

But Jay Griffith was really interested.

"Sure," he said, "besides, I have a temporary flying license."

"Okay," said Thomas, "pack your gear, you're going to transfer to the cruiser *Astoria.*"

He was then slated to fly as an observer on the plane that was catapulted off the cruiser. His job was to observe the landing and to keep headquarters aware of what was going on.

The poor guy went down with the ship during the early morning of August 9 when the Japs knocked the hell out of our Navy off Savo Island. We later heard that they tried to catapult his plane once the battle started, but it took a direct hit. Both Jay and the pilot were killed. Who knows what would have happened to him if he'd stayed with the 1st Marines? I guess I'm talking about the old adage about your number being up no matter what. Hell, Jay may have been killed by a falling tree on Cape Gloucester.

Another incident I can recall concerned one of our men and his rifle. If you remember the '03, it had an elevated sight. While cleaning this sight, a knucklehead in my platoon dropped it over the side. Bales wanted to find out how we could get the guy another.

"Sergeant," I told him, "we don't have any extras of anything, but I'm afraid we're going to lose men in the landing. Tell that joker to pick up a rifle from one of our men who won't need it anymore."

So on the morning of August 7, as we were going in, I could hear all this firing. I remember thinking that our man is going to have his pick of a lot of rifles after we land.

What a laugh! The firing I heard had come from men in the 5th Marines who had gone in ahead of us and were shooting coconuts out of the trees. We didn't take a single casualty during the landing.

This turned out to be a blessing. If we had been met with the kind of resistance the Corps had at Tarawa or Iwo, it would have been murder. Nothing went right. We would have been sitting ducks.

Our initial job was to move ahead toward the airfield. My 3rd Battalion ended up spending the whole first day hacking through the toughest jungle you can imagine. We later found out that if we had gone a ways up the beach, we'd have come to a clearing that would have allowed us to go straight to the airstrip. You can't win 'em all.

I mentioned earlier a lieutenant named Ed Gilson, a hell of a nice guy who seemed to be plagued with bad luck at all times. He was just one of those guys who could do everything right, but it turned out wrong.

Ed was from Wellesley, Massachusetts. I can remember that very well because he lived on Gilson Road. To a guy from Milwaukee, this was really impressive. If you had a street named after your family in your hometown, you had to be important.

Well, shortly after the landing, he was bitten right between the eyes by some damn insect. We never found out what kind of a bug it was. Christ, his head swelled up like a pumpkin. You couldn't even recognize the poor guy. It took our corpsman about five days to get that darn poison out of his system. During that time he went through as excruciating pain as a human can stand. We used to say the jungle was as big an enemy as the Japs and we were right.

Poor Ed, though. Everybody seemed to hit him one way or another. We lost him during the fighting around the Matanikau in September. He got hit with a shrapnel splinter no bigger than a toothpick. It went straight through him. Blood poisoning set in and before they could stop it, he was dead.

It's a funny thing, I knew men who survived the most brutal wounds you can imagine, while Gilson died from a wound like that. Never belittle a man's Purple Heart, no matter where he was hit. Any wound can kill, particularly in the tropics where infections can run rampant.

The first real battle we fought was over the Tenaru River the night of August 21. When I say we, I really mean the 2nd Battalion of the 1st Marines; it was their area the Japs hit. My 3rd Battalion was strung out that first night on the beach. I guess our headquarters figured the Nips wouldn't attack on the water, so they moved us a few hundred yards behind the 2nd Battalion. We had a bird's-eye view of the Japanese attack even though we didn't suffer from it.

I'll never forget that night though, particularly when I go to a 1st Division reunion. There's a man named Wright who attends almost every gathering we hold. The poor guy, he's spent the last forty years blind because of that battle. I'll say one thing for him though, he adjusted amazingly well to that tremendous handicap. But whenever you see him, you realize that the war has never ended for some people.

Shortly after the Tenaru fight, we started our constant patrolling around the Matanikau River, on the other side of the airfield from the Tenaru. And one of these forages turned out to be a lulu.

It happened around September 8. We were sent out to check reports of a large concentration of Japs. It didn't take us long to find out the reports were true. We kept finding discarded Jap gas masks. Our men got a huge laugh out of this.

"See, lieutenant," one of them said to me, "we're not the only ones who throw away a lot of crap we're not going to use. The Japs do it too."

He was dead right. When you are moving out, particularly in a place as crummy as that jungle, there is just no way you can get troops to lug gear they think is useless.

Anyway, I was checking out all this Jap equipment when one of our forward men came up to me.

"Lieutenant," he said, "those bastards are real close. It's still warm."

As he said this, he opened up a fist that was holding a warm turd.

"It couldn't have been one of our boys," he said, "none of them have let go anywhere near the place I found this baby. It has to be Japanese. Besides, it smells Japanese!"

That may have been a primitive diagnosis, but you couldn't argue with it. I decided we'd found out what we were supposed to and was about to start the men back to our perimeter when the Japs opened up on us. Two of my men, Herman Wrede—I think he's a Baltimore fireman now—and Jim Justice—from one of the Carolinas—went down. I knew they would probably both make it—they did—if I could get them back, so I set up a field of fire defense with my BARs, and told the rest of the men to take off. The Japanese fire stopped so my BAR men soon followed the rest of us.

After I returned to our company command post, I was immediately called to division headquarters to make a report. Roy Hunt, Merrill Twining, Merritt Edson and Gerry Thomas—I think they were all colonels then—were waiting for me. I told them exactly what had happened. Then Edson spoke up.

"Do you think they are there in strength?"

"Yes," I answered, "at least a battalion, maybe a regiment."

"You see," he roared, "just as I said! They're not going to hit our flanks again, those sons of bitches are going to come at Henderson from behind." He kept nodding at me as he said this, as if I were someone important. Of course I kept nodding back.

And how right he was! A few days later we had the brutal battle behind the airport we now call Edson's Ridge. Just like on the Tenaru those Japs kept coming, only there were a lot more of them on the ridge. It ended up the same though—the Japs were completely repulsed.

Now here's one for you. You think there are a lot of crazy things that happen in today's business world, just listen to this. In the confusion surrounding the Jap attack on my patrol, one of my sergeants— his name was Louie Hipwell—lost his BAR belt. I didn't think twice about it. One of our majors looked at it a little differently.

"What!" he yelled at me, "You lost a BAR belt? That's government property; get your ass back there and find it!"

I thought he'd lost his marbles, but remember, he'd been in the Corps during the Depression when they had to account for every nickel. You just didn't lose a BAR belt.

At any rate, another lieutenant, Art Weiss, a friend of mine, was to take his platoon to the same area the next day. An order is an order, so I joined Art and returned to the scene of the missing belt. I found the exact spot in the jungle where we had the fight—you could see our expended shells on the ground—but no belt. I was afraid they would take the cost of the belt out of my pay, but they never did.

We didn't find any Japs on that patrol—sometimes you did and sometimes you didn't—but we found more than enough on another patrol Weiss and I went out on a week or so later. After all, there were plenty of Japs to go around.

There had been a foul-up and a good many Marine mortar shells had been left quite a way up the Matanikau. This was a hell of a lot more serious than a BAR belt. If we didn't get the shells, the Japs would and send them back right at our heads. This time we went out as a reinforced company.

By this I mean, along with the full company, we had light and heavy machine guns, a mortar platoon, and additional men from another company. We also had a truck that we drove down the beach to haul the shells back in. My platoon was on the river bank flank. Major Bill McNulty was in command.

I can't tell you how far we went before we found the shells, but just before we did find them, we spotted a couple of Japs. We fired, but I don't think we hit them. Anyway, now they knew we were coming.

A little later all hell broke loose. It was really hot. It was hazy as hell on the river and all we could do was fire where we thought the Japs were concealed. I assume we were hitting some of them, but sure as hell they were hitting us.

Art Weiss had his platoon next to mine. He took a bullet in his spine. Amazing enough, figuring we had to get him back to our perimeter with the bullet in his back, he lived and is still alive out in San Diego. He's paralyzed, but he manages. What guts that guy has!

Another one of the men who got hit in that fight was a young corpsman, Danny Joy. He was everywhere trying to patch up our wounded until a Jap shot him dead. Danny was posthumously awarded the Navy Cross. It is not the fault of the Marine Corps, but I've always felt our Navy corpsmen never got the credit due them. Sailors or not, they were Marines to us.

In the meantime we were in touch with the perimeter. When they found out how rough it was, they said the hell with the mortar shells, we were to pull back and pronto. I guess they figured it was better to lose these shells than to have a company shot to hell out there.

A few days later, my platoon was ordered to fill a gap in the 7th Marines who had arrived on the island a few weeks before. We were going to go part of the way in trucks. It was raining like hell.

Wouldn't you know it, I slipped getting into the truck and went ass over tea kettle into a huge shell hole. I heard a tremendous crack as if a leg were broken. I got back into the truck and went into the lines, but the next morning my leg was up like a balloon. Our corpsman took one look and shook his head.

"Lieutenant," he said, "you're no good here. I'm afraid your ligaments are all torn. You'll have to go back."

They carried me to a truck and drove me to a medical hospital right near Henderson Field. My first evening there turned out to be the night the Japs sent a battleship into the area planning to shell Henderson Field back into the Stone Age. They came darn close to succeeding. It was one night I'll never forget.

By the time I had reached the hospital tent, I could barely hobble with a cane. When the shelling started, all I could do was lie abed and recite the Rosary. The Japanese ships kept sending those shells in like there was no tomorrow for the whole world. The next morning I had a bird's-eye view of the damage because half the side of our tent had been blown away.

Oh, my God, what a sight! It looked as if our whole Air Corps had been destroyed. I could see wrecked planes, jeeps and all kinds of gear scattered everywhere. I was later told that this was our low point on the island. Washington was seriously thinking of either getting the Marines out of there or just writing us off. It was pretty grim.

Anyway, I spent a few days lying there resting my fouled-up leg. I needed an operation and they were trying to figure out where to send me. Finally they decided on Efate in New Hebrides. When the *U.S.S. McFarland* pulled into the bay, I was at least able to hobble aboard.

There were about fifty other Marines slated for evacuation who also went aboard. Included in this group was a Marine pilot named Olson from Arizona. He had been wounded in the neck during the shelling.

The *McFarland* was an old fourstacker that had been converted into a sea tender. When we boarded her, she was in the process of filling a barge with aviation gas for Henderson Field. We weren't aboard more than a few minutes when a sailor came running by, yelling at the top of his lungs.

"JAPS, JAPS—GODDAMN JAP PLANES!"

We were dead in the water and so was the barge. And with all that gasoline we were both prime candidates for Dante's Inferno.

One of the ship's officers quickly grabbed Olson and me.

"Over there," he said, "those axes. Grab 'em and cut us loose from the barge."

What a sight. I can hardly walk and Olson can't move his neck. Talk about the blind leading the blind. Somehow we chopped the cables and got us loose, but in the long run it did no good. The planes kept coming in. They finally hit us down at the fantail, doing a hell of a lot of damage and killing several of the wounded Marines who were down there.

Then the rescue. It was like the cavalry in one of those John Ford movies coming to the aid of a stagecoach. A Marine Air Corps major named Bauer had just arrived at Henderson with a squadron of Wildcats. They wrote finis to the Jap bombers in a hurry.

In spite of Bauer's heroics we were in a bad way. The barge had already been blown up. That lost gas was as precious as gold to Henderson.

They succeeded in getting all of us injured men into PT boats and then took the *McFarland* over to Tulagi. Amazingly enough they patched her up and she put out to sea again. How the hell they did that I'll never know!

At any rate, we moved over to a transport and took off for Efate. I had gone into the Canal weighing 220 pounds and came out at 165. If you want to lose weight, I suggest a diet of moldy flour made into pancakes and flavored with Japanese jam. Add to that C-rations and fish heads mixed with rice. You're bound to get the runs and you'll shed pounds like a duck shedding water.

I finally got to Efate where they quickly operated on my leg. I guess the operation was a success because five or six weeks later a major came to see me.

"Barry," he said, "they tell me you're fit for duty again. We're going to send you over to New Zealand to join the 2nd Division."

This was a real shocker. It took a minute or so to get myself together.

"Oh no, major," I pleaded. "I'm a 1st Division Marine. I have nothing against the 2nd but, damn it, I want to stay with my outfit."

You see, by this time we had begun to think the 1st *was* the Marine Corps. I don't know about the other divisions, but if you were in the 1st, you stayed there.

Anyway, I was lucky enough to latch on to a flyer buddy of mine, Doug Bangard, who was taxiing torpedo bombers to the Canal. I bummed a ride from him back to the 1st Marines.

In the meantime, they were getting ready to pull the 1st Division off the island. We'd taken plenty of battle casualties, but the real problem was the health, both physical and mental, of the troops. The division had really had it by December '42. God almighty, were the men beat! Half of them looked like walking zombies. There would be worse combat than Guadalcanal for the Marines during the war, but I don't think the Corps ever experienced more devastating living conditions for such a long stretch at any other time in the Pacific.

Our next stop was Australia. After a few fouled-up weeks at Brisbane, we moved to Melbourne and a bit of good luck. Our colonel, Cliff Cates, was the senior regimental commander in the division. He got the chance to pick his spot. Our regiment ended up encamped at the Melbourne Cricket Club. The other regiments were out in the boondocks, but we were sitting pretty—real good duty, believe me.

By this time I had been made captain of I Company. My job was to meld our replacements in with the Guadalcanal men and come up with a working assault company. Besides, we had to get the health back of our men from the island. It was no easy task.

Finally, late in the summer of '43, we took off again, this time for Goodenough Island, about fifty miles off the eastern tip of New Guinea. It was here that I ran afoul of "chicken shit" in its worst form.

It seems that the fellow who had read me the riot act about losing the BAR belt was still around and still living by the book. You know the type, a guy who would pull a white glove inspection in the middle of the jungle and not give you any advance warning.

I got the word one day to expect this guy in about an hour or so —he was going to inspect my company with the well-known fine tooth comb. The men really turned to and squared that place away. We were going to be ready for Mr. By the Book.

He arrived on schedule, all right and you have never seen such nitpicking. But, by and large, I thought he was happy with what he found. The only negative crack he made was about my men not knowing how to properly fold their extra skivvy drawers. I did not think this was a capital crime.

I was wrong. The next thing I knew, I was relieved of my command and made a regimental staff officer. The duty itself was quite good. I helped set up the move from Goodenough to Finschhafen directly across from New Britain and also got a chance to watch the Australians in action against the Nips. But damn it, I was still sore as hell. I thought I'd run a damn good company. I still think that today.

We moved across the bay from Finschhafen to Cape Gloucester on New Britain Island, landing there on December 26, 1943. My old battalion, the 3rd, had gone in with the first wave, while I landed with regimental headquarters a few hours later.

Christ, as I landed on the beach, I was greeted with some very bad news.

"Tom," a friend of mine told me, "we had very little resistance when we came in, but snipers killed both Joe Terzi and Phil Wilhert just as we made our first turn. Colonel Whaling wants you to take over King Company right away."

This was a hell of a blow. I'd known both these men since the beginning of the war. Terzi had been an outstanding football player at Niagara University near Buffalo, New York. I think Phil Wilhert was from Atlanta. They were both great guys but I guess those are the kind that get killed.

Anyway, I was back in command of a line company. I never did find out how old BAR Belt felt about it, but I figured the hell with him. Bill Whaling was the boss of our regiment, period.

I had no trouble moving in with my new company. I and K Companies had frequently worked together and I knew many of King Company's sergeants. The top soldier of K, First Sergeant Schmidt, was a hell of a Marine and he pitched right in to help me get squared away.

A day or two after I took over K, my old company, I Company, got pinned down by tremendous fire in a small area not far from the beach. The word came down for me to take K right through I Company and eliminate the Japs who were holding my old company up.

This made no sense at all to me. If I Company couldn't move, what the hell made them think K could? What would happen would be the bunching of our men in a concentrated area and a lot of dead Marines without anything being accomplished. I decided to question the order.

"Look," I pointed out, "if K moves over on the Jap flank, which is the only dry spot in the area, we can hit them from the side while I Company can come at them from the front."

"No, goddamn it," I was told, "you're to hit them straight on, and right away."

That was that.

So I quickly went back to my company and got them into position. There just wasn't much room for any maneuvering. We would have to go through a narrow route to get at them. Something inside me said I would have to lead them. I don't know what it was, but it never dawned on me not to.

Christ, I'd hardly started when, *wham*—it felt like someone had hit me in the chest with a baseball bat. I hadn't the slightest idea what had happened. All I knew was I was down on my knees bleeding like a stuck pig. I thought I was dying.

The next few minutes are a little hazy. I guess I was in shock. I kept trying to stagger away from the Jap fire, but I kept falling down. Why in the hell I didn't get hit again, I'll never know.

Finally, a couple of men from my company forced me down and wouldn't let me up. Then a couple more showed up and hauled me back to an aid station on a stretcher but not before a very unsteady moment.

You see, you really need four men to a stretcher—but I had only two. They're carrying me through the early surf when one of them loses his grip. I went off the stretcher, still bleeding like hell, right into the water. As I lay there, all I could think of was what an undignified way for an officer and a gentleman to die.

A buddy of mine from Boston, Mike Ahearn, commander of C Company, had run over to see how I was when I fell. He quickly dragged me out and helped me get back on the stretcher.

As it turned out, my biggest problem was the blood I had lost. They patched me up, but no one could figure out what had hit me.

In the meantime, K Company, with the help of I Company and some tanks that had moved through the dry field I mentioned earlier, had wiped out the machine guns that were holding us up. It turned out these Japs were on the fringe of the airstrip we were on Cape Gloucester to capture. Small as the action had been, those men of K and I had to show tremendous guts to knock out those Japs.

I also found out from my men what had hit me. I was carrying a Thompson submachine gun at the time. They found the Thompson all right, but it was twisted way out of shape.

It seems that a Jap bullet had hit the magazine of the Tommy gun, blowing it up. Why the hell it didn't blow my head off I'll never know. I ended up with part of the magazine all over my chest, but none of the parts hit a vital spot. I guess it just wasn't in the cards for me to get killed.

At any rate, I was evacuated to a field hospital in New Guinea. The wounds weren't too serious, but my God, you just don't know how much blood you have until it starts to flow from several holes. Believe me, the human body is a walking blood tank.

After I'd spent four or five weeks on New Guinea, I got the word to report back to I Company on New Britain. I was once again put in command of my original company I, the one I had before the episode of the incorrectly folded skivvy drawers. Who can figure out the workings of military command? I can't.

By the time I returned we had taken the airstrip. Our main function was to constantly patrol the jungle where we'd occasionally run into some Japs, but basically we had little in the way of combat. Apparently the real squabbles were going on between MacArthur and the Navy brass.

You see, we'd gone into Cape Gloucester under the 6th Army, not under the Navy. General MacArthur knew how good the Marines were—remember, it was the Corps he picked for the Inchon landing seven years later—and he didn't want to let them go. It finally got ironed out and early that spring we headed for Pavuvu in the Russell Islands once again under the Navy.

We had now been in the Pacific about two years. Most of us were getting a little antsy about going home. Then my old nemesis who had originally canned me from I Company called several of us into his tent.

"Look, gentlemen," he said, "many of you will be going back to the States very soon, while others will be staying with the regiment. I wanted to ask who you feel should stay here and who should go home?"

What a spot he put us on. You can bet your life every man there wanted to go back to the States, but what do you do, start quibbling about how you should go and your buddies stay? I later found out it had already been decided who was to stay and who was to leave. That SOB was just toying with us. What a sense of humor!

The incredible ending to all this was that an officer named Ronnie Slay and myself were the ones ordered back to the States and we were the only men in the tent *not* married. Thank God none of the others was killed when the 1st Division hit Peleliu later in '44.

One of the men in that tent who didn't go home, a buddy of mine named George Hunt, was so sore he got himself a bottle of Scotch and holed up in his tent for a day or two. He ended up taking K Company of the 1st Marines into Peleliu. If you want to know how rough that hellhole was, read his book, *Coral Comes High*. It's a magnificent account of dreadful combat.

Well, I arrived back in San Francisco and took a train to Chicago. Here I was met by my long suffering fiancée, Rosemary, and her mother.

"Great news, darling!" Rosemary said. "The Church has dispensed with the banns and we can get married at once!"

Wait a minute, I thought to myself. I was in no great hurry to rush things that fast. But I took one look at my future mother-in-law and I knew I didn't have a chance. As it turned out, marrying Rosemary was the smartest thing I ever did.

After a thirty day furlough I received orders to report to Marine Sea School at the Norfolk Navy Yard in Portsmouth, Virginia. So we newlyweds headed south for what I was afraid would be a very short stay in the U.S. before another trip to the Pacific. I just wasn't in that big a hurry to go back overseas. Besides, I was a Milwaukee boy. You didn't have swimming pools in the Thirties the way you do today. I could hardly swim, plus I knew very little about ships.

Then I got lucky. I ran into a buddy of mine who had come home after Guadalcanal. He apparently knew the people who assigned the officers to the various ships and was willing to help an old pal. He got me assigned to a brand new aircraft carrier—the *U.S.S. Randolph* (CV-15).

This turned out to be a great break for me. A new construction like the *Randolph* wasn't going to leave for the Pacific for a few months, which was just what I wanted, and it certainly wasn't going to hurt my selection of a detachment. The PFCs would all come from the classes at Sea School, but I could pick the two lieutenants and the sergeants.

As for the officers, I only had one restriction on my selections. They both had to be about my height (6'2"). The Corps is very picayune about the appearance of its seagoing detachments. Looking snappy is part of the game. I had no trouble at all getting two 6'2" tall officers. They were both former football players, the type the Corps was loaded with.

The real key was my sergeants. Most of our PFCs had gone directly to Sea School from boot camp. I needed some top NCOs to make real Marines out of these kids.

For my first sergeant I got Don Sandborn. Hell, he's the guy who actually had written the Sergeant's Handbook. What he didn't know about the Corps hadn't been written. For my gunnery sergeants I signed up two men named Rice and Markle, another couple of real pros. Before I was through I think I had the best group of non-coms in the fleet.

At any rate we commissioned the *Randolph* in the fall of '44 and headed for our shakedown cruise around Trinidad. We didn't seem to have any trouble ironing the kinks out. Things went so well they decided not to send us back to our home port, Norfolk. We headed straight through the Panama Canal for San Francisco. The Essex Class carriers (CVs) were doing such a great job in the Pacific the Navy wanted to get as many of them as possible out there in a hurry.

Now for a coincidence. Our air officer was a commander named Larry Simpler. He'd been on the *Wasp* off Guadalcanal when it went under. Before she was sunk, one of her aircraft had knocked a Japanese plane down in the middle of the jungle. Simpler decided he wanted to study the 20 millimeter gun that was on the Jap plane so he asked for a Marine patrol to take him into the boondocks. I got the duty.

Let me tell you, if there was one thing my platoon, including myself, didn't want to do, it was go out in that stinking jungle and look for a Jap plane Of course, we went.

Not only did we have to find it, we had to dismantle the damn gun and lug it all the way back to the perimeter. While we did all this, Simpler and the three or four swabbies he had brought with him just watched. They didn't do a lick of work.

Anyway, when I first met him on the *Randolph,* I asked if he remembered me.

"Well, I'll be an SOB," he said, "you're the guy who got the Nip

20 millimeter for me on the Island. I'll bet your men are still cursing the Navy."

"You can count on that!" I said.

We both laughed and got along famously after that.

I did get a chance to have Rosemary come to San Francisco for the two weeks before we headed out. We knew at this time she was pregnant and I wanted to see her before we left. I was to be one of the many, many Marines busy with the Japanese when his first child was born.

Anyway, we headed for the Pacific to join the fleet. We were to see a good deal of combat in the Pacific, particularly off Okinawa, but strangely enough, the only time we were really hit was when we were anchored in the harbor at Ulithi.

We had just finished watching a movie on the hangar deck when this Betty came out of nowhere. It crashed into the flight deck, taking part of our ship with it. Unfortunately, we also took a great many casualties.

Most of us felt they'd try to get the *Randolph* back to Pearl and go to work on it, but what we didn't know was a ship like ours carried enough equipment and planking to practically make the whole thing over. It was amazing how quickly they were able to get our ship ready for combat.

It was also at Ulithi that I met some old friends. This was just before the invasion of Okinawa. It turned out that part of the huge armada building up there at Ulithi included the transports of the 1st Division.

Well, you can bet your life I got the signals going back and forth to find out if the 3rd Battalion of the 1st Marines were there and, much to my delight, they were.

It wasn't long before I had my buddy, Red Haggarty, and a couple of other officers from my old battalion aboard for lunch. These "Dungaree Marines" couldn't believe it.

"Christ," laughed Red, "this is like fighting a war in a hotel! Where are the land crabs and the mosquitoes?"

They were right. You had plenty of chances of getting hit on something like the *Randolph,* but if you were going to get killed, you died with a full stomach and clean skivvies.

They just didn't give me the business about being in fat city though. They told me about the horrors of Peleliu and many of the good men we'd lost there. There were so many that I knew. That place must have been hell. Then they got around to the future.

"Tom," Red asked, "do you have extra BARs? You know that is something we never have enough of. This next fight (Okinawa) is going to be close to Japan. If you have any, we could put them to good use."

It turned out each detachment like mine did have two BARs. My first sergeant bitched like hell, telling me I could be court-martialed for giving them away, but the hell with that. The 3rd Battalion, 1st Marines made that April Fools' Day landing on Okinawa with the *Randolph*'s BARs. What was I going to use them for, repelling boarders?

That same Okinawa battle ended up being the largest operation the Marine divisions participated in. Along with the 1st and 6th Marine divisions, at least four Army divisions also fought. The 2nd Marine Division was there also, but they didn't do much. Their real war had been Tarawa and Saipan.

As for the Navy, it was all over the place. Ask any American sailor who was on a carrier and the chances are he will tell you he was off Okinawa.

Our ship wasn't hit there but, my God, so many of the other carriers were. I saw the *Bunker Hill* really catch it. I think they lost about four hundred men.

Admiral Mitscher had his flag on the *Bunker Hill;* she was hit so badly he changed over to the *Enterprise.*

Then, about three days later, the "Big E" caught it badly, so Mitscher changed again, this time to the *Randolph.*

After Okinawa, our planes kept applying pressure to the Japanese. We were all trying to get ready for Olympic, the November invasion of Japan. Thank God we dropped the Big Bomb. That final battle would have been Armageddon. I did get a chance to take a company of seagoing Marines into Japan after the war and, believe me, the Japanese would have been all ready for us.

When I finally got home, I saw my baby girl for the first time and moved from active duty to the unorganized reserves. I ended up in the magazine business and am still in it. I'm the publisher of a monthly publication called *Control Engineering.*

But I'll tell you, the older you get, the more you look back. I've become very active in the 1st Division association. As a matter of fact, I'm the association's president. If you told me thirty-five years ago that in 1982 I would be this active, I would never have believed you.

Don't misunderstand this. War is the height of man's stupidity. But the truth of the matter is, you are more apt to look back on the camaraderie you experienced than on the bad stuff. You form a relationship with the men you served with during combat that can't be equaled anywhere else. You don't meet with them to refight old battles, you meet with them just to be with them again. It is as simple as that.

Parris Island

A group of newly arrived boots were on their way to the Parris Island delouser. A young Marine dressed in khaki, which indicated he had finished boot training, spotted the group and immediately grabbed his crotch. One of the new arrivals asked the man in distress what his problem was.

"Oh, Jesus!" the Marine yelled. "They just gave me the square needle in the balls. It's horrible!"

Parris Island, at least during World War II, was a Marine Corps Jekyll and Hyde situation. On one hand, it may well have been as outstanding a recruit depot as one could find anywhere in the world. On the other hand, it was a complete snow job. The square needle in the privates was just one of the many falsities that made the rounds at boot camp.

Another distortion concerned a boot's record on the rifle range. The word was that if a boot did not qualify when firing for record, there was only one place for this wretched creature after boot camp —Cooks and Bakers School. As middle-aged men look back on the possibility of such an assignment, it must dawn on many that such duty would not have been all that bad. But to an aspiring young Marine the thought of spending the war in a mess hall was appalling.

Of the men in this author's platoon who did not qualify with his rifle—and there were four or five—not a one went to Cooks and Bakers School.

Another piece of nonsense was the word boot. While the term boot camp was prevalent when referring to Parris Island, I did not once hear a recruit called a boot. The common term for the recruit was shitbird. There were other and more obscene words but the prevalent one was indeed shitbird.

In self-defense the recruits had a ditty of their own that went like this: "I'm a shitbird, I'm a shitbird, I'm a shitbird 'til I die, but I'd rather be a shitbird than a fucked up DI."

One final piece of claptrap featured the poor fellow who had tried to swim to the mainland a month before each platoon arrived at PI. He was, of course, devoured by sharks, as it was told.

But sophistry aside, the boot was on Parris Island to become a Marine and this he became.

Assigned to a platoon of seventy or so recruits, the Marine-to-be almost never left his platoon while on Parris Island. Every night an assigned boot would take orders for the PX from each man. This was mainly to keep the platoon supplied with such essentials as toothpaste, razor blades, shaving cream and the like.

There were evening movies, or in my case a movie. My platoon was twice taken to an outside theater and each time we witnessed the same film, *Salute to the Marines,* with Wallace Beery. It was a barnburner.

The two most important people in the lives of each man during his stay on Parris Island were his drill instructors, or as they were called, "DIs." These two men, normally a sergeant and a corporal but occasionally a corporal and a PFC, had power over their charges that was awesome. Their orders were never questioned and they were always called "sir." They lectured and drilled the platoon with one thought only in mind—to teach the men how to be Marines. The reason behind the constant togetherness of the platoon was to help the DIs teach the men to work as a team.

The high point of boot camp was the three weeks on the rifle range. Every possible minute of this period was spent studying or firing infantry weapons, the major one being, of course, the M-1 Garand rifle. This was indeed the most important item of a Marine's possessions. No matter where a Marine would go after boot camp, he was considered available to serve as a rifleman at a minute's notice. A bit far-fetched but that was the theory.

After the period on the rifle range the whole platoon would normally take a week's tour of mess duty. You were still shitbirds but a tiny bit of salt was beginning to appear. Your return from the rifle range meant you had spent seven or eight weeks on Parris Island. You could tell the newcomers to keep moving on the chow line.

Another important factor was your hair; it was beginning to grow back from the skinhead haircut you had been given when you first arrived. You could always tell how long a boot had been on Parris Island by the length of his hair.

Then it happened. You took your final inspection; almost everyone passed this last test; they wanted to get you off the island at this point. The next step was to get your emblems for your dress greens. You were now a Marine and headed out.

On my platoon's final night on the island, the piss call duty was given to a great guy named Jim McKay. The two of us had shared an upper-downer sack throughout our boot camp. This duty called for McKay to wake up our number one DI, a corporal named Robert Glass.

McKay entered the corporal's quarters and sang out:

"I'm Corporal of the Guard, I'm Corporal of the Guard. Get off your ass, Corporal Glass. I'm Corporal of the Guard."

Platoon Sergeant Robert Glass was killed on Iwo Jima and PFC James McKay was killed on Okinawa. It was that kind of a war.

"Ahoy, Raiders"

They say that the Raiders
Are coming to Tulagi.
But Colonel Carlson says no;
It isn't the season.
But that's not the reason.
They're in Hollywood
Making Gung Ho."
—One of the Pacific verses from
the song *Bless 'Em All*

The above verse, like so many wartime songs, is utter nonsense. But, believe me, it was sung all over the Pacific.

The Raiders not only went to Tulagi but captured the place. As a matter of fact the Raiders fought on most of the Solomon Islands. The dense jungle terrain of Guadalcanal, New Georgia and Bougainville was tailor-made for them.

As it turned out, the span of the Raider battalions was a short one. Two of their companies first appeared on the scene at Midway, reinforcing the Marine Defense Battalion in place when the Japanese threatened the island in the spring of 1942. The Raiders were disbanded in early 1944.

But between these two dates, wherever they fought, they fought very well indeed.

Above all, they were extremely good copy. Even Hollywood got into the act, producing the film, *Gung Ho.* Starring the veteran actor Randolph Scott, the film depicted the 2nd Raider Battalion's attack on Makin Island in August '42. The publicity given to an elite group within an elite group did not sit well with the men who ran the Marine Corps.

The two most famous Raiders were Evans Carlson and Merritt Edson, both of whom came to tragic ends.

Carlson was transferred out of his beloved Raiders after Guadalcanal. Wounded on Saipan as a staff officer of the 4th Division, he returned to the United States and was put on the shelf. He died shortly after the end of the war of natural causes. When former Raiders have imbibed too much of the grape, they will tell you the "Old Man" died of a broken heart.

Edson's demise is equally tragic. He also ended up doing staff work and also died before his time. The facts of his death are not easily obtained. However, it has been said that despondency over personal matters drove him to suicide.

Five of the Marines I interviewed were former Raiders. Three of them—Sam Griffith, Irving Reynolds and Dick Washburn—are featured in this section.

I visited with Griffith in Maine and again in Rhode Island, Reynolds at a 1st Division reunion in Kansas City, Missouri, and Washburn in West Hartford, Connecticut.

Brigadier General Samuel Griffith (USMC-ret.) served twenty-six years in the Corps. A graduate of the Naval Academy ("I picked the Marines over the Navy because I wanted to get married, not go to sea. It must have been worth it because we're still together"), he later obtained a doctorate in Chinese studies at Oxford University. He is the author of several books, including the excellently written *The Battle for Guadalcanal*. He holds the Navy Cross.

Irving Reynolds was raised in Kentucky and enlisted in the Corps shortly after December 7, 1941. As a PFC he served as a BAR man on both Guadalcanal and New Georgia. He now lives outside of Washington, D.C., and works as a mechanic for the Greyhound Corporation, a position he has held for thirty-six years. As he puts it, "I guess you can say I have a steady job."

Richard Washburn joined the Marine Reserves while still a student at Wesleyan University in Middletown, Connecticut. He was called to active duty about a year before the United States entered World War II. He fought on Guadalcanal, Bougainville, Peleliu and Okinawa, a combat record that is hard to match. He returned to the States for a few months between Bougainville and Peleliu and managed to attend Command and Staff School and get married. He recently retired as an executive with the Travelers Life Insurance Company; he had first gone to work with that firm shortly before entering active service. Dick is a retired USMCR colonel.

BRIGADIER GENERAL SAMUEL GRIFFITH, USMC (ret.)
1st Raider Battalion

I think many of the original Marine Raiders gained a great deal of their knowledge of guerrilla warfare from campaigning before World War II in places like Nicaragua. I know I did. Fighting those Sandinistas was tough, hard work, believe me; the same kind of rugged jungle combat we had on the Solomons.

Americans, particularly the group that had come into the Corps in the 1920s, believed in a stand-and-fight philosophy which is exactly what jungle warfare is not. And it's a good thing those Sandinistas didn't believe in that stand-and-fight business because if they did, I would be dead, killed in an ambush in Nicaragua in '31. Here's what happened.

Normally I'd take a patrol out, maybe twelve men. But the time I'm talking about, I'd gone out in platoon strength, maybe thirty-five or forty men. I know we had four BARs and four Thompson submachine guns in our group. That was heavy firepower in that area of the world. We were a formidable force—not all Marines, mind you, mainly hill Indians, but we were still a tough bunch.

Anyway, these Sandinistas had set up an ambush for a twelve-man patrol. They probably would have killed the whole patrol if we had been the normal number of ten or twelve. But, as it turned out, they didn't fire a shot. They took one look at our firepower and said, "The hell with this," and took off. You try and kill as many of the enemy as possible without taking heavy casualties yourself. You don't stand and slug it out, not in guerrilla warfare anyway.

Incidentally, I found out about that aborted ambush later on from one of the Nicaraguans who seemed to know everything. He took me out and showed me exactly where the ambush was to take place. Sometimes it was hard to tell the good guys from the bad guys down there.

In 1935 I was ordered to Peking, China, for embassy duty, one of the reasons for this being my desire to learn everything I could about the Orient, particularly China. After I retired from the Corps, in 1956, I earned my doctorate in Chinese Studies at Oxford University, but that's another story.

In the meantime while in China I did get some first-hand knowledge of what the Japanese were trying to do. I did not get involved with any of that 8th Route Army stuff that Evans Carlson did. Hell, he literally served with that Chinese Army against the Japanese before we entered the war. He was quite a guy. I had first met him in Nicaragua in the early Thirties and I can tell you a little story about him that pretty much sums up his character. It happened down in Nicaragua.

It seems that Carlson was at a hill station called Jalapa. He had to travel about twenty miles through hill country that was pretty much controlled by bandits. The area was near the Honduran border where the Sandinistas used to get most of their weapons.

So he got himself a mule and started off. He was dressed like a native with a serapé covering his body. You know, one of those long waterproof cloths with a slit in the middle for your head; it hangs over your shoulder. And underneath the serapé he had a Thompson submachine gun. And that's the way, all alone, he rode those twenty miles. How's that for guts?

Of course there was a lot more to the man than raw courage. He was quite well-read and had a deep belief in people and their ability to overcome obstacles. He was kind of like a prophet out of the Old Testament, strong and righteous. Unfortunately, this was a period when it was easy to label someone like he was anything from a pinko to a card-carrying Communist. I think he was just an extremely brave and intelligent man who didn't like to bend on principle.

Anyway, in the late winter of '40–'41 I was assigned to the staff of the 1st Marine Division that the Corps was building up. This was to be the first full Marine division in history.

Then in the fall of '41 I was sent to England along with another Marine Corps officer, a man named Wally Green. And if you recognize the name, yes, it is the same Green who was later to be the Marine commandant. We were sent over to study the British commandos.

Both FDR and Frank Knox (Secretary of the Navy) were in awe of these British commandos. Unfortunately, a great deal of the Marine brass felt differently. They couldn't understand having an elite group within an elite group, a feeling that was always just under the surface at Marine Corps headquarters. But, come what may, Roosevelt wanted to have the Raiders, that's all there was to it, and that's why Green and I were in Great Britain on December 7, 1941, studying the commandos.

During that eventful first Sunday in December we had spent the day hard at work in the field and late that afternoon had returned to the Hotel Argyle, a charming spot where we were staying. We cleaned up and went downstairs for dinner, where we were greeted by a British brigadier, a hearty, red-faced man who was also staying at the Argyle.

"Okay, Yanks," he said, "stand the house."

Frankly, we'd been getting a little sick of buying drinks for every nationality fighting Hitler just because we were the so-called rich Americans, so I decided to give them the word.

"Listen, just because we're Americans don't think we're all John D. Rockefeller. When is someone else going to pay for a round?"

"But, Yank, you have something great to celebrate."

"Oh, general, is that so? It's a long time until the Fourth of July. What is today?"

"Haven't you heard? The bloody Japs have hit your fleet a real nasty blow at Pearl Harbor—the bloody bastards. You're really in this now, old boy. No more playing soldier."

"Well, I'll be damned," I said. "That's the stupidest goddamn thing those Nips ever did. The Japs are a lot stronger than most Americans want to believe, but they're not in our class."

Then I caught the bartender's attention.

"Stand the house. You bet I'll buy everyone a drink."

After that, Wally bought everyone a drink. Hell, I even think the Britisher bought a round. You might say we all ended up hitting the rack a little warmed up.

From then on Wally and I really went to work, studying those commandos and in March '42 we were ordered back to the U.S. for reassignment. I was sent to the 1st Raider Battalion under Lieutenant Colonel Merritt Edson. It seems that Edson remembered me from basic school several years before and had checked my record book. Apparently he had been greatly impressed with my experience, as he had specifically asked for my services.

Then, in April '42, Edson shoved off for Samoa with the first echelon. We pulled out in June, also heading for Samoa, but we stopped there only long enough to pick up the first group before heading for New Caledonia. That was it, the end of the joy ride. Our next port of call was to be the Solomon Islands.

Now, the 1st Division was to assault Guadalcanal on the morning of August 7, 1942. Our 1st Raider Battalion, now attached to the 1st Division, was slated to go ashore on Tulagi, across the bay from Guadalcanal, at roughly the same time the other Marines were to hit the Canal. We left New Caledonia in five destroyers and headed for our appointment on Tulagi. We arrived on time.

There always seemed to be a certain element of luck when it came to combat and on Tulagi it leaned in our direction. We went in on the eastern end of the island, while the Japs were on the western end. The eastern side was mainly coral beach, and I guess the Nips just figured there was no chance of our going ashore there.

The tides were also in our favor which was a real break because we had no dope whatsoever on the currents. The tides around the Solomons were very erratic anyway, so you just had to take your chances. All in all, our landing was just about as easy as they come.

It wasn't quite that way over on Gavutu, a smaller island near us. A unit of Marine paratroopers hit that island from Higgins boats and ran into a hornet's nest. I believe they suffered well over a hundred casualties before they secured that place. They received quite a fierce reception, the exact opposite from us. But it would soon be our turn to meet the Japanese.

Tulagi itself is not a big island and we certainly weren't there to dig in. As soon as we landed, we headed for the former British residency on the other side of the island. We reached there at about 3:00 P.M. The Japs had been there all right, but the minute our Navy had started to shell them, they had taken off for the bush. We knew they'd be back.

In the meantime we looked over the place and what a sweet deal those British had on that island! The Solomons were a British protectorate and their commissioner lived in this beautiful white frame house with a veranda on three sides. They'd even set up a five hole golf course and I believe a cricket field right there at the residency. This must have been great duty for the British before the Japs came.

We quickly set ourselves up there, but we knew there were three or four hundred Japanese soldiers on Tulagi who weren't going to surrender (not a one did). We also knew they would hit us sooner or later and we figured the golf course would be as good a place as any to meet them.

Colonel Edson gave me the responsibility of the right flank and I put our men to work digging foxholes. We didn't have long to wait. They hit us on the second night with a classic banzai charge. Hell, they were yelling "banzai" all over the place. It was real touch and go for a while.

When they'd hit you with a charge like that, particularly during the early stages of the war when they felt we'd break and run, the only way to stop them was to kill them. As we weren't about to hightail out of there, the Japs ended up wasting all their strength on the charge, which was exactly what we wanted them to do.

They had guts all right, those Japs, no question about that, but so did we! One of our BAR men, a young lad named John Ahrens, had his foxhole right smack in the middle of our lines. He seemed to have his weapon going all night.

As soon as daylight came, Johnny was spotted in his foxhole shot to pieces, barely alive. One of our officers, Lew Walt, picked young Ahrens up in his arms. Johnny was obviously dying, but he opened his eyes and looked at Walt.

"Captain," he said, "they tried to run over me last night, but I don't think they made it. Did they?"

"No, they didn't, Johnny, no they didn't," Walt replied softly.

Then Lew looked around. He counted thirteen dead Japanese.

And by the way, in the light of today, some people might be startled by the feelings of young Ahrens. If he didn't realize that he only had a short time to live, he had to at least know he was very badly wounded. Yet his main concern was, had he stopped the Japs? Out of his head?—I think not. We had a great many guys like Johnny in the Raiders.

Another Raider with a lot of moxie was Jimmy Roosevelt. Do you remember one of the campaign buttons the Republicans had in 1940? "Daddy, I want to be a captain too"? Well, they can shove that button! Jimmy was a hell of a good Marine and his father also had great courage.

Jimmy was with Carlson in the 2nd Raider Battalion; I think he was Carlson's executive officer. And when they started to get ready for the raid on Makin Island, Carlson didn't want young Roosevelt along. His thinking had nothing to do with Jimmy as a Marine. The raid was a hit-and-run operation from a submarine. Carlson just didn't want to be worrying about the President's son during an in-and-out raid like that one. Just think what hay the Nips could make if Jimmy were captured.

So Carlson called Admiral Chester Nimitz, trying to get Roosevelt out of the raid. Then Jimmy found out what was going on and blew his top. He called his father and now FDR is also furious. He got Nimitz's boss, Admiral Ernest King, on the phone.

"Look," he told King, "my son's an officer in that battalion; if he doesn't go, no one goes."

That was it. Jimmy was in a delicate situation. Oh, he could have said nothing and not gone. I don't think anyone would have held it against him. But Jim was a Marine Raider. He knew he should go and he did.

Okay. Back to Tulagi. We ended up killing most of the Nips on the island during the banzai charge that night. A few of them eventually swam over to Florida Island where I'm sure the natives made short work of them. There was no love lost between the natives of the Solomons and the Japanese.

After the banzai charge, we started what one has to call great duty. We didn't know about the naval disaster off Savo Island, so we weren't very worried about anything.

Then the word came through about the food. Apparently the Japanese had big plans for Tulagi. They were probably going to use it for the capital of the Solomons, the same as the British had done.

Whatever, the place was really stocked with great food. Delicious crabmeat, excellent rice and above all medium-rare, thinly sliced roast beef, packed in soy sauce. It sure beat the hell of out C-rations. Of course, we knew our stay here would be short, but it was great while it lasted.

Then, I think it was August 24, we were ordered over to Henderson Field on Guadalcanal. By this time the battle of the Ilu (incorrectly called the Tenaru by most people, but this scholarly old Raider insists on using the proper name) had been fought and won, and we did get there in time for the Ridge fight—you know, Edson's Ridge, even though my group didn't see much of it. I had a Raider company and a company of engineers over on the right flank at the time. If you look at the Ridge itself, then look to its right, you'll spot jungle. Colonel Edson wanted my group to guard this jungle flank; he felt the Japs would be sure to hit us there. As it turned out, they really didn't bother much with that flank, but we did get a lot of sniper fire.

After the Japanese were stopped on the Ridge, General Vandegrift decided to extend his western perimeter to the east bank of the Matanikau. I was given command of the 1st Raider Battalion and told to chase the Japs the hell out of the area, which also meant I'd have to kill a great many of them. They didn't kill easily! And by the way, the reason I was given the Raider command was that Merritt Edson was put in charge of the 5th Marines. Maybe they wanted to get a little Raider spirit into the 5th.

Well, we took off after the Japs and trouble began early in the sweep when they hit us with automatic fire, killing my executive officer, Ken Bailey. Poor Ken, he'd spent the battle of Edson's Ridge right in the thick of it, constantly exposing himself to Japanese fire.

Ken ended up getting the Congressional Medal of Honor for the Ridge. Then, a few weeks later, without any warning, a Nambu opened up on him over by the Matanikau River and he was really butchered. I guess that's the way war is.

Later that same day it was my turn, only I was luckier than Bailey. I caught a rifle bullet in my shoulder from a Jap sniper. He must have been at least four hundred yards away when he shot me. My first reaction was, "Wow! What a great shot!" So much for that baloney about all the Japs having buck teeth and bad eyes. I don't know about that Nip's teeth, but there was nothing wrong with his eyesight.

At the time the sniper's bullet hit me, I was on a hill overlooking the Matanikau, kneeling down in the kunai grass. I was scanning the east with my fieldglasses, trying to locate the Japanese soldiers. The sniper must have been on another hill because he had to be firing on a level with me.

Then, bango, I was knocked down the hill, going bass ackwards. A doctor was beside me in a hurry. He looked at my shoulder, saw where the bullet had gone in and come out, patched me up, gave me some morphine and a pat on the back. I figured I was all right and I went back to work.

[But not for long. Sam's wound was more serious than at first thought. He put in lengthy hospital duty but did recover in time to lead his Raiders into New Georgia on June 30, 1943.

Now back to Edson's Ridge as seen through the memories of PFC Irving Reynolds.]

PFC IRVING REYNOLDS
1st Raider Battalion

Sure I was on the Ridge, in Joe Chambers's outfit. What a guy he was, he got the Medal of Honor on Iwo.

How did I get into the Raiders? Right from boot camp, joined them when they were just getting started and stayed with them until they were disbanded the first part of '44.

Okay. Guadalcanal and the Ridge. I'd been in the field hospital with a damn fungus infection I picked up on the Tasimboko raid. We didn't find no Japs over there, but we did get a lot of the materiel they'd stashed away. They were going to use all that gear in the big push we knew they were going to make against Henderson Field. This was during the first week in September '42 and the hold on that little slice of the Canal we had was shaky as hell.

So we destroyed everything we found that we couldn't use and hightailed it back to our perimeter. But this damn fungus had gotten so bad I could hardly get a boondocker on, could hardly walk. I just had to turn in to sick bay.

Anyway, I guess it was maybe September 10 or so, the Japs hit my outfit with antipersonnel bombs. I heard about it and figured something was coming down over there. My foot was somewhat better so I turned to and got myself back to Chambers's Company.

The night of the Ridge we were strung out pretty thin, each man maybe ten yards apart. The Nips hit one of our flanks and killed four or five of our men. The Japs gave those poor guys a real broadsider.

Anyway, Edson figured we'd have to shorten our lines some, you know, consolidate 'em. So we pulled back a ways and I ended up in a hole protected by sandbags. I figured this is it, so I set up my BAR, took off my belt and got all my ammunition ready. I was going to rise or fall right there.

Not so. We got the word again to pull back. But this time them Nips had sky lights going up. If the Japs could pick you up in them lights as you fell back, you were a dead duck.

Jeez, a BAR and its equipment weighs twice as much as an '03 and, remember, my foot was still sore. I figured they'd get me for sure. So I made a short spurt then fell in a hole as if they'd hit me. Then, a few minutes later, I took off as quickly as I could and I made it down into a valley even though I stumbled a couple of times.

Then the word came through as Edson was supposed to have said it:

"Okay, Raiders, this is it. We stand here. If those little bastards get to the airfield, the whole 1st Division is in big trouble."

Of course you don't know if the colonel really said this or not. Who cares? We knew we had to stand and we did.

In the meantime, all that dragging of the BAR had knocked the hell out of it. It just wasn't about to work and there was nothing I could do about it.

So when the Japs hit us I started to help with the wounded. I grabbed some sulfur from a corpsman and all the grenades I could scrape together and kept handing 'em out and going back for more.

Now, you'll read about front lines like everything is set up perfectly. BS! There were Japs mingling with Marines all night. Christ, you could smell 'em!

I'd stopped to try and help a Raider who was gut-shot—don't know if he made it or not—when, wham, a Jap appears out of nowhere and throws a grenade. Maybe he was throwing it at someone else because it either went too far over my head or was a dud, I don't know which. I know it didn't touch me, but that's the way it was; the Nips seemed to be everywhere.

And let me tell you something: I think the grenades we had played as big a part as anything else in stopping those Nips. Our men were throwing 'em down at those Japs all night.

Okay. Don't let me forget the 11th Marines, our artillery. Maybe some of their shells fell short and maybe they didn't, but a hell of a lot of 'em fell on the Nips. I question if we could have held without that artillery. It was great.

Anyway, that's what I did all night, dish out the grenades and try and help the wounded. I did get a pretty good idea of how things stood, and damn it, I don't remember seeing a single Raider taking off. They just seemed to stay where they were and try and stop the Japs.

One more thing about the Ridge. Can't prove it, but I'll bet you at least half the Marines on the Ridge had malaria at the time. But, then again, I guess the Japs did also—hell, mosquitoes ain't choosy.

[With the steady erosion that was caused by both sickness and battle casualties the 1st Raiders were fast being decimated. Then around November 1, Carlson's 2nd Raiders came to the Canal and with them a young Raider officer named Dick Washburn. Enter, Captain Washburn.]

MAJOR RICHARD WASHBURN
2nd Raider Battalion

Sure I'll be glad to tell you about the Raiders, but first let me tell you about an interesting experience I had on December 7, 1941. I was then on active duty as a Marine second lieutenant at Quantico, Virginia. On the day of the Pearl Harbor attack I had gone to Hartford,

Connecticut, to visit my girl friend, a beautiful young lady who I'm happy to say has been my wife since 1944.

I started back to Quantico that Sunday afternoon shortly after hearing about the attack. The train I was riding on was still in Connecticut when I noticed that everyone in my coach seemed to be giving me these funny glances. I had never experienced anything like this before and it puzzled me for quite a while.

Then it dawned on me what was going on. I was in uniform and their glances were really asking me if I was up to what lay ahead. Some of the civilians even came over and asked me if I felt we could do the job that was needed. Then there were others who came over and wished me luck, while a few shook my hand and said they would be joining up very shortly. And all this just four decades ago. How we have changed!

Okay. You want to talk about the Raiders. Well, in 1941 I was in the 1st Battalion, 5th Marines. Sometime during that year they changed 1/5 to the Separate Battalion and before '41 was over many of the men in this battalion had become members of either the 1st or 2nd Raiders. Of course it was all voluntary; no one forced you into these lashups. Not only did you have to volunteer but you also had to muster to get in. I'd say that for one reason or another about half of the original 1/5 did not become Raiders.

Each of these Raider battalions being formed was to have six companies. After the 2nd—the one I had joined—had the six companies, we set up our training area at a place called Jacques Farm outside of San Diego. Here we started the real Raider training.

I'm not saying that this Raider training was any tougher than the advanced training a regular Marine rifle company went through—hell, it would be pretty difficult to have tougher training than that —but I am saying it was different than that of the other Marine units. We specialized in different things, that's all.

For instance, we spent a lot of time in rubber boat landings. I don't think many of the Marines who weren't Raiders even considered this type of landing but for us it was a natural. We also placed special emphasis on guerrilla patrolling and night action, movements that were essential in our hit-and-run tactics.

Probably the biggest difference between us and the regular training was in the individualistic aspects of the work. The Raiders almost always fought in smaller units than the other outfits and therefore the chances of a Raider getting cut off in the jungle somewhere was quite high.

I guess by May '42 they felt we were trained enough because we shoved off from California headed for Honolulu. The 2nd Raiders were bound for action.

Two of our companies, I forget which ones, were immediately rushed to Midway Island in case the Japs actually tried to land there. When we caught up with these men later on, we found that several of them were bitter as hell.

"For Christ's sake," one of them said to me, "if those Nips had been able to land, we would have been faced with thousands of them. What could two companies have done? We were just sacrificial lambs, that's all. Thank God the Navy saw they didn't get ashore!"

Anyway, on August 7, 1942, Merritt Edson's 1st Raider Battalion assaulted Tulagi in the Solomon Islands. A week or so later two companies of the 2nd Raiders, including Jimmy Roosevelt and the commanding officer, Evans Carlson, went in on the successful submarine-launched assault on Makin Island, deep in Japanese territory. Carlson's attack was a real gutty move, but I think its aftermath was the beginning of some real problems for the Raiders.

That Makin raid was just the type of thing the media love. They built it up way out of proportion with its actual value. To put it bluntly, the noses of many Marine officers who weren't Raiders were knocked way out of joint.

Then, shortly after the raid, the gung ho aspects of Carlson's command came to light and the media really went crazy. Wow! This was tremendous. They even started plans for a film called *Gung Ho*.

But now the brass is really upset. These Raiders are taking the spotlight away from the thousands of other Marines struggling in that goddamn jungle. And what is this gung ho business anyway? Everyone didn't love us.

Well, this gung ho business was originally the property of our 2nd Raider Battalion and to us it was important. Here's how it started.

Evans Carlson was a regular Marine officer who had been assigned as an observer with Mao Tse-tung's 8th Route Army in China. Carlson ended up quite taken with the spirit of those Chinese Communist troops. Gung ho means work together and according to the colonel this is what those Chinese did extremely well. Carlson felt if he could ever combine the inborn individualistic American spirit with the gung ho work-together spirit of the Chinese, we would be unbeatable.

Through the years the term gung ho has been greatly bastardized. Today I guess it means an overly zealous person and is frequently used in jest, sometimes in plain ridicule. But believe me, in '42 and '43, among the Raiders anyway, gung ho was constantly used but not in jest.

Now don't get me wrong. I'm not saying we ran around everywhere yelling "gung ho" and never laughing at anything. Far from it.

As a matter of fact there was one routine that the old man (Carlson was 46 in 1942) had inadvertently fallen into somewhere along the line. He had been giving us one of his lectures—I can't remember where—when someone gave him the so-called perfect squelch. The colonel had just pointed out how we would have to travel from one end of a very thick jungle to the other end:

"But, gentlemen," he had said, "it's only twenty-two miles as the crow flies."

"Yeah, colonel," came from the audience, "but we ain't crows."

This broke up the unit; even Carlson laughed. It became somewhat of a catchword in the 2nd Raiders from then on.

Well, my Easy Company—I was now a captain—and the rest of the 2nd Raiders left Hawaii sometime in September '42, headed for Guadalcanal, but what a milk run we were on. Hell, we stopped everywhere: Canton Island, Vitti Levu, the Fiji Islands, you name it, we stopped there, arriving at Espiritu Santo, about six hundred miles south of Guadalcanal.

Here we intensified our training in hand-to-hand combat, firing live ammunition and throwing real grenades. Whenever you get that serious in your work, two things happen. You really learn something but you also have casualties. I know we did lose a Marine there during this training.

We finally pulled out for the Canal the first part of November. Company E sailed on the *U.S.S. Manley,* one of the original destroyer transports (APDs). By November 4, we were ashore on the Canal. I'm sure these men would have ridden into Balaclava with the famous Light Brigade, anything to get off that ship.

You see, we were really crammed on the *Manley.* Visualize a World War I type destroyer, which was what the *Manley* really was, and add about 130 men to a crew that is already aboard and you can see how things shaped up.

But this wasn't the half of it. When I say we hit heavy seas, I mean heavy seas. They may have given us our helmets for combat protection but in this case we used them to puke in. Everybody, and I mean everybody, was seasick. Some worse than others, but we all were sick. What a mess!

Our ordeal ended when we went ashore at Aloha Bay. Our job was to help expand the perimeter on Guadalcanal. While the 1st Marine Division had been there for almost three months, they controlled precious little of the island. Aloha Bay seemed to be an excellent place to land and ideal for an airstrip. So we went ashore and started moving up the beach toward Henderson Field, making a jungle sweep as we went. You know what this means—heat, sweat, mosquitoes, rain, stink—everything that makes a jungle repulsive.

After a few days of back-breaking hacking through this jungle, we made contact with a battalion of the 7th Marines who were, I believe, under the command of an old regular named Hanneken, H. H. Hanneken—they used to call him "Hard-Hearted Hanneken." He took one look at these fresh new troops and the great equipment we had and gave us the word.

"Okay, captain," he said, "you are now attached to my outfit. We need you."

This put me in a bind. If I followed Hanneken's orders, I'd have to void my orders from Carlson. I thought fast.

"Gee, colonel, that would be great," I said, "but it would foul up the whole operation of the 2nd Raider Battalion. I've got to get to Colonel Carlson with some vital information, then team up with Charlie Company for some special work General Vandegrift has in mind."

[Dick should have said to Hanneken, "FUBID." Charles Ferrier, a buddy of Washburn's at New River, told me this meant, "Fuck you, buddy, I'm detached."]

Hanneken grumbled quite a bit, but he didn't want to mess with both Carlson and Vandegrift.

Now, I just mentioned the great equipment we had and that's the way it was, at the beginning of the Raiders' campaigns, anyway. I don't know if this was because FDR's son was a Raider or because Evans Carlson had been corresponding with the President. Who knows?

But I do know we went into the Canal with M-1 rifles, Thompson submachine guns, plenty of grenades and just about all the BARs we wanted. Hell, we were a walking arsenal.

And this equipment superiority didn't only apply to weapons. We wore a boot that was tremendous, much better than the regular boondockers. It had extremely thick leather that was the cause of my having a very sore ankle for a week rather than a nasty wound.

This all happened over by the Metapona River on the Canal. A Jap bullet caught me in the ankle but instead of going in me, it barely went through the leather and died. I tried to get a Purple Heart, why not? But the doctor just looked at my ankle, put some kind of salve on it and shook his head.

"Sorry, Dick," he said. "No blood."

Well, we caught up with Carlson and I gave him the report. Then we went on the move, a real jungle sweep, the kind of a maneuver we had trained for, and it was grueling as hell. Believe me, that jungle could be an enemy in itself.

For instance, you never hear anything about the liana vines. These nasty things, full of little fishhook barbs, lined the trails. They could actually entrap a man. Of course he could get free, even though he frequently needed help, but those vines would rip at his body. When they would do a real vicious job on the guy, the chances of infection were high. We had men whose cuts from those darn things festered until he got off the island.

And, of course, we had the Japs. We were constantly running into those little characters and having shootouts.

One of the fiercest of these fire fights occurred at a little village called Asamana on the Metapona River. Hell, they call it a village; it was nothing but a bunch of mud huts. Company C, which was ahead of us, surprised some Japs who were crossing the Metapona. We moved up fast and joined the fight. C was hitting them with everything they had and we followed suit.

At the time I was carrying both a .45 pistol and a shotgun, figuring the scatter gun would be great for quick combat. You just don't have to worry much about aiming a shotgun.

But let me tell you, while the shotgun can be great, it can also get you killed. You know the sound of one of those things is a lot different than that of a rifle. I'm sure most of those Nips had never heard a shotgun before I opened up at the Metapona.

Whatever, they came back to me as if I were the whole patrol. That's when I caught the bullet in my boot. After that I was very careful whenever I used my shotgun.

We killed an awful lot of Japs there, probably because Charlie Company surprised them and we came up so fast. It was as simple as that.

My company lost three men there and we buried them in the jungle. My God, but their graves looked lonely! I don't know if they've been disinterred or not, but the sight of those graves was surely a sad one.

[Captain Washburn received the Silver Star for bravery at the Metapona River.]

Well, we spent somewhere around a month or so out in the jungle patrolling, very frequently running into the Japanese. When we did, a fire fight would almost always occur.

But you can take just so much of that kind of living. The Nips were bad enough but the living conditions could murder you. Sometime in December they took us off the Canal and sent us back to Espiritu Santo for a rest. God, we were basket cases. I really felt lousy so I turned into sick bay. I told the doctor how crummy I felt so he gave me an examination.

"No wonder you feel so badly," he said. "Not only do you have malaria—hell, everyone seems to have that—but you've also got a bad case of hepatitis. We're going to rush you to New Zealand.

They've got a hospital that can handle your case better than we can here."

Sick as I was, the next nine weeks turned out to be one of the few lucky breaks I had while in the Corps.

While I was sitting on my butt in the hospital, they moved the whole 2nd Raider Battalion from Espiritu Santo to New Caledonia. By the time I rejoined my outfit the move had been made and our new camp set up. Moving and setting up a new camp is something you can keep.

At any rate I reported back for duty—it must have been sometime in the spring of '43—to find there had been a big change. It turned out that Evans Carlson had left us. They were taking the now four Raider battalions and turning them into a Raider regiment. Lieutenant Colonel Alan Shapley was to command the 2nd Battalion. Colonel Shapley was an Annapolis graduate, a real regular Marine. But what of Carlson?

Well, it turned out that he would never have another line command. He went to Tarawa as an observer with the 2nd Division and was a staff officer with the 4th Division in the Marshall Islands and on Saipan. He was seriously wounded on Saipan at Mount Tapotchau. He went back to the States and never returned to the Pacific. He died a few years after the war ended. He was one hell of a man!

Well, the next move for me was when the 2nd Raiders assaulted Bougainville, which I believe is the largest island in the Solomon chain and is located at the northern end. The 2nd and 3rd Raider battalions were targeted to hit Bougainville on November 1, 1943.

Starting in June '43, U.S. Army divisions and Marine units, mainly Raider battalions, had been either invading or bypassing islands in the Central Solomons. Bougainville is at the top of the chain.

The first thing that happened as we hit the beach was the killing of our battalion commander, Lieutenant Colonel McCafferty. He was brand new to our outfit and I never got to know him very well. Poor guy, he never got started with the 2nd Battalion. Sometimes it happened like that. You could go through some extremely hot action and never get touched and then, bang! One sniper's bullet could kill you right off the top of the barrel. As I was now a major, I took over command of the 2nd Raiders.

The next three or four days were pretty rough, very intense fighting on what was called the Piva Trail. The jungle was just as bad here as on the Canal, maybe worse, extremely dense and loaded with bugs of all types. All the physical disorders you can imagine were here and there was a constant rainfall. The next time someone wants to start a war they should make him spend a week or so fighting in a tropical jungle. He'll change his mind quickly enough.

After those first few days, the 3rd Raider Battalion relieved us. We didn't complain.

Then we settled in for more or less a static situation, slowly expanding our perimeter. My own personal luck seemed to hold fast. Two of us were talking together when some Jap shells started to come at us. We both jumped for holes. I made it, but the poor other guy was blown to pieces.

Now, I don't want to knock the U.S. Army in any way. I lost a brother in the Pacific who was serving with the Army's 77th Division on Okinawa. He was as good a man as any Marine who ever lived. But damn it, I can remember relieving an Army battalion on Bougainville and in this case they sure as hell did things differently than we did.

At that time we were in the field and while I was in charge of our battalion, I was dressed like anyone else—no insignia, no nothing different than our men. I was eating with my men, living with them, if you know what I mean.

God, the commander of the Army outfit had an elaborately built bunker, buttressed by logs. He's got a dinner table, set with silverware and mess boys serving him. It seemed like a different world.

I'll grant you, the Raiders' way of campaigning wasn't typical of the Marine Corps. And I'm not saying that that Army colonel was typical of the soldiers, but to me he was really something else.

Well, when we went into Bougainville, there was never any thought of our staying and slugging it out with the Nips until we had captured the whole island; this would have taken too long and would have been too costly. Our job was to establish a large perimeter so the Seabees could build an airstrip. This we did. Thousands of Japanese soldiers were left to wither on the vine in the deep jungle.

Our battalion was pulled off the island around the middle of January and not too long afterward the Raider battalions were disbanded. Many of the original men who had come over during the first half of '44 were sent stateside. I was one of the lucky ones.

When I arrived in the U.S., I got married, went to Command and Staff School and then found myself back in the Pacific, where I joined the 2nd Battalion of the 5th Marines in time for Peleliu. As a matter of fact I can still remember the loudspeaker on the LST that took us from Pavuvu to Peleliu blaring away with music from *Oklahoma* and the men singing, "Oh, what a miserable morning, oh what a lousy day!" Things hadn't changed much.

One thing that had changed was my job. I was still a major, but I was now in battalion headquarters; Battalion 3 they called me. And when the 5th Marines invaded Okinawa, I was there as executive officer of the regiment. So you can say I fought in the first battle of the Marine counteroffensive on the Canal and in the last one at Okinawa, with Bougainville and Peleliu in between.

I ended up retiring from the Corps as a reserve colonel several years ago and just last year from my position at the Travelers Insurance Company. I have a great family and I hope it turns out I can enjoy them, an occasional round of golf and plenty of sunshine for years to come.

But, you know, as these years roll by, every now and then I think of those days four decades ago when I was a Raider. Believe me, my friend, if you ever were a Raider, you never forget it!

Sir Jacob Vouza

"Sure I remember Jacob Vouza; all Raiders do," says Dick Washburn. "He was our favorite scout. I understand he is now Sir Jacob Vouza, was knighted by the British king. Well, he deserves the title. I believe the Marines also honored Sir Jacob. I know he received a Silver Star. What a story he had to tell!"

Indeed he did.

When the Japanese arrived in the Solomon Islands, they claimed they came as liberators.

"To hell with the white fools," they'd say to the natives. "They were only here to exploit you. We're going to take good care of you."

After making all kinds of promises to the Solomon Islanders, the Japanese then turned around and started to treat the natives like dirt. This is not the way they had been handled by the British. It had taken the English centuries to develop a sane way of treating the natives, which basically meant leaving them alone as much as possible. The Japanese never quite developed this knack.

At any rate, the natives first started to resent the Japanese; then they started to hate them. In the main, these natives ended up being great allies of the Marines, particularly in their natural capacity as scouts.

Jacob Vouza was undoubtedly the most prominent of these scouts. He was also one of the very few natives to survive a brutal questioning session by the Japanese. This all happened shortly before the battle of the Tenaru River on Guadalcanal. Sergeant Major Vouza— he had held this rank in the Solomon Islands's Constabulary—had taken a group of scouts into the brush to check on the movements of Japanese troops. Unfortunately, Vouza fell into the hands of the Japanese, who immediately started to question the courageous scout.

Then bad luck hit Jacob. The Americans had given Vouza a small American flag which he was to take back to his village. The Japanese discovered the flag on the scout and were infuriated. The emperor's soldiers then started to torture Vouza with a vengeance. They smashed his head repeatedly with rifle butts and then jabbed him with bayonets. The scout finally passed out. Believing their prisoner to be dead, the Japs then took off for their attack on the Tenaru.

But this tough Solomon Islander was not quite done for, almost, but not quite. He started to crawl toward the American lines and, astonishingly enough, he reached the Marines' perimeter. There he gasped out what he knew and collapsed.

The sergeant major did survive his ordeal and it wasn't long before he was back again scouting against the hated Japanese.

As of this writing, the venerable scout is still alive. While he is now approaching ninety years of age, he still enjoys greeting Americans, especially Marines, as they come to Guadalcanal. He is, of course, always invited to the reunions of the 1st Division. He sent the following message in answer to one invitation:

"Tell them I love them all. Me old man now. And me no look good no more. But me never forget."

Spooner and Driscoll of the 2nd Division

"It is not our intention to wreck Tarawa. We do not intend to destroy it. Gentlemen, we will obliterate it."
—USN admiral before the attack

When I started *Semper Fi, Mac,* I had only two rules for my interviewing. The men I would talk with had to have been World War II Marines who went overseas, and the overall mix had to represent a cross-section of the United States.

Then, as I came close to my deadline, I realized I had talked with men who had served in every major divisional campaign the World War II Marines fought in except one. My missing battle was Tarawa.

While it had not been my original intention to cover all these campaigns, I quickly surmised that since I had missed Tarawa, its absence would stand out like the proverbial sore thumb.

I began a last minute rush to locate a Marine who had suffered through those three or four days of hell on the tiny island of Betio in November of 1943.

Surprisingly, my search was not easy. Time and again men who someone thought had served on Tarawa ended up having fought at other islands but not on the Tarawa atoll.

Then I took one last stab in the dark by calling Colonel Brooke Nihart (USMC-ret.), the Deputy Director of the Marine Corps Museum, located at the Washington, D.C., Navy yard. I had met the good colonel when I made a speech before the Ends of the Earth Club a few years ago. I asked him where I could locate a Tarawa Marine who had fought on Betio.

"Gee, Henry," he answered me, "we've got plenty of them in this neck of the woods. One of them, Rick Spooner, was in Jim Crowe's battalion. He has a restaurant over near the Triangle. It's called "The Glove and the Laurel" and it's kind of a Marine hangout. Come on down and we can have lunch with him."

I took the colonel up on his invitation, which turned out to be one of my better moves. Not only is the restaurant a delightful spot and serves great fish and chips, but its owner, Rick Spooner, is what we used to call 4.0.

Enlisting in the Corps in 1942 at an age he calls seventeen, for the records anyway, he fought with the 8th Marines on Tarawa, Saipan-Tinian and Okinawa. Then he signed over for what turned into a few months shy of a thirty-year career. His service included the Korean War and Southeast Asia.

Major Spooner (USMC-ret.) naturally has campaign ribbons and battle stars by the bushel—but one of his bravest acts did not come in combat. This was his openly admitting that there on the beach of Betio in the Tarawa group he was scared silly.

Like Henry in Stephen Crane's *The Red Badge of Courage,* Rick first went into combat a very naive young man. But through this first fight he became, as he puts it, "a real Marine." It was not easy for this beribboned, retired Marine major to admit he was once frightened out of his wits, but he did just that and he did it with style.

There was an added bonus at the luncheon. Not only did Colonel Nihart turn up Major Spooner, who had fought on Betio, but also another 2nd Division veteran, Ed Driscoll, who served on islands other than Betio at Tarawa.

Like the major, Ed Driscoll spent World War II as an enlisted man, obtaining his commission during postwar service. He retired in 1980 as a colonel and now does consulting work for the Corps.

Colonel Driscoll was to drive to Portsmouth, Virginia, after our luncheon so he held forth first at our meeting with memories of his days on active duty.

SERGEANT EDWARD DRISCOLL
Scout, 2nd Division

You mentioned Tarawa and I'll be glad to talk about it but, remember, my outfit wasn't on Betio Island where most of the Tarawa fighting took place. I was with a wheeled reconnaissance scout unit. Our job was to try and check how many Japs, or Saps as the Gilbertese called them, were on each island. Tarawa is really a string of islands.

Back to the beginning. I'd graduated from a Catholic high school in Elmhurst, a suburb outside of Chicago, with some pretty good grades and was set to go to Loyola University in the fall. This was the summer of 1940 and it seemed Europe was exploding, France falling and all that. I had itchy feet and didn't really want to go to college.

One day I was boarding an elevated train, heading for Chicago, when I noticed a poster telling what great opportunities the Marine Corps offered a young man.

Oh, this ad was a beauty! It had three different Marines in it. One was riding a rickshaw; another was cleaning the wings on an airplane; the third was in dress blues, presenting arms on a battleship. I was hooked.

When I got downtown, I stopped in to see the recruiting sergeant. I told him how interested I was in the Corps.

"Oh, that's fine," he told me, "but I'd like you to get us a letter from your employer, the pastor of your church and your high school principal. We don't take many guys and we want to get the best we can."

I was quite surprised at this. I'd been working at a temporary job before going to college and I had no trouble with my boss. I'd just been in the first graduating class of the new Catholic high school in Elmhurst where I lived so my principal and pastor also were no problem.

And, by the way, those letters are still in my Marine Corps official files; just about everything connected with a Marine's service is in those files.

Anyway, a month or two later I was called back to the recruiting office to take my written and physical exams. A while later I was sworn in and finally, in February of '41, I was ordered to report for boot training at San Diego, California.

Now, as you know, all recruiting offices did not require these letters. But I guess the Chicago recruiting office wasn't having any trouble filling their quota so they could be real choosy.

Okay, now let me tell a story. It is about the problems these recruiting officers can face. It concerns the case of a young man who looked like he had come right off a recruiting poster. He was Jack Armstrong, the All American Boy with the Hudson High Boys thrown in for good measure. He was also a thief, caught red-handed in a large black market ring that was ringing up big dollars. He was canned from the Corps, but he hired a good lawyer and did not go to the brig because of an enlistment technicality.

What had happened was he had lied on his enlistment papers. When the chief of police in the recruit's hometown found out that this bird had enlisted in the Corps, the chief went to the recruiting sergeant and told him his applicant had a record a mile long. In short, the enlistee was a real bad actor.

But, you see, the recruiting sergeant had a quota to fill and he was behind so he took the guy anyway. The defense attorney based his case on the fact that the Corps was at fault for taking a recruit with fraudulent enlistment papers and the crook got off scot free.

Recruiting duty is just not as easy as it looks.

Well, after I finished boot camp, I went to school at the Marine Corps base there at San Diego to learn Morse code. After I had that down cold, I reported to the 2nd Scout Company, which was part of the 2nd Division's special troops.

The big feature of our operation was these special scout cars. They'd been built by the White Motor Company in Cleveland, Ohio, and had a Hercules engine and bulletproof Seiberling tires. They had a fully waterproof ignition system and could ford anything up to their air intakes. The armor plate was quite thin, but it had a shield that would come down over its windshield. However, this could only stop ball ammunition.

Now, I'll tell you an odd one. Later on when we got to New Zealand, we traded these scout cars to the New Zealand troops for British Bren gun carriers, figuring they'd be a little better in the jungle, but we had a lot of trouble with these Brens. They required a hell of a lot of maintenance so we got rid of those British cars and got jeeps.

Then, after Tarawa, we got rid of the jeeps and ended up with rubber boots and field shoes to do our reconnaissance work.

Well, back to Camp Elliott. I was a private and most of us in the ranks, you know, down the pecking order, were big on liberty. I don't know, maybe General Vogel (2nd Division's CO) was too, but I know we were.

One of our favorite spots was a place between San Diego and Oceanside called Poway. They used to have a winery there and they'd sell you the leavings from the wine vats at sixty cents a gallon. Even poor twenty-one-dollar-a-month privates like us could afford that! A whole platoon could have a ball there.

If we felt flush, maybe a buck or two in our pockets, we'd hitchhike to Los Angeles. Things were less expensive in those days than they are now and you'd be amazed how you could stretch your dollars— you know, ten cents for a draft beer.

The big thing though was Tijuana, down in Lower California. One of my shipmates (Marine Corps term for buddy even though not aboard ship) had a car and we would sometimes drive down the coast. Things were getting a little tense internationally then and we couldn't leave the base in civilian clothes. And you couldn't enter Mexico in uniform.

So, whenever we'd head for Tijuana, we'd put on our khaki shirts, with the slick arms—we had no stripes; we were all privates—and our no-hip-pockets trousers and take off. Once we'd been through customs, we'd put on our campaign hats, minus the insignia. We must have looked like Pancho Villa.

Most of the time we'd stay away from what we called the pesos grabbing area, even though I did go to what they called the longest bar in the world on a couple of occasions. We'd mostly try and meet some of the nicer people who didn't try and make their living on the Yankee dollar and we were successful on many occasions. I'd taken two years of Spanish and could at least get by in the language, which made things a lot better.

One more thing, I never did get to the infamous Red Mill. It was too rich for my blood. But I heard plenty of the sergeants talk about it. I guess you could buy anything you wanted there or at least rent it.

Of course, most of the time we were working our butts off, but on one extended training exercise we lucked out. We must have been gone for close to two weeks. The only place the British were fighting the Germans at this time was in the North African desert. So, they sent us off in columns of scout cars through the desert over to Palm Springs where we bivouacked at the local tennis club. Here they brought out a bunch of young beauties who they wanted to pose with us for some Hollywood promotion. One way or another most of us did get a chance to have a date or two with some of these girls, which was great.

However, most of those two weeks was spent maneuvering in that desert, which was rough duty.

When we finished this extended desert-type reconnaissance work, we headed back to Elliott. I will say that as tough as those maneuvers were, we learned one hell of a lot about our job.

Now, I'll tell you something. We covered a hell of a lot of ground between Elliott and Palm Springs on wheels. A short time before we went out there the 8th Marines, also of the 2nd Division, covered basically the same area on foot. If there was one thing the whole 2nd Division was known for, it was forced marches; it was a fetish with our top officers.

Well, on December 7, 1941, I was on detached duty from the division, going to special school in San Diego. I'd attended Mass that morning and was down in the church's reception room having a cup of coffee, when I got the word of the attack on Pearl Harbor.

Wow! Like every other Marine in town, I rushed back to camp, where I was greeted by First Sergeant Claude F. Satorious, better known as "Peep Sight." It was rumored that he had joined the Marine Corps before Archibald Henderson [early nineteenth-century commandant].

"What the hell are you doing here?" he yelled.

"I figured I'd better come back," I answered.

"But you're on detached duty."

"Okay, then I'll go back to San Diego."

"Like hell you will! Go over to your platoon; they've got work for you to do."

So I spent the night loading .30 and .50 caliber machine gun belts.

Then we went on beach patrol. I won't go into detail about the rumors that were floating around the Pacific Coast at that time because there was a different one every minute. Once we realized what happened to the Pacific Fleet at Pearl Harbor, we could believe anything.

Well, in 1942 the division started going overseas piecemeal. I remember the 8th Marines went to Samoa and then to Guadalcanal. The 2nd Marines had hit Florida Island, right off the Canal on August 7. The Marine brigade that had gone to Iceland with many of our 2nd Division's 6th Marines in it had returned to the States. The 6th then regrouped before going to Guadalcanal in January of '43.

My scout outfit went directly to New Zealand and what a horrifying experience we had on the merchant ship we went over on!

Right off the bat the hole—where the enlisted men were to be quartered—stunk like something I can't describe. We soon found out why.

It seemed that just before the ship had come to San Diego it had hauled a cargo of sheep hides from New Zealand to San Diego; that's the word we got, anyway.

I had just made buck sergeant and when the top called us all together to draw straws to see who would head up the cleaning detail for the hole, I drew the short one. Can you imagine what kind of duty that was?

Well, I know you must have heard a lot of seasick stories in your interviewing, but I'll match mine with any of them. We hit the California groundswells that first night out. I've always had a real strong stomach and I did get to sleep that first night, but when I woke up around dawn, the overpowering stink of the hides and the vomit from the men who had already let go was too much; even I got sick.

The worst part of the problem though came one day while I was in the chow line. They had a big GI can right near the ladder going down below to our sleeping quarters. Hell, I say sleeping quarters; you had five or six racks lashed up on top of each other, hardly pleasant accommodations.

The can was half loaded with leftovers from that lousy food they were giving us. Well, the can was not lashed down properly. As the ship had one great roll, the can went sliding across the deck, bounced off a bulkhead and turned over as it hit the top of the ladder. The whole damn contents of that can spilled down into our hole. So, I quickly tried to round up my working party. The first guy I found was already puking in his helmet.

"No, sergeant," he said, "not me again! You can throw me over the side, but I'm not going down into the hole."

It was the same with the rest of the men who'd been working with me in the hole. They wanted no part of any more cleaning details. Hell, they were still puking from the first one.

Now, I'll tell you what a real Marine officer is made of.

The officer of the day for the hole was an amtrac second lieutenant. When he heard about all that crap in the hole, he gave me the word.

"Sergeant," he ordered, "grab your working party and clean that area up."

"Sir, I can't. My men are all lying down and vomiting. They just as soon we shot them."

"Okay," he said.

Then he collared a couple of sergeants and me, rolled up his own sleeves, and we went down below. That's right, he grabbed a swab himself. And it was quite a sight to see that lieutenant turning to like that.

Well, you don't die from seasickness and we also survived that dreadful chow they were giving us. We were really the raggedy-ass Marines on parade when we reached New Zealand, but we made it.

Now came some great duty and a long stretch of it. We were part of the 2nd Division that didn't go to Guadalcanal. By the time we got to New Zealand, I guess they figured they couldn't use a wheeled reconnaissance group on the Canal so we spent close to a year there Down Under. Many of our men began to look on that place as a second home.

We finally left New Zealand around the end of October, maybe November first. And, in a way, the 2nd Division would never really be the same again.

You see, the original 2nd Division, other than the old-time regulars, was made up mainly of San Diego boot camp Marines, just like the original 1st Division was Parris Island Marines. Naturally, it wasn't completely that way—in things like that it never is—but in the main, we were the West Coast outfit and the 1st Division was the East Coast outfit. This started to change after we began to receive replacements for the battle casualties and sick men of Guadalcanal. After Tarawa it was even more so. And when the replacements started to join us during the Saipan fight, the Division was loaded with men from all over the country.

All right, let's go to the Tarawa atoll. As I told you, I did not go to Betio. Our job was to check out the other islands in the atoll and try to find out how many Nips were on each one. Then the 6th Marines were to go in and secure the place.

Okay. The 2nd and 8th Marines started their own private hell at

Betio on November 20, but we didn't send our small groups into the other islands until the night of the 21st. The Navy coxswain couldn't find the proper place to unload our rubber boats until then.

Personally, I was in company headquarters and did not go ashore the night of the 21st. We were on an LCVP (Peter boat). We tooled around the lagoon, trying to keep radio contact with our men ashore and also keep the brass on the flagship *Maryland* informed about what was going on.

By the way, our LCVP was strafed that night. We never knew if it was an American or Japanese plane. I was crapped out at the time, but that machine gun fire sure woke me up in a hurry.

Early in the morning one of our platoons radioed in that they had two Gilbertese natives with them who had a Japanese prisoner in tow. This was what we wanted so we told them to come aboard. Those natives hated the Japs more than we did. Remember, the Gilberts had been British before the Japanese took them over.

Actually, I guess I was expecting to see natives with bones in their noses and spears because I was surprised as hell when the two Gilbertese turned up dressed in crisp British short sleeve shirts and short pants. They'd been hiding this clothing ever since the Japs had come to the Gilberts. One of these men took a look at our radio and smiled.

"Oh," he said, in perfect English, "a bloody wireless." Then he showed me a diploma, proving that he had passed a British course aimed at making him a wireless operator. I can even remember his name. It was Domingo Mueller.

This was when I found out that the Gilbertese called the Japs Saps. They had trouble with the letter "J"; it came out as an "S." Whatever, we loved their pronunciation of Saps.

Well, we went in and out of those islands, trying to find out how many Japs were on each one. Sometimes we would find some and other times the island would be vacant.

[At this point Colonel Driscoll had to depart for Portsmouth.

"I'm sorry," he told our group, "but I've got to shove off. But Rick here, he can tell you about Betio."]

PFC RICHARD SPOONER
F/2/8th Marines

Semper Fi, Mac, that's a great title. Do you know why the name Mac was used so often? [I did not.] Because of "Marine Amphibious Corps."

There, over on the wall, I have the insignias of the Marine Amphibious Corps during the war, the 1st, 3rd and 5th. When General Silverthorn used to come into my restaurant, he always would look at these because he'd designed the one with the dragon and the numeral III.

Well, just like Ed, I had gone to church on Sunday morning, December 7, 1941. This was in Fresno, California. I'd been raised in San Francisco but was living in Fresno at the time.

So I was walking away from church when I passed a bootblack stand; don't see many of those anymore. The shoeshiner was cussing up a storm. He had a little radio at the stand and this newscaster was giving us the scoop on what had happened. I took the whole thing quite personally.

You see, I'd already been in the Marines for a short time but had been booted out because I was underage, but I still looked at myself as a Marine. I felt the Japs had hit me right in the jaw.

It took me quite a while to get back into the Corps because they now knew my age, but I did get back in, maybe a short time before my seventeenth birthday.

After I went in for the second time, I went through boot camp in a breeze. That entire recruit camp training is great if you really want to be a Marine and that's all I wanted to be.

After boot camp I went to Camp Elliott, which was where we were to learn the skills of our trade and at this time I was learning to be a rifleman.

One thing about Elliott. At this time it was usually just referred to as line camp. You know, it was where you were taught what being in a line company was all about.

Oh, and by the way, I figured I was slated to be in the 2nd Division. Ed said its commanding officer was Clayton Vogel and he's correct. But to us he was just Barney Vogel; I don't know why, maybe because of Barney Google. I think he was later replaced by John Marstons who'd had the brigade that had gone to Iceland in the middle of '41. By the time we assaulted Tarawa, it was commanded by Julian Smith, one hell of a Marine.

Well, at any rate, I soon shoved off for the Pacific. I was luckier than Ed; I went over on a regular Army transport. Of course, we had those long chow lines. Hell, you'd no sooner finish one meal and it was time to line up again for another.

The name of the ship was the *Feland,* and naturally we had no idea where we were heading. You remember the slogans in those days, "A slip of a lip sinks a ship, the walls have ears," and then the poster with the real sleazy Jap with one ear cupped. Written on the poster is, "He is listening."

Actually, we figured we were going to some exotic South Sea island with palm trees and the like.

Well, the first thing we saw was Wellington, which is hardly Tahiti. As for its being tropical, it was actually chilly. We used to wear those khaki-colored flannel shirts which were tremendous. I sure wished I'd saved some of those; can't get them today; they were great! [He's right, it's the greatest shirt in the world.]

As for Wellington, what a delight! I mean both the city and the people were super. These New Zealanders were a lot like the Brits only not so reserved, much warmer and quite friendly. They made us feel we really belonged there at all times. New Zealand truly became a second home to many of the men in the 2nd Division. There were some genuine love affairs and, as I recall, several marriages.

All right, things always change in the Corps. While Wellington was tremendous, we soon found out we'd be at Camp McKay, maybe thirty-five miles from Wellington. It was at the town of Paikakariki, a Maori name. I've just spelled it for you phonetically; hope it's right.

What a letdown this turned into! We first saw this tremendous city of Wellington, then we end up in the boonies. We liked those bright lights of Wellington, even if they roll up the sidewalks real early.

Now, as I've said, it could get chilly there and downright cold at night. Instead of tents we had huts made out of thin tarpaper with six or eight men to a hut. We had these stoves, some woodburning, others kerosene, depending on which tent you were in. Neither of these stoves was much good. The guys with the woodstoves had trouble keeping them going; you had to stoke them and they could get dirty as hell.

As for the kerosene ones, they were downright dangerous. You never knew when one would blow up on you.

I'll tell you one thing about these huts though; I never once heard of anybody pinching anything from another Marine while we were there. We had stands for our rifles and a place to hang our dress greens and you could leave anything you wanted in your green blouse or on your rack. I guess when men realized they might soon be dying together, they just don't steal from each other.

By this time I was a member of Fox Company, 2nd Battalion, 8th Marines. Maybe it was the same with all the battalions in the 8th, I don't know, but it seems to me our outfit had an unusual number of prewar regulars. And, of course, our battalion commander was Major Jim Crowe and if you know anything about the Corps, you know who he was.

Anyway, the big thing when we were at Camp McKay was the hike from the camp to Foxton and back. That was really something!

First, the terrain was rough and ragged, sheep pastures and a lot of rocks. In those days we had boondockers and leggings. Hell, you could wear through those boondockers on a march like that. They told us it was 60 miles, which meant a round trip of 120 miles.

We'd stop every fifty minutes or so and take a break. You know, "the smoking lamp is lit; smoke 'em if you have 'em."

Well, Crowe was a real believer in your feet and I guess he was right. You can't fight a war without them. Every time we'd stop, he was always running around checking the men's feet; if they were in real bad shape, he'd send you back.

He'd also check the Guadalcanal men, particuarly the men who'd had malaria. If he could spot the symptoms of a coming attack, back that guy would also go.

The major had his own command jeep on the march. I never once saw him ride in it. The man was forty-five years old and he marched not only right along with the troops but he kept going back and forth among the men. I can remember on one of our last stops before we reached Foxton, Major Crowe calmly stopped, took off his boondockers and changed his socks. When you'd do this, you were supposed to massage your feet.

Well, the major had trouble getting his socks off because they were caked with blood. The skin on the soles of his feet had just worn through. But he washed off his feet, put on new socks, got up and yelled, "All right, Marines, let's move out." He was waving that swagger stick cane we all got such a kick out of.

We finally reached Foxton and now I'll tell you the most amazing thing about the march. When we reached our destination, we pitched our shelter halfs and crapped out, figuring we were in for a nice long rest, but it was not to be.

While we were bivouacked, a delegation from Foxton came out to see the major. It seemed these good Cobbers (New Zealand for "buddy," used extensively by old 2nd Division men) had arranged a dance for us, but at this point we knew nothing about it, even though we had seen the Cobbers talking to Crowe.

"Now, men," he said, "I know you're curious about what the Cobbers were doing here. Well, many of their young men are in the Near East or North Africa. They've got a great many lonely young ladies in Foxton who are anxious to have a dance with some American Marines. I've told them I'd let any man go who wanted to."

Do you know that these guys all gave a big cheer and other than the men who had the duty at the camp—and were they pissed off—almost every guy in the 2nd Battalion, including the Old Man, went to the shindig?

Then the next day we marched back to Camp McKay.

Now Leon Uris wrote an excellent novel several years ago called *Battle Cry*. This novel is roughly based on his experiences with the 6th Marines.

In *Battle Cry* he uses a composite of many Marines to make up his characters. For instance, I think his portrayal of his commanding officer, named High Pockets, was based on Jim Crowe. He does go into this famous march from Camp McKay to Foxton, but he says it was done by his battalion in the 6th Marines. Maybe they also did it, but, damn it, 2/8 definitely did it and in record time. And we turned right around and made it a round trip.

All right, they made a movie out of *Battle Cry,* starring Van Heflin. They listed Jim Crowe as the technical advisor to the film.

Well, in 1959 or '60, somewhere around there, they gave the General (Crowe) a retirement parade, marking his forty-one years of active service. I attended this parade, along with many other Marines who had served under Jim. After it was over, I got a chance to talk to my old major.

"General," I said, "how could you be a technical advisor to a film where a battalion from the 6th Marines, the pogey bait 6th, got credit for the march made by your own battalion of the 8th Marines?"

Jim laughed like hell.

"Do you know, Spooner, I've received literally scores of letters from men who were on that march," he said, "and they all ask me the same question that you have.

"But," he continued, "don't think I've ever forgotten our old battalion. There never was a finer one. Tragically, so many of those men didn't make it."

One more thing about *Battle Cry.* I've never forgiven Uris for not pointing out that the battalion that did make the march went to a dance that very same night.

Well, after that famous hike, we started to get ready for what we thought was going to be the retaking of Wake Island. We were going to avenge the 1st Marine Defense Battalion that had done such a great job there at the beginning of the war, or so we thought. Anyway, we really went to work getting ready to go into combat.

It's at times like these that the kind of company commander you have is as important as hell and so are the gunnery sergeants. In both cases Fox Company was real lucky.

Our company commander was a man named Marty Barrett and he was a top-notcher. Our gunny at that time was a man named Douglas Gordon. He was one of the younger gunnery sergeants, had only about twenty years in. He had one of those painted mustaches like Crowe had. Gordon knew how to instill pride in a young Marine and that's important.

And speaking of gunnery sergeants, I had one later on at Saipan who was named Johnson. He was older than Gordon and had fought in World War I and he never let us forget it. Whenever things would get rough, he'd just smile.

"Hell, you think this is a war," he'd say, "you should have been at Belleau Wood. That was real war!"

Of course, it got so we'd all give him the business, but he was one hell of a gunny. He'd make us want to show him that we were just as good as those World War I guys.

Anyway, our training intensified. We got the word we were going to the northern tip of North Island—remember, New Zealand is really two main islands, north and south—where we'd practice our landing and then go back to Camp McKay. It didn't work out that way.

We went up to the tip of North Island where we joined a convoy and from there we headed for practice landings on Efate in the New Hebrides. We never did return to New Zealand even though the scuttlebutt always had us going back there. This was extremely hard on many of the men who had spent a good deal of time there. Some had even married New Zealand girls and most of us had strong ties with New Zealand families.

Well, that was surprise number one. Surprise number two was we weren't going to Wake Island. Here I got all worked up over redeeming the Corps at Wake and we find out we're really headed for some insignificant little place I'd never heard of.

The campaign was supposed to be quite simple. Our warships and airplanes were going to knock the hell out of the Japs before we went in. We could expect to find only a dazed and greatly reduced garrison waiting for us. The name of the island we were to invade was Betio and it was part of the Tarawa atoll in the Gilbert Islands.

This brings me around to one of my favorite people, our platoon's lieutenant, a man named Stacy Davis. I'd say he was a father figure, but he was too young for that. He was probably in his mid or late twenties at the time. I know he'd finished college and was managing a movie theater somewhere when he went into the Corps.

At any rate he was a winner all the way. He got to know everyone in the platoon extremely well. Hell, he may even have known their serial numbers. He'd been on the Canal and I don't think a single man in our platoon held a thing against him.

Well, shortly before we went in, he gave the platoon a briefing.

"Okay, men," he said, "now for those of you who were not with the 8th on Guadalcanal, I don't want you to feel cheated when this one is over. What we're really doing is just a little police work. We'll all be coming back right after we secure the place. We probably won't see a single Jap. But don't worry, there's plenty of islands left and you'll get your share of combat. This place is only a little over two miles long and about half a mile deep at its widest point. We've already shelled and bombed it enough to sink the place."

Then he gave us a little bit of his lighter side.

"The few troops the enemy have here are Japanese Marines and I sure hate to see us kill Marines, but after all, they are Japs, so I guess it's all right."

Then he smiled and we all gave him a snicker.

Anyway when we were getting ready to go in, I began to wonder why our ships were still firing at the island if all the Japs were dead. Just playing it safe, I figured.

Then the word came down, "Land the landing force," and we went over the side. Cocky Rick Spooner, who couldn't wait to get his hands on some Japs, was about to become a man, a real Marine, the hard way.

Things got fouled up right at the beginning. It seems to me we went over the side at around 5:00 A.M., but we just hung around in our boats for two or three hours. I don't think we actually started for shore until close to 8:00 A.M.

As our LCI, or whatever it was, moved in, I was still amazed at the amount of fire we were pouring at the Nips. Then it appeared as if our craft had been hit, which surprised me. I looked over toward Lieutenant Davis and almost went into shock. Half of his face looked as if it was shot off. "No, no," I pleaded, "this can't be!"

But it was. I'm happy to tell you the lieutenant lived, but when I first looked at him, it didn't seem as if he could possibly survive.

From here on, things get a little foggy because my main thought was how do I stay alive?

I never did have to worry about getting out of the boat because the Japs took care of that by blowing it up. The next thing I knew, I was in the water up to my chest, still trying to keep myself in one piece. I wasn't thinking about the Corps or all the things I'd been taught. Hell, I would have jumped at the chance to join a mess kit repair unit. In short, the big brave Marine was scared stiff. You've heard of men getting so scared they'd lose control of their bowels. Not me, I was one jump ahead of those guys; I was scared shitless! Hell, I don't even think I peed my first twenty-four hours there on that island!

Actually, I'm sure I wasn't the only Marine in a trance. After all, it was the first battle for many of us. Remember, we'd been told to expect a picnic. Then, when guys start to fall around you, it can become mind-blowing.

Everyone near me seemed to be heading for a seawall to the left of a pier, so I followed the group. With Lieutenant Davis gone—I guess he was back on one of the ships—our platoon sergeant, a Marine named Joe Brown, took over and did a hell of a great job. He wore two hash marks and had been around.

Okay, we made the seawall. Now, don't confuse this with the main seawall over to our right. Ours was smaller, but it did offer some protection. I was crouched under this very short coconut wall. I looked back at the water, wondering how long a swim it would be back to California. I could see tremendous wreckage, including our amtrac, floating in the water. You could also see Marines in the water, wounded and dead. Then I saw the major, Jim Crowe.

Oh my God, he was walking back and forth with that field swagger stick of his; you could spot that pointed red mustache a mile away. He's talking to the men very calmly.

"All right, Marines," he'd say, "try and pick out a target and squeeze off some rounds. You better kill some of those bastards or they'll kill you. You don't want to die, do you? Come on, now, let's kill some of them!"

Well, goddamn it, I wasn't about to try and swim away now. I figured if I tried to, that old tiger would beat me to death with that cane of his.

So, I got ready to lean over the wall and try and get me some Nips. Just as I was about to expose myself to the Jap fire, a buddy of mine leaned over the wall to take aim. The poor guy took a bullet right in his head. That's the kind of a thing that can unnerve anyone, even if you're not an eighteen-year-old Marine who's quickly finding out that combat is not neat and clean. It's seeing your friends stretched out in a funny position with their eyes in a blank stare.

I wasn't hungry at all. The thought of trying to eat anything never entered my mind.

But, my God, did I get thirsty! Not only was my throat dry from the ordeal, but it was hot, oh my God, it was hot! We had gotten some water cans ashore. But the Navy had painted the inside with some kind of a rust preventative. It gave the water a real lousy taste. No sooner had I taken a swallow than I vomited the water. Imagine that, vomiting water!

Another thing that makes me kind of chuckle now was my helmet. I *hated* helmets. But at that point I would have jammed my whole body into that helmet if it would have fit.

At any rate, I reached the point where I knew I had to fire my M-1. I finally got up enough courage so I could let off a clip (eight rounds), but I must admit I didn't really take aim.

A little later we got the word from our company commander, Marty Barrett, who was propped up on his elbows a few yards behind us.

"Listen," he said, "when you fire, be sure you have a target. The ammo you have is all you're going to get. Remember, if you're all out of rounds when the Japs counterattack, you'll be duck soup for them. Take aim, take aim, no supplies are coming in."

Then I remember how so many of the Guadalcanal men bitched about the fleet pulling out and leaving them sucking the hind one. "Oh my God," I thought, "the fleet's going to leave us." In short, I was a wreck.

But I feel my biggest shock was still the stark reality that the Japanese shot back and shot to kill. And kill they did!

There was this one thing that helped me keep my sanity and that was, once again, Jim Crowe. My thoughts of Tarawa always come back to him. Watching the major was like watching a war movie where the good guys don't get hit.

As I look back over the combat, I just don't see how Crowe wasn't riddled. I know it sounds impossible, but, damn it, he was actually calmly walking around. People who would move around in any way whatsoever would be shot. It was almost as if some super-power just wouldn't allow him to get a scratch. I know he received some Purple Hearts at one time or another, but I'm quite sure he didn't get a scratch there at Tarawa.

Well, eventually we moved to the left of the wall and took part of the airstrip; I think we got the taxi strip. But the fight was a long ways from over. As long as there were Japs under arms and shooting, a battle with them was never over.

That first night we all braced for a Japanese counterattack, but it never came, not where I was anyway. They did hit us on the second night and with quite a bit. But by then the issue was really no longer in doubt, not like that first day anyway when we were hanging by a thread.

There is one illusion that a lot of people have about an assault landing that I would like to contradict. My battalion, 2/8, was the only battalion of the 8th Marines that was in that first wave. We took a lot of fire coming in, but nothing compared to what the next battalion of the 8th took when they landed; they were pulverized before they got ashore. I know; I could see them. Those poor guys were dropping in bunches. I don't know what the casualty figures for our regiment were for the whole three days, by battalion, but I know the next group of the 8th to come in had it worse in the water than we did.

My point is, don't by any stretch of the imagination think that being in the first wave always means you catch the worst pasting. It frequently didn't happen that way.

Well, I was on that small piece of hell known as Tarawa for seventy-six hours, but it seemed like seventy-six days to me. My memories are mainly ones of fear. I fought on Saipan and Tinian and received Purple Hearts on each of those islands. As a PFC I even ended up in charge of a platoon on Saipan. Along with the rest of the 8th

Marines, I caught some very nasty stuff at the end of the Okinawa battle.

I stayed in the Corps after the war and served in both Korea and Vietnam. I think if you check around, you'll find that I had a pretty good record when the fat was in the fire. I'm certainly not saying I was never uptight again; a certain amount of tenseness is normal.

But I would like to make a point here. It will be a wonderful thing if the Marine Corps never has to go into combat again, but that's probably wishful thinking. After all, we're supposed to be the first to fight when needed.

However, if any young Marine reads this and finds himself petrified by that first shock of enemy fire, don't let it throw you. It just might turn out that you'll end up a hell of a better Marine when that first battle is over. I know. It happened to me.

The Reunions

"These reunions have sure as hell changed a lot," I was told by a 1st Marine Division man in Kansas City, Missouri. "We used to do a little hell-raising, you know, chase some broads, trying to get a little something extra, but no more.

"And we used to have some real funny things happen. I can remember this one guy—he's not here this year, hope he hasn't died —who was from New York City. Oh, he knew all the angles.

"Well, he thinks he's scored and he takes this doll into his hotel room but she turns out to be a hooker. Not only did he have to give her thirty big ones—this was several years ago, it would be at least fifty now—but she swiped his ring that he'd left on the bureau. Oh, we gave that guy the business—'Mr. Smoothie,' we called him."

"Yeah," chipped in a man from the 5th Marines, "things have changed a lot. Most of the men bring their wives and we go to art galleries and take guided bus tours. We just don't kick the gong around much anymore." [Both these men asked to remain anonymous; their wives were along and they did go on the bus tour.]

"But," he continued, "we have a lot more of the Old Breed turn up now. It's great just to sit around, have a few drinks and shoot the breeze."

This is something I heard at the three divisional reunions I attended. The Marine veterans are at an age where they find sitting down with old buddies extremely enjoyable.

Now for the 6th Marine Division reunion and two incredible coincidences that are mind-boggling. I arrived in New Orleans and checked in at the hotel where the reunion was being held. Then I went to the hospitality suite where the first man I talked to was one Augie Lepore. We exchanged the usual greetings and here's how the conversation went from then on:

Augie: I was sworn into the Corps at Springfield, Mass., in '43. I'd tried to enlist in the Marines the year before, but they told me my eyes weren't good enough. Then when it came time to be drafted, they asked for Marine Corps volunteers. I guess they weren't making the quota then because I was accepted.

Berry: I was sworn in at Springfield also, in August '43. I went to Parris Island in September, Platoon 729.

Augie: Platoon 729? That was also my platoon number! I left Plainville to catch the train in Hartford. I went with a guy named Boomer.

Berry: Boomer, he's the guy who was always saying, "Okay, keep the fifty thousand dollars, the deal's off!"

Augie: That's right, that's the guy. Wait a minute, you were the real young guy; you had a tweed jacket on, Berry, I remember you. Everyone thought you were a rich kid.

Berry: I can remember you also. Weren't you a friend of Freeman's?

Augie: That's right, but I haven't seen him in years. You know, I was eighteen years of age down there, but you were younger than that, weren't you?

Berry: Yeah, I turned seventeen on June 30, 1943; I was the youngest guy in the platoon officially, but do you remember the blond, skinny kid from West Virginia we called "Chicken"? Well, he told me one day he was only fifteen but had said he was eighteen.

Augie: You remember the two DIs, Albritton and Glass?

Berry: Yeah, Albritton had those great white teeth and was always smiling. He was the PFC. I don't know what happened to him, but Glass, the corporal, I know he was killed on Iwo.

Augie: He was the tough one, from Georgia, I believe. A hell of a Marine. My God, what a Marine, even if he didn't seem to like northerners.

Berry: Do you remember when they gave us the tetanus shots and Glass had us doing physical drill under arms?

Augie: Yeah.

Berry: Well, he came over to tell me I looked very pale. Of course I gave him the "I'm all right, sir" crap. What does a seventeen-year-old kid know? Anyway, I started to puke right after that so they took me to sick bay.

Glass came to see me the next day. Of course I wanted to return to my platoon because you had to go back several platoons if you stayed in the hospital too long. So Glass got me out. But you were right. Glass didn't like northerners.

Augie: You know, I have a copy of the list they gave each guy when he left PI, showing where each guy was going. I'd love to run into some of those men.

Berry: You've just run into one of them. Me.

Well, I can tell you John Miller, a Pennsylvania Dutch guy, went to sea school with me. He was still on the *Hancock* (CV-19) when I hurt my shoulder and had to leave the carrier. I haven't seen any of the other men since I left boot camp.

Augie: Diz Anderson, the big, good-natured football player. I wonder what happened to him?

Berry: Oh yeah, he was in that V-12 group that had flunked out somehow. There was a guy called "Pinky" from St. Louis and a Sid something. I'd like to see any of those guys.

Augie: Well, Boomer, he was in the 6th Division's armor. I tied one on with him in China just before we came home. Do you remember those two huge guys from Pennsylvania? We used to call them both "Tiny." They had to go 260 pounds or more. Well, you know me; I'm a little guy. It was the bigger of those two guys, the Polish one—wait a minute, they were both Polish guys—that I had to do that Biddle bayonet drill with.

[At this point George Tremblay joined us. George was with the 1st Armor Amphib Battalion. He was also from New Bedford, Massachusetts, the same hometown as my wife. I asked him if he knew the family. My wife is the daughter of the late Dr. Weeks.]

George: Josh Weeks, the doctor? How could you miss him? My God, he was a big man. Was an All American (football) at Brown, you know. Hell, I worked at the Wamsutta Club. One night when old Josh had downed a few, someone gave him a bad time and the Doc just got on a three-point stance and knocked the guy on his ass.

Well, I myself ended up in K/3/22 at the end of the war and had gone from Guam to China with the 6th Division. So I was there in New Orleans at the reunion not only as an author but as a legitimate member of the division association. I'd already met a guy I went through boot camp with and another man who'd seen my late father-in-law cold cock someone. It was a great visit.

When the Governor Went to War

Orville Freeman

"No, I don't mind being called governor; after all," Orville says, "I was elected to three terms. But I don't go around introducing myself as governor; that would be ostentatious as hell. Do you know of Senator Aiken? Well, he was also once governor of Vermont. I understand his wife still calls him 'Governor' though. It's a nice title."

Governor Freeman also served for eight years as secretary of agriculture in the cabinets of Presidents Kennedy and Johnson, immediately after his tenure as Minnesota's chief executive.

Today he is president of a firm called Business International, a job that constantly takes him to every corner of the globe.

Jane, his wife of forty years, is currently president of the Girl Scouts. They have a daughter in the Peace Corps and a son who is a lawyer in Minneapolis. The Freeman family accomplishes things.

But when the governor sits down with a martini, he can easily return to the time when he was a lieutenant in the 9th Marines and the State of Minnesota came within a fraction of an inch of losing a future governor on the island of Bougainville.

FIRST LIEUTENANT ORVILLE FREEMAN
K/3/9th Marines

Let's go back to 1940. I was studying law at the University of Minnesota. I'd met Hubert Humphrey earlier and we'd become close friends. Hubert was six years older than I. We both firmly supported FDR's foreign policy and decided to campaign that summer for him in the year's Presidential election between Roosevelt and Wendell Willkie. I'm sure you remember Willkie going around the country berating what he called the "third term candidate."

The unusual part of that campaign to me was the position of the

America Firsters. They were firmly against FDR and his plans to aid Great Britain. They seemed to shut their minds to the fact that Willkie and Roosevelt had very similar foreign policies. Willkie was no isolationist. He's the one who later on preached the One World doctrine. The isolationists of the America First group may not have realized it but they didn't have a candidate in 1940. It was a good thing they didn't.

As for my state of Minnesota we had plenty of isolationists at the time but we've always also had a strong international flavor, especially for the Midwest. Take the bigget name in our state politics at the time, Harold Stassen. He certainly didn't believe we should stay out of world affairs. He felt that what was going on in Europe and Asia could drastically affect the U.S. He was right.

And I'll tell you one more thing about politics at that time. I played varsity football that year. When the season was over, Hubert whang-dangled me into a debate and do you know what the subject was?—Resolved, that the stimulation of the economy through the expenditure of federal funds should cease—things never change, do they?

Well, Humphrey became a very close friend of mine during that period, a friendship, I may add, that kept up until he died. He was a great American.

There is one more name I'd like to mention from those prewar years not only because he was a great athlete but also because he was a great person. Poor guy, he died young. His name was Bruce Smith.

When I entered law school in the fall of 1940, I coached Minnesota's freshman football team. Bruce was the star of the team. If you know anything about Big Ten football in the early Forties, you know what an outstanding player he turned into on the varsity.

Well, as 1940 drew to a close I saw the handwriting on the wall. The U.S. was bound to get into the war and I knew I would be going into the service. I figured I'd better go into what I considered the best-trained, hardest-fighting outfit; to me this meant the Marine Corps. So I enlisted in the USMCR.

They told me when I joined up I could finish law school before going on active duty, but Pearl Harbor changed that. I received my orders on the last day of 1941. I figured they were coming but they did give me a jolt and a problem.

You see, at the time these orders came I was planning on getting married. Going on active duty wasn't going to change that unless I flunked out of OCS. In January of 1942 I think a private was still getting twenty-one dollars a month—twenty-one dollars a month and all you could eat, they used to say.

On the other hand, a second lieutenant was making one hundred and twenty-five dollars a month. You couldn't get married on a private's pay, but you could make it as a second lieutenant.

So when I showed up at Quantico for OCS, I really turned to in spite of the fact that I ran into a guy named Sergeant Jones.

Oh, this guy made my life unbearable. He'd stick his face right next to mine and roar at me and he'd spare nothing.

"You stupid educated son of a bitch," he'd yell. Or, "You eight-ball asshole."

Now, let's face it, I'd graduated magna cum laude from Minnesota and had taken almost a year and a half of law school. Besides, I was no bookworm, studying all the time; I'd played Big Ten football and was pretty good at baseball. I knew I was catching on to what we were learning rather well. Many a time I had to control my anger. I honestly think I would have hung one on Jones if it wasn't for the fact I had my heart set on obtaining a commission and getting married.

For a while I felt Jones might have been under orders to ride us, but damn it, we had other sergeants who worked us hard but with a certain amount of intelligence. This guy Jones was a numbskull.

Now, I'd like to say something that might set well with some but not well with others. But then again, I've never been known for not speaking my piece.

Jones was an old-time regular. Well, when I got into the 9th Marines, we naturally had several of those old-line regulars in our outfit. Some of them were great but others just knew too much about "soldiering" and here I mean gold-bricking. They knew all the angles and were great on the parade ground with their spit and polish. But when push came to shove, they could be real bullshitters. What I'm saying is when the chips were down, they weren't any better than those of us who had gone into the Corps for the war and they certainly weren't any more intelligent than we were.

Anyway, Sergeant Jones or no Sergeant Jones, regulars or reserves, the important thing is I did get my commission and very shortly afterward my fiancée and I were married. We then settled down in Quantico where I was to take another three months of training on how a second lieutenant operates. The big difference from my previous training was that now I was a commissioned officer. I didn't have to worry about any Sergeant Jones. I went through that second course at Quantico in a breeze, was given a furlough and reported to my next assignment at Camp Elliott outside of San Diego and the 9th Marines. And so I came under the command of one of the truly great Marines of all time, then Colonel Lemuel Shepherd. I don't know any Marine, enlisted man or officer, who served with Shepherd who doesn't agree with that statement.

Actually, I probably owe my assignment to the 9th to a man named

Overstreet, then Major Overstreet. I heard that when Shepherd was looking over the list of new second lieutenants, my name popped up. Overstreet, already in the 9th, told Shepherd what a great young officer I was and that was good enough for the colonel.

Now, here's a good example of what I meant when I said to you what a great officer Shepherd was in just about everyone's book. While we were in New Zealand, the colonel set up a cocktail reception for all the officers in the 9th Marines. Shepherd stood there and not only greeted each man but also addressed them all by name. That's the kind of thing that a young officer remembers.

Oh, the general was remarkable. I knew it was just a matter of time before we'd be going overseas. I can vividly remember directing my platoon on a problem and going all out while doing it. All of a sudden I turned around and there was a grinning Colonel Shepherd.

"Freeman," he said, "you keep going just the way you are and some day you'll make a fine Marine officer." Naturally I felt great about the whole thing. He was always doing things like that with the young officers. He could, however, kick your ass if he felt you deserved it.

We had an officer in our 3rd Battalion named Tony Walker; Cold Steel Walker, we used to call him becaue he was always talking about how he was going to give it to the Japs in spades. He gave the impression that he was one tough hombre and as a matter of fact he was just that. He had a tremendous record later in the war. He was rugged as hell, mean and strong as a bull.

As a matter of fact Tony was so gung ho he couldn't wait for our 9th Marines to develop before he went into combat so he applied for transfer into the 4th Raider Battalion. His transfer came through while we were out on a training session, maybe ten miles from our quarters. He went over to Colonel Shepherd, trying to get transportation back to the main camp so he could get ready to ship out.

"What?" the Colonel roared. "You got yourself transferred out of my outfit which is about to be the best regiment in the Corps and you expect me to get you a jeep? You son of a bitch, you think you're so tough, you can hike back!" Shepherd wasn't kidding. Tony got back on his own two legs.

I came quite close to such a confrontation with the colonel myself one time in New Zealand. I pulled a tremendous boner and I don't know to this day if Shepherd knows that I was the guilty one.

Well, back to California. Shortly after I reached the West Coast, the 9th Marines moved over to Camp Pendleton, a large new Marine base about forty miles north of San Diego. Once I got settled at our new camp, I sent for my wife. I didn't know how long I'd be at Pendleton, but I wanted Jane with me no matter what.

After my wife arrived in California, she started to look for a place to live and she really lucked out.

It seemed there was a beach community near Oceanside (the town closest to Pendleton) named San Malo. It was populated mainly by wealthy people from the movie community up north in Hollywood. The houses here were truly magnificent. The minute I saw the area I figured Jane had lost touch with reality. I didn't figure we could afford to live in the garage of one of those places. But as Jane had arranged an appointment with the owners of one of those houses, I figured I should go through with it.

You see, I didn't realize that the homeowners in San Malo were afraid the government was thinking about taking over the place for the duration. I guess they thought if several Marine families were already living there, Uncle Sam would leave it alone.

So we were given a guided tour of one of the houses and it was beautiful—two wings, three bedrooms, two fireplaces, beautiful grounds and an oceanfront just a hundred yards away.

After we'd seen the whole place, the owner's wife turned to Jane. "Mrs. Freeman, shall we leave while the men discuss the financial end of things?"

"Oh, boy," I said to myself, "here it comes! How do I get out of this one?"

Then, to my surprise, it was the owner who semed embarrassed.

"Lieutenant," he asked, "would fifty dollars a month be too much?"

"How much?" I replied. I thought my hearing had gone bad.

"Fifty dollars and I'll throw in the gardener."

Naturally I jumped at it. I'd already bought a 1932 Plymouth for twenty-five dollars. Transportation to the camp's gate would be no problem, even though sometimes you had to push that Plymouth uphill.

And by the way, when I did go overseas and Jane went back to Minnesota, she sold the car for the same twnty-five dollars. Not a bad deal either.

However, remember I didn't get to spend that much time at San Malo. We were constantly training at Pendleton, particularly on night problems. Shepherd knew those Japs were at their best after dark and he wanted us ready for them. But when I was there at San Malo, it was idyllic. Several of the other married Marine officers had also latched on to this deal, which made it all the better.

The biggest drawback we had was the ever-present knowledge that we were a Marine infantry regiment. The 1st Marine Division, along with the 2nd Marines, had hit Guadalcanal. Everyone knew there would be a tremendous amount of tough combat ahead, maybe years of it. It was quite doubtful that all officers there at San Malo would be coming back from the Pacific.

As 1942 drew to a close, we knew we were all ready for the Pacific and the thought of what lay ahead dominated everyone's thoughts. I'll never forget that Christmas. Many of the officers and their wives had a tremendous blast. It was really something, everyone trying to have a great time, knowing full well what awaited them.

Then we got the word. The first part of January, almost a year to the day after I had gone on active duty, we were to report to the headquarters of the 9th Marines at Pendleton for transportation overseas. Everyone knew what it meant, a bus ride to San Diego where we would ship out for God knows where.

Well, on the designated morning, Jane and I got into the old Plymouth and headed for Pendleton. We arrived there at 7:00 A.M. on the dot.

Now, do you remember that old bugaboo, "Hurry up and wait"? Well, that's what happened. Four hours later we were still waiting. You can imagine how traumatic this waiting became. Remember, we were heading for combat and real rough combat at that. I knew that both Jane and I were emotionally drained. I could see by my wife's eyes how this was tearing her apart, so I made a decision.

"Look, dear," I said, "God knows how long this will be. We may be here for hours. You'll end up a basket case. You better go back to our place."

She didn't want to leave but finally she realized it was the thing to do and she took off. I longingly watched that old Plymouth drive away.

As it turned out, it's a good thing my wife left. It was 3:30 that afternoon before we finally took off for San Diego. As we headed south on the highway, we went right by San Malo. I could see the top of the roof of our place as we passed. I knew my wife was there. I felt just about as low as a human being can feel. The next time I would see my wife was after I had gone through one hellish experience.

Well, we boarded ship there in San Diego and took off for a direct run to New Zealand, where I found out something I didn't realize. There are sections of New Zealand that have real thick brush, almost jungle. Of course it is not as hot as the Solomons, but it's ideal training grounds if you're headed for somewhere like the Solomons. It was in this area, close to the ocean, where I pulled that boner I told you about earlier. Here it is.

One day we had gone out over the mountains. Everyone was spread out all over the place. I was in charge of K Company and had lost touch with two of my platoons. Hell, I didn't have the foggiest idea of where they were. I had to get them together to properly complete this maneuver I was supposed to do, so I figured the only thing to do was blow my whistle as hard as I could.

Oh, my God, I'd forgotten that this was the signal for the whole regiment to secure the butts. All the companies couldn't have heard me, but of course the word goes down from one unit to another. The next thing you know the whole regiment had crapped out on the beach.

I ended up feeling like a lead nickel but nothing like I did a week or so later when the general called a meeting to review the exercise. He was stating everything that had happened, then he got to my faux pas. He looked up at us; you could see he was boiling.

"Then, gentlemen," he said, "some stupid son of a bitch blew his goddamn whistle!"

He looked out over a silent group and just stared.

I was terrified; I felt I should acknowledge what I had done, but I couldn't do it. Hell, I don't know if I could have stood up even if he had asked the man who had blown the damn whistle to stand up. I might even have run out of the room.

He never mentioned it again.

Our training here continued and I mean it got tougher and tougher. There is so much for a rifle company lieutenant, or captain, to know that it's hard to retain it all.

For instance, did you ever realize how important it is for a platoon not to outdistance its flanks? You naturally think of the danger from the enemy, but what about the other Marines? Do you realize how easy it is for another platoon to shoot into your platoon if you get too far out in front? It happens all the time. And that was the type of problem we worked on constantly.

There was another problem I had to work out and I finally came to grips with it there on New Zealand. It was the strong barriers that are put up between enlisted men and officers. I had always been an egalitarian and the sharp social and military distinctions drawn between those who had commissions and those who did not always upset me. Yet I did know that when we came face to face with the Nips, I'd better be able to draw immediate reactions from my men.

It turned out that there was one happening there in New Zealand that somehow brought this home to me and straightened me out.

You see, most of the time when we had liberty, the enlisted men had to be in camp at 10:00 P.M., while the officers did not have to show up until reveille.

Well, early one morning I was on my way back to camp. It must have been about 2:00 A.M. There were also three NCOs from King Company returning to their tents. If it was that late, you had to walk the last two miles to the camp. The four of us ended up walking together. We shot the breeze during the walk without anything being said about their being a few hours AWOL. When we reached the camp, I let them have it.

"Look, goddamn it," I said to them, "we all know you men are four hours late getting back. I'm not going to say anything to anybody this time, but if it happens again, I'm going to have to run your ass up."

I'm really not sure why, but from then on, I never questioned why I should give an order. If you are going to take responsibility, take it, but remember, it works both ways. Lem Shepherd used to have it down pat.

"Look," he'd say, "rank not only has its privileges but it also has its responsibilities. You are an officer. When you are in the field, you don't eat until your men have eaten and at night you don't get into your hole until the men are in theirs."

And that's the way a good officer is supposed to act, but, of course, they all don't look at it that way.

Well, after training extensively in New Zealand we headed up to Guadalcanal. By now Colonel Shepherd had left us, going to the 1st Marine Division where he became assistant divisional commander. But I never forgot him. He still remains my idea of what a commanding officer should be.

By the time we got to the Canal, the organized fighting had long since ceased, but in the summer of '43 there were still plenty of Japs out in that jungle. Fire fights between our patrols and small groups of the Japs were not that uncommon. However, in my opinion all those Nips really wanted was a square meal. I saw a couple of the prisoners we captured and they looked as if they were starving.

The air raids were a little more serious. Here our division took its first casualties. Our troops, Army and Marines, had started the push up the Solomons, but the Japanese were still in control of most of the islands north of Guadalcanal. Their planes could easily fly down the slot and blast us.

By the first of October we were ready for the real thing and our whole division took a detour over to the New Hebrides for a couple of weeks of dry run amphibious work. Then we moved toward Bougainville, landing at a place called the Empress Augusta Bay. We went in on November 1, with the 3rd Marines going in on the right and our 9th Marines going in on the left. We took some small arms fire as we landed, but not as much as the 3rd Marines experienced.

Our biggest drawbacks were the boats and the Jap Zeros. The beach here was so stiff and the surf so heavy that our landing boats would broach as they landed. You had to get the hell out of them in a big hurry.

The Zeros were shocking. It was the first time I'd ever been strafed and that's one helpless feeling. You are running as fast as you can, trying to find some cover because you know there is really nothing else you can do. I guess some of the men threw some small arms fire at the Japs, but I can't recall any of it taking effect.

Another problem was the coconut log fortifications the Japs had put up. The only covering fire we received while going after those nests was a few shells lobbed in by a destroyer which accomplished absolutely nothing. We had to knock each one of those pillboxes off with small arms fire. As each fortification had at least one Jap machine gun, we had our hands full.

We finally set ourselves up and around four o'clock that first day we had our first experience with what I soon realized was a Bougainville ritual. It rained. As a matter of fact I think it rained at four o'clock every day that I was on that goddamn island. It was almost impossible to keep dry.

Then at night, with the sun gone, it would get chilly. It was always hot and humid during the day but not too bad as long as you were by the water. But then that rain would come, followed by the chill. It was miserable.

There you would be, lying in a hole in the sand with a wet poncho. You'd be soaked and you'd get so goddamn cold you thought you were going to die. Hell, I'm from Minnesota; I'm no stranger to cold. But this was different. It was so bad you'd try to keep your teeth from chattering because you wanted complete silence. Just about the only thing you could hear would be the goddamn land crabs. Any other noise would be apt to draw tremendous fire from our own men. If it turned out that the noise had come from a Marine, the next day the poor guy would really get his ass read off. Hell, I think we would have hanged the guy from the yardarm if they had let us.

Of all the nights we spent there in that dead silence I can probably remember the first one the best. The beach may have been quiet but the jungle wasn't. We'd been told how skillful the Nips were at night infiltration. You thought every sound that came out of the jungle was one of the Japs. I can recall just lying there with my automatic pistol in my hand. I wasn't moving but my heart pounded like a sledgehammer. I was sure the Nips could hear it.

Well, we moved our lines into the jungle, setting up a perimeter that must have been about a half mile wide. The Seabees came in and started to build the airfield we needed so badly and what a job they did.

In the meantime our position was still fragile as hell. We had to find out more about the Nips, which meant we'd be sending out patrols. I picked the short straw on one that looked like a real backbuster, but I really had no choice in the matter.

Now, no matter how you look at it, I was in no hurry to start tramping through that jungle. I'd seen enough fire fights to know they were no fun and to have them deep in that jungle would be dreadful.

For instance, what would I do with my wounded?—a thought that always preys on the mind of the officer in charge. I didn't stop to think how that was going to come back to haunt me.

As for my men, they felt the same way; they wanted no part of it. But when you're told to go, you go. I yelled, "Come along," and every man started out.

Now, keep in mind that I was the exec of King Company, an officer who doesn't usually take out a platoon. But, in combat, things always get changed around like that. If you are available, you go.

The detail itself was quite essential. We were pretty well dug in where we were. Now we had to find out where the Japs were and if possible get a fix on how many we could expect to come at us. We knew there was a trail out there that ran north and south on the island. It was known as the Numa-Numa Trail. The word had come down that we had to find out what kinda Jap movement was running on the trail. The aerial photography we had was useless, probably due to the density of the Bougainville jungle. Honestly, it was a mess!

In any case we headed out, going north through the foothills. I had been told that the best way to go was to head for the Laruna River —I guess it was about six miles into the jungle—cross it and head east.

When we started out, they'd added a machine gun section to my platoon but there was no way we could make any time lugging those guns through that jungle. So, I sent them back to the beach, telling the men to be sure and tell battalion how impossible this jungle was.

Well, we got to the river, crossed it and kept moving. After two days I kept saying to myself, "Where the hell is this trail?"

You know that routine those two guys had—I think they were called "Bert and I"—where one of them asks this old down-easterner directions and he ends up saying, "Guess you just can't get there from here." Well, that's how I was beginning to feel, that there just was no way to reach the elusive Numa-Numa Trail from the beach.

There was one thing I knew for a certainty—we would soon run out of rations and pills to purify the water. This was not supposed to be a sweep, just a patrol.

So, I said, "The hell with it; we better head back to the beach." When I passed this word to the men, no one complained, and we started back.

Somewhere along the line on this return, I decided to take the point. Somehow I felt that an officer should certainly take as many chances as anyone else.

Suddenly, as I was going down a little footpath through this tough, close jungle, I made a turn and there I was, face to face with five or six Japanese. They were just as surprised as I was, but I guess I spotted them a split second before they saw me. I opened up with my carbine and I know I hit two of them.

Then, as I tried to get behind a tree, I felt something hit me in the jaw. I went down and the next thing I knew I was lying behind a big fallen banyan tree. I was paralyzed, couldn't move. Thank God for that tree! The Japs now opened up with a Nambu machine gun, but the tree was absorbing the bullets.

In the meantime, my platoon came over as fast as they could. I was in a complete state of shock. My jaw was obviously broken and God knows what else was shot up. I was sure I was dying.

Well, my sergeant sat me up and a corpsman put sulfur on my wounds and bandaged me up. I was now conscious enough to know I was in terrific pain.

Then the corpsman, a well-meaning guy, gave me just what he shouldn't have, a dose of morphine. I understand this should never be administered to a person with a head wound.

I started to vomit and go back into shock, but there is one thing I can remember and that is a conversation with my sergeant. Keep in mind that as my jaw was broken, I could hardly talk, but I gave him an order anyway.

"I'm done for," I gasped out. "Get the men the hell out of here, fast!"

"Lieutenant," he answered, "we ain't going nowhere without you!"

Thank God for those wonderful guys. The Marines are told you don't leave your wounded and these men weren't about to.

Then they started to half carry, half drag me as we headed back to the perimeter. Things seemed a little hazy for me for a while, but it seems to me Japs were popping out of the brush and firing rather constantly, during the daylight, anyway.

As the time went on I began to gather a little strength. At first I kept going in and out of a stupor but the further we moved along the more my bearings came back to me.

Then came darkness and as miserable an evening as anyone could possibly spend. We were in a swampy area by this time. They had me based against a tree with the water up to my waist. If you have ever been in a situation where time dragged, just visualize what it was like for me, counting the minutes going by in that situation.

Now for some good news. When the dawn came, I seemed to have gained a great deal of strength. Don't ask me how, maybe I got a second wind, but I was able to walk and could think clearly, so I once again took command of the platoon.

I was still faced with one hell of a problem. I might have been back on my feet but I knew I needed medical help in a hurry. Bougainville is about a hundred miles long. Our beachhead was not very wide. First, we had to be sure we were headed for the ocean; then we'd have to hit the beach at just the right spot.

Also, don't forget the Japanese. We had no way of knowing how many of them were near us and just where they were. What a predicament!

Well, our compass didn't let us down. Eventually the Marine we had out in front came back with the word.

"Hey, we're just about there," he said. "I can see the beachhead out in front of us. We've hit it right on the button!"

The minute I realized we'd made it, I crapped out.

"Sergeant," I said, "they can get a jeep in on this trail. Tell them to get one for me. I've done all the walking I'm going to do for a hell of a long time."

The jeep finally showed up and took me to our field hospital where they started to go to work on me.

But this place was no great shakes either. The two nights I was at the field hospital—it was really more of a sick bay—Jap bombers came over. I had to spend those nights in a slit trench right next to two 290 millimeter antiaircraft guns that we had firing at the Japs. What a sound! My ears were sore for days.

On the third day after I'd reached the beachhead one of those destroyer transports we had arrived, picked up several of us who needed more attention and took us down the slot to Guadalcanal, where they had a base hospital. One of the doctors gave me a quick examination and then a bit of a jolt.

"Lieutenant," he said, "it'll be a simple procedure. Do you want me to take the bullet out now?"

"I'll be damned," I answered. "Is it still in me?"

You see, once I started to come out of it after I was hit, the last thing in the world I thought about was the slug. I told him to take it out all right, but to be sure and give it to me, which he did. I still have it, a steel jaggered .25 caliber. If it had been any bigger, I wouldn't be here.

The truly amazing thing was the course of that damn bullet. It had hit the jaw, gone down through my neck to my shoulder. Somehow it just missed my jugular vein and the artery, going between those two. Doctors would come in from all over the hospital just to see how it went through without killing me.

I didn't know it at the time but this was the end of my combat. I was sent to an Army hospital in New Caledonia where they finally set my jaw, which brings me around to my friend, Johnny Alphonse.

Johnny was a Marine pilot and a great guy, a real good friend of mine. We'd gotten to know each other quite well on liberty in California.

As it turned out Johnny ended up stationed on New Caledonia, flying transport planes all over the Pacific. He didn't like the work. What he really wanted to do was fly in combat. He later told me his greatest humiliation was when he found out part of the cargo he had once flown from New Caledonia to Guadalcanal was a new toilet seat for an Army general.

"I didn't go through all that training so some doggie general could warm his fat ass," he said.

Anyway, when I got to New Caledonia, one of the first things I had one of the nurses do was call Johnny to tell him I was on the island. He wasn't in his quarters when the call was made so she left word for him to call back the hospital.

When Johnny was finally located, he was at the officers' club pretty well smashed. He asked the nurse what was wrong with me.

"Oh, he had one side of his head shot off," she answered.

Apparently this shocked the hell out of my buddy. He went tearing around, trying to borrow a jeep. When he couldn't get one, he went out and stole the first one he could get his hands on. Then he took off for the hospital like a bat out of hell.

When he arrived there, he came roaring in, looking for his pal, who he thought was at death's door. He found me all right. I was sitting in a chair, calmly reading a newspaper or something like that.

"Holy Christ!" he yelled. "The goddamn Army nurse had me thinking you were a goner and here you are taking it easy."

Then he started blasting the Army—from MacArthur on down. He might even have included U.S. Grant. He was about as popular at that hospital as Malcolm X at a DAR tea.

Anyway, after that I was sent to the Naval Hospital at Noumea, where my jaw was set. I had started to get some tremendous pain in my head and neck so they sent me back to the States where they removed some scar tissue that had formed throughout the area where the bullet has passed.

But the great thing about coming home was seeing my wife Jane. Remember, when I'd been half out of my head in that stinking Bougainville jungle, I never thought I'd see her again. You can imagine what a reunion that was!

One more thing about Johnny and this is tragic. He came back to the States not too long after I did. We got together for a long session in Chicago, which would not have been approved by the WCTU. As always, Johnny was loaded with funny stories, particularly about the

Army and he was still bitching about the toilet seat he had delivered to Guadalcanal. Then he reported to the Marine Air Corps base at El Torro in California.

Shortly afterward I got word that he had been killed while test piloting. I felt a tremendous personal loss then and I still do.

During 1944, time started to really drag for me. Sometime, I think it was that summer, my old commanding officer, Lem Shepherd, was putting together the 6th Marine Division. Remember how I told you how he knew all his officers in the 9th Marines by name? Well, he found out where I was because he wanted me to take over a company in the 6th. The only question was, could I pass a physical? It wasn't to be. As you can see, here it is almost forty years later and I still do not have full use of my left arm and never will. But I can't complain. I came quite close in November of '43 to losing everything.

Now, let's jump ahead to the mid 1950s. I had been recently elected governor of the State of Minnesota. My old friend, Hubert Humphrey, his wife Muriel, my wife Jane and I had just visited Williamsburg, Virginia, you know, the town that has been restored to eighteenth-century vintage. Hubert was then a United States senator from our state.

I was telling them a few stories about the Marine Corps when I noticed we were close to Quantico.

"Look," I said, "my old commanding officer, Lem Shepherd, is at Quantico. He's the commandant now, you know. Let's stop in and say hello."

Everyone was agreeable so we stopped in to see the general. We had no trouble whatsoever. Three minutes after Lem heard who it was we were immediately ushered into his office. Our conversation went beautifully, then Lem threw in a shocker.

"You know, Governor," he said, "that rifle company I had for you suffered four hundred percent casualties among its officers in Okinawa. You just might not be here if you'd passed that physical."

Enough said.

There is one more thing I would like to say and it concerns how people change under different circumstances.

I spent some time in naval hospitals in the United States. The nurses here were tremendous, but when they got overseas, many of them changed into tyrants. My God, were they bossy! And arrogant! Why, you'd think they were the greatest thing since Florence Nightingale. I've often thought if they were like this to the officers, what were they like to the enlisted men? Now, why do you think it was that way?

Spirit of the Corps

It's a strange hold the Marine Corps has over the large majority of those who served in its ranks. It doesn't always exist; after all, the Corps did have Lee Harvey Oswald. But usually the old saw, "Once a Marine, Always a Marine," does hold true.

Take Bill Woolman. His World War II career featured, among other things, service with F/2/22 on Sugar Loaf Hill.

After his discharge from active duty in 1946, Bill chose to stay in the Reserves as a corporal.

"Don't ask me why I stayed in," he'll tell you. "I stayed in, that's all."

When the Korean War broke out, Bill was called to active duty and served with the 7th Marines.

"I got hit over there," says Bill, "and while I was lying in a sick bay sack, I kept saying to myself, 'Why the hell am I here?' I had no answer."

Probably the greatest example of the Marine mystique that I ever ran into was Colonel Benjamin Finney (USMCR-ret.). As a seventeen year old Ben first enlisted in the Marines in early 1918.

After a quick boot period he was sent to France, where he served with the 5th Marines at Soissons and Mont Blanc. He was seriously wounded near the Meuse River in November 1918.

Between the wars Ben lived a life as a member of what we would describe today as the jet set.

When World War II broke out, he tried to get a commission in the Corps but found himself running into too many stumbling blocks. So he tried the Navy, where he received a much warmer reception. He was just about to receive a commission in the USNR when he ran into Lieutenant Colonel John Thomason. Ben introduced himself to the famous Marine author and described his service with the 5th Marines in France. He also told John that since he had failed to get a Marine Corps commission he was about to go into the Navy.

"The hell you say," said Thomason. "I'll see what I can do about that."

A week later Finney was an active duty Marine officer. His overseas service included sweating out the horrendous Japanese bombardment of Henderson Field in October 1942.

When the Korean War broke out, Ben was once again ready, only this time he had a problem. Ben was now a diabetic.

"No problem," says Ben. "I just substituted someone else's urine when I took my physical."

So Finney was off for Korea, where he once again heard the guns go off.

The years rolled along and Ben finally retired as a Reserve colonel. Then came Vietnam.

Sometime in the mid-1960s Ben was watching a news report on television about the Marine fighting in Vietnam. Ben freely admits he had consumed a certain amount of liquor at this time.

Ben, although then sixty-six years of age, penned off a sharp note to Marine Corps Headquarters requesting a status change to active duty. Naturally, the Corps answered Ben's letter politely, thanking him for his offer and informing him there were no plans for calling retired men to active duty at that time.

Then, at the bottom of the page, there was a personal note that stated, "Oh, come on, Ben, you're too damn old and you know it. My very best regards, Dave Shoup, Commandant."

Ben told me all this while we enjoyed a drink or two at the colonel's favorite slop chute, the "21 Club" in New York City. He also told me his feelings hadn't changed a bit.

"I'm really not a great military man," he said, "but the Corps is something different. Once it gets into your blood, it stays."

L'Estrange of the Regulars

John L'Estrange

Born and raised in a Cleveland, Ohio, suburb, John received a commission in the Marine Regulars shortly after the outbreak of the war, but when he announces himself as "L'Estrange of the Regulars," it is done tongue in cheek.

"You know," he'll say, "like 'Renfrew of the Mounties.'"

Then he'll add, "That regular business was the best deal I ever had. There just weren't too many regular officers in the Pacific and that definitely seemed to give us a preference."

John saw combat from three angles. First, the personal view of his own campaigns. Then, through the loss in action of his only brother, he knows what death means to a family.

"Both my parents took that loss to their graves," he says today.

Finally, the vicarious anxiety of having a son in Vietnam.

"I tried not to influence him in any way," says John, "and I mean that. I sure as hell didn't want him over there in that dung heap. But he got himself a Marine commission and went.

"Those thirteen months my boy was in Vietnam were like reliving a nightmare," John recalls. "The fear of that dreaded telegram haunted me and my wife. I kept asking myself, 'Would they put him in a poncho or a burial bag?'

"Well, the telegram did come, but thank God it was to announce a wound not his death. They gave him a Silver Star and sent him back to us. He's all right now, has a wife, family and a job. I hope we have no more wars. They can hit you in too many ways."

CAPTAIN JOHN L'ESTRANGE
3rd Amphibious Corps

"Always remember the famous last words of the Duke's uncle."
—Catchword of John's company

You know, it's a funny thing, I knew Holland Smith, Lem Shepherd, Pappy Boyington, Whizzer White, all those people and others, before they became famous. And I can't think of one of them who changed later on. They never high-hatted you or anything like that. Just good people, that's all.

As for General Smith, old "Howling Mad," there is something I want to say about him, other than his being a great Marine.

Did you know he was picked up for drunken driving just before we went over? I'm not saying he was a lush, far from it. But he did get collared in California; I'm quite sure there was also an accident involved in the deal.

It was all hushed up, though. What were they going to do, revoke a general's driving license so he couldn't drive on one of the Pacific islands? Of course not.

I was raised in Lakewood, Ohio, just west of Cleveland. I attended Miami University in Oxford, Ohio, for two years. You know Miami— that's the school where all the football coaches come from. Paul Brown went there, so did Ara Parsegian. The list goes on and on. Then I transferred to Western Reserve University, graduating in 1941.

If you go back to the fall of 1940, you'll recall that Selective Service had started. Remember "Good-bye, dear, I'll be back in a year; I'm in the Army now"? What a laugh that turned out to be.

I knew I'd be real choice bait so I enlisted in the Marine Corps Reserves. They let me graduate in June '41 and told me they'd soon be calling me up. In the meantime, I'd become engaged to be married and was more or less marking time.

On December 7, 1941, my fiancée and I were driving along, listening to Jimmy Dorsey on the car radio. I can even remember the song Dorsey's band was playing; it was "Green Eyes" and the singer was Helen O'Connell. Then the whole world changed. They broke into the broadcast to tell us about Pearl Harbor. I turned to my fiancée with a little chuckle.

"Honey," I said, "this is it. We've got to put things on the back burner. I'm afraid I'm going to war."

How right I was. In two weeks I was at Marine Corps OCS, about to become a member of the regulars, and that's a story in itself. It was pure blind luck. Here's how it goes.

Our class had about two hundred candidates and most of us were sitting on this big hill listening to a lecture, a real dull one, I may add. All of a sudden they ran a machine gun maneuver right through us. When it was over, our colonel, I think his name was Hagedorn, started asking us all these questions about what we had seen. Hell, none of us knew our ass from a hole in the ground about machine gun sectors of fire and all that. This infuriated the colonel. His face turned red as a beet.

"L'Estrange," he yelled, "come down here."

I dutifully obeyed his command.

"Look, L'Estrange, when we move the Browning over here, it means such and such, right?"

"Yes, sir."

"And if we do this and that, it means such and such."

"Absolutely correct."

Hell, I didn't know any more than anyone else, but I knew damn well I'd better keep answering in the affirmative.

"Glad to know someone realizes what the hell is going on here," the colonel finally said. And that was that.

Shortly after dinner he summoned me to his quarters.

"L'Estrange," he said, "you're one of the best Marines in the class. I'm putting you down for a regular commission, if you want it, that is."

Saying "no" to the colonel would have been suicidal, so I agreed, thanked him profusely and told him how honored I was to be picked.

I didn't realize it at the time, but it was the luckiest thing that happened to me during the war.

Wherever I would later go, there was always a great scarcity of regular officers and it's the regulars they liked to put on detached duty. I spent a great deal of time overseas sitting on courts martial and the like. When we were on Okinawa, I ended up spending some time as assistant loading officer for the 10th Army. That was really good duty and I only got it because I was a regular.

So toward the end of my Quantico stay they started sending our men down to Camp Lejeune for duty with the 1st Division. Others were flown directly to the Pacific. When my turn came, I was placed in a brand new outfit, the 3rd Division.

As you might imagine, the Corps was growing too fast for production to catch up with it. The result was that we spent about three months at New River with hardly any equipment for the 3rd. In such a situation someone is always coming up with a way to improvise. In my company, which had been designated motor transport, the brainstorm turned out to be motorcycles, and they were something else.

Someone had produced a slew of these two-seaters, the ones with the sidecars. Hell, maybe they got them from an old Hollywood set where they made those World War I movies in the 1930s. Anyway, we went tearing around those North Carolina hills like Errol Flynn and David Niven in *Dawn Patrol*. Every time you'd go around a corner the sidecar's wheel would rise far above the ground. It's a lucky thing no one was killed, though there were a few broken bones.

Then, shortly before we left for Camp Elliott near San Diego, we received a supply of jeeps. Exit motorcycles. I think they stuck them in a museum. Good riddance.

Just before we left for Elliott, I married my fiancée. It turned out to be a bigger thing in my life than getting the jeeps. We're still happily married, which is not all that common these days.

While I was at Elliott, we formed a motor transport battalion of one thousand men. Most of the troops came right out of boot camp while several of the officers were from my original OCS class at Quantico. We had one hundred machine guns, fifty .50 calibers and fifty .30 calibers. We mounted these on our jeeps and recon cars.

After about four months at Elliott we headed for Noumea, New Caledonia. My bride had joined me at Elliott. Shortly before I pulled out, she informed me that she was pregnant. My future son was over two years of age before I finally saw him.

I can't remember how long our voyage was, but it seemed forever. I can remember pulling into the harbor at Noumea late one evening and being startled by the lights. Hell, back on the California coast we had blackouts and New Caledonia, within range of Japanese bombers, looked like Euclid Avenue, Cleveland, on a Saturday night. As a matter of fact, the Japanese did bomb the place our third night on the island. I'm happy to say they turned out the lights for the bombing.

Our stay here turned out to be one of my most pleasant tours of duty while I was a Marine. New Caledonia is truly a magnificent island, perfectly delightful. It was loaded with these beautiful deer whose meat was superb. The French had these black colonial soldiers there. They all seemed to be built like Muhammad Ali in his prime. Their sport was running these deer into the ocean and then cutting their throats. It sounds brutal as hell, but we all ate the deer meat.

The island itself is about one hundred and fifty miles wide and about thirty-five miles long. There was plenty of room to move around there. The French had been there for years and had developed quite a cosmopolitan society, for the Pacific anyway. Here's an example of what I mean.

I was riding in a staff car with a colonel one day when our young driver got nervous and rammed into the back of a civilian's car. Not only did we shake up the Frenchman but also his lady companion, and we put a hell of a dent in the rear of his car.

Jeez, you should have heard him blabbering away a mile a minute. I'd studied his language in college so, in my halting French, I tried to cool him off. I told him we were very sorry and would pay all damages. Could he just give us his name and that of his wife. He calmed down immediately and gave me this sly little smile.

"Monsieur," he said, "my wife, she ees at ze home. Zees ees not my wife."

Then he winked at me. "Ve forget ze whole thing. Au revoir," he yelled as he drove off.

On another occasion a French woman brought attempted rape charges against a man in my company. I think he was a cook. This is a very serious charge especially among allies. So my first lieutenant —I had been made a captain at Elliott—and I went to the lady's house to get the details. Her husband insisted we sit down while his wife brought out the wine. After we had all consumed a glass, she tried to explain what had happened.

It soon became apparent that she had been walking down the street when our man strolled by, slipping her what we called a little goose as he walked by. But I couldn't be sure that was all there was to it. So I asked her if she could show us what happened.

"Mais oui, mon capitan," she answered. Then she stuck one of her fingers you know where, uttering a shrill little "woo-woo" as she did.

At this point her husband started to clap, shouting, "Bravo! Bravo!"

We all drank more glasses of wine. I told her I had to be quite sure. Could she please show us once more? She complied again, finishing up with "woo-woo."

We then seriously attacked the wine. By the time we left, everyone was yelling, "woo-woo." We immediately transferred the cook to an island where his dangerous finger couldn't get him in trouble and that was the end of the matter.

Well, we weren't in the Pacific for woo-wooing. Sometime in the late spring of '43, we were sent off to Guadalcanal to get ready for some serious business.

The fighting on the Canal was over by then and the Marines were using the island as a staging area for assaults on other islands in the Solomons. A special Raider battalion, along with some Ohio National Guard GIs, went to New Georgia around the end of June. Our slot was to be a small island near there called Vella Lavella. It wasn't much of a place, but intelligence told us it would be an ideal spot for an airfield, especially as the Marines were getting ready to hit Bougainville, the largest island in the Solomons.

Our whole battalion wasn't going to Vella, just my company. Two of my platoons went on an LST, while the other two, including me, went on the *D.L. Ward*, a destroyer. The *Ward*, incidentally, was earlier credited with firing the first American shots on December 7, 1941. I think they were fired at one of the Japanese midget submarines. The *Ward* was later lost in a typhoon in the Philippines.

We landed on an August morning and were greeted almost immediately by a Japanese air attack. Hell, I don't think it was more than five minutes after all the Marines were ashore that they hit us. The hospital unit and the Seabees were fortunately also all ashore.

The LST half my company had arrived on took a direct hit exactly where my two platoons had been quartered. If those Nips had come a few minutes earlier, I would have lost half my men.

Now let me tell you about Marines and beer. My men had stored several cases of brew in a locker near the ramp of the LST. The way the ship was burning it was obvious that the ammunition aboard was probably going to blow the LST any minute. Nevertheless, three or four of my men dashed back aboard and rescued the beer. I should have recommended them for action above and beyond the call of duty.

At any rate we all sat back, drinking the beer as we watched the LST go to kingdom come.

For the next few weeks those damn Jap planes came over and gave us the business. We lost four men killed and several more wounded. The amazing thing, though, was that we didn't lose more men because those bombers—they were probably from Bougainville or even Kolombangara—came over constantly. It seemed that most of their bombs would burst in the trees and while there was a lot of fragmentation, it never seemed to be concentrated.

I caught a piece of one of those bombs in my right hand about a week after our landing. It hurt like hell. Like a damn fool I didn't take care of it and the next thing I knew I had a vicious infection, and almost lost my damn hand. That infection developed much faster in that jungle than it would have at home.

Along with my outfit we had some New Zealand troops on the island. They were rugged as hell. We used to sit around with them, playing chess. They'd get the word about some Japs being spotted on the island. They'd go find them, shoot the hell out of them, then return and finish the chess game.

Their favorite sport was playing with the crocodiles. First they'd rifle them up, then toss them some bacon. The bacon would be wrapped around a hand grenade. The next day they'd look for another crocodile.

Our biggest problem was the lack of available military intelligence. No one knew who was where.

One morning a member of my company came running over to me.

"Captain," he reported, "there's a whole crew of doggies marching by. I don't know who the hell they are."

I went over to find out. They were American soldiers all right, and they looked as if they'd had a rough time. They paid absolutely no attention to us, just kept moving by. To this day I don't know who the hell they were. Can you believe that?

The Seabees were trying to put together a landing strip, which was no snap with those Jap planes coming over constantly. Part of our job was to guard the airstrip and to keep the supplies coming in.

We had no soft touch because every single jeep and truck we landed with had been blown galley west by the Jap planes. How the hell those Seabees finished that airstrip I don't know, but they did.

The first group to arrive on the strip was a squadron of Marine Corsairs. What an airplane! They knocked those Jap planes down in no time flat. That was the end of the enemy's bombing runs.

Our airfield was part of the overall plan of the Solomon Islands fighting. Most of the combat action in the central Solomons was an Army show, but there always seemed to be a Marine Raider battalion involved. The fights here may have been small compared to later actions, but they could be nasty as hell.

I found out later that Kolombangara (right across from Vella Lavella) was the one island we didn't want to invade. Our brass figured that if we could set up airstrips on New Georgia, Vella Lavella and Arundel, we could surround Kolombangara and let it wither on the vine. That's just what we did and my company had a grandstand seat for part of the show.

As our troops took more and more of New Georgia, the Japanese started to evacuate their men. We could sit on a high rise and watch the gunfire as our PT boats tried to sink the Jap ships. This is when I met Whizzer White (Heisman Trophy winner and Supreme Court justice). He had one of those PT boats that kept blasting the Japs.

Anyway, it was fascinating at night to watch the flashes of naval fire and wonder just what was going on—that is, until some Japanese destroyers decided to move over to Vella and shell us. We really didn't have much room to hide. Naval gunfire was a hell of a lot more accurate than aerial bombing—it can be horrifying.

Well, on November 1, the 3rd Marine Division, along with some Raider battalions and Army troops, went into Bougainville. From then on the action moved more and more away from us. That old bugaboo, boredom, set in. The old adage about idle time causing problems appeared.

Four of my lieutenants came up with the brilliant idea that this would be an excellent time to be circumcised—anything to relieve the boredom.

"Listen," I told them, "that's for babies. Any adult who lets a doctor cut his penis is crazy."

They didn't pay any attention to me and went ahead with the operation.

A day or so after the operation, orders came through making them all captains. In the meantime my prediction had come true. Their healing process was complicated and very painful. So I found myself with four newly made captains with very sore peckers. To make it worse, we're on an island with nothing to do. What a mess!

We finally left there sometime in March '44, moving back to Guadalcanal. And it's there that I met "Duke" Peasley.

As you know, the Corps takes great pride in its characters. The Duke was truly one of these. He had obtained the magical Marine Corps rank of warrant officer. This meant you were neither an enlisted man nor a commissioned officer—you were a very pleasant half way between the two. We called them gunners.

The Duke's rank, or rating, whatever you call it, did allow him to play poker with the officers, a game at which he had become extremely proficient. It was during one of these games that he told us of his uncle's dying words, an utterance that should live forever.

Duke's uncle had been a real old-time Marine—Boxer Rebellion, Philippines, Banana Wars—all those spots renowned in the Old Corps. He finally retired after what is referred to as long and honorable service. Shortly after leaving the Corps, he passed on, cause of death being listed as loneliness.

And it was on his deathbed that he left his beloved Corps a true heritage. Shortly before cashing in, he thrust his dying body forward one last time and bellowed:

"FUCK 'EM ALL!"

He then lay back and expired.

I don't know about other outfits but from then on, particularly on Guam and Okinawa, the old man's last words became a catch phrase with our company. Whenever things would be real rough, someone would yell out, "Remember the dying words of the Duke's uncle."

Well, the next big show I was involved in was the invasion of Guam, the first pre-World War II American real estate that we recaptured from the Japanese. This is what we had been training for on the Canal. And it opened up with a very unfortunate experience for my company.

They loaded us aboard LSTs so we naturally thought we were going right into action. We didn't know where we were headed; the scuttlebutt, wrong as usual, had us headed for the Japanese stronghold at Truk. It turned out to be Tulagi, right across the bay from Guadalcanal. Here we sat on those goddamn LSTs for about four weeks. It was miserable.

At any rate, they did have an officers' club on Tulagi, called the

Iron Bottom Bay Club. Naturally, the poor enlisted men could not enjoy the club; for better or worse rank does have its privileges, so we figured at least the officers could go knock down some cool drinks. Along with a few of my lieutenants, I went ashore to try the club out. Unfortunately our combat fatigues did not go over with this naval officer at the entrance to the club.

"Sorry, captain," he said, "uniform of the day is khaki."

"Hell," I answered, "we're sitting over there on those LSTs, loaded for combat; our khakis are all stowed away."

"I can't help that; those are my orders. Good day, captain."

Talk about being pissed off. I was livid. I guess those clowns thought it was the "21" club.

Naturally I couldn't let it drop at that. I went to a telephone, called the club and asked for the head man.

"Commander," I said, "this is *Captain* L'Estrange," hoping this bird would think I was a naval captain. "We have several Marine officers on LSTs here," I continued, "with only combat attire available. They should certainly be able to drink at the club, correct?"

"Oh, of course, captain," the commander answered, "tell them to ask for me."

So we spent several hours at the exclusive Iron Bottom Bay Club over the next four weeks. It was a godsend.

We finally took off for our destination, Guam, in the Mariana Islands. The Marines were to land in two groups. The 3rd Marine Division was to strike an area between Asan Beach and Adelup Point, while the 1st Marine Provisional Brigade, containing the 4th and 22nd Marines, was to land south of the 3rd. The 77th Army Division was going in with the brigade.

They divided our battalion in half. Major Murphy was to take two companies in with the brigade, while I had command of the other two companies. My group was going in with the 3rd Division. Both commands were going in with the first wave.

I had thirty DUKWs for the invasion. This was an amphibious vehicle, propeller driven in the water, with rubber wheels for land travel. They were mounted with 37 millimeter guns. We were to take in all types of equipment and deliver it when needed. D-Day was set for July 21, with H-Hour around 0830.

Now, when you start in on one of these landings, you never really know what to expect. However, on Guam, we weren't kept in the dark very long. I lost three of my DUKWs from enemy fire on the way in, with the worst still to come.

Where we were landing was really like a huge amphitheater, surrounded by hills and cliffs. It was this high ground that turned the beach into an inferno. The Japs could actually look down on our every movement. It took us three or four days to really clean up the area. During that time the beach was under constant fire from everything the Nips had. I believe we suffered somewhere between two and three thousand casualties from their pasting.

Along with the Japanese fire, I was faced with a tremendous problem with the DUKWs. No one had bothered to tell us about the coral reef. Every one of the damn rubber tires had been cut to ribbons coming in. There was no way we could move our vehicles on land. So while we could unload them, we couldn't move the equipment.

Pretty soon I got the word from a ship-to-shore telephone; I think it came from Admiral Conolly. Anyway, he was boiling.

"L'Estrange," he yelled, "why aren't you moving those DUKWs?"

"I can't, admiral," I answered, "every single rubber tire has been destroyed by the reef."

"We can't have that, L'Estrange. You stand by. I'll get you some tires, even if we have to have them flown directly from San Francisco."

Oh, he got me the tires all right. Sent directly to me. Do you know when they arrived? The next year, when I was on Okinawa. Hell, I was up to my ass in tires then! Of course, I didn't have any DUKWs at that time, but so be it. I got the tires.

Well, there really wasn't much you could do about the Jap fire. We just dug in and hoped. Our own artillery and riflemen finally cleaned out the high ground, but it really was bad until they did.

We did find out later that it could have been worse. The Japanese had moved several of those large guns to Guam they had captured at Singapore but they had never mounted them. Those guns could have blown the whole beachhead to smithereens. Thank God they didn't set them up!

After our infantry and artillery had cleaned the Japs out of the high ground, we all began moving up. My company more or less started spreading out where it was needed. We were part of a special motor transport battalion, attached to corps headquarters, but we frequently ended up with machine gun companies, artillery units, reconnaissance details—you name it and we did it.

For instance, the craziness of their banzai charges must have reached its height on Guam. Hell, they seemed drunk half the time. Maybe they were, but we made mincemeat of them.

Anyway, they broke through one night and hit our hospital. My company was one of those that was rushed over to stop them.

What a sight it was! The walking wounded, bandages and all, are banging away at the Japs. Some of the more seriously wounded men were firing from their beds.

After it was all over, they even found several dead Japs in the surgical tent. The Marines lost some men, of course, but we killed the Nips in bunches. Those banzai charges could be scary as hell, but when they were over, the Japs never seemed to have accomplished much. They called them suicidal charges and they were that all right.

I mentioned earlier that we also went on reconnaissance and that's how I ended up being one of the first Marines to enter the Piti Naval Yard when we recaptured it. I walked into one of the buildings at the yard and the first thing I saw was a desk calendar. It was still open at December 10, 1941, the day the island had been captured. Not a thing had changed. I guess the Japs felt time was going to stand still for them. Talk about wishful thinking!

Another thing that should be said about Guam concerns the 77th Army Division. As you know, there were several times when you had a lot of friction between the Marines and the Army.

Take the 27th National Guard Division. Whenever those guys fought alongside the Marines, there was hell to pay. I don't want to get into any big rows between Americans, but I do want to go on record about the great turnaround of the 77th on Guam.

When the 77th first went ashore, they didn't accomplish much. Then something happened, maybe they regrouped, I don't know what, but they really turned to. Any Marine who badmouths the 77th on Guam should blow it out his sea bag.

I have one more personal note about Guam. My brother was a Navy flyer. The carrier he was on, I think it was the *Franklin*, furnished some of the planes that flew in our support during the landing. I used to wave at them whenever I could. I was sure that the pilots could not distinguish one Marine from the other, but I always felt one of them dipped his wings at me. He knew I was there, anyway.

I'm sorry to tell you my brother was killed by Japanese naval antiaircraft fire some months later. My parents took this loss with them to their graves. If anyone wants to realize how dreadful the aftermath of war is, let him talk to the parents of a lost son.

Well, we left Guam that fall and headed back to Guadalcanal, and I'm happy to tell you my return trip to the Solomons turned into one of my company's finest hours.

Our ship was of Dutch registry out of the East Indies. Its captain was a man named Rommel, a first cousin of General Rommel. But the captain was certainly not pro-Axis. He hated them all. Our shipboard accommodations, both for officers and men, were superb. I had not seen anything like it during the war and I wasn't to experience such a deal aboard ship again while I was in the Corps.

All the ship's hands were natives of the East Indies. They must have thought we were first class passengers because they waited on us hand and foot.

The captain was one of the most interesting men I've ever met—a real philosopher. He felt the Japanese phase was temporary, the sooner it was ended, the better. He also felt the colonial aspects of Asia would not return after the war and that it would be interesting to see what direction his part of the world would take after the war.

There was one thing that upset me. He seemed to be giving my men mess duty way out of proportion to the other troops on board. I complained to him about it. He just smiled.

"Go talk to your men about it," he told me. "If they want a change, we'll do it."

So I went to my men to get the word. I found several of them in the galley, eating Danish pastry.

"Christ, captain," they said in horror, "please, please, don't take us off mess duty. Most of us have never eaten like this in our lives."

Needless to say, the matter was closed.

Another thing Captain Rommel did was break out some one-armed bandits for the men. He knew most of the troops didn't have any change, so he'd put on his carpenter's apron, load the pouches with silver and walk among the men, passing out coins.

What a great guy he was! I hope the postwar years were good to him.

After we landed back in Guadalcanal, we started to get ready for the next island and, believe it or not, this time the scuttlebutt turned out to be right. I don't know how he found out, but one day one of my lieutenants came into my tent with the word.

"Captain," he said, "this is a screwy war. Our next stop is to be an island with a woman's name. It's called 'Nancy.' "

What he was actually saying was "Nansie," a Japanese word for Okinawa, a Japanese island 350 miles from Kyushu. It may have had a woman's name, but it sure as hell was no tea party. Before it was secured, the Marines, Army and Navy were to suffer almost 50,000 casualties. It was the worst American bloodletting in the Pacific war.

Well, we left the Canal for the Ryukyu Islands sometime around the middle of March '45. Our company was on a pretty good-sized transport—I think it was an APA. Before we reached Okinawa, we had become part of the largest convoy I'd ever seen. It was so huge you could look back a mile or so and see the Japanese airplanes attacking ships in the rear of the convoy.

The one thing I can remember about that trip is the tremendous sheet of fire our ships threw up at those Japanese planes. You couldn't believe it. It saturated the air. Every time a Jap plane went down someone would send up a cheer. It was like a football game. You didn't stop to think you were watching a man being killed. It just didn't work that way.

We landed on April 1 near a couple of Japanese airfields, Yontan and Kadena. I was expecting a greeting similar to the one we received on Guam. Instead, what a pleasant surprise we received. If the Marines experienced any hostility during the landing, it wasn't where we went ashore. I can't remember hearing a shot being fired.

Shortly after we went ashore, I told my men to dig in. Intelligence told us we could expect a great deal of air action from the Japs and for once they were right on target; so were the Nips.

We were stationed on a ridge right between the two airfields when they came over. They bombed the living hell out of us with magnesium bombs. Our casualties were very light simply because we had dug in so well, but what a job they did on our gear.

The next morning when we started to move around, we were greeted with a scene of utter devastation. The magnesium had even burned the wood off our rifles. We had to draw all new equipment in order to survive.

Then there was the incredible attack the enemy made at Yontan. They came over on one of their normal bombing runs but not all of their planes were along for bombing. Several of them were full of Japanese suicide soldiers, loaded with grenades. Much to my astonishment one of their planes does a belly landing on the airstrip.

God, the first thing you know several Japs jumped out of the plane and started throwing hand grenades everywhere.

All hell broke loose. Their surprise was complete. The Marines killed every one of them, but not before they did a hell of a lot of damage.

During this time my company was still on the ridge between the two airports. The Japs had this large artillery piece somewhere. We never found out exactly where but for three straight weeks they shelled us three times a night. Do you know that they'd first shell one side of the ridge, then the other. They *never* hit the ridge itself. I didn't lose a man from that gun, but we did lose a lot of sleep. But the way things were going on Okinawa you were damn lucky if all you lost was sleep.

Once again, my company was officially a motor transport battalion, attached to Corps headquarters. But, just like on Guam, it was a misnomer because we did so many different things. We served with three different units, the 1st and 6th Marine Divisions and the 96th Army Division.

One of our jobs was moving materiel for the 22nd Marines (6th Division) at Sugar Loaf Hill. The combat there had to be seen to be believed. Those poor riflemen kept going up and down that goddamn place and each time they'd suffer brutal casualties. The Marines brought some tanks in to try and help out, but they were sitting ducks for the Nips. I saw one of those Shermans take a direct hit from Japanese artillery. After Sugar Loaf Hill was finally taken, I counted thirty-three tanks that had been knocked out by the Nips.

My company spent some eighty-four days on Okinawa, doing just about everything imaginable. All in all, I think the action there was just about as vicious as any battle the Corps ever fought in. Christ, it wasn't until around the middle of June that General Buckner was killed. At that time we were trying to flush the Japs out of caves. The fighting was intense right up to the bitter end.

By July I had served three years in the Pacific. They told me it was time to go home for a while, and who was I to argue!

When I boarded an LST for Maui, where I was to board an APA for the States, I was sure I'd be home for a while, then come back out for the invasion of the Japanese homeland.

We were somewhere between Guam and the Hawaiian Islands when we got the word about the Big Bomb. We were all happy as hell. We still weren't sure the Japs would surrender, but we figured the Air Force could now bomb Japan into oblivion before we went in.

The big news about the armistice came a few nights later. Now we realized we weren't going to invade at all. We were traveling under full nighttime security with not a light anywhere, but the minute we got the word, the Pacific turned into a Christmas tree. What a sight!

From then on it was smooth sailing. Not only did I get to be with my wife again but I saw my son for the first time. The lad finally had a father.

There was one thing hanging fire. Remember, I was officially a regular Marine, even though I never had any intention of staying in after the war.

This colonel got hold of yours truly back in the States and went to work on me.

"L'Estrange," he said, "as of right now you are a major. Stay in. There are bound to be some real interesting things going on and you can be part of it. Stick with me and we'll both be generals in the next war."

Hell, if I'd stayed in, I'd probably be dead. The next thing I heard about the colonel he was over in Greece, helping the Greek Army in their civil war. I would have been with him. No thank you. I love the Corps, but one war was enough!

"Or So They Said"

"Where's Tiny?"

"Oh, he took off like a big-ass bird."

I had never heard this expression before I went to Parris Island and I never did figure out why a big-ass bird takes off faster than any other kind. But a great deal of rational thinking did not go into the expressions of the Corps.

For instance, who was Mr. Kelsey and why were his nuts any colder (or deader) than those of any other person?

But then again, who was Mr. Hogan and why was his goat any more fucked up than any other goat?

And is it true that a Christmas turkey has a stronger ability to fertilize the barnyard than any other turkey? Many's the time I was told that I was full of more shit than that Christmas turkey.

Anyway, like any other military organization, Marines developed certain expressions that they seemed to cling to.

Some of these had legitimate meanings that were enlarged upon. To secure the butts meant to close the firing range, but it was expanded to mean: stop anything. A working party would frequently hear, "All right, you guys, secure the butts."

While Marines are reluctant to admit it, the Corps is part of the Navy. If you heard, "Shove off, coxswain; you're loaded," it meant that the speaker did not particularly care for your act. "Fire in the paint locker" told you to move fast.

On the other hand, Army expressions rarely made it in the Corps. A Marine spotted anywhere writing "Kilroy was here" would have been frowned on.

Then there was the outhouse humor.

"Hey, have you seen Ski?"

"Yeah, he went to shit and the hogs ate him."

Or:

"Where's Paisano?"

"He's in the head eating a sandwich." A variation was, "He's in the head beating his meat."

Any such reference to the head or bodily functions was almost always a subject of ridicule. If you really wanted to give someone the business, you told him to go shit in his mess kit or his shelter half. If you were talking to a sailor, it was suggested that he defecate in his flat hat.

Probably the most common of these everyday putdowns, however, was a bit more on the gamy side.

"Hey, Mac, got a cigarette?"

"No, but I got a White Owl for you."

At this point the Marine would grab his crotch.

Then there was the grand old Anglo-Saxon word for sexual inter-course. This word, which seems so vulgar to many, was probably used by Germanic warriors as they moved on to the island of Britain in the Dark Ages.

Whatever, the word *fuck* was used by Marines in every possible form. *Fuckin' A* was extremely popular and frequently was accom-panied by additional words. *Fuckin' A told* or *Fuckin' A right* were everyday expressions, but the phrase that I always found colorful went like this:

"Hey, Bull, you going on liberty?"

"Fuckin' A doodle de doo."

Where the *doodle de doo* came from will always be a mystery.

Probably the gamiest of putdowns was told to me by one Richard Murtaugh, an eager seventeen year old who went into the Corps in August 1943 fully intending to go to war. Instead of fighting the Japanese, he ended up learning the ways of the world from a lady of questionable repute named Tiger Lil. Murtaugh's overseas service was two years of guard duty in Panama.

Shortly after his arrival in the Canal Zone, Private Murtaugh went to see his first sergeant to obtain a seventy-two-hour pass.

"We called him 'The Wheezer,'" remembers Rich, "because he would always start to wheeze when he got riled up. He must have been close to sixty since he had stupidity marks (service stripes) all over his sleeve. I presented my case to him. He started to wheeze and his huge beer gut actually seemed to move up and down.

" 'What, a seventy-two-hour pass,' he said, 'and you've only been here a month? Listen, chicken, you wouldn't get it even if I was fuckin' you. Shove off!' "

From Bats to Bullets

Hank Bauer

By the time World War II ended, the majority of professional ball-players were in uniform. True, many of them were playing on base-ball service teams, but that is where the government wanted them. Many others, however, did fight a war.

Warren Spahn was wounded while fighting in Europe as was Hoyt Wilhelm. Frank (Creepy) Crespi, second baseman on the 1942 World Series-winning St. Louis Cardinals, was so badly injured that his play-ing career was ended.

Then there is the tale of Lou Brissie. In 1948 he was pitching against Ted Williams. The great slugger lined a baseball so hard off Brissie's leg that Ted ended up with a double. A concerned Williams then asked Brissie if he was all right.

"Oh yeah," answered Lou, "it bounced off the plate I've had in that leg since it was almost blown off in Italy."

But when it came to fighting a war, it is doubtful if any ballplayer contributed more than the Marines' Hank Bauer.

Hank joined the Corps right after Pearl Harbor. He shipped out to the Pacific toward the end of '42 and did not return to the States until thirty-six months later. He was an original member of the 4th Raider Battalion. When the Raiders were disbanded in early 1944, he be-came a member of the new 4th Marines. The original 4th had moved from China to the Philippines in November 1941. It had ceased to exist as a serviceable regiment after the fall of Manila. Platoon Ser-geant Bauer was wounded in the assaults on Guam and Okinawa and was awarded a Bronze Star for bravery in both these actions.

After the war, he spent fourteen years as a major league outfielder and eight years as a manager. He guided the Baltimore Orioles to a world championship in 1966.

Hank lost four prime years from his playing career due to his Marine service. This is heavy duty when you figure such a career is usually over when a player reaches his mid-thirties. This is something that does not bother Hank.

"I guess I knew too many great young guys who lost everything out there to worry about my losing part of a baseball career," he says.

As always, Hank means what he says.

PLATOON SERGEANT HANK BAUER
4th Raider Battalion
4th Marines, 6th Division

"Bauer was one tough guy. It would sometimes scare the hell out of me to tell him that Woodling was going to play in right field instead of Hank."

—Casey Stengel

There is one thing the Marines and the New York Yankees have in common—it's called pride. You know, once you put those Yankee pinstripes on, you knew you had something to live up to.

Well, I think it's the same with the Corps. Once you got that green uniform, damn it, you knew you had to shape up. After all, they're both winners—I mean, the Yanks and the Corps.

I was raised in East St. Louis, Illinois, which is a pretty tough town. That's how I learned to throw and run—throwing rocks at street gangs and running from them if they started after me. I guess you could say there was plenty of ethnic crap going on in those days—you know, black kids against white kids.

My first year in organized baseball was 1941, when I played outfield and infield—hell, I even pitched some—with Oshkosh in the old Wisconsin League. I didn't do too badly for an eighteen-nineteen-year-old kid. I had high hopes of moving up to the major leagues after a few years in the minors.

Then came Pearl Harbor. I quickly swapped my seventy-dollar-a-month job, and lousy meal money, for twenty-one bucks a month, good food and great medical care, at the Marine Corps boot camp, San Diego, California. It was not that bad a deal even if they took six dollars and some change out of my pay every month for life insurance. Those insurance payments came damn close to being a good investment, at least for my father, later on.

The one amazing thing that I can recall about those boot camp days was this feisty little corporal we had for a DI. Hell, the son of a bitch couldn't have weighed more than 140 pounds. Yet he never hesitated to really give guys like me the business. I could have chewed him up and spit him out, but I guess he had us all buffaloed.

After boot camp, I was sent to the Marine Sea School, also in San

Diego. I thought this was great—spend the war on a nice clean ship, maybe get to wear those dress blues, real good duty.

Then the Marine colonel on Mare Island found out I was a professional ballplayer, so he sent for me.

"Bauer," he said, "all our team needs is a catcher. I want you to take that spot over."

"Sir," I told him, "I've never been a catcher in my life."

"Oh, that's all right; you're a real ballplayer; you can catch."

Well, hell, I became the Mare Island team's catcher and what a team we had! The colonel was a real baseball nut and he was getting us games all over the place. Christ, we went 63 and 13, which would have been a good record even in the Lassie League.

Now, I'm not saying this wasn't good duty. Hell, you could go down to the slop chute and get a pitcher of lager beer for a quarter. You could get drunk for fifty cents. But if I'd wanted to play ball, I could have stayed a civilian and probably moved up a couple of notches in the minors.

But every time my name would come up for a ship, the colonel would take it off.

"Can't lose my catcher," he'd say. "This is the best team I've ever had!"

Then Jimmy Roosevelt came back from the Makin Island raid to form the 4th Raider Battalion. It was strictly a voluntary thing and there was no way the colonel could keep anyone away from Roosevelt if Jimmy wanted him.

So, me and this guy named Quackenbush—I don't know what the hell ever happened to him—put in for the 4th Raiders.

Everything is going fine until they ask me if I can swim and I had to tell them no. Oh, I could swim a little, but not what they wanted. When I told Quackenbush what had happened, he blew his top.

"Why you gutless son of a bitch," he says, "why the hell didn't you say yes?"

So I went right back to the Raider sergeant and told him I could swim. The sergeant just laughed.

"Christ, you learn fast," he said, "but we'll take you."

Remember, I was really in top shape, weighing in at about one-ninety. I guess they figured I'd make a good Raider, no matter what.

Anyway, it didn't take long to find out how good I could swim. We went up the California coast to the Oceanside area, where we were to practice that amphibious landing stuff. They had us making a landing from those little bitty rubber rafts when, wham, a big wave knocks us over. I ended up going straight to the bottom.

Do you know the old expression, "sink or swim"? Well, I swam.

What they were doing at this time was giving us a real crash course in survival. They needed us overseas fast and the first thing I knew we were aboard ship, headed for Espiritu Santo in the New Hebrides Islands, where I had my first bout with malaria. I was to have twenty-two more attacks of that damn bug before I got it out of my system.

Later on, I think it was on Guadalcanal, I went swimming and picked up fungus in my right ear. That was another delight. If there is one thing you can do in the damn jungle, it's pick up every disease known to man.

Well, we went from Espiritu to Guadalcanal sometime during the first part of '43. We arrived in time to catch the tail end of the fighting there. Then we started some real tough Raider training.

After I had been in combat, I appreciated how essential the training was and how many lives were probably saved by it. But, you didn't look at it this way while you were doing it. Hell, some of it could be worse than combat.

One of the things that the Raider officers were always harping on in combat was the firing group—hell, I think the Raiders invented it. You would have two men with M-1s on either flank with a BAR man in the center and back some. First one M-1 man would move up and start firing then the other M-1 guy would do the same.

Then the BAR Marine would move up, plant his weapon, and start firing. This way he could cover the other two Marines as they went forward. Someone would always be shooting at the Japs. Oh, it was quite successful.

There were plenty of Japs still on the island when I got there, but my outfit didn't have much contact with them. Occasionally we'd have fire fights, but they didn't amount to much.

One big fight I can remember on the Canal was between our planes and those of the Japs. Hell, the sky was filled with planes going at each other just like in the movies. We could see all this right over the bay between Guadalcanal and Tulagi. All of a sudden two of the planes broke off and headed for us. We saw them drop what we thought were bombs. Someone later told us it was their gas tanks, but of course, we didn't know this then.

Well, hell, we all started to jump around looking for a hole. One of my buddies thought he had a great spot so in he goes. He didn't realize we'd moved the head a few days before and that's what the poor bastard jumped into—the old head.

Christ, he ended up covered with shit—it might have been our imagination, but we all thought he stunk to high heavens for weeks. We all gave him the business, you know, looked at him and held our noses.

That brings up a problem we did always have in the jungle and it was no laughing matter. You were constantly getting the runs. And if you'd go into the brush, the minute you'd take your pants down every fly for miles would gather—just like they were going to a party. And when I say flies, I mean real flies! They were the size of sparrows. Some of the men would even let go in their helmet, wash it out and either shave or cook in the same helmet. Jungle living could be crummy as hell.

And speaking of our helmets, the one thing I never did use it for was combat. When the artillery and mortars started to come at us, I wanted to be able to move fast. I just couldn't move as fast with a hunk of steel on my head. When I was platoon sergeant, fighting on Guam and after that on Okinawa, I just wore that Raider fatigue hat.

Well, late in the spring of '43 our battalion took off for the New Georgia Group, further up in the Solomons. The plan had been for several coordinated landings on June 30, but the word came down that the Nips were going to fortify a place called Segi Point on the southeastern tip of the main island in the group.

So, our company was rushed up to beat them to it. After we reached the Point, they put us ashore in my old friends, the rubber boats. Thank God this time we didn't capsize. We had no trouble at Segi, but we were told our ordeal was just starting.

Our next job was to hike through that goddamn jungle to a place called Viru Harbor. And when I say jungle, it was undescribable— worse shithole you have ever seen!

We started out with M-1s, BAR's, machine guns, Thompsons, mortars and .37 antitank rifles. Hell, those .37s were impossible—you know, they're those big long things. Every time you'd take a step, they'd get caught on some kind of a vine.

Finally, we figured, what the hell, if the Japs have tanks, we'll just have to handle them one way or another. So we tossed the .37s into the bush. They're probably still there and would make one hell of a great souvenir if someone wants to go get them.

But you can have them as far as I'm concerned. What a waste! The only souvenir I wanted to get home was my own ass!

Well, back to the jungle. As I remember, we hiked through that stuff any way we could. At best we averaged a half mile per hour, maybe less. The only good thing about the next three days was them dark chocolate bars. I think they were called D Bars. They were real good. I just about lived on them for the rest of the time we were on New Georgia.

Now, as we were moving, we'd occasionally take fire and some of our men were hit. But for me, the real shoot 'em up came near the end of our three-day ordeal. After walking through all those swamps and jungles, we reached a point where we could look out on this bay. We spotted this barge, full of Jap soldiers, out on the bay—hell, never did see a barge on the land, did you?

Anyway, I was a machine gunner then. Me and this other machine gunner opened up on them with crisscross fire. We just shot the hell out of this barge with everything we had. Do you know, we *sank* the damn thing—with machine gun fire, and that's no bullshit!

My next stop after New Georgia was once again Guadalcanal. Here we had more of that tough Raider jungle training. What made it particularly tough for me was the constant malaria. Hell, I think half the Marines in the Solomons had that bug while we were doing that jungle crap.

We went out again—I think we were headed back for New Georgia —when malaria really clobbered me. It was a combination of the fever and the diesel fumes I was inhaling from the back of the LST. They had to send me back to the Canal so I could get some treatment.

This was really the end of the Raiders for me, and sometime during the first part of '44 it was the end for everyone.

In March of that year we went out on the greatest invasion of the entire Pacific War. This was because the island we hit, in full battle gear, ended up not having a single goddamn Nip on it. Those were the invasions I loved.

It was called Emirau, in the St. Matthias Group. Once we found out it was unoccupied, we quickly laid out an airstrip. They told us that Emirau would help cut off the supply line to Truk, an island that was supposed to be the Gibraltar of the Pacific. Whenever our bombers would operate in the vicinity, they'd always save a few extra bombs to drop over Truk on the way home. They just never gave that place any peace, even though we never did invade it—we let it wither on the vine.

After Emirau it was back to Guadalcanal to get ready for the shot at Guam.

And what a change had occurred on the Canal since my first visit there in January '43. Hell, we even had movies. I can remember sitting on a coconut tree log in the rain watching Bill Bendix in *Wake Island.* Every time those Marine machine gunners would knock off the Japs, we'd cheer like hell.*

But the all-time winner was *Gentleman Jim* with Errol Flynn. I must have seen that two or three times on Guadalcanal and a couple more times on Guam. Flynn had recently had all that publicity about the girl he and some other guys had nailed on their yacht. The men

---

*Author's note: Ben Finney told the author that *Wake Island* was one of the first films brought to Guadalcanal. The first time it played there the sound track of the Jap bombings could be heard for miles. Many of the Marines jumped for foxholes when they heard it.

really got a huge kick out of that last line when Flynn says something about his being a gentleman.

Another change was in the food. It was a lot better on the Canal in '44 than when I'd been there earlier. We had a great deal of that horse cock which was great. You'd stick it in a sandwich and cover it with mustard. Hell, it was as good as a sandwich in an East St. Louis delicatessen. Don't tell anyone today you like horse cock though; they'll think you're talking about part of a horse's anatomy. They won't realize you're referring to those different types of cold cuts you'd get in the Corps.

The cooks weren't much good though—they couldn't be. They had to work as if they were on a production line. I can remember seeing one of them whipping together a huge batch of pancakes. The joker cut his finger but that didn't stop him. He just went right on making those wheat cakes with the blood dripping into the batter. He didn't give a shit.

There was one thing they never could change on the Canal though —those damn land crabs. They were everywhere. If you'd kill them, you had to bury 'em in a hurry. Christ, did the dead ones stink! Trucks and jeeps were always running over 'em and the smell would be stifling.

And the crabs weren't the only wildlife you had to worry about. You'd always sleep covered by mosquito netting. Then, when you'd wake up in the morning, you'd have to empty out your boondockers to make sure them little things hadn't crawled into your shoes for the evening. If you didn't, you'd be apt to get one hell of a nasty bite from some damn insect.

Well, the next trip we took headed us for the invasion of Guam, where I picked up my first Purple Heart, but first we'd had to spend about two months cramped like sardines on LSTs. You see, we were originally to act as floating reserve for Saipan. Maybe it was planned that way. If you spent two months on an LST, you'd be willing to storm the gates of hell just to get off the damn thing.

One of the worst things about those two months was we just weren't eating too good. I don't know, maybe they hadn't counted on our being on board that long, but the food became worse and worse.

There was this old guy working in the galley who used to bake fresh bread every morning at about two-thirty—damn, did it smell good. I was a platoon sergeant by then so I was able to get friendly with this guy. I'd go into the galley and shoot the breeze with him. It wasn't long before he started giving me a loaf of that hot bread and a half pound of butter. I'd throw the butter on that bread and, Christ, was it good—it was like eating steak!

As I look back, I think the time I spent on that flat-bottomed son of a bitch was just about as bored as I've ever been. We had a guy aboard—his name was Bud Herrick—who was married to Kathleen Winsor, you know, the woman who'd written *Forever Amber*. You remember that book—it was considered real hot stuff in those days.

Well, Bud—he'd been a great football player at California—had several copies aboard. Christ, I think every guy on that LST read his wife's book. Jeez, were they horny! Anyway, if you've ever seen books that were completely worn out by reading, it was the copies of *Forever Amber* on our LST. I think even the chaplain read it.

We finally hit the beach on July 21. Our outfit, the 4th Marines, went in alongside the 22nd Marines. We were part of the 1st Provisional Brigade under Lem Shepherd, who was the general later put in command of the Sixth Division when it was formed.

Now, let me tell you one thing. When you get into combat like Guam, everyone is scared shitless, unless he's drunk or crazy.

Take the Japanese, on their banzai charges on Guam anyway. I know they were drunk when they hit us, because we could hear them drinking up a storm before the charge.

We were bivouacked that night, constantly in our foxholes and constantly shooting up flares because we could hear this jabbering in Japanese. Every now and then we'd hear a bottle break. Then you would hear this high shrill laugh the Nips had. You know—yah-ta-ta, yah-ta-ta, yah-ta-ta—that's what it sounded like.

Then, this one old Jap, he could speak English, yells out, " 'Merican Maline, you die tonight! 'Merican Maline, you die tonight!"

Well, we had this real tough guy from Texas, and he yells out, "Tojo eats shit, yuh slant-eyed son of a bitch!"

Jeez, that really riled up the Japs. The Nip who could speak English yells something out in Japanese. I guess he was telling the other Nips what the Texan had said. The noise then was deafening; it sounded like a hundred cats fighting in an alley.

A little while later one of our men yells out, "Here come the bastards!"

It was the craziest thing you ever saw. Hell, some of them were falling-down drunk. They were all laughing or cursing in this hysterical tone. We literally shot the shit out of those poor bastards. I'm sure many of them were dead before they really knew what was happening.

After it was daylight, some of us went out to see how many we'd knocked off.

All of a sudden this so-called dead Jap officer jumped up and came at us, swinging this big samurai sword. I don't think he was more than ten yards from me, but he was closer to the guy in front of me—he was the one the Jap took a swipe at.

Christ, my buddy parried the sword with his M-1 just in the nick of time. Then this other Marine, standing right next to me, let a whole clip from his M-1 go at the Jap officer. I was in the Pacific from Guadalcanal until Okinawa and that's as close as I came to a live Jap during the war and it's as close as I wanted to come.

However, don't think everything those Nips did was as stupid as that charge. They were really clever as hell. They had most of the American habits down cold and they tried to make the most of 'em.

For instance, if you spent the night in a hole up on the lines, you'd probably have to go to the head in the early morning. The Nips knew the Americans didn't like to crap, or even take a leak, in the same hole they were staying in. So their snipers would all be on the lookout when the dawn started. It was the most dangerous goddamn time of the day.

Well, I picked up some shrapnel on Guam, and a Bronze Star— can't remember exactly what for—but I got one. Hell, they could have given those Bronze Stars to our whole outfit for some of the things we did.

We had one little kid in the 4th Marines we called Chicken Wilson, that was his name. I don't even think Chicken shaved. He had this early peach fuzz all over his chin. He was a little bitty guy, don't think he was even seventeen years old. He was a BAR man—the damn BAR was as big as he was.

I can recall one time he had that weapon going like the devil, really doing a number on the Japs. Then he caught something in his stomach, came right out his back. The poor kid, he couldn't find a corpsman, so he had to walk a mile or two before he could get attended to. Hell, he had to hold part of his gut in while doing the walking. He made it though. When I'd go to Cleveland later on with the Yankees, I used to stop in at this pizza parlor he was running. I hope he got some kind of a medal; he deserved it.

Well, it was on Guam where I received a tremendous blow. I got a telegram—don't remember how they got it to me, but they did— telling me that my brother had been killed in the fighting at Saint–Lô in France. We'd had a lot of rough stuff at the time and I was feeling pretty low as it was. When I got the word on my brother, I really felt lousy. I told one of our officers about it. He said he was sorry to hear it and then he snapped me out of my doldrums fast.

"You must want to get even with those bastards," he said. "Japs, Nazis, they're all the same. I'll send you out on a patrol so you can kill some of them."

"Bullshit," I answered, "I've been taking out all the patrols; let someone else take it out."

Jeez, wouldn't it have been great to have my family get a telegram telling them they'd lost another son. Baloney!

The officer wasn't a bad egg. I just think he put two and two together quickly and came up with five.

But that's the way it was with officers. Some of them were good guys; others were assholes.

Two of the best I had came from the Raiders. One was named Ray Luckel. I think he got out as a full colonel. Boy, did he look like a fuckin' Marine! He had that flattop haircut and he always seemed to have a great tan. You'd get a fair shake with Luckel.

The other was Alan Shapley. He ended up colonel of the 4th Marines. He was strict as hell about the training. God Almighty, he made you train! But once a week he always made sure we had a day off to play some kind of a sport.

Wait a minute, don't let me forget Lieutenant Gutsporn. He had charge of my machine gun platoon when we were training on Guadalcanal. The enlisted men couldn't get no liquor here, but we did get a couple of cans of beer every now and then. It was piss warm so we used to tie a rope to it and throw it into the ocean. Then, if you learned how to hit it right with your bayonet, you could put some foam on it.

Well, old Gutsporn used to go over to the officers' club on the Canal, pick up a bottle of Scotch and then set up a meeting with me. After all, I was platoon sergeant, we did have important business to discuss. Then we'd both sit there and kill the fifth. Now, *there* was a *great* officer!

Well, our next fight after Guam was Okinawa and what a ballbreaker that turned out to be! Hell, even the generals could get killed on Okie.

Old Simon Bolivar Buckner, Jr.—what a name—was the lieutenant general in charge of the whole operation. He got it after I was hit, but I heard what happened to him. He just got nosey on why the hell we weren't moving forward and them Japs nailed his ass.

And poor old Ernie Pyle. You know, the writer. He did such a great job in the European theater. Then he came over to see what the Pacific was like. Hell, he got his over on a real nothing island off Okinawa. Christ, he was almost the only guy killed on that one.

Actually, the first part of this campaign was a breeze. They gave the 4th Marines three days to take the Yontan Airfield—hell, we walked across it in thirty minutes! Then we quickly set up a perimeter, overlooking the water.

And what a sight! You could look out over the water and see nothing but American ships, every possible kind you could imagine.

After we had been set up there for a few hours, we got one hell of a shock. Out of nowhere, a goddamn Jap plane tried to land on the airstrip. I don't know if the poor clown just didn't know we had captured the place or if he was just off his rocker. Anyway, he calmly started to get out of the cockpit when everyone opened up on him. Shit, he never even did get out of the plane—must have been hit a hundred times.

Well, a couple of weeks after we landed, we started south, looking for the Nips. And when you looked for those guys, you'd always find them.

Now if any Marine who was with a rifle company tells you he had some close shaves on Okie, believe him. Once we really went after them, your getting hit, or close to it, happened every day.

Here's what I mean. We were moving forward, going down a trail. Our company captain was leading, Gunnery Sergeant McGinney was second and I was behind the gunny. Jeez, the Nips had the trail covered by a Nambu machine gun and they let us have it.

I jumped over to the side, trying to get some cover, and believe me, they actually shot the canteen off my cartridge belt. The poor captain never knew what hit him; he was practically cut in two by the machine gun fire. McGinney was lying over near me. One of the bullets had grazed his nose.

"Bauer, Bauer," he's yelling, "did the bastards shoot my damn nose off?"

"Hell, no!" I answered. "You just have a scratch, but look out, we've got to get those bastards before we get killed."

It turned out his nose did get infected and they sent him home, but look how close he'd come to getting killed. We did end up killing the Japs but not before they hit a couple more of our men.

That was the story of Okie though. Those Japs knew damn well they'd get killed, but they wanted to get as many of us as possible before they got it.

At any rate, when they moved us south, it seemed everywhere we'd go we'd run into them. Christ, they'd hole up in them caves and we had to get them out, or just seal them up. It seemed to me they almost had underground cities and every time we'd try to get them, we'd take casualties.

You might remember that after the war when I was playing with the Yankees, the Old Man (Casey Stengel) used to platoon me a lot —you know, Gene Woodling against right-handers and me against left-handers.

Okay. I didn't like it one bit, but I wish to hell they could have platooned me on Okie. I sure as hell wouldn't have minded someone else playing for me there. Hell, it wasn't until the fifty-third day on that island that I caught it. And that's a long time to be in a fight in the Pacific.

Here's how it happened.

We had a young kid in our outfit who caught a Jap machine gun bullet in one of his knee caps—shattered the hell out of it. Me and a guy by the name of Chester Hash—he was an old-timer, had been on the *Arizona* at Pearl Harbor—ran out to carry the kid back to an aid station. We dropped him off and the corpsman gave us a load of blood plasma to carry back to the lines.

Well, on the way back we started to run into artillery fire. It was a bright sunny day and I could actually see the reflection from the sun on one of the goddamn shells coming at us. That's the baby that nailed me. A piece of shrapnel went into my thigh, almost coming out of the other side. If it had gone through, it would have taken the head of my dick off.

I'm lying out there, bleeding like a stuck pig, when this guy from our mortar platoon—can't even remember his name—comes out and drags me into a foxhole. A corpsman came over, put a patch on the wound and gave me about half a bottle of blood plasma. Then they stuck me in a jeep and we took off.

We had just started up when the driver noticed these shells dropping all around us.

"Goddamn," he tells me, "they're starting to zero in on us. I'd sure like to go faster."

"Well, get your ass going," I said. "I can stand it."

Oh boy, he started going about seventy miles an hour over them Okie hills. What a ride! But he safely delivered me to an Army hospital where they gave me something and I went out like a light.

About five or six the next morning a medic was making his rounds.

"How do you feel?" he asked me.

"Okay," I told him, "but you better take a look at the wound. I think something happened down there last night."

He pulled back the blanket and I was lying in a pool of blood. My wound had hemorrhaged. What a mess!

So they fixed me up again and moved me out to a hospital ship in the bay. They had real mattresses and clean sheets on the ship. Christ, I hadn't slept on one of those things since before I hit Okie. I conked out and must have slept for twenty-four hours.

Then they took me back to Guam where they were going to operate on me. They wheeled me into the operating room where this real good-looking nurse started to shave the area where they're going to cut. I was only twenty-two years or so old and I hadn't even talked to a woman for months. You can imagine what happened to me. She just smiled and gave me a shot of something. The last thing I can remember before going out was looking into the eyes of that beauty.

Do you know that when I came to from the operation, that thing was still standing up. Didn't do me any good though.

Well, I ended up spending about four weeks there, after which they sent me back to my company in the 4th Marines. Hell, I could hardly recognize anyone. Most of the old-timers had been killed, wounded or just plain rotated home. I was beginning to wonder when the hell my time would come.

Anyway, it wasn't long before there was one thing I didn't have to worry about, the damn invasion of Japan. They dropped those Big Bombs and that was it. But darn it, they still wouldn't let me go back to the States.

"I'm sorry, Bauer," one of the officers said to me, "we're about to go to Japan for occupational duty. We don't know what will happen there. You're just too good a man to lose now. Remember, you did join the regulars, you know."

So, I had to pack my sea bag, go aboard the *U.S.S. Polk* and head for Yokosuka, Japan. And what a pleasant surprise we got when we landed. Why, we had no trouble at all with the Nips. As a matter of fact, we felt a little sorry for them. They seemed to have had such a bad time.

Then we saw those long sticks with the knives attached to their end that the civilians were going to greet us with if we had invaded their island. Wow!

Well, I finally got home in December '45, almost exactly three years after I had originally left the States. I went back to playing ball as soon as I could, and you know what happened to me after that.

There is one thing more I should add. In 1955 the New York Yankees went on an Oriental tour. First we stopped in Okinawa. Hell, you wouldn't recognize the place. They had a hamburger joint near where I had been wounded.

Then we headed for Japan. I can't remember which city it was—Hiroshima or Nagasaki—but Stengel and I had drawn the duty to lay a wreath on a memorial to the dead from the atomic blast. As we walked over to the memorial, Casey noticed I was a little nervous.

"Christ, Hank," the old man said, "what are you so jumpy about?".

"Hell, Case," I answered, "I might have killed some of the relatives of these people. I hope they don't know it."

The Young Marine Remembers—I

Boot camp is normally a severe shock to most new Marines. The YM was no exception.

He vividly recalls his first supper on the island when his platoon was served franks and beans, not a bad dish at all.

The YM was just about to put some mustard on his franks when he got the word.

"Hey, buddy," he was told, "pass me the baby shit."

At first the YM was puzzled. Then he realized his comrade meant the mustard. The YM ate his franks plain the rest of his stay on Parris Island.

He had consumed a good deal of beer on many occasions and a limited amount of hard liquor. He had never ordered a mixed drink at a bar. Therefore, he was taken back when the waiter at the Old Arch Inn in Boston approached him first.

"What'll it be, Marine?" the waiter said.

The Young Marine thought fast. He knew the two Marine sergeants with him, Welch and Kenny, were going to order liquor. On the way to the bar he'd heard someone order a sidecar. It sounded great to him. He put on his most nonchalant look.

"I'll take a sidecar," he said.

"*Sidecar?*" the two sergeants yelled in unison. "Baloney, bring the kid a shot and a beer!"

That was that.

The YM treasured his cordovan loafers. They were the only link he had between his gray flannel days and his present service in a Marine detachment aboard an aircraft carrier.

His gunnery sergeant on the carrier was a crusty regular from West Virginia who could recite the *Marine Corps Manual* backwards.

The gunny pulled a quick inspection on the three men at gun number 14. There was the YM with his cordovan loafers.

"*Jesus H. Christ!* What are you doing topside with your goddamn bedroom slippers on?"

Those cordovan loafers from Barrie Brothers Booters in New Haven, Connecticut, ended up in the Atlantic Ocean.

While doing a short tour of duty at the Pendleton brig, the YM fell afoul of an old-line platoon sergeant who quickly felt he had found an easy mark.

The YM wore a reasonably expensive wristwatch that his father had given him. The sergeant greatly coveted this watch.

One night at the PX slop chute the sergeant offered to swap what he said was his very expensive watch for the YM's. While the YM was no expert on timepieces, he didn't feel the sergeant's watch really looked like much. Besides, in one of the sergeant's weaker moments, he had mumbled something about being given a choice, in Georgia during the early Thirties, between reform school and the Marine Corps. The deal was not consummated.

For the rest of his days at the brig, the YM pulled constant duty in the tower, a duty generally considered the pits. He did, however, learn a lesson about power.

After he got out of the hospital the YM walked a post on the East Coast. He had done guard duty before, with a sidearm. On his current post he was armed with a club. This was in the fall of 1944, and the chances of trouble with German saboteurs was rather slight.

Anyway, it was about 2:00 A. M. and raining very hard. The YM decided to sit in a doorway rather than adhere to the General Orders. He thought of General Order Number 11: "Walk My Post From Flank to Flank and Take No Shit From Any Rank." He laughed.

Then, out of nowhere, sprang the gunnery sergeant. He was an old-timer who used to love to say, "Boy, you're pissing on my leg and telling me it's raining."

That was it. The YM received his one and only court martial—ten dollars a month out of his pay for two months and thirty days restriction to base.

The humiliating part was the Sunday formation where the sentence was read. It was a rather informal post and many of the guilty Marine's friends cheered lustily.

Six months later the YM ran into the gunny in San Diego. They had a couple of beers together. The gunny said he hoped the court martial had made a better Marine out of the YM. Of course the YM agreed, but at the time he certainly doubted it.

The Gunny and the Private

Keith Renstrom and Stan Ellis

Keith Renstrom and Stan Ellis are very different men indeed.

Mr. Renstrom is a devout member of the Mormon church who neither smokes, drinks nor uses profanity—an unusual combination for a man who spent six years in the Marine Corps, most of the time as a gunnery sergeant. Born in Utah he still lives there with his wife and six children.

Mr. Ellis, a native of New York City, comes extremely close to being the exact opposite of Keith. Stan not only drinks and smokes but his language is sprinkled with salty expressions, many of which he obviously learned during his wartime service.

Be that as it may, the two men are extremely close friends—a friendship forged when they both served in Fox Company, 2nd Battalion, 25th Marines.

Today, Stan is an insurance investigator in New Jersey. Gifted with a keen sense of humor, he is inclined to downplay his days in the Corps. Like so many other Marines in their late fifties, he does this with a smile. One suspects that underneath it all he is intensely proud of his days as a Marine. He should be.

Keith takes a more serious approach to the Corps. He realizes that his no-nonsense adherence to his religious beliefs makes him different from most Marines. But he never patronizes those who do not share them. He takes a "that's your business" attitude toward such matters. It is easy to imagine him telling the men of Company F to do what they want on their own time, but to be on deck for the 6 A.M. roll call.

I visited with these two Marines at the reunion of the 4th Division in Philadelphia. Jody Renstrom and Jeanne Ellis, their wives, were also at our gathering.

Keith did most of the talking. Gunnery sergeants usually do, with Stan occasionally throwing in some pearls of wisdom.

Actually, it was Stan who was a little hesitant at first.

"I'll have to clean up my language," he said.

"Not on your life," replied Keith. "The last thing in the world we want is to change you."

GUNNERY SERGEANT KEITH RENSTROM
PFC STAN ELLIS
F/3/25th Marines

"When I first met my gunnery sergeant, I couldn't believe someone like him existed, in the Marine Corps anyway. A gunny who didn't smoke, drink, swear or chase women—it never happened!

"Then I began to think he was a mean, ornery cuss—real bad news. It didn't take me long to realize how wrong I was.

"Now, gunny, don't let your head get any bigger by what I have to say, but Keith Renstrom is truly a Marine's Marine. Our company would have gone to hell and back for this guy, and I guess we just about did."

—Stan Ellis

Keith: My dad was a Marine in World War I. He raised the American flag in my hometown of Huntsville, Utah every single day. When he started to get feeble, he turned the flag over to the local American Legion post—they still raise the same flag every morning. Dad truly loved our country and he instilled that same feeling in the hearts of his children. I'm proud to say I love America. Oh, we can get off track, but we usually end up straightening things out.

I enlisted in the Marine Corps on June 13, 1940. I was nineteen years old at the time and I guess I just wanted to get out on my own. The Corps sure obliged me in a hurry, quickly shipping me out to the recruit depot in San Diego where I was soon given the word. I think those DIs are always on the lookout for each boot's first mistake so they can straighten him out.

In my case it was these two white lines that designated where we were supposed to walk. Being a small-town boy, I paid no attention whatsoever to the lines, didn't even know what they were there for. I soon found out.

"Hey, Marine," this sergeant yelled, "those *lines* are there for a reason. You don't walk outside those *lines*; if you did, we wouldn't have had them there. Now you get your fanny back inside those *lines* and stay there!" [It is quite possible that the sergeant did not use the word fanny, but fanny is what you will get out of Keith.]

I thought, "What in the world is happening now?" But from then on I made sure I walked where I was supposed to. The next morning when they yelled, "Hit the deck!" at 5:00 A.M., I turned to and did the same the rest of the time I was there.

After boot camp I joined Fox Company, 2nd Battalion, Sixth Marines at Camp Elliott and it was here that I found out what being a Marine really meant. This was an old-line regular Marine regiment that had really fought in World War I. Most of the men in the 6th had at least one cruise (six years) in the Corps, even the privates.

One of the most interesting men was my squad leader. He had been very successful as a civilian but had gone through a real sad ordeal. One night while dead drunk, he had been driving home with his wife and little girl. His wife had pleaded with him to let her drive, but, as you know, reasoning with a drunk ain't always easy.

Well, he finally rolled the car over. He was thrown from the car and in his drunken state watched his wife and child burn to death.

He eventually joined the Marine Corps. On the fifth and twentieth of every month (payday) he would drink himself into a stupor. Other than that, he was a heck of a good Marine.

We had a great many other super NCOs and while I thought very highly of these men, I did run into trouble with them through no fault of my own.

I was then a BAR man and had become darn good with it. I was firing away at the range one day when my weapon started to foul up. I knew the weapon inside and out, so each time it went haywire, I'd take it apart and fix it in a hurry and get back on target.

When I had finished, they brought the target over to me. In spite of all my trouble, I had really done a job. Then one of the officers who had seen this spoke up.

"Make that man a PFC at once."

[Ellis then called Keith an earbanger.]

Well, I was dumbfounded. I'd only been in the Corps a short time then. You just didn't make PFC that quickly in those days. But the officer who gave the order was Lieutenant Colonel Poindexter. What he said was gospel.

As you might guess, my gunnery sergeant was not very happy about the whole thing. To make matters worse, our company commander thought it was quite funny, which really made the gunny boil.

The next time we were on the range, he called me out in front of my whole platoon.

"Okay, Deadeye Dick," he said, "let's see how good a shot you *really* are!"

Fortunately, with a prayer in my heart, I shot my best score ever that day. There was one thing about those old-line NCOs, if you showed them you could produce, they respected you. They gave me no trouble whatsoever after that. I ended up a PFC with less than six months in the Corps, a very unusual thing in those days.

In the meantime, the war in Europe had really blown up. Everyone knew the 6th Marines would be going somewhere, but no one knew where. The scuttlebutt had us shoving off for Martinique, a French island in the Caribbean. The word was we had delivered several airplanes to Martinique before the fall of France and the Vichy government down there wouldn't give them back.

After a great deal of guesswork and waiting, we finally boarded ship at the Broadway pier in San Diego, headed, we thought, for Martinique. We didn't realize how wrong we were until we went through the Panama Canal and headed north. We stopped off at Charleston, South Carolina, where we all drew winter gear. Now we knew it wasn't Martinique.

Remember, this was the summer of '41. The U.S. was not at war and censorship was quite loose. Plenty of people who were very much against America getting involved were wondering just where in the heck we were headed. I remember that man in Congress from Montana (Senator Burton Wheeler) *demanding* to know what was going on.

Well, we left Charleston and headed north. Our next stop was Newfoundland. Now the plot is really thickening. What are American troops doing in Newfoundland? Canada is at war with Germany. The U.S. is neutral. What is going on?

When we took off from Newfoundland, our course was straight out into the Atlantic. Now things are serious. Every available U.S. capital ship in the Atlantic is trying to protect us. We all knew that German submarines were tracking our ship; if there was going to be an incident, it would be a big one.

Next thing we knew, one of the men came running into our quarters.

"I just saw the gyro compass," he said. "We're now going directly north; it must be Iceland."

He was right; we pulled into the Reykjavik harbor where we saw several ships that had been scuttled to make sure the Germans couldn't come in. It was quite a sight.

Iceland, which is about five hundred miles west of Scotland, is officially part of Europe. I believe we were the first American regiment to appear in the European war zone during World War II.

The island was then part of Denmark, a country the Germans had taken over in 1940. The British had sent troops there to make sure Hitler didn't move in. Roosevelt was very much in favor of this because he sure didn't want a bunch of Nazis that far out in the Atlantic. It was the British troops that we replaced.

One of the first things that amazed us about the English barracks we took over was the way the hot water was furnished by the nearby hot springs. Many of the places I went to when in the Corps had a scarcity of hot water for your showers but not Iceland. The big problem there was getting cold water.

We all got a kick out of two British Army orders that were posted on the wall where we took showers. The first sign read like this:

"Under no conditions will there be a withdrawal from this position. You will hold this position at all cost."

The sign next to it read:

"This is what you will do in case of a withdrawal . . ."

We thought that was so dang funny, we took it out of the shower room and put it in the mess hall.

A good deal of our time in Iceland was spent on working details. I was to be wounded three times in the Pacific, but I think I came the closest ever to being killed while on one of those working parties when I was caught between two trucks. Golly, it felt like my intestines were pushed into my chest. I was lying there in brutal pain, waiting for an ambulance when two Marine privates came over to me.

"Want a cigarette?" one of them asked.

"No, I don't smoke."

"How about a drink?" the other said.

"No thanks, I don't drink."

"Jeez," the first one then said, "what the heck can we do for him?"

That may be something only a Mormon can enjoy, but I still look back and chuckle about it.

Well, the doctor arrived and gave me a shot of morphine, but it seemed like an eternity before a British lorry came and took me to the hospital. Here they put me in a small room and gave me a complete examination. Then the two doctors had a conference outside of my room. They left the door open and I could hear every word.

"He's pretty bad," one said.

"Yes," came the reply, "I don't think he'll live to morning."

Gee whiz, what a shock! I said to myself, "Golly, I'm not that bad!" I started to pray to God the way I always had, but I also made Him a promise. I told Him that if I lived, I'd follow His teachings completely for the rest of my days. Between my prayers and the tremendous work the doctors did on me, I pulled through and outside of some late-developing back trouble, have had no serious aftereffects.

After I got out of the hospital, I was assigned to guard duty in Reykjavik. The purpose of this was to make sure only authorized Marines were allowed in town—the last thing the Corps wanted was any problems between us and the Icelandic people. We were different, the Americans and the civilians, believe me.

One time, after our tour of duty, my buddy Sammy and I went into a restaurant to order steak and chips. I quickly finished mine, but Sammy was only half done when the waitress came over.

"What kind of steak is this?" Sammy asked her.

The waitress, who had been in the U.S. and could speak English, answered:

"Why that is fresh pony; we just got it this morning. Isn't it delicious?"

My stomach turned a little, but it didn't really bother me.

Not old Sammy. He started to turn a shade of green, ran outside and vomited. He never ordered steak and chips again.

Poor Sammy. His full name was Charles Samuels and he was from Montezuma, Iowa. He went all through the war right up until it was almost over. Then he was killed in Okinawa. It is something that you can't dwell on, but it certainly is sad when I think of all my good buddies who didn't come home from the Pacific.

Well, as time went on, the U.S. and Germany were getting closer and closer to war. Each day a German plane would fly over our base and check things out. We did our best to camouflage things, but I don't think we did much of a job.

Anyway, one day the German plane came over and dropped a little parachute with a letter attached. We finally got nerve enough to open it up:

"Dear Marines," it read, "if you will camouflage your position in this way"—they had enclosed a diagram showing us what we should do—"it will be much more difficult for us to see it."

The things that really unnerved me though were the broadcasts of Lord Haw-Haw. He would start his program this way:

"Hello, Marines. I hope you enjoy your dinner tonight of such and such."

Unless the menu was real late in being set up for the evening, he was always right. There was definitely a leak somewhere. The Germans seemed to know everything we were doing, down to the smallest detail. There were all types of rumors floating around, but I never found out for sure if the spies were Icelanders or Marines. Anyway, we never saw combat while we were there, so I guess it made no difference.

When the war did come, it was halfway around the world. I had the duty when the news of the Pearl Harbor attack came through. The commanding officer of the Marines in Iceland was a general named John Marston. He was an old-timer who had done plenty of campaigning in places like Haiti. He had to be woken up out of a sound sleep to be told the news.

"My, my," he said, "well, the Japs can't bomb us here. You better put the men on alert. I'm going back to sleep. We can discuss it when I get up."

And you know he was right. It really didn't affect us at all.

Anyway, we came back to the States in February of '42, arriving in New York City the day the *Normandie* blew up. I had no interest in New York City though. We were all given a furlough and my only concern was to get back to Utah and see my family.

I had a great furlough. One way I've been lucky in life concerns family. I grew up in a close one and I have a great one now. The core of the Mormon faith is the family life. I think you'll find most of us are lucky in that respect.

My orders called for me to report to the 9th Marines in San Diego. The 3rd Division hadn't been formed yet and my job was to help build up the 9th, which was to be part of the 3rd Division.

After several months in California, I was transferred east to Camp Lejeune to start a new outfit, the 23rd Marines of the brand new 4th Division. When I arrived at Lejeune, I joined Fox Company of the 23rd. We had nine men in the Company then, which is just about as new as you can get.

One of these nine was a man named Sergeant Gallagher. I'd served with Gallagher before and thought he was a top Marine. I'd made corporal by then—I think anyone in Iceland who had taken the corporal's test was promoted once the war started—and old Gallagher, he wanted to go higher.

"Look," he says, "study for sergeant; we need some good ones."

"But," I said, "I just made corporal."

"No matter, Keith, we're going to have a brand new outfit. It's going to take good sergeants to turn this lashup into a real Marine Company."

So, I easily made sergeant.

Our captain, Joslyn, was a really good officer, one of the best. After the 23rd was filled, he went over to F Company of the 25th Marines of the same division. I went along with him as did about half the company, including Ellis. By now I had made gunnery sergeant.

Once we joined the 25th Marines, we moved fast. They marched us aboard a transport and sent us through the Panama Canal and up the Pacific to San Diego. From there we went by truck to Camp Pendleton. The 1st, 2nd and 3rd Marine Divisions were already in combat and Washington wanted to get the 4th out in the Pacific as soon as possible. At Camp Pendleton I took a gamble that could have really gotten me in trouble, but I'm glad I took the chance.

As I've told you, my dad was a World War I Marine. So he, along with my twelve-year-old brother, came from Utah to see me. There wasn't much trouble getting them on the base, but keeping them there was another story.

It was easy enough for dad; I just gave him one of my uniforms, but brother Pete was another story. I got the smallest man in the company to give him some dungarees. They were still a little big, but we fixed them up. He looked pretty good.

The big test came when Colonel Hudson, the battalion commander, walked by. Pete and I were standing by my tent talking to one of my friends. We all saluted the colonel and of course he saluted back. As he walked by, Colonel Hudson smiled.

"Good night," he said, "we're sure getting them young these days, but you'll make a good Marine out of him. Carry on!" You see, it never dawned on him we'd have a twelve-year-old boy on the base.

Dad and Pete stayed with me about four days. I even took them out on a night problem with actual firing. Pete thought he was in a real war. You can imagine what fun he had telling this to the kids back in Utah.

Incidentally, when the Korean War broke out, Pete became a real Marine and did fight over there. Thank God he came back.

Now, we all knew we would be going to the Pacific. Everyone really turned to. When the 4th went into action, we wanted to bring as many back alive as possible. The more trained a Marine became, the better his chances of making it.

During this period we knew we were going into combat, but didn't know exactly when. The men were getting a little edgy. I was always trying to keep them out of fights and making sure they got back to camp even when they were dead drunk. I may not drink or smoke, but I've never looked down my nose on people who do. Golly, if I did, I would have disliked practically my whole company. It did get very touchy before we pulled out of San Diego. A couple of my men barely made it—

[Enter Stan Ellis]

Stan: Just before we went over, Tommy Healy, a buddy of mine known as T.K., and myself were on authorized liberty. We ran into Platoon Sergeant Tucker who told us we better get our ass back on time because we're probably going to ship out a week earlier than we thought. We were pretty well oiled up, but we knew this was serious business.

Anyway, we started to hitchhike. We got as far as Highway 101 near Balboa but no further. Now we're really concerned plus we're still pretty loaded. We spotted this pickup truck with the keys in the ignition. T.K. puts on his most austere face.

"I commandeer this truck," he said, "in the name of the United States Marine Corps. Amen."

I told him I was duly impressed.

So we took off. What a trip! We're naturally picking up all doggies, swabbies and jarheads we see with their thumbs out. We're bellowing out every song we know and having a ball.

All of a sudden we hear a siren. Sure enough, it's the state police. The next thing I knew we were behind bars with this big police sergeant looking at us. I decided to try and con him.

"Look, sergeant," I said, "we're not regular criminals."

"Maybe not," he answered, "but in California we figure stealing a truck is a good start."

"Come on, sergeant, we've got to get back to our regiment. We're going to ship out."

He must have done something because about an hour later a jeep comes up with a Lieutenant Coates in it. They ran our ass up to a justice of the peace who starts reading off all these grand larceny charges. By now I'm getting a little bored and quite a bit hung over. I knew what we did. What the hell! I figure, why don't they get the darn thing over with and let us go overseas?

Finally, after a couple of hours of baloney, they transferred our charges over to Marine authorities, put us in the jeep and headed us for the troopship. When we got to the pier, they raced us up the gangplank and, wow, I don't think we were there more than ten minutes before the ship pulled out.

Anyway, the thing was a long way from over. Now we have to face Colonel Hudson, a real beautiful man. I figured I better give T.K. the word.

"Tommy," I said, "when we go in, let me do all the talking. I can handle the colonel; we're old friends."

I'll say we were old friends. When we were run up to him, he just put his face in his hands.

"Ellis, Goddamn, not you again."

"Yes, sir, but I have an explanation."

"For stealing a civilian's truck. This should be good."

"Well, colonel, when we found out the regiment was shipping out, we took the situation into our own hands like a good Marine should. After all, it is the first and utmost duty of a good Marine not to let his outfit and the Corps down—both Private Healy and myself rather die than do that."

I glanced over at Healy and he's biting his lip to keep from breaking up. The colonel's mouth is open wide enough to stick an apple in it. Then I continued.

"Furthermore, if an emergency like that happened again, I would do the same thing. The Corps comes first." Then I saluted.

"Ellis," the Colonel said, "I'm proud of you; the whole Corps

THE GUNNY AND THE PRIVATE

should be proud of you; we can't lose this war with men like you and Healy. However, we do have this little matter of grand larceny charge. If you two come through this friggin' invasion, you'll have to pay the civilian $150 each. If you don't make it, I'll see the charges are dropped." My, but this was comforting!

Anyway, we both came through the campaign (Marshall Islands) in good shape. The division was sent to Hawaii to get ready for our next beachhead (Saipan). Liberty wasn't much, but Healy and I could have sure used that dough. We got our captain to write the civilian and point out we had worked very hard for that money and could he find it in his heart to send it back? We did get a letter from the civilian wishing us luck but no money. I wonder, did that SOB ever find out that my dear buddy T.K. ended up being killed on Tinian.

Keith: Well, the Marshall Islands fight was a lot easier than what came later, but we still took enough casualties to make it bloody. Whenever you have to kill a lot of Japanese, it's always rugged.

Our battalion first went ashore on Ennubirr Island of the Kwajalein atoll. There weren't many Japs on the island, but there were enough to put up a fight.

The beachhead was unopposed, but shortly after the landing, as we were moving inland, I spied a figure in a green uniform over on my left. I figured he was a Marine. Then, *wap*, a bullet went into a tree right beside me. I don't know how in the heck he missed me.

I hit the deck, but the Marine in front of me made a quick decision. I guess he figured no Marine would be firing at us, so he quickly shot the man who had fired at me. It turned out that it was a Japanese soldier the Marine had shot, but one of the many unfortunate things about combat is that you have to make snap judgments like that. You are not always right.

Our casualties here ended up being quite light, but one of the men we lost was a seventeen-year-old lad named Chris, and that's a story in itself.

It starts with his life insurance policy. While it wasn't mandatory to take out that $10,000 policy, almost everyone did. And we were under instructions to try and make sure that the men who balked ended up taking the policy. Chris was a hard case. He just wasn't about to take a policy. I had to go to work on him.

"Chris," I told him, "they're really on my back on this. Hurry up, take out the darn policy."

"No, gunny," he said, "my parents abandoned me when I was very young. My mother's no good and my father's a drunk. The only one who raised me was my grandmother and she died a while back. My parents ain't getting any blood money from me. No one back home would miss me."

This went on and on. Finally, he came up with a solution.

"Gunny, look, you've been great to me; I can't let you get in trouble because I don't take out a policy. I've named my two buddies in our fire team as beneficiaries. They'll each get $5,000 if I get it."

Golly, poor Chris ended up being killed right there in Ennubirr. When I turned over his body and looked at that young face—the poor guy hardly shaved—I broke down for the only time during the war. He looked just like a kid brother. I took myself away from the company and bawled like a baby. I never did it again.

Chris was wrong about one thing though. Maybe no one back in the States missed him, but several of us did. I still do. I hope somehow he knows this.

There is one thing more about Chris's story. After I put his dogtag in his mouth and slammed it shut as we were instructed to do, I started to really hate the Japanese. His body had already begun to putrefy in that tropical climate. Honestly, I think I could have killed all the Japs in the world.

As a religious man, I knew this was wrong. It was the Japanese government, not the people, who had started the war. I wrote my father and told him how I felt. He wrote back and told me to do my job as best I could but to try and not hate a whole people. I did try, but it wasn't easy, not after we put little Chris in a burial bag. To me the only good Jap was a dead one, at least 'til the war was over.

Of course, all our men weren't like Chris. There will always be some men who, once they see what combat is all about, don't want any part of it. We had a young fellow like that who came up with the brilliant idea of blowing off his big toes. Do you know, he was so scared, he couldn't even hit the toe. All he got out of it was a powder burn. We squared him away after that, but he certainly took a razzing from the rest of the men. Nobody said anything to him about what he tried to do; it was the fact that he *missed*.

"What the heck kind of Marine are you?" they'd say. "You couldn't even hit your toe—from three feet away. You have got to be the worst shot in the Corps!"

After the Marshall Islands operation was secure, we found that our battalion had suffered very little. Other parts of our division, the men who had gone in at Roi-Namur, saw most of the fighting, but overall it was the easiest operation the 4th Division experienced during the war. It was a good thing it turned out this way because we ended up invading Saipan three or four months later. Saipan was to be a different story.

From the Marshalls we went to Maui in the Hawaiian Islands. Here we went into extensive training for the Mariana Islands. In May '44 we boarded LSTs for the trip to Saipan. Our first stop was Honolulu and it was there that the seven LSTs blew up. I was on liberty when it happened, but Stan was on the first one to explode.

Stan: I'll say I was and there was nothing funny about it. They never found out for sure how it happened, but there were sailors doing some welding near the bow where some high octane gas was stored. They figured some sparks got to the gas.

Anyway, it happened on Sunday, May 21. I think the number of my ship was LST 274. We were tied up at a place called Westlock when our ship went up. The blast threw me into the drink. I don't remember going through the air; I guess I was stunned. The next thing I remember was coming out of it actually underwater. I swam to the surface, still not knowing what the hell had happened. I got back aboard the LST, but by this time the fire had also reached the rest of the LSTs lined up there.

The word was to abandon ship, so I jumped back into the bay and swam to shore.

By the time I reached land everything was blowing up. One of my friends, named Van Ness—I think he was from Connecticut—was already ashore and trying to run away from the explosions.

Part of an amtrac motor went sailing through the air like shrapnel, cutting off both his legs. The poor guy bled to death before anything could be done for him. There were several other men killed from my LST, but I can't give you the exact number. I do know it was a horrifying experience, no enemy to fight, just plenty of dead Marines and sailors.

And, remember, I'm just talking about *my* LST. There were six others that also went up. It affected not only our outfit but also the 2nd Division. They also lost plenty of men. I think it was probably the most dreadful accident in the Pacific during the war.

Keith: Yes, I guess it was. Anyway, we still had to go about our business which was to invade the Mariana Islands on June 15. Saipan, the island we were to hit, was the first island where we knew we'd encounter thousands of Japanese civilians, so we were joined by several Japanese-Americans who were to act as interpreters. Naturally, we were quite suspicious of them—that's the way things were at that time. We even placed a special guard on them without their knowledge.

Golly, do you know that every one of them turned out to be one hundred percent loyal and also did an outstanding job. As I look back, I'm embarrassed that I ever mistrusted them.

Well, Saipan turned out to be the largest operation the Marine Corps had ever participated in. It was the first time two Marine divisions had fought side by side in a campaign. We (the 4th Division) landed on the southwest end of the island simultaneously with the

2nd Division who were a little north of us. The Army 27th Division was being held in reserve.

We were immediately hit with Japanese fire coming from a ridge away from the beach. As a gunnery sergeant, part of my job was to try and keep things moving. Remember, all Marines aren't heroes and sometimes keeping things moving isn't easy.

There was one young Marine who was lying flat right there on the beach. I could see he wasn't hit so I went over to see what was wrong.

"I can't move, gunny; I just can't move," he said, "I'm just too scared."

I could see him shaking all over, almost as if he were having convulsions.

"Come on, Marine," I said, "the fire isn't that bad. Besides, you're just as apt to get hit lying here as you are if you keep moving."

"I know, I know, but I just can't move."

I tried everything I could think of but he just wasn't going to budge. He wasn't necessarily a bad kid, just paralyzed with fear. It happens.

Anyway, I had to keep moving as our company made our way up near this railroad crest. We were constantly receiving small arms fire; then the shelling started. Some of our small army tanks had come ashore and I remember seeing one of them take a direct artillery hit. There wasn't much left of it. We did have air support so we called in a strike from some of our carrier-based planes. They got rid of the artillery in a hurry.

We're now trying to get to the ridge, still taking fire and very concerned with hidden Japanese who would spring out of nowhere and make a suicidal lunge at us.

I'll be darned if I know where one of their officers came from, but all of a sudden he was in front of me, pointing a pistol at my head. He pulled the trigger and I heard this click. Either Sergeant Ralston or Pappy Peck, I can't remember which one, shot him before he could fire again. I picked up the pistol and gave it to the Marine who had shot the Jap, but I kept the cartridge that had misfired. Still have it. You can see where the firing pin touched the bullet but, thank God, didn't ignite it.

One of our Company E officers wasn't so lucky. I saw another Jap jump up and go for him, only that Japanese was waving a big samurai sword. A Marine BAR opened up on the Jap. You could actually see the bullets going through the Nip, but before falling, he almost cut our man in half. The poor Marine officer just lay there groaning.

"Stop the blood, please stop the blood!" he was moaning. "For God's sake, stop the blood!" His cries got weaker and weaker, then he died.

We finally got to the ridge where we settled down, trying to tie our line together. It was now real late in the day and it dawned on me that I hadn't eaten anything. This was my first day of intensive combat and I had forgotten all about food. I started eating all the rations I could lay my hands on. Part of being glad to be alive, I guess.

The next move we made was the taking of the Jap airstrip. One of the things we captured here was the Japanese paymaster's safe. We didn't know how to open the dang thing, but E Company had a guy who had served time for safecracking. He had the reputation of being able to open anything—a real professional. When he saw the safe, he started to glow.

"Oh boy," he said, "oh boy, just like old times!"

He had that safe open in no time at all, just as slick as a whistle.

"Any time I can help out, just let me know," he offered.

Then he walked away as proud as a peacock. You'd have thought he'd just discovered the cure for cancer.

After that we started to move north, past Magicienne Bay toward Mount Tapotchau, the highest point on the island.

When you're moving up like this, you never know when the Japs will open up on you. You are constantly having fire fights, some of which develop into real slugfests.

We ran into one of these situations one day when one of our flanks was on the beach. A BAR man named Gapota was on the beach flank. We heard firing and Gapota went down. I yelled over at him.

"Gapota, are you hit?"

"Not really," he answered, "just in the arm."

Then a man named Mike Plasure ran out to get Gapota. Just before he reached him, the Japs cut Mike in two with a Nambu machine gun.

At this point we knew we were faced with more than sniper fire so we had to regroup and figure out how to get rid of the machine gun. When we finally did get to Gapota, we found him dead from chest wounds. You see, the shock of being wounded had stunned him. He knew he had been hit in the arm, but he didn't realize he had the chest wounds. The poor guy probably didn't even know he was dying.

Stan: That's right. When you do get hit, the shock of it can be devastating. We had another guy in our company get shot in the shoulder on Saipan. It was a clean wound that went right through him without hitting a vital spot. Yet he died instantly. The shock had been too much for his heart. And remember, this was a young guy in tip-top shape.

Keith: That's true. I know it's hard to understand, but it happens in combat. Well, as we moved north, we started to run into Japanese civilians. One of them, a teenage boy, jumped out from behind a rock and just stared at me. The poor kid was shaking all over.

Then he pointed at my Thompson machine gun and made a motion which was really asking me if I was going to shoot him. By this time he was sobbing. I finally convinced him we didn't kill young boys. When one of our interpreters came up, we found out an amazing thing about the lad.

It seemed that his parents lived on Maui. He had been sent to Japan several years before so his grandparents could rear him like a Japanese, not like an American. After the war broke out—I guess he was actually an American citizen—the Japanese had put him to work on Saipan. It turned out to be one of the few bright spots on a real bloody island. The young fellow did get back to his parents on Maui. Thank God for that!

Stan: You couldn't always trust those civilians though. I was holed up on a knoll along with a guy named Gleason. No, poor Gleason had already been killed—it was Madunick and Tommy Healy.

I had just lit up a cigarette when I spotted three beautiful nude Japanese women. Hell, I thought it was a mirage, but they were for real. They were bent over with their tushies pointed toward us. They had twisted their heads so we could see they were smiling.

Jeez, we're taking this all in. I can remember one of my buddies nodding his head.

"Not bad, not bad," he says. "We should defintely liberate these beauties."

Then Jap fire opened up on us from both sides. Fortunately the Nips fired too soon. We were all able to hit the ground without getting a scratch.

Personally, I've always felt that was the cheapest trick the Japs pulled, tempting a man like that—those dirty bastards!

Keith: Yes, sometimes the Japanese women could be as tough as the men. We had a Marine officer named Billen. One of their women came over to surrender to him and when she got close enough, she threw a grenade at the poor guy. They could be nasty!

As I've said, when we were moving up, we were constantly having contact with the Japs. There was one night, however, when they didn't hit us and thank the Lord for that. We had found a cave of sake that afternoon. This was really great for bargaining.

You see, when you'd send men back to the beach to get ammunition, if you had something like sake to give to the men handling the supplies, you'd not only get fast service but you'd get all you wanted. We were badly in need of illuminating mortar shells. So, I figured if I sent the sake back the next day, we'd be all set.

Goodness, there was just no way to keep that sake away from our men. They'd been fighting for several days, living on rations; they were just in no condition to hold their liquor. The first thing you knew, half the company was drunk. I can see them now, laughing, singing, dancing, just having a real old time.

At about two-thirty the next morning the drunk ones had all passed out. You know how drunks snore; you could hear them all over the place. Those of us who hadn't been drinking were on the line, waiting for the Japs. We figured they must have known what was happening—if they didn't, they had to be deaf.

Well, dang it, we started to hear this crunch, crunch, I was sure this was it. I called for flares and guess what? A herd of cattle was coming toward us.

Our first reaction was amazement, followed by laughter. Then we realized it wasn't funny. I mean, what should we do? Maybe the whole thing is a typical Jap trick. Maybe they want us to fire at the cows and give away our positions. Maybe the Japs were coming in right after the cows. It sure wasn't a joke.

We ended up taking a gamble and doing nothing and we won. There were no Japs that night and thank the Lord. If they'd ever thrown one of those banzai charges at us, we would have been in real trouble.

Stan: Gunny, I do have to admit that when you took gambles like that, they usually paid off. Remember the night we had already dug our foxholes and you came by and gave us the word to move back and dig some more?

Keith: Sure, the line was too long.

Stan: Sure, hell. We all thought it was chicken shit. We'd already dug the goddamn holes. All the guys are bitching like hell. The gunny couldn't have been elected dogcatcher that night. Then came the banzai. If we hadn't shortened and strengthened the line, we might have been overrun. As it was, we lost very few men. He may say "gosh almighty" and "gee whiz," but gunny was one hell of a Marine.

Well, my war was over before we actually secured Saipan. I'd already had several of the close shaves that everyone in a place like Saipan runs into, but when they did get me, they did a good job.

I'd been standing with Captain Joslyn, who was having one of those deep discussions with Ellis (no relation) and Shoup, two other company commanders in our battalion. We were near a railroad track.

Jeez, you know how those officers get going in a discussion like that. Jibberty, jibberty, jibberty—a lot of bullshit. I didn't know what they were talking about and I'm not sure they did. I did figure the Japs had spotted us and when a shell landed over on our right, I knew they had.

"Begging the captain's pardon," I said to Joslyn, "but we better get our ass the hell outa here!"

"Ellis, this is one time you're right."

We hightailed it away from there and just in the nick of time. The Nips pulverized the area.

The Japs kept up their heavy fire and those brutal mortars. We're trying to move up, but it isn't easy.

A little later one of our lieutenants collared me—I don't remember which one; I tried to keep away from those birds.

"Ellis," he said, "we're real low on mortar shells. Take two men and go get some."

Oh, this is great. I'd be going away from the Japs, and it was legit. We needed the shells. So I grabbed two of my buddies and we took off.

God Almighty, we hadn't gone far at all when the Jap artillery spotted us. Their goddamn shells are coming in like gang busters.

"Disperse, disperse!" I yelled. Where the hell I got that word, I don't know—must have been from a movie. Hell, I couldn't even spell it.

I spotted this big hole and jumped in. Oh, this is tremendous. Our artillery had started in on the Nips. The shells are going over my hole in both directions, but I'm cozy as hell. You know, "Three cheers for the old Red, White and Blue!" I figured I may spend the rest of the battle in my hole.

Well, you know the old saying, "You never hear the one that has your name on it." Oh, that's a lot of bullshit, believe me!

Womp, womp. I hear this shell getting closer and closer.

"Holy shit!" I yelled out. "Not me, not me!"

Then, *wham!* I vaguely remember going up in the air and the next thing I knew, I was on a hospital ship. It was three days later. It was touch and go for a while, but I pulled through.

Keith: You were lucky, all right. But with all your baloney, you were a heck of a Marine when the shooting started.

Well, after Saipan, they moved us across the water a few miles to Tinian. We landed on a beach the size of a postage stamp. I can't say this was as rough as Saipan, but our battalion had some bad moments. One of them was when we lost Stan's great buddy, Tommy Healy. T.K. was actually up on a tank, trying to direct their fire when a Nambu machine gun riddled him. Immediately after he was hit, the tank blasted the Jap machine gun, but it was too late to do Healy any good.

Stan: I remember hearing about it in the hospital. I still miss him. What a guy!

But, gunny, they also racked you up there, didn't they?

Keith: Yeah. It was right after we thought we'd gotten rid of all of them. We'd called for naval gunfire and they'd saturated the area. It was one time I could actually see our shells landing and body parts of the Japanese soldiers going in every direction. It was pretty gruesome, but after all, it meant that those Japs weren't going to kill any more Marines.

Unfortunately for me there was one Japanese sniper that our Navy didn't get and after the shelling stopped, he put a slug near my ear. I let go a long burst from my Thompson in his direction, but missed. Then I started to move over to where I thought I'd have a better chance of nailing him and it was then he caught me in my right leg. It spun me around and knocked me down. I managed to crawl away from his line of fire, but my gosh darn leg started to stiffen up on me. Pretty soon I couldn't move it at all. I tried to get one of my corpsmen to patch it up so I could stay with the company, but he just shook his head.

"I can't stop the bleeding," he said, "You have to go to the hospital back at Saipan to get that leg fit for duty."

He was right and I knew it. I went back to Saipan where our doctors really worked on the leg. They seemed to have done a good job, but they didn't know how to stop the draining. This seemed to drag on and on. Finally, I said the heck with it, leg draining or not, I had to get back to the 25th Marines. I'd gotten the word that they were beginning some rugged training. If the regiment was going to invade another island, I wanted to be there. I'd made the first three assaults and saw no reason for missing the fourth.

So I packed my sea bag, got a discharge from the hospital, and hitched a ride back to the company. No one knew I was coming, so when I showed up at Tinian Town, Captain Joslyn couldn't believe it.

"Gunny," he asked, "what in tarnation are you doing here?"

"Why, captain, I figured you could use a hand with some of the replacements, so here I am."

That was that. We headed back to Maui to gear up for Iwo Jima, which, as you know, turned into a real nightmare. I was on that seven-by-five-mile island for ten days and I can't remember a day when we didn't take casualties. But when things were as bad as they were on Iwo, you are apt to sometimes think back more on the lighter moments than on the horrible ones.

I can remember seeing a young lad named Massey being thrown by a shell's concussion, but the only shrapnel that touched him had caught him in the right buttocks. I ran over to see if he was all right. He was sitting up, with his dungarees off and, of all things, a cribbage board in his hand. A piece of shrapnel was sticking out of the cribbage board.

"Gunny," he said, "look where it ended up; all that and not a drop of blood. I thought I'd be getting off this lousy island!"

Then there was Lieutenant Cragg. Our first night on Iwo, he had jumped into a shell hole and gone to sleep. He didn't realize it but a Jap soldier was also sleeping in the same hole. They both woke up at the same time when the dawn was breaking.

"Wow," the lieutenant told us, "he took one look at me, I did the same toward him, and we both ran in the opposite directions."

One of our men then asked Cragg why the dickens he didn't shoot the Nip.

"What?" he answered. "You don't shoot someone you've just slept with!"

I can also remember trying to get one of our young Marines to move forward. He just looked up at me with these big innocent eyes and said, "Golly gee, gunny, a fellow can get killed around here!"

Of course, he was kidding me over the fact I didn't swear, but he said it loud enough so some of the other men could hear him. This was great because it relieved a little of the tension.

We had another fellow in the company named Tiny Villeret—he was from Texas. In the Corps you always seemed to call the real big men "Tiny" and Villeret was huge. Tiny was a sergeant and one of our best, but on Iwo he developed a bad habit that worried me. It seemed that everywhere I went Tiny was always with me—he just stuck to me like glue.

"Tiny," I finally said to him, "don't stick to me like this. Together we're just too big a target."

"Gunny, you're the only guy around here who *might* know what's going on. Ah figure that if ah stick with you, little ole Tiny might not get one of them Japanese packages."

It didn't work. Tiny did get hit—with his size, he was bound to—but he pulled through.

Well, you know the story of Iwo. We landed on the southern end of the island and had to move north with the Japs trying to kill us as we went along. On the fifth or sixth day we ran into a Nip pillbox that was just too tough for us to destroy, yet we had to take it. I soon figured out that we needed some artillery support if we were going to keep moving. I passed the word down to the beach to see if we could get a pack howitzer sent up. They had to dismantle one, bring it up in pieces, and then put it together again, but they got it up. Then they sighted in on the pillbox.

Gee, the first man who tried to fire the howitzer got a bullet right in the head. The second man had more luck. He missed with the first round, but the second one was right on the money. Then we charged the gosh darn place and wiped it out. Now we started to really roll their line up but were constantly taking casualties.

I think it was about this time that Captain Joslyn caught part of a mortar shell. Joslyn had to be evacuated from the island, but he did survive. Three of four other men, hit by the same shell, were buried on Iwo.

One of our lieutenants then took over the Company. He had been with us since Camp Pendleton and was a solid officer. What wasn't known at the time was how close he was to the breaking point.

An hour or so after he took over, he sent me back to the beach to bring up some wire. It didn't seem to me that we really needed wire at the time, but of course I took off for the beach. I realized there was something wrong, the way he had said, "Wire, wire, go get lots of wire." It just wasn't like him.

By the time I got back to Fox Company, the poor guy had completely cracked up. They were leading him to the beach as I arrived.

Now, he was just as much a casualty as any of our other wounded men. After you had seen as much killing as he had, you were bound to be on the edge. Who knows what pushed him over. The same thing could have happened to me, but I'll never know for sure if it would have, because my turn to get hit was right around the corner.

Shortly after I had got back with the wire, one of our platoon leaders, a brand new second lieutenant, was killed by a sniper. Line officers were getting very scarce so I took over his platoon. The very next day I was trying to move the platoon forward when a Jap jumped out of one of those spider holes. He had a grenade and was looking to see where to throw it. I quickly shot him but not before he had lobbed the grenade in my direction. It landed in a small tree right next to where I was standing.

Now, if you shot one of their grenades, it would blow up without doing much damage. But in this case there was no time for that. All I could do was try and duck. I ended up being hit in my arm, face, neck and back. I tried to stay in command of my platoon, but it was no use. It was the end of Iwo for me. They sent me back to the States where I ended up a DI at San Diego until my discharge.

I'll tell you something though. When I come to a reunion and talk to so many of these men, I realize what a gutty bunch of Marines we had in F Company. Why, there's a man here who was hit in the neck on Saipan and bayoneted on Tinian, yet when he was wounded again on Iwo, he didn't want to be evacuated. Maybe we were all nuts, I don't know, but I'm darn proud to have been with these men.
Stan: Yeah, and so am I. We had an outstanding record. But we also had some great liberties!

You know, I was a runner in combat, but I was also company bugler. Do you remember this call? Ellis took out his trumpet and played liberty call. It went like this:

Who's going ashore?
Who's going ashore?
Who's got the price
Of a two-bit whore?

The Horrible Scene

It is difficult to pinpoint the most horrible scene witnessed by the Marines in a war that produced more dreadful sights than all the Boris Karloff and Bela Lugosi films put together. But the mass civilian suicides and murders on the island of Saipan must stand at the top of the list of terrors.

As was their custom, the Japanese soldiers fought on Saipan with an unyielding, dogmatic will to conquer or die.

It must have been apparent to the Japanese senior officers soon after the Americans landed—certainly no later than the fall of Mount Tapotchau—that since the Emperor's soldiers could not conquer, they would have to die. But what of the thousands of Japanese civilians on Saipan who had been caught up in the insanity of war? Must they also sacrifice their lives to a medieval code that called for either the annihilation of the enemy or their own destruction? Apparently so. It was one thing for a battle-hardened Marine to watch a group of Japanese soldiers form a circle and play catch with a live grenade until it went off. It was something else to watch a Japanese mother with an infant in her arms jump off a cliff. Both scenes were witnessed on Saipan.

As the Marines pushed northward on Saipan, they did not realize the macabre scene that awaited them. To be sure, there had been civilian suicides, but the large bulk of the Japanese civilians were being fed and given medical care by the Americans. They were in stockades and would stay there until after the island battle was over.

But hundreds of civilians had chosen, for one reason or another, to stay with their troops. Along with the Japanese soldiers they had been cornered near the cliffs of Marpi Point. As these Japanese began their self-destruction, many Marines watched in horror.

Japanese men would stab what appeared to be their wives and children and then jump into the sea. Women were seen adjusting their hair and then, clad in their finest kimonos, leap to their deaths. Elderly Japanese literally had to be carried to the edge of the cliffs and then hurled into the sea.

Some of the civilians, finally realizing the absurdity of what was happening, tried to flee but were shot down or bayoneted by their own soldiers.

While this self-inflicted genocide was going on, a Japanese-speaking American pleaded over a loudspeaker with the civilians to stop their senseless self-destruction. One Japanese who had surrendered also spoke to his people, pointing out that the Americans would not harm them, that they would be fed and taken care of. It was to no avail. Only a handful of the Japanese civilians at Marpi Point survived.

There can be no disputing these facts. Many of the events were recorded on film by the Americans. During 1945 just about every Marine viewed these films. It was part of the indoctrination prior to Olympic, the coming invasion of Japan. The thought of invading an island whose inhabitants were that willing to die was sobering indeed.

The Lawyer Who Went to War

Buck Schechter

Irving Schechter is another World War II Marine who was decorated several times for bravery yet who hardly seems to fit the mold of a fire-eating Chesty Puller.

Buck (a Marine Corps sobriquet) fought in three campaigns as a rifle company commander and was decorated after each campaign. He received the Silver Star for bravery on the Marshall Islands, the Navy Cross for heroism at Saipan-Tinian and the Bronze Star for bravery at Iwo Jima. He was also wounded on Saipan.

Mr. Schechter is currently the president of the Bank of Smithtown on Long Island and quite active in his own law firm in the same town. If one ever makes a wrong turn in Smithtown, Buck is a good man to know.

Buck serves as a model for all Marine Corps Reserve officers. He had never planned to be a military man. A graduate of the University of Iowa, he later received a law degree from New York University and was about to hang out his shingle when the threat of American involvement in World War II convinced him to enter the Marine Corps. He could have easily obtained a job in the Corps's legal department but that wasn't why young Mr. Schechter had joined the Corps. He would be the last one to brag about it, but Buck joined the Marines specifically to fight for his country. And he did.

Mr. Schechter retired from the United States Marine Corps Reserve a few years ago with the rank of colonel. But he still looks as though he could lead a company into combat.

Our interview started when I asked him if he ever wondered how he had survived all his arduous Pacific combat.

Here is his answer.

CAPTAIN IRVING (BUCK) SCHECHTER
A/1/24th Marines

"To lead is to serve."

Yes, I have wondered why I'm still walking around after all the combat I went through. You would think the best I could have hoped for was a major disability, but I really can't say that I am bothered physically by my Marine service.

The time I think about the most occurred on Saipan. I was leading my company through a wooded area. I had just climbed a small ridge when I heard a shot. I turned around and saw one of our flamethrowers lying on the ground. He was the man closest to me when the shot rang out. He had been hit in the head.

You see, it was very common for the Jap snipers to wait until we had walked by so they could pick out their target. They frequently would try and knock out the officers if possible. But above all they wanted the special equipment men, especially the flamethrowers. My God, how they hated those men! If I had not had a flamethrower behind me, the sniper would have gone for the officer. It's as simple as that.

Well, let's go back to the fall of 1940. France had fallen and the Germans could do anything they wanted to do. I'd just got out of law school and had passed my bar exams. I was vitally interested in what was going on all over the world. The best way to keep abreast of events was through the radio.

Anyway, I was listening to a late news program. One of the advertisements on the program carried a message from the Marine Corps. It called for college graduates to send in an application to see if they could qualify for the Corps's officers training program.

Well, my dad had immigrated from Austria before the turn of the century. He had worked hard and prospered. I figured the Schechter family was a vital part of the American success story and I also felt there was no way this country could stay out of war. So I wrote in for an application.

Now, you may think writing in like this—like sending in box covers for a free sample of something—doesn't sound like the Marines, but remember the Corps was real small at the time. Due to Hitler's war, they'd been authorized to expand and they were trying to do it fast. I should add they very quickly answered my application and told me to proceed to 90 Church Street in lower Manhattan for a physical. I did and much to my surprise I found out I had a weight problem.

I don't mean I was overweight, just the opposite. I think the minimum was 133 pounds and I weighed in at 130. Believe me, it's a lot easier to put on three pounds than to take it off. I returned to the recruiting office a week later well over the minimum. They told me to go home and wait for orders.

In the meantime, although I had passed my bars, I had not yet been admitted by the appellate court of New York State. I petitioned the court to hasten the procedure as I was about to leave for Marine OCS training at Quantico, Virginia. I had to have the court's approval if I wanted to practice in New York State and I did not want this hanging over me while I was on active duty. The minute they heard this I was whisked through the court. When I arrived at Quantico early in 1941, I was a bona fide New York State attorney at law.

The next six or seven months were spent in various forms of training all aimed at making me and my fellow OCS candidates Marine officers. I can't recall any real difficulty here for myself or for most of the other candidates. By September '41 most of us were in place as second lieutenants at the new Camp Lejeune in North Carolina. By now there had been quite a change in the international situation.

You see, when I first went into the Corps, I didn't think about Japan at all. I am Jewish and my father still had relatives in Europe. It was Hitler I was concerned about. If the time came when the U.S. made an amphibious landing in Europe, I wanted to be there.

However, by the fall of '41 you could not ignore Japan. The situation between Tokyo and Washington seemed to be deteriorating rapidly. The Corps now had begun the greatest expansion program in its history. All you had to do was look at a map of the Pacific and realize that the Marines' specialty, the amphibious assault, would be in great demand if we went to war with Japan.

Well, on December 7, 1941 I, along with some other young officers, walked into a hotel lobby in Kingston, North Carolina. The radio was blasting away, giving us the word.

"ATTENTION! ATTENTION! ALL CAMP LEJEUNE MARINES REPORT BACK TO THEIR QUARTERS IMMEDIATELY!"

This was it. Then the radio started to broadcast news of what had happened to Pearl Harbor.

We returned immediately and found everything in a condition of chaos that was to continue for quite a while. The scuttlebutt ran wild. One of the stories that most people believed had German dirigibles bringing paratroopers across the Atlantic to be dropped at our camp. The fact that Germany had not as yet declared war on the U.S. had not impressed anyone but neither had the Japanese before Pearl Harbor.

Anyway, we started immediately digging trenches all over our camp. We were going to be ready for the Nazis when they came. In the meantime, the possibility of some kind of action against the Panama Canal seemed a lot more logical, especially after Germany declared war on us on December 11.

Later in December, twenty-two young second lieutenants were ordered to report to Norfolk, Virginia. I was included in this group. We ended up at Newport News, near Norfolk, on December 31. Here we were quickly joined by some five hundred recruits from Parris Island. These new men had been in the Corps only a few weeks. They hadn't even done their three weeks on the rifle range. Part of our orders were to set up a mini boot camp when we reached our next designation, Panama.

Well, sometime in January we boarded transports in Norfolk. We were to be part of a large convoy—I know the battleships *Mississippi* and *Idaho* were in the convoy—that was headed for the Pacific. Our group left this convoy at Panama.

Our job now was to reinforce the Marine garrison already there and to help them prepare the area for a possible attack. Our men were also to board all ships going from the Colon side of the Canal over to the Balboa side to act as a guard detachment. As we had to spend a good deal of time putting our men through the second part of their boot camp, we had our hands full. We also received the Marine detachment from the *U.S.S. Erie* when the Germans sunk her off South America. Those U-boats were having a field day throughout the entire area at the beginning of the war.

In the meantime, all of us second lieutenants who had left Norfolk became first lieutenants and in August of '42 most of us were made captains. By this time we were all angling to get out of Panama. There was a big war going on and we didn't want to spend it nurse-maiding ships through the Canal. Fortunately for us the Corps felt the same way; they had no intention of letting a crew of young, eager captains wither on the vine in Panama. We soon received orders to report back to New River.

Then came a slight problem. There were still plenty of German submarines cruising the Caribbean, and transport back to the States wasn't that easy. We ended up aboard a PC Boat which was used for anti-U-boat work. It got us as far as Guantanamo Bay, or as the men called it, Gitmo, in Cuba. From here we fended for ourselves, hitching plane rides to the States. One way or another we all got back to Camp Lejeune where I was able to get what most of us wanted, command of a rifle company. My task was basic—namely, give the men rugged infantry training.

After several weeks of this we were told to stand by for shipment to Camp Pendleton, California. All of the troops knew this was to be the last stop before the Pacific and for the first time I became concerned about men going over the hill. I had about 230 men in my company and it was possible that some of them felt that combat against the Japanese might not be a piece of cake.

I called them together and gave them a pep talk about sunny California, with special emphasis on all the goodies they would find in Tijuana, on the Mexican border. I also informed them that we still had a lot of work to do at Pendleton before we shipped out to the islands.

Whatever I said, it must have worked. I didn't lose a single man on the train ride across the country.

When we got to Camp Pendleton, we became Able Company, 1st Battalion, 24th Marines of the newly formed 4th Division. I'd guess this was around the early summer of '43. It was to be several months before we went into action, but starting in February '44, we fought on the Marshall Islands, Saipan, Tinian, and Iwo Jima. All of this fighting happened during a little over a year's time, which is about as concentrated as combat can get.

There is one incident that occurred while we were at Camp Pendleton that concerns the son of a famous man who insisted on going into combat as an enlisted man. He paid for this act with his life and I think he should be remembered.

The story starts one night in the summer of '43. I was over at the HQ when my first sergeant called me on the phone.

"Captain," he said, "I have a young PFC here whose orders say he is to report to A Company."

"Okay, sergeant," I answered, "process him in and square him away in the morning."

"But, captain, there is something screwy about the address of his next of kin."

"Why's that, sergeant?"

"It's the White House, Washington, D.C."

As you might assume, I was a little taken back.

"Oh," I said, "well, what's the name of his next of kin?"

"Harry Hopkins, sir."

This did make things a little interesting. I decided to go to my office and have young Hopkins meet me there. His first name was Steve.

He arrived at my office and gave me the proper salute. I asked him to sit down.

"Hopkins," I said, "I see you have been in officers' training and I'm somewhat puzzled as to why you should show up here. There is no mention of your flunking out of OCS."

"No, sir," he answered, "I did not flunk out; I just got damn sick and tired of getting the needle about my having some kind of an easy job because I was Harry Hopkins's son. My dad has believed in this war since it started and so have his sons. I'm anxious to go overseas and back up what my father stands for because I stand for the same things."

"Okay, Hopkins," I told him, "we'll get you into machine guns in the morning."

Well, when we finally left San Diego, we were stationed aboard our transports until we reached the Marshalls. We had a chance to go ashore some at Honolulu but never overnight. And when you spend a long period aboard a transport, you have plenty of time to study the men you live with in such close proximity. This is what I did concerning Steve Hopkins. I wasn't trying to be fatherly, mind you; he was only a few years younger than I. I just wanted to make sure he was for real. He was.

There he was, every day, field stripping that machine gun of his, cleaning the barrel, checking the ammunition, and above all, fitting right in with his fire team. He was gung ho all right.

Well, we went into the Roi-Namur part of the Marshalls around the beginning of February. Our battalion went ashore on Namur, a small island right next to Roi—the two were practically twin islands. It seemed that there were many more Japs and pillboxes on Namur than on Roi. The Nips were dazed from the shelling, but they were fighting. And whenever you have to kill a few thousand Japanese, you always lose men yourself. One of the Marines we lost here was young Hopkins. He had kept his machine gun going right into the middle of a banzai charge until he took a bullet in his head.

Another Marine we lost was our battalion commander, Lieutenant Colonel Aquilla (Red) Dyess. I think he was from Georgia. He was killed by a sniper right at the end of the campaign. And this brings up the old story of death premonition, which would sometimes come true and other times would not.

You see, one day when we were aboard the transports, Colonel Dyess asked to see me in private. We went over to the fantail and he put a hand on my shoulder.

"Buck," he said, "I know you're a lawyer. I also know I'm going to be killed on this operation. I want you to help me make out my will."

"Oh come on, Colonel," I answered, "I'll be glad to help on your will. My fee will be your picking up the check when we have dinner after the war back in the States. You're not going to get killed."

"Thank you, Buck, but I just feel in my bones that I am going to get killed."

And, of course, he did.

Anyway, we secured the area in a day or two. Our division suffered about seven or eight hundred casualties, which would later seem a rather inexpensive fight. Remember, this was our first combat. We had a lot to learn but we did pick up some very valuable experience there at the Marshalls. We now also had first-hand experience of something that was to cause us a lot of grief on islands to come. Meaning, the Japanese did not often surrender. You had to kill them. And that was costly.

After we did our job in the Marshalls we headed for Maui in the Hawaiian Islands. This was to be our staging area for the rest of the war. It was here that we trained for both the Marianas and Iwo Jima. And we would be on Maui when the Japanese surrendered.

One of the first things we discovered when we reached Maui was that there had been a change in our landing craft. The Corps had figured that one of the worst problems the 2nd Division had experienced on Tarawa was getting their landing craft hung up on reefs. Now we had these new Alligators that were supposed to go over the reefs with no trouble. I can't remember that they gave us any trouble when we finally did go to Saipan and Tinian.

I'm not trying to put myself up as an expert but it seems to me that the invasion of Saipan that we trained so hard for was a definite turning point in the war. I understand it was the reason for the Japanese government firing Tojo as prime minister. Since the capture of Saipan was quickly followed by the seizures of Guam and Tinian, surely the Japs knew their navy was no longer able to hinder our movements or reinforce the places we would invade. I'm sure informed people in Japan knew by September of '44, before MacArthur's men invaded the Philippines, that their war was lost.

We landed on Saipan on June 15, nine days after Allied armies had invaded Normandy half a world away. Naturally, the European landing grabbed all the headlines back home; but, believe me, those first two or three weeks were just about as bad as things could be. And incidentally, it was the first time the Corps sent two full divisions into combat at the same time. The 2nd Marine Division also landed at Saipan when our 4th Division went in.

So we landed and started to move in. I can't recall that my battalion's landing was rugged, but it didn't take the Japanese artillery very long to open up. This meant that while we moved in, the beach area could be just as dangerous as the front lines. Sometime that first afternoon I received word that we had once again lost a battalion commander. His name was Lieutenant Colonel Nayard Schultz, but we called him Heinie. He was a big guy, from Detroit, I believe. He took a piece of a shrapnel in his head. It was a small sliver so it had to hit him in just the right spot to kill him.

You know, come to think of it, being a battalion commander in the 4th Division was a pretty risky job. We lost two of them, Dyess and Schultz, and our artillery regiment, the 14th Marines, lost Harry

Zimmer on Tinian. I know the division lost at least two more battalion commanders on Iwo.

That first night we dug in. I don't know how far we were from the beach, but we had made some progress. The sergeant in charge of my weapons platoon, a man named Tucker, crawled over to where I was lying to give me a report on our light machine guns and 60 millimeter mortars. The sergeant—he was from Oklahoma—had won the Navy Cross on Namur in February.

The poor guy had just started to crawl back to his platoon when he caught a full machine gun blast in his stomach. My God, was he riddled! Even today I can see him, literally cut in half. I used to wonder what the people back home thought when they saw the name of someone they knew on a KIA list. Did they think the corpse looked like the one they'd seen in a funeral parlor back home? Because if they did, they were sadly mistaken.

After the death of Tucker, none of my men moved because our people were apt to fire if they heard even a snapping twig. Tucker had definitely been killed by Japanese fire, which meant that along with their shelling we could expect more small arms fire and probably infiltration.

Well, after that first night we started to move north, and when you're moving north you always faced danger from your own artillery no matter how good they were, and our 4th Division's 14th Marines were good.

At any rate, we ran into this friendly fire one time on Saipan while going through some canefields. I immediately had some green star cluster fire shot up in the air, which was supposed to be the signal to our artillery to let up. Then I got on the phone with our battery to give them the word.

"Hey," I told them, "one of our own shells had almost taken a leg off one of my men. Will you please cease fire."

"Are you sure they're our shells?" the reply came back. "Maybe they're coming from the Nips on Tinian."

This did get to me. I had no time to get into a debate so I started to shout.

"No, no," I said, "they're ours all right. Please stop."

Then to my utter amazement the voice on the other end of the line said, "What size are they?"

"What size?" I bellowed. "Circumcise, that's what size!" Then I hung up.

I wonder what he expected me to do, go out and catch one?

Anyway, they stopped the shelling, but the Japanese didn't. The rest of the campaign seemed to be one continuing drive during the day and waiting to see what the Japanese would do at night.

As this action was going on, my main concern was Company A. What I was doing was trying to keep the lid on. I'd told the men when they went in that they had to wear their helmets. But I wouldn't put my own helmet on until I felt things were really bad. This way the men could look over at me and see how things were.

Of course, I never did put my helmet on during combat. I remember one of my men asking me after we stopped the crazy banzai attack on Tinian what I meant by things being rough. I just smiled. Naturally I was as scared as any other Marine in Company A. I just tried not to show it.

At any rate the Marines' job on Saipan was to hurt the Japanese to such an extent that they were no longer able to mount a serious counterattack. This way the Seabees could square away the airfield and our two Marine divisions could move over to Tinian. In anticipation of this move our regimental commander, Colonel Hart, called me into his tent.

"Schechter," he said, "I like the way your company operates. I'd like to have Company A lead the assault on Tinian. How would you like to go in?"

"Well, colonel," I said, "I'd like to land with my entire company in one wave. This way I'll have my riflemen, mortars and machine gunners all ashore at the same time."

"Schechter, that sounds like a good idea. I think I'll land the whole regiment in company waves."

And I believe that's the way we landed. It worked.

Now, Tinian was a good indication of one thing that so many Marines were to see on Iwo Jima. We watched our Navy lay down a tremendous barrage, but when we landed, it didn't seem as though our shelling had killed anybody. Several Japanese soldiers appeared out of nowhere to greet us with small arms fire. And, once again, that phrase called "pure luck" showed up for me.

As I waded in, I turned to give some orders to my radio operator only to see the poor guy floating in the surf. He had been hit in the head with a bullet. It was the same situation as the one I told you about earlier—you know, the flamethrower. The Japs would almost always go for the man with the visible equipment. That's the way it was.

Our main objective was, as always, the Jap airfield and we started to go after it shortly after we landed. As my company was the first one ashore, I was asked to give a priority for equipment. I expected an early counterattack from the Nips so I asked for plenty of barbed wire, which turned out to be an excellent choice.

On our second night ashore we took the barbed wire and strung it up in front of the company. I also set up two 37 millimeter guns that could fire canisters when and if the Japs came at us.

They came all right, maybe at about half past two that morning. My company was quite undersized by this time. We were protecting the left flank of the whole beachhead with about one hundred men.

It was at this time that my barbed wire became invaluable. God, did we pile those Japs up on it!

The Japs would yell "banzai" and my men would yell it right back at them, along with some choice obscenities. The most remarkable thing to me was that every single one of my men stayed put. I don't think one of them broke and ran. I was constantly circulating as best I could among these Marines, trying to keep the lid on things.

Then we did get a lucky break. The shells from those two 37 millimeters were devastating. I think the Japs came at us three different times and after their third charge, those 37s ran out of ammunition. I don't know if we could have stopped another charge without more shells.

Well, when dawn came, I could take stock of the situation. We had suffered about thirty percent casualties, which is pretty bad for one early morning battle. However, we later counted some four hundred dead Japanese soldiers in front of our lines. Some of these Nips had actually been killed in the same holes occupied by our Marines.

[Schechter received the Navy Cross for that early morning work. Characteristically, he feels it was the men of Company A, not he, who earned it.]

Anyway, as you know, the Corps doesn't give you much time to rest. The next day we started moving again and it's here I should mention Colonel Otto Lessing, who was now our battalion commander. Lessing was not only a top officer but he also had an interesting background.

His parents had separated when he was a kid. His mother was American and his father was German and an ardent Nazi. As a matter of fact, the senior Lessing was one of Hitler's top censors in Berlin. Maybe this was why Otto tried to be such an outstanding Marine.

At any rate, we had been on the go for seven days, always facing some resistance. We hadn't had any food other than our regular combat rations. I should also point out that we had run into some heavy rain. In short, things were pretty miserable.

Then I received a call from headquarters. I don't want to mention any names, but it was from a pretty high source who claimed he was interested in finding out how my men were.

"Just about all done," I told him. "Perhaps it's time to pull them out."

"Oh, we're all shot," he answered. "Why, I have a slight touch of dysentery myself."

Oh, my God, I thought, he's back there on the beach with hot rations, coffee, the whole works and he has a slight case of the runs. Tough.

"Schechter," the ranking officer continued, "I have a bet with someone over in the 2nd Division that we will take Tinian before they do."

Now I was thunderstruck. How the hell could anyone make a bet like that, playing with other people's lives? But our orders were to keep going and we did.

I won't go into details, but a little later I received orders to go into an area that meant certain disaster. I complained to Colonel Lessing, who sympathized with me, and even tried to get a hold put on the orders but was unsuccessful.

I started to execute these orders, but the first three Marines in line were immediately killed. That was enough for me. I had the three bodies put in ponchos on the back of a jeep and sent back word that I just didn't have enough clout to go any further.

Shortly after this Colonel Lessing showed up. He spotted the ponchos.

"Buck," he said, "what's that?"

"Colonel," I answered, "that's the bodies of the first three men who tried to move into the area I told you about. We just don't have to end up putting what's left of my company into ponchos because someone back on the beach is a nut."

So Colonel Lessing picked up the phone and called back to the beach. He was obviously asked how things were going where we were.

"Not so good," he said. "I'm staring at three Marines who are covered with ponchos because of that stupid order I tried to get changed. I hate waste."

That was it. In the movies Colonel Lessing would be a big hero, as he was to me, but in the real world he was relieved of his command. I don't know if he's still alive, but if he is, I'd like him to know I salute him.

Anyway, things like that happened. We also had another great guy in our battalion, Captain Cokin, who had B Company. I can't think of one thing I did during the war that Cokin didn't equal. Yet I got much more recognition than he did. So be it.

We finished up on Tinian and went back to Maui to get ready for our next assault. This turned out to be Iwo Jima, as horrible as any action in Marine Corps history.

At Maui we started to train and I mean really train. Perhaps that is why we did end up taking the place. But you could train until doomsday for a place like Iwo and you still would suffer tremendous casualties before the end of that battle.

One of the reasons for these casualties was the Japanese commander, Lieutenant General Kuribayashi. I think he knew his cause was hopeless from the beginning, but he also knew the natural defenses on Iwo were extremely formidable. He had over twenty thousand men under his command, plenty of artillery, mortars and strong fire power. His troops had several months to prepare for the attack and they had pre-registered every inch of that rock. I guess Kuribayashi figured that if his men could make the taking of Iwo bloody beyond belief, the Allies would think twice before invading Japan. This might give Japan a way of getting out of the war without unconditional surrender. Who knows?

There is one thing that is definite, though. I don't think it could have been possible to defend the island with any more tenacity than was shown by the Japanese.

By the time we assaulted Iwo, I had been made a major and was the 1st Battalion's operational officer. The battalion's commander was an Annapolis graduate named Major Paul Treitel. He was a career man and naturally resented the fact that he hadn't been made lieutenant colonel, the rank his job called for. Regular officers were always more concerned about their rank than reserve officers. After all, they meant to wear the green uniforms when the rest of us became civilians.

We went in on February 19. We weren't in the first wave, but if there was one island where that didn't matter, it was Iwo. Once we went ashore, shells started to land all around us. One of our first men killed was a major who had always been in our rear echelon. He had reached a point where he couldn't stand all his friends going into combat while he never got near the front lines. He actually begged for a combat command and finally got it. I don't think he was on the beach five minutes before he was dead. I've never stopped thinking about that. He could have stayed aboard ship at Iwo, but he just couldn't stand being out of things any longer.

Well, we started to try and move north, while the 5th Division centered on the southern end of the island around Suribachi. After the 5th had secured that southern end, they started to move north on the west coast, with our division doing the same over on the east coast. Two regiments, the 9th and 21st from the 3rd Division, also came ashore and moved north, or tried to. None of us was moving very fast. And every time we moved, you would have dead and wounded Marines. There was no escaping this.

My old Company A now had a commander who was a graduate of

the Citadel. I think he joined us on Maui just before we left for Iwo. If I'm not mistaken, he lasted two days in combat before he was killed.

Another officer from Company A was a man named Steve, who had charge of the weapons platoon. He was the strongest man I've ever seen—he had been a wrestling champion somewhere. But he wasn't strong enough to stop a shrapnel sliver from going into his brain.

That's the way it was. It really depended on the exact spot where you were located. There were so many shells coming that if you were going to survive, you just had to be lucky, that's all.

Anyway, you couldn't possibly take the casualties our battalion was suffering without consolidating your troops. We did get some replacements, but it seems to me they were getting hit at a faster clip than the original men.

A week or so after the landing we formed two companies out of what was left of the battalion. Even then these new companies were woefully understrength. I then actively took command of one of these two companies. I supposed it was called A, but what difference did that make?

Shortly after I took over A Company again, I had a chance to know for sure that I had saved another Marine's life. Something like that didn't happen often and I've always felt very good about coming through when the chance popped up. Of course I had to kill a Japanese to do it, but I guess that's what we were there for.

At this time we were moving through this volcanic ash when all of a sudden a Jap jumped out of one of those spider traps. They actually had camouflaged holes with ladders going down into them that allowed the Japs to come up quickly, fire and disappear.

I saw this Jap start to take a bead on a young Marine who was walking ahead of me. I fired my carbine without even taking proper aim and, thank goodness, I caught the Jap in the back. It all happened so fast that I didn't realize what went on until it was over. But I'll never forget it. I think that young Marine the Nip was hoping to kill made it through the campaign, and that still gives me a good feeling.

That happened around March 8. As rugged as that terrain was we did start to really move right after my quick shot at the Jap. It was then that Lieutenant Colonel Brunelli took over command of our battalion; he had been the regiment's executive officer. I can't remember if Paul Treitel was wounded or just used up. Treitel had been in command for sixteen days and very few battalion commanders lasted throughout the whole campaign.

Well, things continued pretty much the same way up until we left Iwo, trying to move north, blasting their caves, eliminating their mortars and reducing those pillboxes one by one. It didn't seem possible we could ever blast out all their mortars. I can hardly remember a day when those grotesque ashcans didn't come at us.

The end came officially on March 16, but there still was plenty of mopping up to do—there always was. Our division pulled off Iwo before the end of March and headed back to Maui to regroup for our next invasion. There were very few of us left who had originally gone ashore in the Marshalls, even though our first combat had been a little over a year before Iwo.

We never did go into action again, and thank God for that. We were the first Marine division sent back to the States, where we were deactivated. I believe this was in October '45. The years have gone by and the whole world has changed tremendously. I still frequently look back and hope I did my job as an officer. I think of the many things I did do, not on the spur of the moment but after calculated thought, that I hoped would produce a good example for the men.

For instance, I never cussed a man, officer or enlisted. I know this policy was rare, but I just didn't think you gained a man's respect by calling him a "&!@*" when he had no recourse against you. You walk into a bar and call someone a bunch of vile names and he'll probably knock your block off. So, why should you curse him just because you are his military superior? That's baloney.

Since then, the years have been good to me. I have had certain successes and honors, there's no denying that. But if anyone from Company A of the 24th reads this and says to himself, "That Buck Schechter was one hell of a good officer," well, it would make me feel pretty good.

Friendly Fire

"Jeez, I lost a young lad near Sugar Loaf," recalls David Curtin, "a beautiful kid, a real fine, decent Marine, killed by one of our tanks. He was barely eighteen, if that. It was not a case of a round falling short; it was just a freakish accident, that's all.

"This tank, you see," continued Curtin, a second lieutenant, L/3/22, "thought it had spotted a Nip target; maybe it did—and it let go with some heavy fire.

"Damn it, instead of a Jap the shell struck a real thick tree stump. The full blast of it came back and tore into this fellow's chest. I ran over to him and tried to take his dogtags out of his chest where the blast had shoved them.

" 'Oh no, Lieutenant, you ain't taking my dogtags,' he said. 'I ain't going to die.'

"Unfortunately he did die and it was a tragedy I've never forgotten. We had more men killed by accidental fire than will ever be known."

Lieutenant Curtin is correct. There will never be an accurate count of how many Marines were killed by friendly fire due to two reasons.

First, it could easily happen without anyone knowing what actually occurred. A battle is just too confusing for any kind of count of who killed whom.

Secondly, even when it was established that a Marine was accidentally killed by American fire, how would it be handled? How many officers are actually going to write the parents of a dead Marine and tell them the man was killed by his own people?

At any rate, the point is that in one way or another men were killed by friendly fire. And sometimes they were killed in bunches.

Carl Nichols was a second lieutenant in the Pioneer Battalion of the 2nd Division. He had participated in the fake landing of April 1, a landing which he claims was not known to be a fake until the invasion crafts were turned around and sent back to their transports after making a pass on Okinawa.

A short time later Nichols's Pioneer Battalion was attached to the 8th Marines for a full combat landing on Iheya, an island north of Okinawa.

"This time as we went in," remembers Carl, "our Navy seemed to be hitting that island with everything we had. When I lifted up my head, I could see several bodies lying on the beach, so I knew it was going to be rough.

"Well, as it turned out, the bodies were American Marines all right, but there wasn't any Japanese resistance at all. These Americans, and there were plenty of them, were killed by rocket fire from our Navy. Of course it wasn't intentional, just a foul-up. I guess you cannot fight a war without horrible mistakes like that."

There was another glaring tragedy that came out of my interviews that was even more crushing than the deaths from friendly fire. It concerned three Marines who were with Lieutenant Ken Cosbey.

"When I left Iwo Jima headed for Maui," recalls Ken, "I had a group of Marines under my command, or let's say my responsibility. Well, our ship was about three or four miles from Honolulu and it looked like it was going to take at least three hours to get us into port. The ship's captain decided he wanted to get his mail that was on shore so he ordered a small boat sent into the port. Three of my Marines, all of whom had fought on the Marshalls, Saipan, Tinian and Iwo with the 4th Division, asked me if they could accompany the sailor who was going in for the mail. I figured, why not; after what they'd been through, they should do anything they wanted, within reason.

"Oh, my God, their boat smashed against the side of the APA and went down. The men all got caught in a net in the water and were drowned.

"As I'm sure you know, the 4th Division never went into combat again, but just because a captain wanted his mail those three Marines were dead.

"Well," continued Ken, "as you know, I became an Episcopal priest after the war and when I give services, I pray as much for those three Marines as I do for anyone."

The 8th Marines' Mustang

Bob Stewart

If there was one thing the late John Stewart taught his four sons, it was love of country. One, George, was an Army second lieutenant in the Philippines when the war started. He was killed while a POW.

A second son, John, was wounded with the 22nd Marines on Okinawa, while son Jim worked on the Manhattan project.

Billy, the baby of the family, enlisted in the Navy shortly after the war ended.

Son Robert enlisted in the Marine Corps in 1942. After completing his Parris Island training, he became one of those awesome figures known as a drill instructor. Here he showed such outstanding leadership qualities that he was sent directly to OCS at Quantico, Virginia.

After receiving his commission, he joined the 8th Marines and fought with them on Saipan, Tinian and Okinawa. He holds two Purple Hearts.

Today, Bob is vice-president of an important advertising agency. Like so many others who for years would not talk about the war, he now expounds on it at length, particularly venting his feelings about the dropping of the atomic bombs.

"We went into Japan the latter part of August 1945," he says, "over near Nagasaki. I saw what had happened and it was horrible. But what the hell do you think that November invasion would have been? Look how tough it was to defeat the Japanese soldiers on Okinawa. And many of those were Okinawan conscripts. Do you think the Nips would not have fought as hard on their home island? After all, there were something like a million and a half Japanese soldiers in Japan proper. Can you imagine how long it would have taken to kill them all? And unless they made a complete change in their tactics, we would have been forced to kill at least ninety percent of their soldiers. God only knows how many civilians would have been killed! In turn, our American casualties would probably have equaled what we had suffered up until that point in the war.

"I have seen one of the plans we were considering for the invasion. The 2nd Marine Division was to be one of the spearheads of the attack. The plan makes no mention of the 2nd after D+4. In other words, our losses would have been so great my division would no longer have been a serviceable division after the fourth day.

"Let's face it. The bombs gave the Emperor a chance to end the war and thank God for that!

"And besides, history does not say we started the war by bombing Japan."

1ST LIEUTENANT ROBERT STEWART
C/1/8th Marines

> Now here's to Daddy Claxton
> May his name forever stand
> And always be remembered
> By the 'boes throughout the land.
> His earthly days are over
> And the curtains round him fall.
> We'll carry him home to glory
> On the Wabash Cannonball.
> —from the song, Wabash Cannonball

We had this guy in my platoon named Rich, Red Dog Rich we used to call him. He was from the mountains of western North Carolina. Red Dog had a guitar. I don't know where the hell he kept it but he was always showing up playing away on that guitar. He'd appear like magic on top of a supply truck, a tank or what have you, playing away with the "Wabash Cannonball." I never did figure out who Daddy Claxton was but I certainly did learn that song by heart. I must have heard it a thousand times.

Okay. Back to December 7, 1941. My dad and I were listening to the Redskin-Giants football game on the radio when they broke in with the news of the Japanese attack on Pearl Harbor. My father's head went back as if he'd been slapped in the face.

"Oh my God," he said. "George!" George was one of my brothers. He was a second lieutenant in the infantry with MacArthur. It didn't take much imagination to realize that if the Nips could bomb Honolulu, they sure as hell could hit the Philippines. George was eventually captured and put in a POW camp. We learned through the Red Cross that he was alive but it wasn't until after the war that we found out what had happened to him.

It seemed that when the Nips realized they were losing, they started to ship the American prisoners to Japan. The ship George was on was sunk by American bombers. The Japs had made no attempt to identify those ships as carrying a POW cargo. The American pilots undoubtedly thought they were sinking regular Japanese transports. You can't blame our pilots, what the hell, that was their job.

In the fall of '45 my father learned the War Department had placed many of the repatriated POWs from Japan in the Walter Reed Hospital in Washington, D.C. Dad then immediately went down to see what he could find out about my brother. He did locate a buddy of George's and, amazingly enough, the guy's name was also Stewart. Unfortunately, the news he gave Dad was bad.

"I was in the same prison ship with George when the planes let us have it," he told Dad. "There were only a handful of us who survived."

Then he related one of those crazy quirks of fate that seemed to happen in war.

"We all had dysentery," he said, "and the Nips had set up a big trough that hung over the side. Along with eight or nine other Americans I was sitting on the trough when the attack came. The only Americans who weren't killed were those of us on the can when the ship was hit."

I've often thought that if my brother had only been doing you know what at the time, he'd probably have survived. I guess that's the rub of the green.

Well, shortly after the war started, I went down to 90 Church Street to enlist in the Naval Air Corps. I was quite anxious to go to the Pacific and I felt going as a Navy pilot would be a pretty good way to go. I knew George was fighting for his life and this bothered me a great deal. I passed all the tests and was told to go home and await my orders. I was not, however, sworn in and this was going to be very important.

So I went home and waited and waited and waited, but still no orders came.

Finally, in the fall of '42, I said the hell with it and joined the Marine Corps. There was no waiting here. They quickly called me up and sent me down to Parris Island.

Three weeks after I'd arrived at PI, I got this official-looking envelope from the Navy Department that my mother had forwarded to me. It was my orders to report to the Naval Air Corps. I immediately showed it to one of my drill instructors, a big Polish guy from Pennsylvania.

"Christ, Stewart," he said, "I don't know what the hell to do with this. You better go see the captain."

He called up the captain and told him the story and away I went.

Incidentally, this was to be one of the very few times I talked to a commissioned officer as a boot.

I walked into the captain's office and saluted.

"Private Stewart reporting as ordered, sir," I said, just as I had been taught to do, and gave him my orders.

The captain told me to stand at ease while he read the naval orders. I'd already had my hair cut off, had blisters on my feet and was pissed off at everything in general. I was visualizing heading for Chapel Hill and those great white uniforms the Navy pilots wore. Then the captain put down my orders.

"Tell me, son," he said softly, "were you ever actually sworn into the Naval Air Corps?"

"No, sir," I answered.

"Well, my boy, I suggest you go to church every Sunday and do a lot of praying."

I didn't know what the hell he was talking about.

"Why?" I answered.

"Because you better give your soul to God. Your heart may already belong to your mother, but your ass belongs to the Marine Corps!"

Then he tore up my orders and sent me back to my platoon.

It didn't take me long to realize what he meant. If there was one thing that Parris Island did, it convinced you that your ass certainly did belong to the Corps. I didn't mind the work and the exercise but the petty crap did get under my skin.

I remember one Sunday when a group of us were standing out near the drill field. Sunday was the only time you could stand around like that. A couple of gals, about my age, walked by. They were the first women we'd seen on the island. The shock was too much for us. We all started to hoot and whistle, you know, generally making asses out of ourselves just like we were standing at the corner drugstore back home. Christ, those dolls must have gone directly to a telephone and rung the bell on us. Was there hell to pay!

Both our DIs called the whole platoon together. Then one of them —not the guy I'd given my naval orders to—let us have it.

"All right, you Romeos," he said, "all sixty-eight of you shitbirds, go into the head."

At first we didn't think this was too bad. After all, we were in regular barracks at the time and we had to keep the head spotless. If we didn't, the DIs would have kicked our ass. But as time dragged on, things became rough. There was just no room for anyone to move around. We had been told the smoking lamp was lit, so you can imagine what happened to the air. Talk about your smoke-filled room, hell, this place became the black hole of Calcutta!

Then there was, to put it politely, elimination. After we'd been there about half an hour, the urinals and thrones started to get full usage. Something was being flushed constantly. After an hour or two, this sight can really turn you off.

Finally the DI opened the door.

"All right, you idiots," he yelled, "I hope you learned your lesson. The next guy who thinks he's Errol Flynn can move his sack into the head. Now get the hell out of here before we have to fumigate the place."

We headed into our barracks figuring it was still Sunday and the DIs would leave us alone. By this time most of us are really disgusted. I was standing next to the open door, trying to get some fresh air and sounding off to one of my buddies.

"Christ," I said, "I can take anything these birds can hand out physically, but this petty chicken shit is driving me nuts!"

One of the DIs was standing next to the door and he heard everything.

"Is that so, Stewart?" I heard. "Turn out for physical drill under arms."

This DI, the one who had sent us into the shit house, was Sterling Hayden, the actor. You know what a big guy he is. But I'll be damned if I was going to let him make an ass out of me.

We went out to the parade grounds, both carrying our rifles.

"Okay, muscle man," he said, "both of us are going to start. Let's see how long you can take it!"

You know the drill, you lift your rifle up in the air, then bring it down, then you do the same thing to both sides, then start all over again. The rifle weighed about nine pounds.

We did this for, oh hell, I don't know, it felt like hours to me but I guess it was for about thirty minutes. Anyway, Hayden finally put his rifle down and started to laugh.

"Okay, Stewart, I guess you are pretty tough, but knock off being a wiseass."

Now, let me tell you something. He stopped right in the nick of time. I was beginning to feel nauseous. I think if we'd gone on just a couple of minutes longer, I would have puked all over his boondockers.

Anyway, that ordeal was over but Hayden wasn't through with me. A few days later we were told to fall out with our pith helmets on—those things Frank Buck used to wear in his movies. As I always tried to look salty, I put mine on on a slant. Hayden did not like this.

"Stewart," he bellowed, "who do you think you are, Lou Diamond? Square away that helmet." Then he pushed it down on my head as far as possible. It ended up coming down to my nose.

"There, Stewart, now you look great. And wear it like that until evening chow."

God, I felt like that little guy Benny in the comic strip. You know, the guy with the overcoat down to his shoes and the derby pulled over his ears. Everybody in the platoon thought this was hilarious, everyone but Stewart, that is.

But let me tell you something about Hayden. After I was through with boot camp, I became a DI myself. And I got to know him somewhat. Believe me, he's one hell of a man! He eventually became one of the Marines who went into Donovan's OSS unit. I know he ended up behind the German lines in Yugoslavia, which must have taken a lot of guts.

After boot camp, I stayed on Parris Island as a DI. This was good duty but not getting me to the Pacific. I did learn a hell of a lot about leadership which probably helped me get to OCS. I also met a great guy named Sinkovitz. Don't confuse him with Sinkowitz, the Georgia All American. Sinkowitz went through Parris Island in a V-12 platoon when I was a DI but was surveyed out—something to do with his feet.

Anyway, my friend Sinkovitz was also a great football player, starring at Temple University and the Pittsburgh Steelers. When I left PI for Quantico and OCS—around July '43—Frank went with me, and do you know whenever we were teamed up in any of that hand-to-hand combat training, my partner was always Frank. Could that monster cream me! I was lucky to get out of OCS alive.

Sinkovitz was also the start of what I call my Polish connection. We went separate ways after getting our commissions but from then on I seemed to be serving always with Polish-American officers. This was particularly true when I joined the 1st Battalion, 8th Marines sometime during the first part of '44.

Wow, you could have called this outfit the Polish battalion. We had John Bochynski, a football star from Temple and a guy named Kleinewski. I never could remember his first name because everyone called him Ski. He'd been one of the stars for Holy Cross in that tremendous upset of Boston College. You might remember that BC was set to have a big victory dinner that night at the Coconut Grove restaurant in Boston. They cancelled the dinner, and thank God for that. The Coconut Grove burned down that night with a huge loss of life. Ski was from Pawtucket, Rhode Island—oh Christ, was he ever! All he ever talked about was Pawtucket, Rhode Island.

Still another Polish guy was Ray Slous from Chicago. He must have played football somewhere, all these Polish guys did. I'd also served with a guy named Sebasteanski before I joined the 8th Marines. How the hell he missed our battalion I'll never know. I think he'd been one of the Seven Blocks of Granite at Fordham.

Bochynski was the one with the great sense of humor. He had a dry wit that could put you down in a second. After Saipan we'd received a lot of replacements, including a new colonel, a man named Hayward. He'd somehow been connected with Hollywood and was always telling us about his escapades with the stars. I can remember him coming out of the shower one time when Bochynski walked over to him.

"You know, colonel," John said, "I was in the movies."

"You were? When?"

"Oh, lots of times. It cost me a buck each time."

Of course John said it with a very straight face. It took the colonel a few moments to realize he was getting a needle, but when this dawned on him, he started to laugh and naturally we all broke up.

Okay, Saipan. This was my first fight and it was brutal. I don't know how it could have been any worse, at least for the 8th Marines. Many of the men told me how rugged Tarawa was, and they were certainly right, but it only lasted three days. Saipan seemed to go on and on.

The 8th Marines went into Saipan on June 15, 1944, but my group didn't go ashore until the 16th. We started in on the 15th, mind you, and that's a story in itself.

You see, my amtrac was literally picked up by a shell and knocked over on its side. Some of the men in my platoon were wounded but not that seriously. Amazingly enough, I don't think any were killed.

Now, the amtrac wasn't about to sink but there was no way to turn it over. So we all clung to that damn thing, trying to figure out what to do. Even if we could swim to shore, and it was quite a ways, we would be landing without any damn equipment whatsoever.

Then we noticed a frightening thing—the bloody amtrac was drifting away from the landing area. We started to visualize ending up in an area where there were no other Marines, just Nips. Christ, those Japs would have had us for breakfast!

Finally, after what seemed like hours, we were able to flag down an empty amtrac that had dropped its cargo off at the beach and was coming back to the ships.

Our next move was to try and scrounge some equipment. We finally got all geared up and headed back for the shore, but it wasn't until the next morning that we reached the beach where I immediately received a hell of a shock. The first dead Marine I saw was a man by the name of William Bolin. Willie the Whip we used to call him. He'd been a DI the same time I was one. For all I knew, he was still back at Parris Island. The poor guy, he looked as if he was sleeping.

That first day didn't turn out too badly, but that evening became a nightmare. The trouble was, you weren't going to wake up and realize it was all a bad dream.

Now as I've reached this point, I wonder, is it really possible to accurately describe what happened? I know it's difficult as hell for me to re-create the terror of that night so I guess it will be hard for people to believe it.

Our job was to just lie there and make sure the Japs didn't drive us back into the ocean. Hell, I don't think our perimeter was more than three hundred yards deep. The enemy's guns were on the back side of a ridge, set up in such a way that it was hard as hell for our naval support to hit them. The Japs could let us have it at will. All you could do was hope one of their shells didn't have your name on it.

Even now, thirty-five, forty years later, the more unreal it becomes. There you are, curled up in a foxhole, absolutely helpless. One would come over and it doesn't hit you, but you hear somebody scream. "Christ Almighty," you say to yourself, "who got that one? It sounded like so and so." Of course, you have this moment of relief, knowing it's not you, but what the hell, it was probably a friend of yours. And, you knew there'd be another one coming soon. Every moment you keep saying to yourself, "The sons of bitches are going to get me; they're going to get me—when, when, when are they going to get me—which one, which one?"

Then one comes over that you know is going to be close.

"Here I go," you say, "here I go, oh sweet Jesus, here I go!"

You'd only get a real sense of relief when the Japs would fire short. There was an area called Lake Suppie between us and the Japs. Lake, hell, it was just a big swamp. When one of their shells would land there, you'd either hear a muffled explosion or a thud. You knew they'd wasted one.

"Please, dear God," you'd say, "let them blow the hell out of that fuckin' swamp." But most of the time they didn't fall short.

My turn finally came at about four in the morning. It wasn't a hit right on my foxhole, but it couldn't have been too far away because a piece of shrapnel lodged in my side. It bled for quite a while but I figured it wasn't going to kill me.

The shelling eased at dawn and a corpsman came and patched me up. If we hadn't taken such a beating, they probably would have evacuated me, but our battalion had lost so heavily, particularly officers, that I just had to stay.

My sergeant, a man named Fink, wasn't so fortunate. He'd been hit by some kind of phosphorus shell. I'm sure he never knew what hit him—the poor guy was burned to a crisp. He was a perfect example of our helplessness. He was not only a great guy but one hell of a Marine. If knowing what to do would have made any difference —and plenty of times it did—he probably would have made it. But in a situation like the one we were in, all the training and knowledge in the world didn't mean a thing. It was just plain luck, good or bad.

Now I'll tell you about something that just happened last year. I'd been taking annual chest X-rays for years, all negative. On my last one the doctor told me to take a complete scan. A day or two after the examination he called me on the phone.

"Bob," he said, "were you ever shot?"

"No," I told him, "but I was twice hit by shrapnel."

"Once under your right arm."

"Yes, on Saipan."

"Well, a part of that baby is still there. It's about the size of a pea. Does it bother you?"

"Not a bit."

"I can take it out if you want me to."

"If it stays, can it kill me?"

"Hell no!"

I thought about it for a minute and decided to leave it in. I figured someday it might set off the alarm during the screening you take before you board a plane. Think what fun it'll be to tell the guard— not to worry, it's just my shrapnel from Saipan!

After that night of horror, we broke through and started going north, heading for Mount Tapotchau. Sometimes we'd move so fast we'd run out of essentials, especially food and water.

There was one night—I think it was while we were on the top of Tapotchau—we had no water at all and were also short of chow. Some Seabees who were on Saipan for construction work, not to fight, volunteered to lug the stuff up to us.

They get to the top, puffing like hell. There were maybe ten or eleven of these guys, not a one under forty, and I swear one of them must have been in his mid-fifties.

Just as they get to us, the Japs opened up with mortars then some of them tried to infiltrate our lines. It was no big deal; we didn't lose any men, but it did get rather hot for a while. It was all over by the time dawn came. You should have seen these middle-aged Seabees then. I mean, they were real combat veterans now. I'd love to hear the stories that flew around after they got back to their unit. Don't get me wrong, the Seabees did a great job out there and there were times when they were called on to fight, but fighting wasn't what they were there for. I did get a huge kick out of listening to them that morning though; you'd have thought they'd won the war.

Now, I don't want to take any shots at other American outfits. What the hell, guys were fighting and getting killed everywhere. But there was an Army unit on our right that didn't move anywhere as fast as we did. Perhaps their tactics didn't call for them to move that quickly. Whatever, we started to get some fire from American artillery. This type of thing happened more than our people liked to admit. Sometimes the Marines got it from their own artillery, but not this time. These shells were from the U.S. Army.

At any rate, one morning it was my turn to have the lead platoon. I was talking to our colonel, a great guy from Georgia. The colonel had his arm on my shoulder and was pointing to the area he wanted me to cover when some shells started to fall short. One of them landed near the colonel's radio operator. There was hardly enough left of the poor guy to bury.

Then another one landed a few feet over to my right. I received a shot to my jaw just as if someone had hung one on me. I was stunned for a moment. Then, as I began to get back with it, I couldn't figure out what had happened. Hell, it was a big shell. I should have been blown sky high.

Do you know, the damn thing was a dud! What had hit me was a flying piece of coral that had been dislodged when the shell hit the ground. How lucky can you get? That's why I never play the New York State Lottery. I figure I've used up all my luck.

Well, we kept moving north. A few days after we'd crossed Mount Tapotchau, one of our men made a startling discovery. The guy came across a huge supply of Japanese money. We thought this was a big hoot. All this funny money. Guys are lighting cigarettes with the bills, wiping their you know what with it—all the things you could think of to give everyone a laugh.

As it turned out, the laugh was on us. After the war ended we went to Japan. That darn gook scratch, as we called it, was legit. We could have lived like millionaires in Japan. Oh well, what are you going to do . . .

Anyway, after a while they sent us back to a rest area. We were there only a couple of days when the Nips pulled a massive banzai charge against an Army battalion. They threw three or four thousand troops against our lines, including everything they had, even their wounded.

Now when you throw that many men at a position, particularly if the men are willing to die, you are bound to break through somewhere. Part of the Jap charge even broke into the 10th Marines, our artillery; but remember, every Marine is first trained as a rifleman. They succeeded in stopping those Nips cold. We were called back to help in mopping up, which was a real nasty job because they weren't about to surrender. We had to kill just about every one of them.

After that operation the Marines and the Army pretty much put the lid down on the Japs even though, as always, it would take months to hunt down all of them. Naturally we expected a long rest period.

Baloney! We got the word that the 2nd and 4th Marine Divisions were to move over to Tinian, about four or five miles southwest of Saipan. This is always called the perfect campaign, but I know our battalion suffered a good many casualties here, not as many as on Saipan, but enough.

The big thing for me was taking the airstrip that was used by the Enola Gay when it dropped the Big Bombs in '45. After the war I saw a film showing the Gay taking off for that raid. I couldn't help but say to myself, "Hey, Stewart, you helped take that airfield and you were almost killed doing it." Let me explain.

I was standing on the outskirts of the field, talking to Red Dog, you know, the guy who had the guitar. Incidentally, that same Red Dog was a hell of a Marine.

Well, as we started to move closer to the airstrip, I started to tell Red Dog where I wanted his squad—he was a corporal and squad leader—to deploy. I had my arm on his shoulder when a Jap sniper zeroed in on us. Just as I turned my head to look in the other direction, a slug came between the two of us. It hit the field glasses I had on the top of my pack, knocking the hell out of them. If the bullet had been an inch or two either way, it would have nailed either Red Dog or me. Between that and the dud on Saipan, I guess the man upstairs was looking after me. Come to think of it, He must have been looking out for all of us who lived through those rugged island campaigns.

Two days later I did get hit. I picked up shrapnel in both my legs. One of our corpsmen patched me up but, damn it, I still get floored by cellulitis—you know, the same thing Mickey Mantle had. All that over a few pieces of shrapnel.

They sent me to a field hospital for a week or so. My platoon was then taken over by a nice guy named McGuire. The poor guy was killed the day before I rejoined the outfit. Of course I probably wouldn't have been in the exact same spot he was in when he was hit, but I felt pretty lousy about someone taking my place and then getting killed.

Shortly after I got back to my company, the Americans hoisted the flag in Tinian town and stated the battle was over. So, all the people back in the States are reading about the invasion being over and my company is fighting its fool head off every day.

Then they gave us a bummer. They took the whole 2nd Division back to Saipan, the whole division *except* the 1st Battalion, 8th Marines—my battalion. We had to stay put and keep going out on those damn patrols, which had become a real pain in the ass.

This leads me into my real disaster on Tinian which, I may add, did not come from the Nips; it came from a fellow officer. I was lucky I didn't end up in the Portsmouth Naval Prison.

After things tapered off some, they started to get an officers' liquor ration into the island. We had to pay for it, but it was dirt cheap. The reason it became so dear to us was its scarcity, not its cost.

They put up a special tent where we would keep this booze, each bottle having the owner's name written on it. You just didn't drink another guy's liquor unless he gave it to you, period.

I went over to the tent one night, really needing a couple of belts. There is a new officer in our company there with a buddy of his, not from our company, and they've just about killed off my bourbon. The stranger was a captain but that didn't stop me. Maybe I'd been in the field too long, I don't know, but I really blew my top.

"Who the hell told you guys you could drink my whiskey?" I yelled.

You know, if they'd been apologetic, I probably would have cooled off, but they turned arrogant as hell.

"Take it easy, lieutenant," the captain says, "you're talking to your superior officer. Stand at attention."

That cut it! I don't really recall what happened next, but I soon realized I was standing up and the captain was on his ass.

Now there's hell to pay. Oh, the SOB is going to send me to the salt mines. A lieutenant just cannot go around cold cocking captains. Fortunately for me our colonel, the Hollywood guy, Hayward, was really a square shooter. He just marked it down that I was suffering from battle fatigue, which may have been correct, but he did give me the word.

"Stewart, there is absolutely no sense in throwing the book at you. But don't get any grand ideas. You will have to end up with a few shit details. I see you graduated from Pace College. Perhaps you could do some graduate work. Stand by."

The next thing I hear, the word comes down from headquarters that we have to send one officer to Troop Transport Quartermaster School over on Saipan. Of course it's Stewart who goes. This is the pits! You're living in transient officers' quarters. You have to dress in uniform each day but you can't get your laundry done and to top it off, the work is boring as hell.

So I finished the school and went back to Tinian. By now the fighting was pretty much over and I figured on resting up some, like the rest of the battalion. What a dreamer I was!

The next thing I hear is the battalion has to send an officer to Fire Marshal School. Of course it's Stewart. Back I go to Saipan and some more crap. Believe me, I'm beginning to wish I hadn't clocked the booze stealers.

After I became a bona fide fire marshal, I once again returned to Tinian only to be told to get my ass back to Saipan for Chemical Warfare School. Christ, by the time I finished that course I must have had more specialty spec numbers in my file than any other lieutenant in the Corps.

The final blow occurred when I once again returned to Tinian and got called up to Hayward.

"Stewart," he said, "or should I call you professor? No more school for you. You are hereby made censorship officer. You can read all the letters written by the men until we move into action again."

Then he took out the charges against me for striking a superior officer and tore them up.

"Bob," he said, "this will not appear on your record." And it didn't.

Well, the next move for the 2nd Division was to Okinawa and a very strange job for our outfit. The 2nd had fought on Guadalcanal —our three infantry regiments had anyway—Tarawa, Saipan and Tinian. It wasn't to be quite that way on Okie. My regiment, the 8th, was the only part of the division that actually saw combat on Okinawa.

We headed for shore on April Fools' Day, but it was a fake. I was told our job was to make the Japanese think we were the main landing while the 1st and 6th Divisions made the real landing. We never knew if it made any difference or not.

My regiment finally went into combat the second week in June. The other two Marine divisions had been fighting for weeks where we went in—the southern end of the island—and had sustained horrendous casualties. I think it was a shot in the arm for them to have a fresh regiment move in.

Our initial position was about four miles from a beach area that our people had under control. But the Nips were still there in force covering those four miles. Then came a typical Marine order.

"Your food, water and other additional supplies are on the beach. Go get them."

If we didn't get through those four miles, no food or water. We made it all right, but lost some great guys doing it.

One of these KIAs was an officer named Sneider who had been an outstanding pitcher at college. During the several months between the fighting on the Marianas and Okinawa we had set up battalion baseball teams. Sneider would pitch on the officers' team and then when the enlisted men's team played another battalion, he'd put on a dungaree jacket with sergeant's stripes and pitch for them. I don't think he lost a game. What a great guy!

Anyway, we left Okinawa sometime in July and headed back to Saipan. Wow, when I arrived there, the first thing I heard was that my brother John, who had joined the Corps at the end of '43, had been wounded on Okinawa and was in the hospital on Guam. John, a PFC, is ten years older than I am. The last thing I'd heard was that he had been boxing kids ten or fifteen years younger than he on Parris Island.

At any rate, I had no trouble bumming a flight from Saipan to Guam. I'd picked up a couple of bottles of Old Crow. Brother John may have been a PFC, but he was about to break a bottle or two with a newly made first lieutenant.

When the plane landed on Guam, I ran into some luck. One of the first men I spotted was a Texan named Stone Quillian. Stone had gone through Quantico with me. When I told him why I was on Guam, he smiled.

"Bobby, ole buddy," he said, "I'm going to take good care of you. I'm now Major General so-and-so's aide. The good general has left the island for a while. I don't know why, maybe he's got a little something going somewhere. His jeep and his driver are doing nothing. He'll be glad to pick you up tomorrow and drive you to the hospital and if your brother is ambulatory, you'll both get a tour of the island."

What a deal! The next morning the general's driver showed up bright and early and we drove to the hospital. Brother John had been hit in the leg but by now was in pretty good shape. The three of us drove all over Guam, constantly whacking that Old Crow as we proceeded. We had a great day.

Our driver dropped us off back at the hospital around six o'clock in the evening. It was hot as hell so John and I just sat there with what was left of the Old Crow, looking out at the ocean and chewing the fat. I had stripped down to just my khaki pants and skivvy shirt.

The first thing we knew it was ten o'clock. Then the old battle axe of a nurse spotted us.

"What the hell are you two doing here? Get into your sacks or I'll put you on report."

I figured this was as good a place as any to bed down so, what the hell, I stood at attention and answered, "Yes, ma'am."

The next morning I got over to the airfield and bummed a ride back to my outfit. During the flight I kept thinking how great it had been to see my brother and what a great guy he was. John is about seventy now and, hell, if they wanted him to go again, he'd be ready. He's a real gung ho American.

One of the things we'd talked a great deal about was the coming invasion of Japan. We knew we'd be in it and the chances of us both coming out of it were not good. We didn't know if brother George was alive or dead but we realized he'd probably never come home.

Hell, our parents could easily lose three sons before the war was over.

It all became academic a few weeks later when the Enola Gay took off for Japan. The 2nd Division did go to Japan but without a shot being fired and thank God for that.

When we did go ashore, it was under full battle conditions minus a bombardment. All our weapons were at the ready. We set up our perimeter, dug our foxhole and waited.

We were attacked the next day all right, by hordes of Japanese kids crawling all over our machine guns. We fought them off with chocolate bars. We felt a little foolish, but the kids had a great time. I remember one of our men, a real hard-nosed guy, shaking his head.

"Christ," he said, "they're just like the kids back home. Why the hell did we have to have a war?"

You know, he was right. The next time there's a lot of saber rattling maybe we should get the kids together on both sides and let them play a game. Presto—no war! There's good and bad in all people. You can't change that.

A good example of this was the two POW camps we took over near Omuta. They were like night and day.

The first one was run by a professor from the University of Tokyo. He made sure that the sanitary conditions were excellent and that the prisoners got all their rations and any Red Cross packages that came through. To top this off, he even bought oranges and sugar for the prisoners out of his own pocket. The poor guy went broke doing it, but there are undoubtedly people alive today because of him.

The other camp was brutal, a real atrocity camp. The prisoners were forced to work in the mines. Christ, many of them hardly ever saw the light of day. They had to go in those mines seven days a week.

Outside of those mines they had a statue of a Japanese miner. Early each morning the prisoners had to bow toward the statue before going down into the shaft. Naturally the statue became a symbol of hatred to the prisoners.

Boy, did we take care of that detail shortly after we arrived. We gathered as many Japanese who had helped run the camp as we could and made them watch us blow that statue sky high. That was the end of that.

There was a bright side though. We found out from the prisoners that if it hadn't been for the Nip peasants who also worked in the mines, many of the Allied prisoners—and there were Americans, English, Dutch, just about every nationality there—would have starved to death. These Jap workers would always try to bring an extra ball of rice down into the mines with them. They could see that the prisoners were hungry as hell and they'd do their best to get them food.

We also knew how to handle that one. We found a large warehouse full of rice. We lined up all the Jap miners we could find. Then we unlocked the warehouse door and told those miners to go to it. It was quite a sight to see.

Then there was a double cross on the double cross. It seemed that in China the Japanese instituted a policy of paying any Chinese soldier a certain sum of money if he would come over to the Nips and bring a serviceable weapon with him. So, some three thousand Chinese came in at one clip and turned over their weapons. The Nips then paid them off.

After the Chinese were paid, they promptly nabbed them as POWs, took the money back and shipped them over to Japan to work in the mines.

Well, how do we treat these Chinese soldiers who are now yelling like hell about being Allied soldiers and, above all, want the money back the Japs had taken from them? It was quite a foul-up, believe me.

The Chinese had a leader named Chang who had once worked as a cook in Brooklyn. He was the only Chinese who could speak English. Just to shut him up we made the Japanese give him a lot of money to distribute among the other Chinese soldiers.

Then Chang takes off with the money. Fortunately, we caught up with that bandit and made him give the money to the other Chinese soldiers. Our instructions were that the Chinese should then buy new uniforms so they could stand guard duty. In turn we'd feed them. It all ended all right, but what a pain in the butt the whole thing was.

In the meantime we'd taken over a hotel run by a Japanese who was small even for a Nip. I'd say he was about 4'2".

Anyway, we told him the U.S. Government would pay for everything and we'd just sign for it. He thinks this is great and is running around bowing a mile a minute.

God, you should have seen some of the signatures: Barney Google, John Dillinger, Dick Tracy, Charlie McCarthy—it was great!

There was, however, another business this little guy ran that was cash and carry and he dealt only in real good-looking young things. To top it off his name actually sounded like "nukie bookie," which went over great with the men. We had a special armband made for him with the big letters "NUKIE BOOKIE" on it. He used to love to bounce around and and point to his armband saying, "Me NUKIE BOOKIE, me NUKIE BOOKIE."

He was a shrewdie though. He made sure all his best ladies were made available for the Marines. There was one in particular who looked like a little doll. She was strictly for the Americans. What we didn't know was she was trying to feed her parents and also put enough money aside so she could marry her Japanese boyfriend.

Well, it didn't take her too long once we arrived to get her dowry. When the wedding day arrived, half our company showed up. All the men knew she'd be going out of business, but they wanted to give her a great send-off.

Now in case anyone is revolted by this, let them remember that the U.S. has never been bombed out of its gourd and then been occupied by foreign troops. Things can be pretty rough.

Well, we left Japan in time to arrive in San Diego on New Year's Eve. We had been the first Marines to go to Japan so I guess we were there about four months. And to tell you the truth, most of us had a great time. No real problems at all.

There's one thing more that happened there that may tell you something. It occurred on November 10, the Marine Corps's birthday. As you know, if at all possible on that date, the Corps furnishes the troops a turkey.

Well, they got us a real big bird there in Japan, it must have weighed twenty-five pounds. I don't think most of the Japanese had ever seen a turkey. They had chickens, most of which were scrawny as hell, but I don't think they had many turkeys, if any.

So, our cook is making a big deal out of cleaning that turkey in front of a large crowd of Japanese. Finally, he picks the turkey up and waves it at the Japanese.

"This is an American chicken, you idiots," he says, "and that's why we won the war!"

One of the Nips translates this for the crowd, which is followed by choruses of "Ah so, Ah so."

When you come right down to it, that's as good a reason as any.

The Young Marine Remembers—II

The Young Marine had never been on a horse in his life. So, when his platoon went on mess duty and the mess sergeant asked if any of the men had ever done horseback riding, he did not respond. The first three men who claimed they were expert riders were put on special duty—they had to clean the stove. The YM learned a great lesson—never volunteer.

Luck plays a big part in the life of any Marine. The YM's stay at boot camp was loaded with it, both good and bad. At boot camp he stood second in line for both the tenth and fortieth day inspections. The man on his right was asked to detail field strip his M-1 rifle, while the man on the YM's left was asked to detail the nomenclature of the rifle's trigger housing group. This was on the tenth day inspection. The same two boots received equally difficult questions on the fortieth day inspection.

Not the YM. He was in the middle. On both days he was asked to name the date of the Marine Corps's birthday.

"November 10, 1775," he answered correctly both times.

Then he shuddered when he thought of detail field stripping the M-1.

There was a slop chute in Newport, Rhode Island, called the Blue Moon Cafe. It was a great hangout for swabbies and Marines.

It happened that there was a rather sensuous waitress whom the Young Marine had designs upon.

After a few trips to the watering hole, where he had tried to make points with this beauty, the Young Marine made his move.

"How about a bite to eat after the Blue Moon closes?" he asked.

"Like hell," she answered, "I don't half-mast my skivvy drawers for no bellhop!"

Oh well, thought the YM, you can't win 'em all.

The Young Marine had a stretch of guard duty at the Camp Pendleton stockade. The brig was under the command of a gunner with about twenty years in the Corps, including a long stretch in China.

It came to pass that a newly arrived prisoner—charged with a long stay over the hill—had served in China with the gunner. The prisoner was only a PFC due to a long list of foul-ups.

When the gunner first saw the incarcerated Marine, the prisoner smiled at him:

"Ding Hao, Gunner," he said.

"Ding Hao, shit," came the reply. "I've got more time in China than you got in the Corps. Butt out!"

The Young Marine had scored. The young lady was no beauty, but not that bad, pretty face, a little chunky, maybe about 150 pounds. But when the normal eighteen year old spends all week in a barracks, weekends are apt to be dominated by unrelenting lust.

The lady in question was living with her sister, so they could not go to her apartment. For the first time in his life the YM registered at a hotel as Mr. and Mrs. The desk clerk smiled and gave the young man the key.

As the YM and his "wife" started for the elevator, the "Missus" made a request.

"Honey," she said, "could you pick me up a pack of cigarettes?"

"Sure, sweetheart," the YM replied. "What brand do you smoke?"

The desk clerk went into hysterics.

On a hot day on Guam in August 1945 the YM had no thoughts of peace. As a matter of fact, he had snickered at breakfast when a fellow Marine had said:

"Golden Gate in forty-eight

Breadline in forty-nine."

The YM felt anyone who thought he'd survive the coming invasion of Japan was quite an optimist.

Then came the big news. The Army had dropped a bomb on Japan that had destroyed a city. Everyone seemed to believe this might end the war. There was no thought of the poor Japanese civilians. They could blow up the whole island as far as the YM was concerned. He wasn't going to have to hit Japan with an M-1 rifle in his hands. Thank God for that!

The Milwaukee Kid

Jim Doyle

Jim Doyle was just shy of fifteen when the Japanese bombed Pearl Harbor. With what he calls the innocence of youth, he couldn't wait until his seventeenth birthday so he could join the Marine Corps.

"It was a different world then," he recalls. "Everybody I knew wanted to go."

Jim fought on Guam as a rifleman and on Iwo Jima as a radio operator. He was wounded on Iwo, half his right thumb and the complete first finger on the same hand were amputated.

He is currently a vice-president of the Emery Air Freight Company.

Recently, Jim had an occasion to visit the Marine Corps base at Quantico, Virginia. While there he went to the PX. He noticed they were selling neckties with the 3rd Marine Division insignia. He tried to buy one.

"May I see your ID card?" the girl behind the counter asked.

"Oh, I'm a civilian," he answered, "but I was on Guam and Iwo Jima with the 3rd a long time ago."

"I'm sorry, sir," the girl said, "but we're only allowed to sell to active duty people."

As she said this to Mr. Doyle, she kept looking out the window at two salty Marine sergeants.

Jim took the hint. He went over to the sergeants and gave them his story. One of them just smiled, took Jim's money and went into the PX to buy him the tie.

"Jeez," said Jim, "they both looked like an old China hand I knew on Iwo. Only their names change in the Corps, you know.

"Anyway, I thanked the sergeant graciously for doing me the favor, but he just shrugged his shoulders."

"Look, mate," he said, "remember one thing about the Corps; we take care of our own."

PFC JAMES DOYLE
Signal Company
3rd Marine Division

> "When my son joined the Army Reserve, I asked him why he
> didn't pick the Marines.
> " 'Hell, Dad,' " he said to me, 'living with you, I feel as if I've
> already done my twenty years in the Corps.' "

With a name like Doyle, my ancestry is obviously Irish. There used
to be quite an Irish colony in my hometown of Milwaukee when I was
growing up, probably still is. Both Pat O'Brien and Spencer Tracy,
the actors, came from this bunch.

There were also very large Polish and German groups in the city.
Allen Bradley, one of Wisconsin's largest manufacturers, has a huge
clock on the top of his main building. It's supposed to be modeled
after Big Ben in London. In Milwaukee they call it Big Stash. It was
in this Polish area on the south side of the city where I grew up. I
was known as Doylinski in those days.

Politically, it seems to me, those Polish-Americans limited their
politics to the corner taverns. And these politics were aimed more
at strengthening their unions than at anything else. The city's other
large ethnic group, the German-Americans, were a little different,
being much more set up in a political way.

These German-American bunds were very large organizations indeed. You were always seeing posters on telephone poles, and the
like, announcing their coming meetings, meetings, I may add, that
drew huge crowds. I wouldn't say that these bunds were overly
pro-Hitler—even though there must have been some Nazis in them
—but I do think they were quite in favor of America keeping its nose
out of Europe's problems. I do remember a large strike at Allis
Chalmers in 1940 or '41. There was talk at the time of Chalmers
furnishing war materiel to Great Britain. I don't know if this had
anything to do with the strike or not. But I do know that after Pearl
Harbor Milwaukee became one hell of a pro-American city, the same
as it had been in World War I.

My dad had gone to France in 1918 with the 32nd Division, which
was made up of the Wisconsin and Michigan National Guard. He told
me that his outfit was loaded with first- and second-generation German-Americans who did a great job fighting against the Kaiser's
Kultur. It was the same in 1941. Milwaukee went to war with a vengeance.

Well, December 7, 1941, was on my sister's confirmation day. The
whole family went to the service and returned home with our hearts

full of religion. My father turned on the radio and, oh my God, how things changed! Dad was livid. Mother started to sob. I was only fourteen years of age and probably couldn't fathom the depth of what was going on. Hell, I didn't even know where Pearl Harbor was. All I knew was that we were at war. It was all as exciting as hell!

The country was in absolutely no danger of being bombed, but we didn't know this at the time. Dad became an air raid warden. I was a Boy Scout and part of our task was to make sure that no one had a light showing after dark. Of course it was all ridiculous, particularly in mid-America, but it was going on all over the country.

As the months wore on, the urgency of protecting ourselves against a bombing attack started to peter out. By 1943 I was faced with the ordeal of watching all my friends a year or two older go off to war. Jeez, it was awful! I began to develop this haunting fear that the war would be over before I could go. I feel like an idiot telling you this now, but, darn it, the world was different in '43. Many sixteen-year-old kids felt that way.

Toward the end of '43 I was in my junior year at the local seminary —that's right, I was hoping to become a priest. But more and more I just couldn't concentrate on my studies.

Then I had a real traumatic experience. You know how kids are. You are apt to idolize the football heroes a few years older than you are. We had this guy in Milwaukee named Phil Mushovich. He was three or four years older than I. What a football star he was. Wow!

Well, word came back to Milwaukee that Phil had been killed in action. I was stunned. However, rather than impressing me with the stark realities of war, it made me want to go more than ever.

That December one of the priests called me into his office.

"Jim," he said, "I see you have signed up for Greek next term."

"That's right, Father," I answered.

"Well, son," he continued, "you are now the only junior in the school who hasn't passed ninth grade Latin as yet. How do you think you can tackle Greek?"

He had me cold. I couldn't really answer.

Then he went on:

"Jim," he said very softly, "have you ever thought that God hasn't called you?"

This was not as cold-hearted as it sounds. He was really trying to let me down gently.

Then he put a great big smile on his face.

"James, my boy, why the deuce don't you join the Marine Corps? That's what you really want to do."

That cut it. I was going to be seventeen very shortly, so I went home and told my parents what the priest had said. Mother was very upset, but I think my father was secretly quite proud. He had tried to get back into the service but had been turned down. Anyway, they both signed my enlistment papers and on March 15, the old income tax day, I boarded a train for the San Diego recruit depot and began my growing up.

When the train reached Chicago, I found that I had a five- to six-hour delay. I'd teamed up with a twenty-two-year-old guy who was also heading for boot camp. He suggested that we go to a burlesque show. I'd never been to one but I'd heard they had some great comics. I'd loved that type of thing ever since I'd done the old Smith and Dale Dr. Cronkite skit in a school play. Remember, this was back in the days when the skin part of the show was not as raunchy as it is now. The comics were great and I've been hooked on good burlesque ever since.

Well, it took us about three days to reach San Diego, but when we did arrive, we knew the place was all Marine Corps. It was the biggest place I'd ever seen. We saw this platoon, drilling and doing the manual under arms. They were really on the ball, snappy as hell. I was in awe.

It didn't take us long to realize that we were the lowest form of animal life on the base. Our platoon number was 646. One of the theories about boot camp is that you spend almost every minute with your platoon. This way you learn to work as a unit. Our two drill instructors, Sergeant Pratt and Corporal Vogel, made sure we did just that.

We'd break out at 5:00 A.M. for the formation each morning except Sunday. At this point you'd be freezing your ass off. By noon you'd be roasting. And if anyone screwed off, Pratt would yell out:

"The whole platoon, high port around the parade grounds."

So we'd put our rifles over our heads and start out at double time. We wouldn't stop until Pratt said to stop.

Vogel's specialty was drill. He was a little guy, about 5'6" or so. He'd been hit on the Canal so he had a stiff leg. But he knew how to call that cadence. I think we learned how to drill as well as any other platoon at San Diego.

Our DIs also knew all the little tricks that made life tedious. Some eight-ball would foul up so each boot had to run down to the ocean and fill his bucket with sand. We then returned to our tents and spread the sand on the deck. Then we'd do the same thing, but this time we'd bring back salt water. The final step was to really scrub that deck. What a pain in the ass!

Then there was the guy who called his rifle a gun. That was truly a sacrilege in the Corps. The poor guy had to stand outside his tent with his rifle in one hand and his gun, if you know what I mean, in the other. Over and over again he had to repeat:

"This is my rifle.

This is my gun.

My rifle's for doing;

My gun is for fun."

My turn came after we'd been boots for about five weeks. None of us had even spoken to a woman since we'd arrived. Pratt had the platoon at parade rest and was giving us one of those long-assed lectures of his when I spied this BAM (Woman Reserve Marine—also called Beautiful American Marine or Broad-Ass Marine—take your pick) waltzing down the parade grounds. She had this cute little fanny and did she know how to twist it! My eyes kept following her until she disappeared out of sight. My eyes then returned to Pratt; he was waiting for me.

"Losing your power of concentration, Doyle? My, my, that's bad, boy. Could cost lives in combat."

At five o'clock that evening he had a special detail for me. I was to double-time back and forth through the BAM's area with my rifle at high port, yelling, "I'm an idiot; I'm an idiot!" And I was to keep this up until told to stop.

The women must have been alerted because they were all standing around waiting for me. And how those ladies gave me the business! Everyone enjoyed it except Jimmy Doyle. I guess it was just my turn to be in the barrel. Pratt tried to make sure that each one of us got a little special attention at one time or another.

My moment of glory at boot camp came during our stay at the rifle range. This was the two or three weeks when you really lived with your rifle, and I mean really lived with it. You studied it, took it apart and put it back together blindfolded, snapped in with it (dry run rifle fire practice without any bullets, from every position, done by the hour) and finally fired for record with it.

When the record day rolled around, I was pretty nervous. We'd been told that if we didn't qualify, we'd go to Cooks and Bakers School. As I look back now, I realize that it wouldn't have been bad duty, but when you're seventeen years of age and there is a big war going on, you sure as hell don't want to spend it in a mess hall. The innocence of youth, I guess.

Anyway, my first clip was a bummer. Hell, I think I even had a Maggie's Drawers (completely miss the target with one round). Then I spotted Pratt.

"For Christ's sake, Doyle," he yelled, "check your windage and elevation."

I did what he told me to and he was right; they were all off. I squared them away and then I got hot. I believe I ended up with 320 out of 340, which is expert in anybody's league.

Then the big day came. We were no longer shitbirds. Now we were Marines. When they gave us the globe and anchor to put on our piss cutters (also called cunt hat, overseas cap and garrison cap) and our green blouses, well, sir, we thought we could lick Napoleon's Grand Army.

Our whole platoon was now slated for a ten-day leave, but it wasn't set to start for a few days. While we were waiting for our leave to start, we were free to go on liberty into San Diego. So, a buddy and I took off to see the town. Naturally I wanted to head for a burlesque show. We soon found one. While inside the theater, I had an experience that I think perfectly demonstrates how naive a young lad could be in 1944 compared to the youth of today.

We were sitting about ten rows back from the stage when I noticed that this civilian sitting next to me was rubbing my leg. I told my buddy what was going on, so he said:

"Here, let's change seats."

Apparently the civilian started to do the same thing to my friend. My buddy picked the guy out of his seat and let him have one right in the jaw. Then my friend said:

"Let's get the hell out of here."

After we went outside, I got curious.

"What the hell is wrong with that guy?" I asked.

"Why, he's a fairy," I was told.

Hell, a fairy to me was a little thing with gossamer wings. Then my buddy gave me a detailed explanation of what a homosexual actually was. Do you know that I didn't really know? Things were sure a lot different forty years ago than they are now.

Two days later we received our ten-day leaves and I once again had a chance to see America from a railroad car window. Between the trip from San Diego to Milwaukee and my return to Camp Pendleton in Oceanside, California, I ended up spending seven of my ten days leave on a train. This is not recommended.

Be that as it may, shortly after I arrived at Pendleton, I was put to work helping to build what they called "Little Tokyo." What a job that was! I never worked so damn hard in all my life!

At the same time, we were trying to take advanced infantry training. Jeez, all week long, work, work, work. Occasionally we could dash down to San Diego and once we made it to Los Angeles, but basically we worked our ass off. There was a saying going around that went like this:

"Don't bother bitching to the chaplain. He's had so many complaints, he's gone over the hill."

Things just didn't get any better. Finally, one of my buddies got in a shouting match with a platoon sergeant. We were on a real shit detail at the time, so three of us backed our mate to the hilt. Then a top sergeant got into the act.

"Listen, you clowns," he roared, "shut up or the four of you are going overseas pronto."

"Hell, Top," one of us answered, "you're not big enough to send us overseas."

Christ, the top blew a fuse.

"Not big enough, huh?" he said. "We'll see about that!"

Two days later the four of us boarded the *Alcoa Patriot,* one of Kaiser's coffins, headed for Honolulu. A week or so later we landed in Pearl Harbor, not really a member of any units, just casuals, I guess. I never did know who was in charge.

I spent five days there, not knowing what was going on. I did manage to sneak into Pearl one night and headed for Motor Street. I had been told they had a good burlesque show there. So when I saw this long line, I got into it. They had two squawk boxes hooked up on the side of some building with this pitchman giving a spiel.

"This is what you've been fighting for, boys—beautiful girls—this is what you want!"

I have nothing against beautiful girls, believe me, but I was hoping they'd also have some comics.

I asked the guy in front of me when the next show started.

"What next show?" he answered. "This ain't no burlesque; it's a cathouse. The broads ain't much, but they're as good as any on the island."

I was in a state of shock. My desires are quite normal, but mechanical sex is for someone with less morals than Jim Doyle. So I went over to a place called the Edgewater Beach Hotel for a drink. They took one look at my ID card and sent me packing. As you might gather, Pearl Harbor was a real bust for me. I headed back to the *Alcoa Patriot,* pretty much down in the dumps.

A few days later the ship shoved off. I still didn't know where the hell I was going or what outfit I was in. I did know if we kept going west, we were bound to find the war. We found it on an island that the Army and Marines had invaded about three weeks before we arrived. It was Guam. It was supposed to be just about secured.

Now, I've never been able to know just what they meant when they said an island was secured. The big problem was no one bothered to tell the Japanese. I do know that thousands of them were waiting in the hills, the jungles and the caves for us to come and get them. This was to be my job for the first five or six weeks I was on the island.

After we had landed, they lined up most of the riflemen from the transport, gave us combat gear and put us in units of the 3rd Division. We were to go where needed to help flush the Japs out. It was called "going on an island sweep."

My first such jaunt turned into a real confrontation. My question has always been, "Who found whom?" I've always felt they were waiting for us.

We were moving up this hill when all of a sudden we heard a lot of firing. Someone yelled for us to hit the deck, so we all went down. Another guy then yelled out:

"They're over there, the other side of that ridge."

It really hadn't sunk in to me that those other people were shooting at us. I stood up to see if I could find out just what the Japanese looked like.

"Get down, yuh fool," someone blared out, "you'll draw more fire!"

He was right. No sooner was I down than the Nips opened up again. Now the thing became personal. For the first time I realized that the people over on the ridge wanted to kill me. Hell, I didn't even know them. It was a weird feeling.

That's the way it went for the next five or six weeks. We moved from place to place, usually in trucks, always looking for Japs. We'd toss explosive satchels into caves, then seal them off, fire up into trees, the jungle, anywhere where we thought Japs were holed up. I can't tell you how many times I fired my M-1 during these sweeps, but it must have been a lot. However, I never once knew if I hit anyone. That's the way it was.

Several of the Japs did surrender—not nearly as many as we hoped would—but they did come in in lots of twos and threes. Others stuck hand grenades in their guts and pulled the pin. I've never really understood why they did that. I guess it was part of their culture.

Then, sometime in October, I found out that the Marine Corps did realize I was alive. I got the word to report to a radio school they were setting up over near the airport. This was a great break for me. My father had been a signalman in France during 1918. He had a short-wave set up in our attic. I became quite accustomed to listening to Morse code and could identify many of the characters. They called the place the Caribou School. I heard the caribou is the symbolic animal of Guam. To me a caribou is an Alaskan deer up there with Dan McGrew. Heaven knows what it has to do with Guam.

So I ended up assigned to a signal company, which is what you call in the Corps "fat duty." By the time I left the school, I had become quite good in both receiving and sending code.

The only pain in the neck detail we had was when we pulled guard duty. One of these details made me unequivocally realize there is a hell of a lot of difference between the officers and the peons. I believe it happened on November 10, 1944, the 169th birthday of the Marine Corps.

It seems a group of officers decided to have a party at the Officers' Club that night. Naturally the bash had to be guarded. I was picked for part of the patrolling detail. Up until that time I hadn't seen any American women on the island, but the brass showed up with a slew of them. I guess they were nurses.

We were outside with our M-1s, trying to walk our posts in a military manner and we could hear all this singing, laughing and clinking of ice cubes. It was frustrating as hell.

After the party had gone on for two or three hours, we noticed some of the officers sneaking off to the beach, always with one of the lovelies in tow. It was dark by this time. When I say lovelies, remember, I hadn't seen an American woman in months. They may have looked like Powerful Katrinka, but they were lovelies to us.

Anyway, we were really boiling by now. I remember one of our group letting out with a dirty laugh.

"I think there may be some hanky-panky going on down at the beach," he said. "Besides, most of the officers are probably half-bombed by now. I know one of the guys working at the club. I'll bet I can get us a bottle or two."

"Good luck," we said, "our hearts go with you."

Jeez, about a half an hour later he came back with three bottles of Scotch. We had our own little party. No nurses, mind you, they were officers' stuff, but we had a hell of a time.

You see, liquor was always a big thing among the enlisted men, maybe because we knew the officers could frequently get it and we couldn't.

Take the time when a guy in my tent got two cans of grapefruit juice in the mail from his father.

"For Christ's sakes," he moaned, "if there is one thing we're up to our ears in on this lousy island it's grapefruit juice!"

He took the two cans and threw them into the jungle.

"Let the Japs have 'em," he yelled.

About a week later he got a letter from his sister.

"Wasn't that ingenious of dad," she wrote, "drilling a hole in those grapefruit juice cans, pouring in bourbon, soldering in the hole and sending them on to you?"

"Mother of God!" the guy roared, and took off into the jungle. He was in luck—it was pure Jack Daniels, and he shared the cans.

You know, it's funny how such little details like that can come back, but frequently the rough stuff isn't that easy to remember.

Take the time we wanted to get some coconuts. This young Guamanian—hell, he was probably as old as I was—was walking by.

I went over to him, flashing a quarter.

"See," I said, "one quarter? You climb tree, see, get-um *co-co-nuts*, see."

"Screw you, buddy!" he answered. "I won't do it for less than a dollar."

I didn't stop to think that the Guamanian natives were American citizens. They had been taught English in their schools before the Japanese had come. Most of them looked upon themselves as very proud Americans. They'd had it real rough under the Japs and to them we were liberators. They told us they knew Uncle Sam would come back some day and throw the little brown men out. They treated us royally, particularly with the pig roasts.

When the Japanese had first come to Guam, the natives had turned most of their pigs loose in the jungle so the Nips wouldn't get them. These hogs had reverted to the wild stage and multiplied like rabbits. A couple of times we actually went on boar hunts. We'd bring the pigs back to the islanders and they'd prepare a feast fit for a king. They'd make a pit with the coals on the bottom. Then they'd put the pig in the pit and throw in sweet potatoes, pineapple, any number of good things. What a delicacy! They always had this drink called tupa to go with it. It came from the top of the coconut trees and had this milky-white juice—something like white honey. When properly treated by the natives, it had a ferociously high alcoholic content. In other words, it would knock you on your ass, but what a beautiful way to go!

Don't think we weren't working at the same time though. Hour after hour we'd transcribe messages from Pearl Harbor. We'd also go out in the field with the troops. The 3rd Division was gearing up for its next campaign. This is when the training really intensified. We knew our next shot would be closer to Japan and we weren't expecting any rose garden. This was a good thing because we sure as hell didn't get one.

Now, one way you could tell an outfit was getting close to combat was the increase in church attendance. I started going to every service I could, no matter what the denomination. I'd never been to a Jewish service so when I heard that a rabbi was going to officiate at our little thatched-roofed chapel, I decided to attend. I sat right in the front row. I was really quite impressed.

When the service was over, the rabbi asked me to join him in the tent they'd put aside for the clergy. He was a naval officer so I dutifully complied. He sat me down and started to give me the eagle eye.

"Young man," he said, "I watched you at my service. You are obviously not Jewish. I'm curious. Why did you attend?"

"Well, sir," I answered, "the way I look at it, we all believe in the same God. I figured I could get to Him while praying with you as well as any other way."

"I'll be darned," he replied, "Well, a nice gentile boy like you deserves a drink."

He reached into his footlocker and broke out a bottle of Scotch. We spent a very pleasant half hour or so before he had to take off. We discussed everything under the sun. I've often wondered if that rabbi realized how much I appreciated the whole thing. What a guy!

Well, the campaign we had been training for turned out to be Iwo Jima, which came as a big surprise to me. Right up until the invasion I thought it would be Formosa. Scuttlebutt always ran rampant in the Pacific, especially when you were headed for a beachhead. I've always felt the brass started these rumors just to confuse the troops. I'd never heard of Iwo until the day we went in.

I moved from Guam to Iwo on APA 44. This was a Navy ship which was a lot better than the Merchant Marine one I'd gone to Guam on. I've been told this was usually the case. The Navy seemed to treat the Marines much better than the Merchant Marine did.

The day of the landing was February 19, 1945. We'd been told that it wasn't going to be rugged because the Navy had been shelling the place for something like sixty-eight straight days. Our division, the 3rd, was to be held in reserve just in case it was needed. My signal group, however, would probably go in that first day to support the 4th and 5th Marine Divisions. Some members of the divisional band were going in with us to act as litter bearers. These litter bearers, I may add, were heavily armed. Somehow it just didn't look to me like it was going to be a snap campaign.

We headed for the beach in LCVPs, frequently called by the troops "Landing Craft, Very Pregnant." The closer we came to Iwo the worse it looked. Crippled landing craft, discarded equipment and yes, dead bodies gave testimony to the fact that Iwo was a very hot spot indeed. Then one of our Weasels took a direct hit. This was a small amphibious craft that was self-propelled in the water. It looked something like a tank. The one that was clobbered was the one that we had stored extra rations and some beer in.

The minute we hit the beach I headed for our designated spot. I couldn't move very fast because I was lugging an SCR radio. Wham! Right off the bat, a Jap sniper put a slug in the radio. I jumped into a hole already occupied by a Marine sergeant. I figured the radio was ruined so I got ready to toss it when the sergeant grabbed my arm.

"What's the matter, kid, don't you know that's government property? Give it to an old China Marine."

Then the guy started to fiddle around with the radio. Bullet hole or no bullet hole, he got the damn thing going. He must have been a valorous SOB because he immediately stuck up the radio's long aerial which started to make me nervous.

"Jeez, Sarge, pull the aerial down; it'll draw more fire."

The sergeant just laughed. "Take it easy on your first cruise, son. If you're going to get it, you're going to get it; that's all there is to it."

I spent my first night on Iwo right there on the beach. Hell, there was nowhere else to go. We were supposed to set up a command post at the airport nearest Suribachi. They called it Motoyama number one.

In the meantime, my friend, the old sergeant, had taken off. I never saw him again, but I sure hope he made it through the campaign. He probably did; those old salts were tremendous survivors.

Another one of those China Marines had given me some great advice before I left Guam when he told me to buy several condoms.

"You stick your extra socks, skivvies, cigarettes, anything you want to keep dry in them skins," he told me. "Smartest thing you can do."

How right he was!

Of course the sailor working in the PX thought I was crazy.

"Where do yuh think you're going, Marine," he asked, "to the liberation of Paris? You're some optimist!"

Well, after that first night the days and nights seemed to run together. The 5th Division was moving to isolate Suribachi by cutting off the southern end of the island. This way they could also take the airfield. We were to move in right after them and we did.

Now, there is one thing to remember about Iwo. While we had taken the airfield, that doesn't mean it wasn't under fire. There was constant pressure on it from artillery, mortars and snipers. When we first had to cross that damn field, everyone was running but me. The damn radio weighed so much I just couldn't move fast. I tried to pretend I was strolling down the street in Milwaukee on a Sunday afternoon. I didn't get a scratch.

The Seabees arrived at about the same time we did to work on the landing strip with their bulldozers. They knew they'd be fair game for the snipers while driving the machines. So, one of them would set a straight course for the machine, start it up and jump into a hole. When it reached the point where it was to stop, another Seabee would jump out, stop the machine and send it back the same way. This probably saved some lives, but it sure looked funny seeing a bulldozer moving around on that airfield with no driver.

The important thing is those Seabees got the airfield shipshape in no time at all. The first thing you knew American planes were on Motoyama I long before the battle was over.

This brings up a great story, the type of tale that always floats around any campaign. You never know if it's true or not, but who cares?

It seems that one of our early B-29s to land on Iwo came limping in. It had been shot up pretty badly over Japan and would have undoubtedly ended up in the Pacific Ocean if it hadn't been for the capture of Motoyama I.

After the plane landed, out steps this flyboy type with the white scarf, goggles, the whole bit. At the same time a group of exhausted Marine riflemen were walking by. They'd been on the lines for several days and were really beat. The flyer greets them with a sarcastic chuckle.

"Hi there, fellows," he said, "the Air Corps is here; you lads can go home now."

One of the riflemen calmly puts down his rifle, takes off his helmet and pack, walks over to the flyer and cold cocks him with one punch. Then he walks back to his gear, picks it up and goes on. He didn't say a word. How the boys loved that tale!

I spent five days at the airfield, then I was switched to another outfit. You see, they were moving the radio people where they were most needed throughout the fight. In this new lashup I had a radio jeep that was used for air-to-ground liaison. We had both a receiver and a sender. We'd get the coordinates from the forward observers and send them to the planes. Other times, we'd send them to an artillery command post.

During most of this time you were vulnerable to Jap fire of one kind or another. The thing we feared the most was a Jap mortar attack. We caught a vicious barrage from their mortars one night that was just about as bad as it could be and I didn't even know it.

Physically, at the time, I was bordering on sheer exhaustion. I'd had it. I'd lain down next to the jeep on the side facing away from the Nips. No sooner had I shut my eyes than I was out like a light.

I woke up a little after dawn and looked around. What a disaster! Broken equipment everywhere. Several men hit. And the jeep, well, the side facing the Japs was pulverized. The radio was beyond recognition. A buddy of mine came over to see how things were. He shook his head.

"Jim," he asked, "how the hell did you live through that?"

"I don't know. I slept through the whole thing."

"You what? You mean you didn't hear a damn thing?"

"Not a thing!"

"Jesus H. Christ!"

Shortly after that night I joined still another group over near Mottoyama II, the second airfield. Here I was to help in laying and repairing telephone line. The problem was we'd sometimes get lost. Remember, the lines were not like World War I trenches. It was very easy to find yourself over on what was really still Japanese real estate. This is exactly what happened to us around the 10th of March.

At the time we were trying to extend our telephone coverage. Shortly before dark we spotted an empty pillbox. We figured this would be an ideal spot to put up our switchboard. So, we set the thing up and called back our position.

"Oh, my God," we were told, "you're behind the Nip lines. Don't try to come back tonight. Our own men will probably blast you. Stay in a hole. We should reach you sometime tomorrow." So we burrowed in for the night.

The next morning this guy in our outfit moved out a ways to do what most people do in the morning. He had picked up a Colt revolver somewhere and he wore it slung low on his hips, western style. Suddenly, we heard several shots. Then our buddy came running back.

"Godalmighty," he yelled, "I was all set to drop my dungarees when this Jap appeared out of nowhere. I guess he was out to do the same thing as I was because he looked as startled as I must have when he spotted me. He had just put his rifle down. He started to pick it up when I pulled out my Colt. Thank God it worked! I kept firing low because the Colt pulls up on me. The Jap went down and I hauled ass. Christ, it was just like the movies!"

A little later in the day we moved back to our own people who were moving toward us. Fortunately there was no mistaken identity concerning us. Apparently the Marines had been given the word.

But, you know, that episode was not unusual. Iwo Jima is a small island. The Japs had taken months to fortify their positions. It wasn't unusual at all to have them on all sides of you.

Well, around the middle of March things started to quiet down some. I think the place was secured on the 20th. Anyway, we were slated to leave on the 27th.

Would you believe it? On the night of the 26th a Jap snuck into our area and tossed a grenade at me. I guess it was another case where no one bothered to tell the guy the battle was over.

I caught part of it in my chest, but that was superficial. It was my right hand that really was clobbered. My right pointing finger and half of my right thumb suffered what they call traumatic amputation. It is one strange sight to look down and see two bleeding stumps on your right hand—really strange.

There were plenty of corpsmen around who immediately went to work on me. Then I was flown to San Francisco with long stopovers at Guam and Pearl Harbor. The doctors spent months working on the rest of my hand and what I have left is in pretty good shape. All in all, I guess I was pretty lucky. The Marines suffered close to six thousand dead on that lousy rock so I can't really complain. But if I was going to lose a couple of fingers, I would have been just as happy if it had happened my first night on the island instead of the last.

One more thing—a few years ago I took my lovely wife on a vacation to Pearl Harbor. We walked over to Motor Street. The buildings were still standing even though they were quite decrepit and deserted. One of the squawk boxes was still hanging by a wire. Then we went over to the Edgewater Beach Hotel. It is now quite a luxurious place. I ordered a drink and they served me. I guess they figured I was now old enough.

The Enemy

When Dick Bennett first heard of the Japanese attack, his immediate reaction was, "Where the hell is Pearl Harbor?" His mother probably did not know where Pearl Harbor was either, but on the night of December 7, 1941, she cried. She had three sons and had correctly surmised they would all go into the service. Two of them, Dick and his younger brother, Gordon, were seventeen when they joined the Corps.

"Come to think of it," Dick will tell you today, "not only was I unaware of Pearl Harbor's location, the only Japanese I'd ever seen was a little creep who used to stand outside of Stoughton's Drugstore, in my hometown of West Hartford, Connecticut, and demonstrate yo-yos. This Nip was a marvel; he could wrap that yo-yo around his head. Several of us discussed that little guy the next day and we all came to the conclusion he was a spy.

"Most of my friends," Dick goes on, "were hardly impressed with the Japanese; we all thought initially America could handle them easily, once we got going.

"But the night before I was to leave for Parris Island, my family had most of the neighbors over for a gathering. At this time we had an elderly retired Army colonel living next door with the magnificent name of George Washington England.

"Shortly before our party broke up, he pulled me aside.

" 'Dickie,' " he said, " 'I saw those Japanese troops when we went to the relief of Peking during the Boxer Rebellion. They are disciplined as the devil and tougher than a cob. Watch out for them!'"

Dick was to see how tough these Japanese were on Okinawa.

His feelings were quite common in the U.S. when the war started. To most Americans, on the East Coast anyway, the Nips were short, buck-toothed little fellows, always bowing and saying, "So solly, so solly." Of course, since they all wore horn-rimmed glasses, they could not possibly shoot straight.

Also, Peter Lorre's portrayal of detective Mr. Moto (Japanese) couldn't compare to Warner Oland's Charlie Chan. Even Chan's number one son could outfox Moto. This was the feeling at the beginning of the war. The Americans were completely in the dark concerning their new enemy.

In reality, Japan had been basically on a war footing since 1931, when they started to fight in Manchuria. Emperor Hirohito had tremendous spiritual power but rarely used it. The civilian government had on occasions tried to thwart the military, but could never succeed. A political assassination in Japan was not uncommon and it was done with brutal thoroughness.

A squad of soldiers would surround the house of the intended victim. Then the actual murderers would simply go inside the home and execute the doomed fellow. There was no major country in the world whose military had greater control than Japan.

The Japanese did, however, have one weakness. This was a total commitment to their spiritual beliefs and their own invincibility. The Anglo-Saxon powers didn't have the stomach for a long drawn-out war. As the Americans had greatly underestimated their Oriental enemy, the Japanese greatly underestimated the Americans.

One of the Japanese leaders who did not share the belief of so many of his countrymen was Admiral Isoroku Yamamoto. He had spent too many years in the United States not to realize how the American people would react to a war with Japan.

But even the prestige of Yamamoto could not curb the power of the Japanese military. Yamamoto could talk forever about the might of Detroit and Pittsburgh but his words fell on deaf ears.

Knowing this, Yamamoto sponsored the Pearl Harbor attack. He was banking on a sweeping victory and hoping for a short war in which both sides would give a little at the peace treaty table but where America would recognize the dominant position of Japan in Asia.

It wasn't to be. In spite of the discipline that time and again found the Japanese hurling themselves against the American troops, and a willingness to die on the part of the kamikaze pilots, the old adage that says, "A good little guy can't beat a good big guy," held true.

The Tank Man from Yale

Prate Stack

Whenever I get the blues I look at my white shoes.
—Old college song

Lee Prather Stack, Jr., was one of a great many young men attending a prestigious college who opted for the Marine Corps after the attack on Pearl Harbor. Prate was a junior at Yale when the war came. He immediately joined a Marine Corps unit that allowed him to finish his college education before entering active duty.

A tall young man—6'3" was a lot taller in 1943 than it is today—and athletically inclined, Stack easily adapted to the physical aspects of Marine life. His first ten months of active duty were just about as pleasant as they could be.

One of the reasons for this cheerful duty was the fact Prate came from a family that in 1944 would be called "well-heeled." During his duty in California he had a new Buick at his disposal for weekend liberties. It's hard to imagine this tall, well-turned out Marine officer driving that Buick on the West Coast without a young lovely on the seat beside him.

Then the time came for Stack, as he puts it, to pay the price for wearing the uniform. He went ashore on the first day at Peleliu in command of a tank platoon. By the time his outfit landed on Okinawa, he had become an intelligence officer in the 1st Tank Battalion. Toward the end of that grueling campaign he received a devastating leg wound from which he would never fully recover.

"It took me twenty-three years of operations to get my leg as good as it is now," he says. "It can't get any better, but what the hell, I can play eighteen holes of respectable golf without a cart and at sixty years of age I have no desire to go mountain climbing."

LEE P. (PRATE) STACK, JR.
1st Lieutenant, 1st Tank Battalion
1st Marine Division

I was probably one of the last to hear about the Pearl Harbor attack. I was a member of the Yale Dramatic Club at the time. We never received as much publicity as Harvard's Hasty Pudding, but we always felt we were as good if not better than they.

Anyway, we were about to go on tour for the first time over the 1941 Christmas holiday. We had locked ourselves in one of the Yale halls on December 7 for a hard-working rehearsal on a show called *Waterbury Tales*. It was a takeoff on Chaucer's *Canterbury Tales*, I guess. That evening, maybe around eight or so, some guy came running into the hall.

"Jesus Christ," he yelled, "haven't you heard the news? The goddamn Japs have bombed Pearl Harbor. I don't know where the hell that is, but we're at war."

Do you know, not a one of us could tell him where Pearl Harbor was. Can you believe that? Here is a group of young so-called scholars, attending one of the great universities in this country, and none of us knew the location of our country's main naval base in the Pacific. The East Coast just wasn't oriented toward the Pacific.

The next day things started to really hop at New Haven. Everyone was talking about the same thing—what the hell each guy was going to do. I was in my junior year and already a member of the Naval ROTC. But my brother Steve, a year behind me at Yale, decided to join the Marine Corps and so did my roommate, a guy named Jack Tilliey. The two of them talked me into switching over to the Corps. Besides, the Marine program allowed you to finish college before going on active duty. I figured there'd be plenty of war left by the spring of '43—it wasn't going anywhere in a hurry—and I was right.

Yale, I may add, was a tremendous place to be that first year of the war. You know, weekends in New York City, meeting some lovely under the clock at the Biltmore, those great jazz bands on Fifty-second Street and, of course, the football games at New Haven. I was a member of Chi Psi Fraternity and we had great times. I don't think the country really got drab until the first part of 1943. By that time casualty reports were beginning to show up and you really knew you were at war.

One other thing that made New Haven great then was the Glenn Miller Band. We had a large Army Air Corps group at Yale so they based Miller's Air Corps Band there. Can you imagine being at college and listening to those great musicians all the time? "Chattanooga Choo Choo," "Tuxedo Junction," "In the Mood," "American Patrol." It was tremendous.

It all ended in June 1943 when both my brother and I got the word to report to Parris Island on July 14, which happens to be both my birthday and Bastille Day. I was lucky my parents didn't name me Napoleon or something crazy like that.

Well, you know the old expression, "Be sure and get off on the right foot." Unfortunately that's exactly what Steve and I didn't do.

Here's what happened. My father had loved railroads all his life, he knew all about them. He was even on the boards of directors of a couple of them. He felt that riding on a government ticket could get pretty crummy south of Washington, D.C., and he was right. All the college guys headed for the officers' candidate platoon that we were going to be in found this out the hard way—all of them except the Stack boys, that is.

Dad insisted we have private accommodations on a Pullman train that would get us down there a little ahead of the regular group. He even wired ahead saying when we would arrive. The only problem was the other train was on time and we were late.

Oh Christ, we stepped off the train, dressed in seersucker jackets, button-down shirts, striped ties and, of course, white shoes. The rest of our bunch, the ones who had been on the cattle cars, and a very irate Marine sergeant were waiting for us. We both felt about two feet high.

Our crushed feelings did not impress the sergeant one bit. He was fuming.

"I've already got what is undoubtedly the dumbest bunch of college bastards who will ever come to Parris Island," he snarled, "and now I have a couple of big-time clowns like you two. You college guys are a swift pain in the ass."

Naturally he's got the whole crew very concerned and Stack and Stack are about as popular as Billy Graham in a cathouse. Then the old sarge let go a beauty that relaxed everyone.

"Besides," he yells, "you know what college does to you morons; it makes you more stupider, that's what!"

Well, you didn't have to be an English major to know this guy was something else.

So we started our training and one of the first things we had to learn was to use nautical terms. Most of us knew what they were, but we'd never called the ground in an open field a deck or the wall in a wooden barracks a bulkhead. It could get confusing as hell at first and sometimes hilarious.

Take the new platoon in the barracks next to ours. Similar to our own setup, their back door had wooden stairs leading up to the second floor. I can't remember if we had to call the doors latches or not, but I don't think it became that absurd.

Anyway, we did call the stairs ladders. One morning their DI was standing right outside the barracks. He yelled for the platoon to hit the ladder. You know the old routine: "Assholes and heels and I don't want to see them very long."

Now, they did have a fire ladder, I mean a real ladder, leading to the roof inside the barracks and the predictable happened. Before the DI could stop them, half his platoon is out on the roof trying to stand at attention. The DI was livid. He made those poor bastards go up and down the ladder / stairs for the next hour. I will say one thing, those men knew what he meant the next time the DI told them to hit the ladder.

Back to my own platoon. I still don't know what one of our DIs was trying to prove, but he seemed to get huge joy out of pitting me and my brother against each other. The first time he did this I was amazed. I was coming out of the head when he collared me.

"Stack," he whispered, "your brother just told me you were chicken shit. Tomorrow I'm going to match you two up against each other for some hand-to-hand stuff."

Well, damn it, my brother and I have always been rather close, even for brothers. Naturally I went over to Steve and asked him what was going on.

"Prate," he laughed, "I was going to ask you the same thing. That idiot just told me you said I was a big yellow baboon."

So now we knew what our DI was up to even if we didn't know why. We gave our platoon a good show the next day, but we would have done that anyway. See that scar on my lip? Steve gave me that a week or so later in bayonet drill. We weren't going to learn anything by playing games so we really went at it. But whenever it was one-on-one, it was always Stack against Stack.

There is one more thing I'd like to say about Parris Island and that concerns a great football player from Georgia named Frank Sinkowitz. I say this because I think he got a bum rap. Okay, he wasn't very modest, but why should he be? He was just about the best football player in the country at the time.

All American or not, the guy had flat feet—hell, they were flat as a board. Maybe that helped him with his balance when he was running. Maybe he could easily put all his cleats on the ground at the same time, I don't know. But I do know his feet were pure misery after an all-day hike with full marching gear on his back. He was eventually surveyed out of the Corps. The scuttlebutt was that the Corps wanted to get rid of him but that was baloney. The poor guy had real flat feet, that's all.

Another guy in my platoon was James Whitmore, the actor. I knew him from school days. I'd played football against him when he was at Choate and I was at Pomfret. He's got a peculiar kind of build; I think he's bowlegged. We called him "Alley Oop" after that prehistoric cartoon character who used to be in the funnies. I never did hear what happened to him after boot camp.

Our platoon's next move after Parris Island was to Quantico, Virginia, where we were to have three more months of training as PFCs. It was during this time that several of the men did flunk out. After all, it wasn't cast in stone that we had to get commissions. It was no snap course, I'll tell you that.

One thing above all that they pushed at Quantico was decision-making. They'd try and set up as many situations as possible where you'd be forced to act under extreme tension. I guess they wanted to see how each guy would react. If you couldn't take pressure when you got into combat, it would be too late to do anything about it. Your mistakes could not only cost your life but those of the men serving under you.

After three months of OCS we got our commissions, which also meant a new life. We still worked just as hard but had about every weekend off. This meant some great liberty in Washington, D.C., for the next three months.

So on my first trip to the nation's capital I reserved a double room each weekend for the next three months. I told the hotel my wife would be joining me each weekend. Of course I was a bachelor at the time, but I didn't want any nosy clerk poking into my affairs. My room was always registered under Mr. and Mrs.

Do you have any idea how many unescorted young damsels were floating around Washington at that time? Why, a one-legged man with BO and bad breath could have made out there. And I mean there were some real good-looking dolls, not dogs. It was a bachelor's dream.

One of my favorites was a real stylish lady who worked for American Airlines. Her job was handling the priorities for the flights. If you put in for a flight, you'd get a rating from one to four, depending on how important they felt your trip was—the higher the rating the better your shot at getting aboard.

At any rate, my friend let me in on a little trade secret. They also had a fifth rating, which was unofficial. It was called PF, meaning personal friend.

Here's what it meant. If you had some clout, you could usually get someone a PF rating, which meant they were almost certain of getting into Washington. That's how they kept a supply of exciting young beauties coming into town. After all, we had to keep our hard-working politicians relaxed, didn't we? They liked variety.

Well, these great weekends ended, or at least had a change of scenery late in February 1944, when I was ordered to report to Camp Elliott. I was assigned to, of all things, a tank battalion. This really surprised me as I'm not exactly the most mechanically minded man in the world. I did a little nosing around and found out why they put me in tanks. The reason was really something.

It seemed that when I enlisted, I had filled out a rather lengthy questionnaire. One of the questions concerning experience asked you to put a check mark next to each of the following vehicles you had driven. One of the listed vehicles was a tractor. Hell, I'd driven one at a summer camp when I was about fifteen years old, so I checked tractor. And that's why I ended up a tank man.

At any rate I soon turned to and tried to do the best job I could. It wasn't that I had much trouble in the mechanical end; it was just that such things bored me.

Bored or not, I reported to the tank farm, as they called it, near Camp Elliott, which is over by San Diego. We were situated back in a rock canyon. The Sherman medium tanks were just beginning to arrive, but we trained on nothing but light tanks. I didn't get a chance to work with any of the Shermans until I got overseas. Come to think of it, I never could figure out why they called the Shermans medium tanks; I never saw any bigger one while I was in the service.

In any case, we had three tanks to a platoon and five men to a tank. Then you also had servicemen attached to each platoon. We had the G.M. diesels, which were damn good motors.

Of course, you were cramped as hell in the tanks. I wouldn't recommend this duty to anyone who suffers from claustrophobia. And could it get hot! Jesus, there was one time later on, at Peleliu, when the thermometer reached well over a hundred degrees outside the tank. Then our blower went out of kilter. God knows what the temperature became inside. I knew we'd soon start passing out so I stopped the tank and had us all crap out until we could get things straightened out. Oh, it could be miserable all right.

I spent about three months in California and managed once again to pull some great liberty. My family knew a retired admiral who lived nearby in La Jolla. He had two new Buicks but very little gas, while I had no car but the tank farm had plenty of gas. I used to borrow one of his cars each weekend, always returning it on Sunday night with a full tank. Can you imagine what it was like driving up and down that West Coast in 1944 in a new Buick? I was not exactly the loneliest guy in California. I knew it couldn't last forever, but I was in no hurry to take off for the Pacific.

Sometime in the spring of 1944 it all ended when I received my orders for the Pacific. I ended up in charge of a replacement battalion and that's a story in itself. They placed me in command of what was called a casual company. I thought this was a little odd, what the hell, I was only a second lieutenant. Command of a company called for a captain and there were plenty of them around.

Remembering that great rule for a good officer—get to know your men—I started to ask these guys where they'd come from.

The first four or five had the same answer.

"They pulled me out of the brig to put me on board."

One of them even tried to pull my leg. "Didn't you see me come aboard with leg irons and handcuffs on? I was the guy who had the guard with the carbine walking behind me."

He was giving me a load of crap, a real wiseass, but it did seem to be true about my men having been in the stockade. Hell, here was Lee Prather Stack, an officer and a gentleman, by act of Congress, setting forth to fight for his country and I'm in command of a company of brig rats. Do you know something, I got along famously with them, particularly with a group that had come from Michigan, which was a story in itself.

A whole crew of men had joined up together in Hamtramck, a Polish-American district outside of Detroit. Somehow they'd ended up in a big hassle in San Diego and most of them landed in the brig. They had a natural leader with them named Bogard and once you had his trust, you were all set with the rest of them. They were one tough bunch of cookies. More about them later.

Well, the ship we were on was a newly commissioned Army transport manned by the Coast Guard. Among the crowded troops were Marines, soldiers and sailors, and what a mess it was, particularly the chow lines.

Fortunately for everyone, we had a no-nonsense Marine colonel aboard who knew what was going on. He went to the ship's captain with a proposition.

"Look," he told him, "we've got some great cooks in our group. We'll put them to work in your galley if we can also put some Marine MPs on guard at the chow lines."

Okay. The captain went along with the deal and the whole situation cleared up at once. There were complaints from some of the wise guys in the line who ended up with a club stuck up their rear ends, but it sure as hell worked.

We did have one more problem on our trip. Somewhere out in the Pacific our engines just plain stopped. I mean they stopped producing any power at all. This was around the middle of May, 1944, and there were plenty of Japanese submarines in operation. We just sat there dead in the water for about twenty-four hours. I can assure you every guy on that ship was on pins and needles.

We finally got under way to the relief of everyone and a day or two later pulled into Noumea on New Caledonia. We stayed here a few days after which the Marines boarded another ship for transport to our staging area on Guadalcanal.

While I never did get to see any of New Caledonia, I heard a great story about the famous Pink House, renowned throughout the Pacific. You see, there was very little chance for contact with any women in the Pacific, particularly if you were an enlisted guy. The Pink House was an exception. Of course you had to pay; the Pink House was a bordello, or in plainer words, a cathouse.

It never lacked for customers. As a matter of fact, you had to stand in line. When you reached the head of the line, a very corpulent madame would be waiting. You had to whip it out and if it wasn't already standing at attention, you had to go to the back of the line. It seemed that many of the men had been whacking off just before getting in line so they could last longer when it was their turn. The madame wanted no part of this foolishness.

So be it. It seemed we no sooner reached New Caledonia when we were off again. I can't remember when we reached Guadalcanal, but I'd say around the first part of June. Here I still had my company of brig rats and they really came through for me.

In such a situation you are supposed to keep all hands busy, you know, idle hands mischief makes and all that crap. So I took my stalwarts out on some kind of foolish exercise. Jesus, every officer who drove by us had his own jeep. This finally got to me.

"Christ, every officer on this goddamn island has his own jeep but me," I shouted, more or less to myself.

About two o'clock the next morning I was awakened by a gentle voice. Remember, an enlisted man cannot lay his hands on an officer, so this bird can't shake me.

"Lieutenant, lieutenant," I heard, "we have a present for you."

I looked up and it was my friend from Hamtramck.

"Bogard, what in the hell do you want?"

"Would the lieutenant please step outside with me? You don't have to dress."

So I stuck on my boondockers and, still in my skivvy drawers, walked out of my tent.

"Your jeep, sir," said Bogard as he saluted. "We found it."

That was it. There were no marks on it. My orders had arrived, so I drove it for the few days I had left on the Canal. Then I left it for a fellow officer and never heard of it again.

My new designation was Pavuvu, some 60 miles away on the Russell Islands. The time had come to start paying the price for wearing the green uniform. I was now an officer in the 1st Tank Battalion of the 1st Marine Division. My new outfit was getting ready for its third island invasion of the war. We were to hit a place about 600 miles east of the Philippines. The Japanese had heavily fortified this island and we had to take the place to support MacArthur's coming invasion. That's what we were later told, anyway. The island was Peleliu.

In the meantime, the 1st Division had left New Britain in April '44 to come to this island of Pavuvu, first for R&R and then to build up for their next fight. I don't think they could have picked a worse spot for rest. But by the time I joined the outfit, I had no time to worry about the location or the next invasion. I had to get to know all I could about the Sherman tanks and the men of my platoon. They had the 1st Tank Battalion on a perimeter where we worked our butts off for tank-infantry team training. Our tank operation was slated to play a big part in the coming invasion.

The landing on Peleliu was set for September 15, which turned out to be a month or so before MacArthur's invasion of Leyte. I went in on D-Day along with my platoon but no tanks. As you can imagine, this had the scuttlebutt running wild. My men were convinced that the brass figured all the men who had their tanks ashore on D-Day were going to be casualties and we would replace them. It didn't quite turn out that way even though the tank battalion had its share of casualties on Peleliu, but then so did everyone else.

Anyway, I spent the first night ashore in a foxhole. I'm sure the thought of an easy campaign promised by Major General Rupertus went out the window that very day. Not only did the Japanese artillery knock the hell out of our beachhead but we weren't ashore very long before the Nips started their counterattacks. I know they hit us with one shortly before dawn on the 16th.

Now, as I said, my platoon did not have our Shermans as yet but other tankers did. And it's a good thing, because on the first afternoon, the Nips sent down their own tanks toward our lines. They even had Japanese infantry riding on the tops of those tanks.

As I recall, the Marine tanks showed up in the nick of time and blasted the hell out of the Nip machines. We had noticeably heavier firepower than the Japs and it really was no contest. You could see their tanks burning all over the beachhead.

My platoon's tanks became available on the third day, and that's when I found out just how bloody hot it was on Peleliu. Even when the blower was going on inside the tank, it was torrid as hell, but when that conked out, you just couldn't exist in the tank. Peleliu is just not that far from the equator. I don't think the Marines ever fought on any other island where the heat was worse than on Peleliu.

Well, the big stumbling block was a place we called Bloody Nose

Ridge. We had shelled the devil out of it but it seemed as formidable as ever. We later found out that it had something like six different stories of tunnels. You can imagine what a problem that place was, especially as the coral made it real tough for the Marine riflemen to dig in.

Anyway, they decided to temporarily bypass Bloody Nose and move us north. My platoon was then in support of the 5th Marines, who succeeded in taking the Jap radio station on the northern end of the line.

So as we were moving north, there was one night when we had to change tactics. Plans called for armor to pull behind the lines each night to rearm, refuel and have any needed maintenance work done.

But one night as we were moving north, we were told to stay right on the lines. It seemed a certainty that the Nips would counterattack and the colonel wanted all the firepower he could get.

The colonel was right. The Nips did hit us and our guns seemed to be going all night. You always had spare barrels and when one got too hot, you just put on your spare barrel.

There was another time when our tanks really piled those Japs up in stacks. Our riflemen had bottled up a large crew of them in one of those caves. It would have been madness to try and go in after them so the Marines saturated the place with flamethrowers.

In the meantime, we had our tanks lined up where we figured the rear entrance to the cave was located. Naturally the tremendous concentration of the flamethrowers screwed up the oxygen in the cave. So the Japs came running out the back side, which turned out to be just where we figured it would be.

My God, it was like shooting fish in a barrel. And remember, this was daylight; we could see our machine guns turning those poor guys into mincemeat. It wasn't a pretty sight. Then again, what was the alternative? With that damn code of theirs, they weren't going to surrender. The Germans were tough soldiers, but when they knew it was hopeless, they'd call it quits. The Nips weren't like that. Most of the time they'd blow themselves up before surrendering.

It was this type of action that used to really concern the tankers. We knew all about the kamikaze satchel chargers long before they had the suicide pilots. We had to be constantly on the lookout for them. They'd load themselves with dynamite and wait in some kind of a spider hole. When the tanks would appear, these nuts would jump out of the ground and run against the tanks. Someone had to plug them before they reached the tanks or the Sherman and every-one in it would blow sky high.

The closest call I had on Peleliu, though, didn't come from a satchel charger even though on two different occasions Marine riflemen shot down those suicide nuts coming at my platoon. It came from a split-second shootout where the alertness of my gunner saved our hide.

It all happened over near Bloody Nose Ridge. As I opened up one of our ports to get some air in, I saw this Marine field piece go sky high. I didn't know where the Japanese fire had come from, but my gunner had spotted this Japanese gun going in and out of one of those tunnels they had set up on a ridge. It was maneuvered on a railroad track.

"Lieutenant," he said, "when that baby comes out again, it is going to take a crack at us. Permission to fire to, sir."

"Hell yes," I answered. I'd say their gun was about a hundred yards away.

Sure enough, a minute or two later, out comes the Jap gun. I could see it now and so could my gunner.

Wham! he lets go with our 75 and blows the hell out of the Jap gun. It was like a shootout in one of those western movies we used to see. Thank God our gunner was a crack shot.

Well, sometime around the first part of October, they started taking my tank outfit off Peleliu and I think the rest of the 1st Division was off there toward the end of the month. The Army then had complete control. The Marines had done the job they were supposed to do in spite of suffering over seven thousand casualties. But just because we left, that didn't mean the Army didn't have plenty to do. The 81st Division had been landing piecemeal since late September. They did their share.

One more thing before leaving Peleliu. Shortly after my tank had knocked out that railroad gun, I had occasion to make a report to the colonel of the 5th Marines. While I was at regimental headquarters, Chesty Puller showed up. He was in command of the 1st Marines at the time.

"How many second lieutenants have you had killed so far?" he asked.

He was told the number—I can't remember what it was—and he sure as hell wasn't satisfied.

"What the hell are you doing, having a Sunday School picnic?" he bellowed.

Chesty was a real charismatic leader and he just didn't know what fear was all about. However, there were several Marines who thought he was a little off his rocker. You know, you can hear too many guns go off.

So they pulled us off Peleliu and much to everyone's disappointment took us back to Pavuvu. I will say, however, they had made a lot of improvements on that island since we took off for Peleliu. Regular showers, movies, even a few Red Cross ladies; the greatest improvement was a regular beer ration for the men. It was limited, of course—hell, you couldn't have the division falling down drunk— but it was there.

There was also a sadness, as far as I was concerned anyway. We had several suicides on Pavuvu, which was really a crying shame. I guess you had to expect this. The traumatic experiences the men had gone through on Peleliu were enough to affect anyone's mind. But to have a young guy go through all that misery and then take his own life after it was over was a real pity.

There was one officer I met at Pavuvu whom I should mention because he was such an unusual man. His name was Paul Douglas, the same Paul Douglas who was a senator from Illinois after the war. It wasn't unusual to have a regular officer as old as Paul, but Douglas was a reserve and not one who'd spent many years as a reserve between the wars. His reasons for being there were unique.

As it turned out, these reasons went back to World War I. It seemed Douglas had either been just a shade too young to go into the service in 1918 or else he'd stayed in college at the time. Anyway, he felt he owed his country a war and when this one came along, he enlisted as a private. He didn't end up with some cushy job back in the States either. He was right there in the Pacific. I think he came out a major when the war was over. He was quite a guy.

Well, we overhauled the division to get ready for the next move. It turned out to be the biggest campaign the Marines fought in divisional strength. Our 1st Division and the newly formed 6th Marine Division were to land on the island of Okinawa with the 2nd Marine Division in reserve. Why the hell they kept the 2nd in reserve as long as they did, I'll never know. We kept hearing about their landing on small islands near Okinawa with no Japs on them but never the main event. The 8th Marines of the 2nd Division did come into some nasty stuff toward the end of the campaign, but the 2nd and 6th Marines never came to the main island. We could have used them.

At any rate, Okinawa was the largest island any Marine division fought on. We felt it would be the closest thing to a land mass type of area we would run into and therefore ideal for tanks. I was switched into intelligence with our tank battalion so I had a general idea of what we did with our tanks on the island.

But, as I look back, the first thing I can recall is the old saying that no matter what goes on, someone will always figure a way to make a buck. I guess it's just a plain old American custom. Things were pretty quiet in the north when we first went in and the agile mind of one of our battalion officers quickly went to work.

It seems that we had taken over what appeared to be the headquarters for the Japanese Imperial Marines. The place was loaded with hundreds, maybe thousands, of the Nip Marine insignia.

So this enterprising officer dug up some sewing machines, got some cloth and put everyone he could find to work making Japanese Imperial Marine battle flags. I must confess they were a hell of a lot better than the ones from the Nip army.

Then he took the flags out to some of the hundreds of U.S. Navy ships off Okinawa. My God, did he clean up! But he was generous to a fault. Somehow he managed to buy a tremendous amount of beer for all hands, enough to last until we moved south. Tragically, it was going to be the last beer many of these Marines would ever have.

After we did move south, we ran into some of the roughest stuff of the entire Pacific war, particularly the Shuri Castle area where the 1st Division had it so rough. My job as intelligence officer took me back and forth between the command posts and the front lines and one of my trips to a CP allowed me to witness something the Corps believes in.

You see, there was this hill near Shuri—I can't remember its name—that had to be taken. But it was turning into a real tough nut to crack.

So the lieutenant colonel in command of the battalion that was really getting the hell knocked out of it was at the CP as was the ADC (assistant divisional commander). As you might imagine, the battalion commander was a walking basket case, he shouldn't even have been on the lines. Unfortunately, the ADC couldn't, or wouldn't, take this into consideration even though he never raised his voice when giving orders to the lieutenant colonel.

"Colonel," he said, "General del Valley (the 1st Division commanding officer on Okinawa) says we have to have that hill tonight."

"But my men are all used up," replied the battalion commander. "Half of them belong in sick bay."

"Colonel, you have your orders. If you don't take the hill, heads will roll."

"Yes, sir."

The battalion commander saluted and walked out. I knew the lieutenant colonel, so I walked over to try and offer some consolation. He turned toward me as I approached him. There were tears in his eyes.

"We'll take the fuckin' hill, but I don't care if I come off it or not."

The battalion did suffer more casualties but they took the hill. I don't believe the commander was hit even though I think he was wounded later on.

But that was the Marine way of thinking and you can argue for or against it. Who the hell knows if they're right or not?

The Corps says if you keep moving against the enemy, flanking them if possible, you lose fewer men than if you stay in a hole and let the enemy work you over with artillery and mortars. Brutal as it sounds, it usually works.

As we continued to move south, we were on the right, with the 6th Marine Division on our left. I think the Japanese had more artillery on Okinawa than on any other island the Marines fought on and they gave our tanks hell. One of the reasons for this was the goddamn rice fields. I mean, you just can't move a Sherman tank through a rice field.

Here's how they'd work. The Nips knew we'd have to keep our tanks on the roads between those rice fields and that's the area they'd zero in on. They'd wait until you had reached that point, then they'd open up.

And it wasn't only our tanks that suffered from those guns. Remember, each tank usually has a supply of riflemen and other troops moving along with it.

Another thing on Okinawa that was a real bastard was those tombs. If you take a look at a picture of them, you'll see a little wall surrounding each one. It was supposed to be shaped like a woman's womb, the reasoning behind this being that you come from a woman's womb and when you die, you return to one.

The Japs would frequently use these tombs as fortresses. You'd never know which ones they might be in. I guess they wanted to put as many of us back in our mothers' wombs as possible.

But, you know, as rough as things could get, you always had these funny stories floating around. Some were true, others half-true and a lot of them just plain fantasies. Take the one about the lieutenant coming across a young Marine in a foxhole. The lieutenant looks down and he sees the young lad is beating his meat.

"Hey, Marine," the officer yells, "what in hell are you doing?"

"Just a little something to keep my mind off the shelling," comes the reply.

And it was always added that the kid didn't miss a beat.

Back to Shuri Castle. Now, you know all about the great picture of the flag raising on Suribachi. What you may not know is that the Marines seemed always to raise a flag wherever they went.

There was this rifleman from Georgia in the 7th Marines who was one of those professional rebel types. You know, always fighting the Civil War over and over. Come to think of it, I guess we had more of that type around forty years ago than we do now—you never see that kind anymore.

Anyway, he'd had a Confederate flag sent to him when we were on Pavuvu and when we finally did take Shuri, the first thing that goes up is the Stars and Bars. He even had a guy with a harmonica playing "Dixie." Most of the Marines, no matter where they were from, got a huge kick out of the whole act, but I heard some stuffed shirt Army general got really pissed off. So what!

Now, I've already told you how that Jap artillery fire had been taking a big toll on the tanks. To be precise, the Jap fire, plus normal maintenance problems, had reduced our battalion to just six tanks ready for duty. We'd gone in with sixty. We had to do something about the Jap artillery or we'd have no tanks left at all.

So as we continued to move south, we ran into one of those real big guns—it might have even been dismounted from a naval vessel —that we couldn't locate. All we could figure out was its general direction; we just couldn't pinpoint it. As intelligence officer I was supposed to know all about the Jap artillery fire on our tanks, so the colonel figured I was the guy to go up in an observation plane and radio back to our artillery the exact location of the Jap gun. I agreed.

The plane was a Stinson LS. It certainly wasn't built for combat, but it was ideal for observing. So they got a pilot, I grabbed some powerful binoculars and we were off.

Christ, try as I did, I just couldn't pinpoint the goddamn Jap gun. But I did narrow it down to what we called an acceptable target.

Then came the big blast. We lined up every available gun for miles around for TOT (time on target). The idea was for all the guns to shell the target at the same time. In other words, a gun three miles away would fire a short time after another gun maybe five miles away. That way shells would come in from every direction at the same time.

Unfortunately for us, no one bothered to tell us what time the big blast was set for and when it did come, the concussion to our plane was tremendous. It literally sent us upward as if we'd been shot out of a cannon. I'm happy to say my pilot kept control of the Stinson and none of our shells hit the plane. Apparently, they did blast the big Jap gun to kingdom come, which made our colonel happy as hell. He greeted us when we got back to our airstrip.

"Stack," he said, "you did such a great job, would you try it again tomorrow? We're having trouble with another one of their big bastards five or ten miles south of where you were this morning."

I've got to tell you I was in no hurry to go up into that mess again so soon, but you know the Corps. I answered the colonel in the affirmative, which turned out to be a very questionable decision on my part.

The next morning turned out to be absolutely crystal clear in all directions. And when you're up in that beautiful setting in a small plane like the Stinson, it seems like the war is on another continent.

But it wasn't and I soon found this out in spades.

The gun we were after was on a reverse slope placed in such a way that it was extremely hard to spot. Once again we had a general location but not enough accuracy to call in a strike.

Then I got lucky.

One of the Nip gunners threw an empty shell case out from underneath the camouflage. Why he did this I'll never know, but I caught the case's reflection from the bright sun. I guess with all their devotion to duty the Japs could fuck up just as badly as we could.

We radioed back the position of the Jap gun, both to our artillery and to several warships which were ringing the southern end of the island. They followed up immediately and blasted the area where I had spotted the reflection to pieces. We later found out that not only did we get the gun but also a large Nip command post in the same area. It was quite a show but it almost cost us our lives.

We were so busy watching the results of the shelling, we forgot how exposed we were to our own shells, particularly the fire from the ships in the bay. One of our naval shells—I think it was an eight-incher—passed about ten feet in front of our plane. Holy Christ, if it had hit us, parts of our plane would have been blown back to San Francisco. It was close enough to scare the wits out of us so we moved out of range. But, petrified as we were, it didn't improve our intelligence any. Looking back over the years, it's hard to fathom why we made our next move. Hell, we just plain decided to challenge the whole Jap Army. Can you believe that?

I guess the best explanation was that we just got too cocky. We'd been up two days in a row and both times we'd been successful as hell. The war had turned into a hide and seek game for us. Find the Japs, tell our people, and presto, no more Japs.

Anyway, we both had Colt automatics. We felt it would be a lark if we strafed the Japs at ground level with our pistols. We made some kind of a bet on who could hit the first Nip. What we forgot was they'd be firing at us with much more accurate weapons than pistols.

So down we went and opened up on them. The Japanese returned our fire with a vengeance. One of the Nips succeeded in putting a slug through our plane that also ripped through my right leg just below the knee.

Now, if you ever shoot a bullet through a piece of wood, you'll note a neat hole going in but a gaping hole where it comes out. That's what my leg looked like. My pilot got me back to a field hospital and my long fight to save my leg began.

From Okinawa I went to Guam and then to an amputation hospital on Mare Island, California. Both these trips were via a hospital plane. At Mare Island they told me that the damage to my bone meant my leg would have to come off.

"The hell with that," I told them, "get me back to the East Coast. My leg can be saved."

Of course, I really didn't know what the hell I was talking about, but I didn't want to lose my leg—who the hell would. I'd really gotten used to having it.

So I ended up at the Chelsea Naval Hospital outside of Boston. Here I ran into two great orthopedic surgeons who went to work on me. Among other things I had to keep my leg in traction for three months. It appeared that my leg could be saved but would it be any good?

In the meantime the war had ended and I had no trouble getting separated from active duty. Then I went into phase two of my rehabilitation, which was to find out if I could use my leg at all.

Now, as I look back, I have no bitterness at all. What the hell, I could have easily been killed at either Peleliu or Okinawa. I have quite a limp, but I can walk and for long distances. I think I'm pretty lucky.

But what about all the men who did lose a limb? Was such a devastating operation always necessary?

At the hospital they frequently would wake a man up at two in the morning and tell him they were sorry but an arm or a leg had to come off. They were probably right most of the time, but there must have been times when the doctors were wrong. Oh well, I guess that's how it goes.

One more thing. During my stay on either Guadalcanal or Pavuvu, can't remember which, I went out on a training exercise. There were no Japs anywhere near us but the exercise was under strict combat conditions, and under the command of one Major McIlhenny. I had a question so I looked up the major.

"Major," I started, but that's all I got out before he stopped me.

"Don't use rank out here. Use my code name, Tabasco Mac. What's your code name?"

Lieutenants didn't have code names, not that I knew of, but I thought fast.

"Ketchup Stack," I answered.

"Good, good. Now, what is it?"

So I told him and that was that. When I got back to camp, I asked another officer what the hell was going on.

"What's all this crap about Tabasco Mac?" I said.

"Oh, don't you know? McIlhenny's family produces Tabasco sauce; he's big as hell on that stuff!"

Well, many years after the war a buddy of mine married a girl down in New Iberia, Louisiana. I went to the wedding and it turned out the bride was my old major's niece, and there he was in all his glory.

"Hello there, Tabasco Mac, how are things?" I asked him.
The major looked at me carefully and then smiled.
"Just great, Ketchup Stack, just great!"

Lewis "Chesty" Puller—the Warrior

To the pre-World War II Marine officers he was Lewis or Lewie. To
those who came later he was Chesty. But whatever he was called, the
stories about him were legendary.

When they showed him a flamethrower for the first time, he asked,
"Where the hell do you put the bayonet?"

Chesty did not marry until his late thirties. When, during his long
bachelorhood he was asked why he wasn't married, he would answer,
"If the Marine Corps wanted me to have a wife, they would have
issued me one."

Once he was walking by a young second lieutenant and a PFC. He
noticed the PFC was standing at attention and repeatedly saluting
the officer. When Puller asked the young officer what was going on,
he was told the PFC had neglected to salute the lieutenant so the
enlisted man was getting a lesson in military courtesy.

"Oh, that's splendid, Lieutenant," Puller told the young officer,
"but, remember, you have to return every one of those salutes."

And so the legend goes.

Renowned as the only Marine in history to receive five Navy
Crosses, Chesty never did get the Medal of Honor. And he probably
never had a chance to obtain this most coveted of all American
decorations. One of the reasons may be that many of his fellow
officers felt Lewis was a little off his rocker.

"I was talking to Lewie," remembers Bill Hawkins, also the holder
of a fine combat record, "one day in Quantico. I think it was the
summer of 1955. I was a major in the Reserves at the time.

"Well, Puller and I were discussing Formosa, or Taiwan, whatever
you care to call it. I said something about Chiang Kai-shek wanting
some American Marines to come over and train his men.

" 'Is that so?' said Puller. You know the way he used to talk out of
the side of his mouth. 'Well listen, when his troops get to a river,
they're all told to jump in. If they can swim to the other side, fine,
they're good soldiers. If they can't, they drown. So he ends up with

the toughest possible men in his army.

" 'Hell, he should be sending officers over here to help train our men!'

"You see," Hawkins went on, "we all admired Lewis as being incredibly brave, but he sometimes seemed to forget that all Marines didn't quite look at things the way he did."

Another Marine officer, who did not want to be quoted, said that Puller was considered an extremist when it came to the assault. This is an image that is extremely hard to gain in the Marine Corps.

But whatever Puller's faults or virtues, the enlisted men loved him. It wasn't always that way among the officers, as Colonel Brooke Nihart relates it.

"Puller would too often make a fool out of a young officer," Nihart said. "I was told that one time Puller, then a colonel, came into a tent area where the men were lounging around. A young officer called the men to attention, which was what he was supposed to do. Puller then read the young officer off, which he wasn't supposed to do."

And so it goes on Chesty. He was badly wounded on Guadalcanal as a battalion commander of the 7th Marines. He went into Cape Gloucester as the executive officer of the 7th, but before the campaign was over, he served in several combat functions.

At Peleliu Colonel Puller commanded the 1st Marines in some of the roughest fighting in the history of the Corps.

Not only was the combat ferocious but the terrain was unbelievably bad. Shrapnel from his Guadalcanal wound began to bother Puller tremendously but not as much as the heat and the battering his regiment had taken. When the 1st Marines were taken off Peleliu, World War II combat was over for Chesty.

Now, some years after his death, it is hard to evaluate this man, Lewis Puller. He is called everything from a warrior, born two hundred years too late, to a madman. Perhaps one more Chesty story shows what the enlisted men thought of him.

It seems that the ranks had set up a shower at the top of a hill. All the water had to be carried up the hill by the men. A new second lieutenant used the shower until the water supply was drained dry. Puller greeted the young man after he came down from the hill.

"Enjoy the shower, young man?" asked Puller.

"Yes, sir," came the reply.

"Good, now get two buckets, fill them with water and take them back up the hill. And keep doing that until you've replaced all the water you just used."

"Yes, sir."

Oh, the ranks loved their Chesty!

King Company at the Point

"It is nevertheless true that, in the final analysis, the battle is won by the individual fighting man operating as a member of a squad, a platoon, a company."

General Vandegrift wrote the above in his forward to *Coral Comes High*, a book in which a Marine captain, George Hunt, traces forty-eight hours that Company K, 3rd Battalion, 1st Marines, fought on the island of Peleliu, September 15–16, 1944.

Acting as the left arm of the 1st Marine Division, King Company was to seize the area surrounding, and including, a place they called the Point and hold it against Japanese counterattacks. Their success was crucial for the battle. If the Japanese held this position, they would have free rein in raking the entire landing area of the 1st Marines.

The Point itself jutted some twenty-five yards into the surf. It was about fifty yards north of White Beach A, where Hunt's company was scheduled to land. The entire area was bristling with Japanese troops.

While in Kansas City, I sat down with four survivors of King Company's fight at the Point on Peleliu. They shared with me their memories of the action and their days as Marines.

While these veterans are still aware of the role Company K played in securing the beachhead, they are quick to point out that each man's memories are based on what he actually did there, not the overall picture.

"That fight at the Point," one of them commented, "is made up of a lot of little incidents and thoughts. I can recall one of our men sharing his rations with me, then taking a sniper's bullet in the head. I can also remember thinking how great it would be not to be there at all."

These four men from Company K represented a cross section of America. Bull Sellers, the company executive officer, was an Alabama farmer who for twenty years has served as a county extension officer in Dawson, Georgia. Ray Stramel, a post office employee in Nebraska, was raised in Kansas. Joe Hendley, a native of Oklahoma, works for TWA in Amarillo, Texas.

And finally Bill Getz, an old friend of mine, grew up in Westchester County and now lives in Lakewood, Ohio. He is an advertising salesman for *Coal Age Magazine* and one of the most respected men in his field.

Their collective story is not one of unbridled bravos. They all feel it would have been better if they'd had another company or two with them to help out, and they speak freely of many fouled-up situations. However, they also realize that you can't fight a war without SNAFUs.

As one of them put it, "There's just too much confusion in a battle not to have things get screwed up."

One who has particularly good reason to feel put out is Bull Sellers.

"I was the company's executive officer on Peleliu. Captain Hunt, who had been with the 1st since Guadalcanal, went home, as he should have, after Peleliu, and I became commanding officer of Company K. I was the only company commander in the division who was on Okinawa from start to finish, and they never did make me a captain. Now that's a shaftin'!"

But if you ask Bull Sellers how he feels about the job King Company did on the Point, his eyes will light up.

"I'm damn proud to have been part of what we did there," he says. Then his voice softens.

"But, gawd almighty, we lost so many fine fellows in doing it."

In the following interview, I have not singled out individual speakers. It really doesn't matter who is saying what. All four of them were with Company K on the Point. That does matter.

1ST LIEUTENANT WILLIAM (BULL) SELLERS
2ND LIEUTENANT RAYMOND STRAMEL
PFC JOSEPH HENDLEY
PFC WILLIAM GETZ
1st Marines, 1st Division

One of the toughest things about our fight around the Point was that so many of King Company's old-timers got killed there—men who had already fought on the Canal and New Britain. Men like Johnny Koval and McNeel, they were killed at the Point, while most of the newer men like myself were the ones wounded.

Koval and McNeel, yeah, I think they were killed while we were actually taking the place. But I've got to disagree with you on the new guys, plenty of them were also killed there. That new lieutenant

—what the hell was his name?—I think he was the first one killed. A sniper got the poor guy, right between the eyes, just as we landed.

His name was Woodyard, he had the second platoon, and you're right about when he was killed. I don't think he'd taken ten steps off the amtrac when he bought it. I should know; he was my boot camp drill instructor at San Diego. Hell, he knew as much about being a good Marine as anyone I've ever known—real gung ho.

Actually, the whole thing between Woodyard and me was quite a coincidence. After I finished recruit training, I was sent to OCS at Quantico, then I shipped out and joined the 1st at Goodenough Island.

And, by the way, that's something that has always irked me. I made three landings with the 1st and I was always hearing how great things were in Australia where the division had spent about eight months before I joined 'em. Damn it, I never did get to see Australia.

Well, in the meantime, after I left boot camp, I forgot all about Woody. Then he ups and joins us when we're training for Peleliu on Pavuvu. He hadn't changed a bit, never would play cards with the other officers, was always brushing up on what he was supposed to do.

That was Woody, all right! I remember him coming up to me that last night on the LST just before we hit Peleliu. He had this puzzled look on his face.

"Tell me," he said, "I've been reading up on what happens when you land, but what actually is the real scoop? I want to do the best job possible."

"Okay," I answered, "first don't worry about it. You know everything you've been taught. Once we land, you'll forget most of it. You'll just think about saving your own hide and losing as few men as possible. It'll come natural to you. Wait and see, there's just too damn much confusion to go by the book."

The poor guy, he never had a chance to do much of anything.

Yeah, well, that's the way it happened sometimes. "Little Wiggy" Wiginton, he was another of the new men killed at the Point, wasn't he?

The platoon runner, Wiginton . . . oh no. He was out on the Point with me. We both got the Silver Star for Peleliu. Wiggy was killed on Okinawa. What a great little guy he was!

Right, he was that; most of our men were good eggs. That's one of the reasons it was so tough to take all those casualties. King Company went in with two hundred and thirty-five men. Seventy-six of us were standing when we left. In other words, close to seventy percent of our men were hit around the Point. Even if you yourself were one of the lucky ones not hit, the chances were extremely high that several of your good buddies were killed or wounded.

Yeah, and remember, we had spent about two weeks crammed aboard LST 227 prior to the landing. They only had bunks for seventy or so guys and we were jammed on top of each other. This meant most of the men slept wherever they could find a spot. You can really get close to guys in a deal like that.

Of course it could work the other way. You could get tense as hell about a guy. Maybe he took some of your toothpaste, or a couple of your cigarettes. Maybe you had a run-in over something, who knows. But you also feel lousy if he gets it, because the two of you were really friends.

That's right. I can remember after we'd taken the area and were trying to set some kinda defense up for the counterattack we knew was coming. There's ole Sutherland and that guy, you know the one, the preacher from Oklahoma, down in that tank trap. I'll be darned if the two of them, good friends, mind you, aren't arguing over how to set their machine gun up. Hell, it didn't make no matter anyway. They were probably both right. Damn it, the Japs are about to hit us and those two are going at it tooth and nail.

Maybe they were just pissed off over what had happened. Remember, we had been told it was going to be an easy fight and here we were, not ashore more than two hours and we'd already been shot to hell.

Maybe so. I think we were all surprised at the rough reception we received. But, damn it, we seemed to hold on in spite of all that confusion.

We sure did. I think one of the reasons we did was men like LaBerge. Why, he was just about as cool a cucumber as you could find anywhere.

No doubt about that. Remember, shortly after we landed, how he fought those Japs at the water's edge with his bayonet. Gawd almighty, I think he handled a couple of 'em at one time.

Yeah, and didn't he take some shrapnel in his back but wouldn't be evacuated until one of our replacements shot him in the shoulder by mistake?

Okay. LaBerge was plenty cool, but to me the coolest guy was my sergeant, Dick Webber. Jeez, nothing could upset him! That first night we were on fifty percent alert. We were always catching something from the Nips so only half of our men, no matter where you were, could be asleep at one time.

I say asleep, but for me that was a joke. It was my first night in combat and I didn't even try to sleep. I don't think I could have if I wanted to, with all that racket going on. Even if I could have, I was too frightened to—afraid of waking up dead, if you know what I mean.

So I'm crouched in a hole, when Webber grabs my shoulder.

"Okay, buddy," he says, "your turn. I'm going to cork off."

Christ, Webber lies down and in a matter of minutes he's out like a light. You'd think he'd just come off a twelve-to-four watch at the Brooklyn Navy Yard.

Oh, he was quite a guy! After the war he got out of the Corps, but then decided to go back in. I believe he went ashore on that bloodless invasion of Lebanon and also served some rugged time in Vietnam. I think he's now an antique dealer in Maine.

Well, it was pretty hard to keep your cool when you're getting shot to pieces, especially if you thought about that crap we'd been handed before we went in.

I'll say, but intelligence just screwed up, that's all. Our aircraft and navy had been hitting that island with everything they had for three days before we went in. It just didn't seem possible that anything could still be alive there, at least near the beaches.

Right, I think it was General Rupertus (1st Division commander) who told us we'd be on and off Peleliu in a week. What he didn't figure on was the animal-like ability of the Nips to withstand bombardment. They were like moles. No matter how hard you hit 'em, you had to eventually go in with a rifle and annihilate 'em.

Yeah, we all heard that and remember, we were also counting on the 1st Division's luck with landings. On both the Canal and Cape Gloucester the division met very little resistance on the beaches. Come to think of it, Okinawa turned into a hellhole but not at first. Peleliu ended up being the only island where the 1st Division did have to fight on the beaches.

Well, we went in as the pivot company. Then we took a left turn while two platoons in the company actually went out on the Point. We managed to take the area by having a bunch of us get killed—it was as simple as that.

But, my God, what a price we paid. Everywhere you looked you saw dead and wounded Marines. It's hard now to reconstruct it all, I mean, to know for sure if the dead men lying there were killed in taking the Point or if they got it when the Nips counterattacked. But I can remember men, so many of them, some horribly mangled, others with one piercing hole—Graham, Mike Pollinger, Windsor and so many others. Hell, I say men, but they were men in death only. Alive, so many of them were really boys, but boys with a pair of balls. I'll vouch for that!

Well, it was then, after we tried to set up some kind of a perimeter, that we got pinned down which meant we had to set up a defense under fire.

And what made it doubly hard was the coral; it was everywhere. Can you imagine trying to dig a foxhole in coral? You were lucky to find a place where you could dig anything. Some of us did the best job we could, then stuck our pack—or a pack whose owner would never need it again—in front of us. It wasn't much, but I guess we felt it was better than nothing.

Don't forget the tank traps. Those were great places!

Yeah, but weren't the guys in the tank traps cut off?

I guess they were. I think most of them were hit, one way or another.

Jeez, I jumped in a shell hole. That's one good thing our naval bombardment did, dig us up a lot of shell holes. Course you had to watch out that one of those Nips didn't jump in with you.

They kept coming at us, one way or another. Can't remember the guy's name, but a Jap jumped into someone's hole and the Marine strangled the SOB. But it seemed every time those Japs came at us, we lost someone.

We sure did. But they kept coming and hitting us with artillery and mortars.

Right, but we sure piled them up! I remember seeing the area in front of us a few days later; it was saturated with dead Nips, in every position you can think of—all dead.

Well, we can thank Joe LaCoy and his mortar group for piling up a lot of 'em. Remember, we had to hold where we were and I don't think we could have done it without Joe's mortar fire.

I'll say. We'd tried to set up some kind of a line, but you couldn't have it straight or anything like that.

Well, old Joe and his men—hell, I don't think they had more than three or four mortars, but plenty of shells—they're laying those things just far enough in front of us to hit the Nips but not us. Can't remember any falling short, but they took those Japs out five or six at a clip.

Over where I was, on the Point itself, we didn't even have a machine gun. But we did manage to take over one of their pillboxes that had a British Enfield machine gun. Don't know where the hell they got it, probably Singapore or somewhere like that. It was in great shape though and we put it to instant use. That helped us a hell of a lot all that day and night.

You just said, "where I was." Lots of groups were cut off from each other, particularly the men on the Point. I was over behind the tank trap. I was the company's executive officer, but I'd completely lost touch with George (George Hunt, K Company's commanding officer) because the radios were out. First the Japs had jammed 'em, then the batteries went dead. We kept getting this military music, then a Nip woman kept jabbering away in Japanese; we didn't know what the hell she was saying.

Well, I was getting more and more pissed off. Finally I gave her the word good.

"Fuck you, you bitch!" I yelled. "Get off the air!"

She didn't pay no mind at all though, just kept on jabbering.

Then, when night came, I kept shootin' up those flares so wherever our men were, they could have some idea of where the Nips were. And George could see we were still alive—we were still in action.

The flares helped. I remember getting a good look at a bunch of Nips. Christ, they were big for Japs! And they knew what they were doing. None of those aimless banzai charges they'd pulled on other islands. They figured they were going to die all right. All they had to do was look out at all the ships we had in the harbor to know it would only be a matter of time. But damn it, they were going to make us pay for that lousy island.

They did that. We later found our their soldiers had come from the Kwantung Army that had been fighting so long in Manchuria. And many of their naval forces were the Jap Marines. Oh, they knew how to fight all right. It's true we outnumbered them on Peleliu, but they had about ten thousand troops there and we just had one Marine division reinforced by Corps troops. Someone said they had talked about sending another Marine division in with us, but one of our brass said we could handle Peleliu by ourselves. What a dreamer he was! The 1st did get reinforced by the 81st (Wildcat) Army Division later on, but only after we'd left the Point. We did get about thirty more Marines sent to us—I think this was on the second day—other than that, the original K Company was all we had those first two critical days.

I'll say the 81st came in! My brother Gene was with that outfit. Of course he knew I was with the 1st Marines. As it turned out he'd heard my company had been shot to hell and he thought I was dead. Speaking of coincidence, we were pulling off the island, I think it was September 24, when Gene's outfit was coming in. Hell, he'd liked to faint when he spotted me, thought he'd seen a ghost. It was quite a reunion.

Yeah, I remember that happening. But you know, I would like to comment on that business about our outnumbering the Japs. That might have been true on the whole island, but it sure as hell wasn't where we were. They counted over five hundred dead Japs in front of us when we moved out. That's more than twice as many men as we had when we hit the beach. Come to think of it, I still don't know how we took that place . . . and how we held it.

Why, hell no, we didn't outnumber them, at any time! Plus, they had plenty of artillery up in those hills they could throw at us. They had one gun that seemed to come out of nowhere, fire three or four shells, then the goddamn thing would disappear again. A little later it would start all over again. Now, how in the hell could we do anything against that?

Oh, that bastard! I think it was the gun that disabled that tank that came up to help us.

At any rate, one of its tracks had been blown and all the driver could do was move the turret around. Other than that, it was a sitting duck.

Well, gawd almighty, down comes a Japanese tank, heading straight for us. I yelled out to the Marine in the tank. "For God's sake, do something now, boy, or your goose is cooked!"

And he did; he turned that turret around and put three quick rounds into that Jap tank. Then these Nips came rolling out of the tank like one of those old Keystone Cop comedies. Naturally, our men opened up on them. No sense to worry about prisoners, no way those birds were going to surrender.

Hell no! One of them came out of a pillbox with his hands up. He was another one of those big guys. We were a little surprised, but we held our fire. He starts to walk toward us when quick as a flash one of our guys shoulders his M-1 and opens up on him. For a split second I'm shocked; I mean, why the hell do you want to shoot a guy who has his hands up?

Jeez, the minute the rounds hit the Jap, the son of a bitch blows up. I mean he goes into little pieces. You could even smell that crummy liquid smell that goes with their explosives. The guy who had shot him had caught a quick glimpse of the stuff the bastard had on his back. The Nip was playing hardball all right. He was planning on walking over to us, blowing himself up, and taking us along with him. I guess he figured he'd go to heaven but not us. Oh, those guys were tough, never doubt that!

Okay, but so were we. I took a long look at that place as we were leaving. Solid coral, it must have risen thirty-five feet above the water's edge. Remember those huge rocks and those pillboxes? We had to be tough not only to take it but to hold. The Japs wanted that back pretty badly.

Well, I think we had more brains than they did. Those Nips were half brave and half nuts. And they were everywhere. Just because we had set up a line, it was nowhere near as neat and tidy as you may think. Japs were in and out of it all night. Our company really didn't know what the hell was going on. I do think we all knew how important it was not to be driven off. But, also remember, if they did overrun us, we would have all been killed. None of us were looking forward to that. It was tough, especially with so many sergeants and officers going down.

That's right. Estey, my platoon lieutenant, got his early, I think it was on our way to the Point. He was hit twice in the right arm, and badly. Most of our sergeants were also hit. As far as I can remember, Dick Webber ended up in charge of my platoon. I tried to stick close to him.

And, by the way, Bull said earlier only seventy-six of us were fit for duty after the second day. What he didn't say was some of that seventy-six had also been hit, including me, but hadn't been reported.

I had taken some shrapnel in my right knee. But, what the hell, the corpsmen—maybe it was only one corpsman by then, perhaps the other had been killed—were busy with guys hit a lot worse than I was. With some of those guys it was touch and go whether they'd make it.

My wound did bleed quite a bit, but later on a corpsman patched it up. But it was never reported. I didn't think any more about this until the following May when I got hit by machine gun fire in my left leg. We were over by the railroad tracks near Naha on Okinawa.

Hell, they'd send you home with two Purple Hearts, but I only had one. No one knew about the atomic bomb; we all figured we'd be hitting Japan in the fall. I figured I'd be better off at home than on the Japanese beaches but that was that—no Purple Heart for Peleliu.

That's right, you did get hit when we ran into that ambush by the railroad track. So did I. Weren't we hit at the same time?

Same time? Hell, Joe, we were hit by the same machine gunner, don't you remember?

I remember when both of you were hit on Okinawa. And we had plenty of other men hit at the same time. It was a Jap ambush, that's what it was, and there was no damn excuse for it. Hell, it was after four o'clock when we moved out. We should have gone into that area in the morning. And no one had reconnoitered the place. We were told to go in there blind. Those Nips were waiting for us.

Anyway, after that fiasco I sent the word back to headquarters we weren't going to move again until we knew what in the hell was in front of us. At least we knew what we were facing on Peleliu.

Yeah, but we didn't know how rough it was going to be when we went in on the amtracs. Remember how some of the guys were playing harmonicas and we were singing up a storm?

You know, I was trying to remember what song we were singing when we did go in, but I couldn't put my finger on it. I know George says in *Coral Comes High* that it was "Give My Regards to Broadway," but damn it, I think it was something else in the boat I was in.

I can't even remember the men singing. But I can remember those sailors from LST 227 sending that hot chow in to us on the third day at Peleliu. What great guys! It was just before what was left of us moved north. I think L Company was with us.

Right! They still called us a company, but they were just being polite. But you know, there was another SNAFU there. We had to move inland, into that swamp, because someone had called for naval artillery where we would have been if we'd followed our original plan. That barrage probably would have taken care of what was left of us.

And when I was going through that damn swamp, some wise guy started passing the scuttlebutt that the Nips had surrendered. I should have known better, but I did believe it, I'll say I did! I even threw my damn rifle into the swamp. Hell, there was plenty of fighting still going on around Bloody Nose Ridge long after we left the Point.

I'll say there was! Our battalion commander, Lieutenant Colonel Hankins, was killed there on the fourth day, hit by a sniper. He was walking around as if the fight was over. I hope he didn't believe that baloney about how easy it was going to be. When colonels start getting killed, things are really rough!

Oh, there was plenty of action left on Peleliu, even after the whole 1st Division left. To our company, their first forty-eight hours around the Point were by far the worst. We stayed on that small island—it was only about six miles long and two miles across at its widest place —for seven more days after we left the Point, but nothing was like the first two days.

I'll agree with that, but hell, what can you expect? The holding of our position had to be done. Maybe we didn't go along with all the big strategies, but we knew the Nips were in front of us and wanted to knock us off.

When you look back and try to reconstruct what happened, what you remember most are the things that directly affected you. On the second day I can remember taking a breather and looking up and seeing this Jap with his rifle pointed right down at me. All I had in hand was my knife which I threw at the Nip, but missed. The Jap ducked as I threw it, then someone else shot him dead.

Right, that's the way it was. Japs, Japs, Japs, and our trying to stay alive in all that confusion, but we did manage to stop 'em. My God, though, so many of our men paid a dreadful price!

Yeah, but old John Henry, he sure fooled 'em. They thought he was a goner but he didn't go along with it. He's dead now, but he loved to tell the story about the doctor on the hospital ship telling the nurses not to bother with John, that he was as good as dead.

"The hell you say," he yelled, "I'm not agoing to die! Now, you just patch me up." And they did.

There's one more thing I want to say. We told you we had come to Peleliu on LST 227 and what a great bunch of guys they had on that ship. You know, they brought all that hot chow up to us and all. Well, after we left Peleliu we figured we'd seen the last of LST 227. We were wrong.

Several months later, on April 1, 1945, our division is going into Okinawa. Our regiment was held in reserve that first day. We kept buzzing around in Higgins boats, waiting to be told what to do. Our problem came with the darkness. Along with the kamikaze pilots, there were supposed to be kamikaze boats about the size of Higgins boats attacking our fleet. We didn't dare go up to any big ships, in fear they wouldn't know who the hell we were, and would blast us out of the water. Somehow we managed to sidle up next to an LST.

"We're King Company, 1st Marines! Not Japs! Don't shoot!" we're yelling.

"Oh Christ, not you guys again!" comes back from the LST.

There must have been thousands of American ships out in that bay and in the darkness we had pulled alongside of LST 227, that's right, 227. Can you top that!

Here and There—II

Bing Bromfield found himself, a thirty-one-year old shitbird, on Parris Island in late 1943. He had tried for a year to obtain a commission but, figuring the Corps had forgotten about him, he entered the Marines as a private.

"I knew I was a little old for a boot," Bromfield said, "but I was shown how to become a Marine by a great DI, Harry Bills."

Bing then set up a luncheon where he and I would join Harry Bills. Bills is one Marine who has kept in great shape; he even runs in the Marine Corps Marathon at Washington, D.C.

Shortly after this luncheon I met with Louis Dubuque, who had spent two years on Bougainville, coming out of the Corps as a captain. He had also had Bills as a DI but didn't care for Harry one bit, which just goes to show everyone didn't like his DI.

When Bromfield finished boot camp, he was called to Parris Island Headquarters.

"Come in, lieutenant," he was told. "You didn't know it, but your commission came through just as you arrived at PI. We figured it would do you good to go through training as a private. You have some back pay coming."

Douglas MacArthur seemed to have a love-hate relationship with the Marine Corps. The word among the Marines was that the good general regularly had something unpleasant to say about the Corps. Yet, once he had the 1st Marine Division under his wing at New Britain, he certainly fought like the devil to keep them.

And Lem Shepherd once told this author that when MacArthur planned the Inchon landing in Korea, he told Lem he couldn't make the amphibious assault without "his" Marines.

Anyway, when MacArthur went into the Philippines, his biggest campaign of the Pacific War, he managed to have a Marine artillery unit under his command.

When the campaign was over, some of the more literate Marines stuck up a sign that read:

WITH THE HELP OF GOD AND A FEW MARINES
MACARTHUR RETOOK THE PHILIPPINES

There was scuttlebutt in the Pacific and then there was scuttlebutt. Certainly one of the great stories concerns Sam Petriello of the 15th Marines. Sam ended up being with the first Marine unit to go to Japan.

"Well," says Sam, "the word that went through the ship like wildfire was that Henry Ford was giving out a free Ford to the first one hundred Marines ashore in Japan. Christ, you had guys swimming ashore when the boat had trouble getting into the dock. You know, I think guys actually believed it."

If you ever go to a reunion of the 6th Division, you will find they do things with class. The name of the bartender is George Booz, once of the 22nd Marines. And Mr. Booz does not drink. He does a great job.

If there is one thing the Marines do, it is to cherish their old-timers. And if these men are ancient and colorful enough, they become members of that great band of men known as the Characters of the

Corps. Such men will always pop up at divisional reunions or gatherings anywhere on November 10, the birthday of the Corps.

But there is one place where even the most historically-minded Marines did not expect to find one of these Old Salts. Not in Japan, in the fall of 1945. However, that is exactly what happened.

In October 1945 a 5th Division patrol came across an internment camp in north central Kyushu. There was only one man still living there, an eighty-two-year-old Caucasian named Edward Zilling. When the Marines entered the camp, Mr. Zilling walked out, aided by a cane, to greet them.

"Marine Zilling reporting for duty," he said.

The Marines were flabbergasted. They asked if Mr. Zilling could document his statement. The venerable gentleman quickly produced papers showing that he had joined the Corps in 1888 and had been discharged in 1894.

Then, when the Spanish-American War broke in 1898, he had reenlisted in the Corps for another cruise.

"My God," said a young lieutenant, "you are the real Old Corps!"

It seemed that Marine Zilling had married a Japanese woman and had lived in Japan for many years. Just to prove he truly was a Marine, Mr. Zilling produced another document.

"Here," he said, "these are my pension papers. I'm supposed to receive sixty dollars a month and I haven't seen a dime since 1941. Tell Uncle Sam he owes me a lot of back pay and I want it."

Edward Zilling was certainly a Marine.

The Rifleman of the Evil Little Island

Jack Thompson

"Ok, maybe I was too gung ho. But, damn it, I seriously question if any outfit other than the U.S. Marines could have taken Iwo."

This author has been a close friend of Mr. Thompson for more than twenty years. As a matter of fact, Jack unknowingly played a major role in my decision to write *Semper Fi, Mac.* As the years rolled by, he became more willing to discuss his days as a Marine than when I first met him. I felt he was representative of Marines in general and that the time had come to record the memories of those men while they still were in their prime. I feel this did prove to be correct.

As for Jack, he is a cool customer who has a very difficult job. The magazine that employs him carries a tremendous amount of advertising. These advertisers desire an excellent placement position in the magazine. As there are a limited number of these desirable positions, it is rugged duty indeed to keep all the advertisers happy. As production director of the magazine it is Jack's job to keep the peace. For years I was amazed at his ability to do just that.

Then I woke up. If one had carried a rifle on Saipan, Tinian and Iwo Jima and received two Purple Hearts in the bargain, why should he allow the ravings of an irate advertising account executive to get to him? Jack doesn't.

Today Jack lives in Old Greenwich, Connecticut, with his wife and two children. Every working day he goes to the local train station, picks up the *New York Times* and heads for his office at the giant publishing firm where he has been employed since his graduation from Colgate University over thirty years ago.

At his office, Thompson immediately goes to work trying to solve his never-ending array of problems. He is assisted by several able associates. On one occasion I pointed out to a young lady that Jack

Thompson had seen the flag go up on Suribachi.

"Suribachi!" she said. "What's that, a pizza parlor?"

And that's the way it goes.

CORPORAL JOHN THOMPSON
B/1/26th Marines

If you talk about real infantry combat to people who have never experienced it, you'll either have trouble getting them to believe you or they just won't listen. But, damn it, just about everything imaginable can happen in combat and frequently does.

Take early one morning on Iwo. We were just getting up, so to speak, but not the way you do back home. Most of us had slept very little, if any, in the type of hole or whatever we'd managed to dig for protection. Let's just say we were stirring.

Anyway, we had this great little guy in our platoon named Frankie Benshadle. Frankie was from Buffalo, New York. As he was the shortest guy in the platoon, he naturally was the BAR man. The Browning always drew more fire than an M-1 and the Corps figured the smaller the BAR man the smaller the target.

So, just as we're beginning to get ready to move that morning, Frankie gets up and lets out a roar.

"Hey, you guys," he yells, "I am eighteen years old today. Happy birthday, Frank Benshadle!"

Bang. It's from a sniper. Down goes Frankie. It doesn't look as if he'll make nineteen. I mean, that's the way things happened on that evil little island called Iwo Jima.

Okay. Let's go back to 1941 when I was a junior at a school in Massachusetts called Mount Hermon. For several years prior to this time I'd had my own fantasy about being a pilot. Someone had told me there was a place in Boston where an American could join the Royal Canadian Air Force at age seventeen years. I'd just turned sixteen in August so I figured what the hell, why not add a year and go into Boston to enlist. The Canadians told me to return to school and sit tight; I'd hear from them.

As it turned out, I did get a letter from the Canadians, but it wasn't until after December 7. They thanked me for my interest but said that as the U.S. was in the war, they wouldn't be taking any more Americans. They also wished me luck. There were plenty of times later, especially on Iwo, when I'd watch our planes fly over and wonder what it would be like to be in a cockpit, but I was too busy to worry about it. Goodbye fantasy.

You ask me if the Pearl Harbor attack surprised me and the answer is yes and no. That the Japanese hit us at Honolulu did come as a surprise, but the fact that they did attack us was not a surprise, not to me anyway.

You see, I'd been extremely interested in the international situation and had followed it very closely. I knew all about the embargo this country had placed on Japan and that FDR had told the Japs in no uncertain terms to stop their aggression in Asia or face the consequences. I knew how important not losing face is in the Orient and I didn't think Japan would back down.

Besides, I had studied the Japanese sneak attack on the Russians at Port Arthur in 1904. It seemed to me that if the Japs decided to attack us, they wouldn't worry about a little thing such as the Western custom of declaring war. After close to a decade of combat in Manchuria and China, they had realized that fighting a war wasn't a game of cricket. Any method you use to win a war was acceptable to the Japanese.

And who's to say they're wrong. Just reflect for a moment on the fact that none of our carriers was at Pearl on December 7. If they had been there, God only knows what would have happened.

As for the Japanese attack itself, while it didn't surprise me, I didn't believe it because of what had been going on at school. Several of the students, including me, had set up intercoms so we could break in on radio broadcasts. Around the first of December the kid across the hall had broken into a regular broadcast to announce that the Japanese had captured Los Angeles and were making all the citizens eat fish heads. I thought the same guy was pulling a fast one on December 7 and I walked over to his room to tell him to knock it off.

"No, no, Jack," he said, "this is no bullshit. It's the real McCoy. Those little bastards have hung one on us."

Well, the fever that now swept Mount Hermon was tremendous. Remember, when you're talking about boys of high school age, you're talking about kids who have just passed the stage of playing soldiers. Everyone seemed to want to go to war, no doubt about that.

Of course my situation now changed. I figured there was no way I could get into the service by lying about my age; I would just have to wait until I reached my seventeenth birthday. I could then enlist in the Marines if I could get my parents to sign my papers. When August '42 did roll around, I approached my father, but he wanted no part of it.

"Look, Jack," he told me, "you just have to wait until you graduate from Mount Hermon. I know your mother will say the same thing. We may be divorced, but this is one thing I know we'll agree on."

He was right. I now decided I'd just work as hard as I could to finish my schooling. It paid off because in the first part of '43 I got Mount Hermon to give me my final exams early and by March 2 was down at Parris Island.

Now, you better be ready for this because I may be the only guy to say it, but I really liked PI. I'm the guy who did everything right down there. I was stoic as hell. I was also in top physical condition. I mean, if they told me to do fifty pushups, I'd do the pushups. If they told me to run around the parade ground with full marching gear, I'd run around the parade ground as many times as they wanted me to.

And you know something, I think this great attitude started when we went to the delouser. It was run by this old-time top sergeant with a goatee. His name was Lou Diamond.

The Corps uses Parris Island for more than one reason. First, they want to get you to learn how to function as part of a unit. That's why you almost never leave your platoon while at boot camp.

But there is something else. They also want to instill in you a real sense of what the Corps is all about. That's why they had this colorful old guy at the delouser.

Lou Diamond was quite a character. While he did have this big beer gut, his uniform was perfection and he had a military bearing that is hard to explain. I can picture him now with this perfectly pressed field jacket. It wasn't an Ike jacket; that came later. It was the one with the zipper on the front. If you washed it enough, it would bleach out almost white. He had red stripes on his sleeve, showing that he was either a first sergeant or a sergeant major, I can't remember which. He also had the 1st Division's patch, showing he'd been on Guadalcanal.

Anyway, he was bellowing at us to keep moving, keep moving. I think that's all he said, but you could just sense he was a Marine Corps legend. He looked to me like something out of one of the John Thomason books I'd devoured so eagerly a few years before.

Well, as I've said, I'm the guy who did everything right. My "junk on the bunk," you know, the 782 gear, was always perfect. When we went to the range, I shot expert, had the highest score in the platoon. When the rest of the boots went on mess duty, I was sent to the sports arena to work as a soda jerk. Hell, I really loved boot camp, and that's the truth.

As a matter of fact, I will tell you something that I don't usually mention. I did so well there that when my training was over, I was offered an opportunity to go into the V-12 program and go to college.

And do you know something? I turned the college bid down. You can't possibly explain to the youngsters today something like that, but I'd gone into the Corps to fight, not go to college, that could come after the war. That was my total attitude, believe me. But, also remember, everything was different in '43 than it is now.

Well, I ended up going to a school anyway, but it was radio school at Quonset Point. I'd always been very interested in radio work and I figured this would be just about as quick a way as any to get overseas. It's amazing when you think how many ways a Marine division uses a radio man.

Anyway, they really crammed electronics down our throats in a hurry and after about three months at Camp Lejeune I was put on a troop train headed for the West Coast. I can still remember one stop that turned into one of the most pleasant surprises I had in the Corps.

The stop I'm talking about was Sweetwater, Texas. Why the hell we stopped there no one ever found out. Of course, the troops were told not to leave the train and of course very few of the Marines paid any attention to this order. No guards were posted and most of us simply walked into town. Those Texans couldn't have been nicer to us. This was in the middle of the war and I suspect most of the town folk had sons or brothers in the service and I assumed they hoped wherever their boys were, they were receiving equally fine treatment. We ended up spending a delightful day there and my hat will always be off to the good people of Sweetwater.

Now for the type of foul-up that is part of any military career. After I reached our designation at Camp Pendleton, they didn't know what to do with me. I kept moving around, doing radio work at various places but not going overseas. I can't remember how long this lasted, but it seemed to drag on and on.

The final indignity came when I was posted with a Cooks and Bakers School. Now I really was pissed off and raised the roof.

"Okay, okay," I was finally told, "you want to go to the Pacific so badly, we'll stick you in the next replacement draft."

Let me say one thing in favor of a military operation—when they want to work fast, they can do it.

The first thing I knew I was put in a replacement ship that boarded at San Diego. We took off for the Pacific and didn't stop until we reached Saipan, where we were attached to the 2nd Division. The 2nd had gone into Saipan on June 15, 1944, three weeks before we landed. While a good deal of the real rough stuff was over, there was still plenty of action left.

As a matter of fact, during the following November, some four months after I left Saipan, the 2nd Division formed a sweep to clear the Nips out of their last stronghold on the island. The Marines suffered some fifty-two casualties cleaning out these diehard Japanese. You could never underestimate the Nips' willingness to die.

Well, on July 24, the 4th Marine Divison that had been fighting alongside the 2nd on Saipan moved over to Tinian, an island maybe five miles away. The 2nd was used as a decoy on the 24th on another part of Tinian. We didn't actually go ashore until the next day.

I should explain that I had gone overseas as a radio signalman. But they had more of these men than they had equipment. So, after all the training I had experienced in electronics, I was given the word that I was no longer a radioman.

"Okay," this sergeant said, "you now have a battlefield promotion from radioman to rifleman."

As I was still a PFC, I really didn't know what the hell he was talking about. Being a rifleman in combat is one of those things you're glad as hell to have been after it's over, but you are in no hurry to be one again. The sergeant was obviously pulling my leg, but from here on I was a rifleman.

Another thing I should point out is what actually does happen in a replacement draft. It doesn't always work out where you are split up piecemeal and are sent to different regiments as permanent replacements. It seems to me our draft just worked as a unit replacement attached to the 2nd Division. Anyway, I wasn't with the 2nd Division long enough to make any difference. The Japanese saw to that. Here's how it happened.

I was lying in a shell hole when a Japanese hand grenade landed behind me. I don't know where it came from. If it had been an American grenade I would have been killed, but as it was my pack absorbed a good deal of the blast.

The Nip grenades were highly explosive and their fragmentations so fine that they covered more ground than ours did. But they didn't have the concentrated devastation of the American grenades.

Anyway, I caught some shrapnel in my side and my left arm. The piece in my arm cut a vein that made me bleed like hell and made the wound look worse than it was. They figured it was bad enough to get me out of there so I ended up in a hospital in Honolulu.

At this point I must say I was feeling good. I'd survived two island campaigns and had a Purple Heart. I felt, as the old expression goes, as if I'd seen the elephant. Thank God, I didn't know what lay ahead. If I had, I would have been shaking in my boots.

I was discharged from the hospital, spent two weeks of R&R at Waikiki and was sent over to Camp Tarawa on the main island of

Hawaii. My short tour attached to the 2nd Division was over. I was now a corporal and squad leader in the third platoon, Baker Company, 3rd Battalion of the 26th Marines. This was part of the newly formed 5th Division. We were in a huge area called Kamuela which had plenty of room for very intensive infantry training.

Now, when I talk about training, I really mean training. You know, constant mock skirmishes, real artillery fire, maneuvering a squad, a platoon, a company and amphibious landings. No one knew where we were heading, but we knew it wasn't going to be a church social.

In any case, we moved out from Hawaii sometime around Christmas. And, I may add, Jack Thompson, who had never missed an order or a train, so to speak, almost got in real trouble as the division pulled out.

We'd been on alert for quite a while before we actually moved out. Tokyo Rose even knew about our coming move. She had been broadcasting that the 5th Marine Division was about to leave Hawaii for a Japanese held island where, of course, we would be annihilated.

At a time like this all liberty is cancelled, but even so some of the men would take off for a few hours.

Wouldn't you know it? Another fellow, a buddy of mine named Mel Dukes from Louisville, Kentucky, and I went into Hilo for a few hours. Shortly after we left the camp, the word came through that we were shoving off. They later told us they'd combed Hilo looking for us but had no luck.

Anyway, we finally returned to our camp to find it deserted. We quickly grabbed a couple of bicycles and headed for the ships. I wouldn't say we got there seconds before the ships pulled out, but everybody was on board and the ship was ready to shove off. Dukes and I had been missed and were on report.

But I'll tell you, it would have taken a real bad guy to jump all over us and our CO, a man named Rea Duncan, was one hell of a good guy. I think we were confined to quarters for what amounted to an hour or so but that was that. If our ships had sailed before we had got there, it would have been a different story.

Our ship was one of those Kaiser APAs. The troops were stacked maybe five or six high; I think we had the whole 1st Battalion of the 26th aboard, including the support troops and equipment.

In any case we were soon all keyed up thinking about our next island. You know how you'd get; you'd think, "Well, this is it! Let's go in and get it over with." But it was never that simple. Here we were pulling away from Hawaii and going to combat, or so we thought, when in reality we were going just a few miles to the island of Maui for a dress rehearsal which, incidentally, I thought went quite well, especially for Baker Company. It should have; we'd certainly spent enough time working on it.

Here I'd like to mention the leader of the 3rd Platoon, Charlie Cusick, a good guy with whom I'd gone to school before we both enlisted in the Marine Corps.

I had no idea who my second lieutenant was going to be when I joined Company B. I got quite a jolt when I saw it was Charlie.

"Well, I'll be damned," I said to him. "Charlie, how the hell are you?"

Charlie showed no surprise whatsoever. He probably knew I was coming and was prepared for my familiar greeting. He gave me a stoney stare.

"It's Lieutenant Cusick, Thompson," he said, "and please remember that."

I'll admit I was a little teed off at Charlie. I mean who the hell did he think he was? He hadn't even seen combat yet.

Then it dawned on me. It wasn't who did Charlie think he was; he *knew* who he was. He was the second lieutenant in charge of my platoon and I'd better remember it.

And, you know, it never bothered me again after I realized the facts of life as they then existed. Charlie found little ways such as occasionally sneaking me some bourbon to show me he wasn't a phoney. We had quite a discussion about the whole thing while having a drink after the war.

"Jeez, Jack," he told me, "I was in a bind. I couldn't have the other men feel I was playing favorites."

"Charlie," I answered, "you were perfectly right. But we're civilians now. Let me buy the next round."

The last time I heard about Cusick, he was living in Cleveland. He was a good officer, no flies on Charlie.

We ended up going into Iwo on February 19, 1945. We went in on amphibious tractors. Our regiment was in the second wave. Strangely enough, I've read where we were supposed to have had it rougher than the first wave, but damn it, I just don't recall it being so bad. We landed on Red Beach, which is to the right of Mount Suribachi, and started moving across the island. Iwo is quite narrow at this point. I'm quite sure we moved over to the other side of the island without too many problems. When it started to get dark, we set up for the evening.

The next morning (February 20) things started to change. Our first shock came when we found we were on the front lines and had been all evening.

Well, I knew that our company hadn't taken a single casualty that first night. As a matter of fact, I don't even recall a single incident being reported. This was very unusual. You could almost always count on those little people trying something every night.

By this time I was beginning to relax a little. When we were coming ashore, our tractors went right by the *U.S.S. New York* as it fired a broadside at Iwo. And it's an awesome sight to see one of those battlewagons let loose like that. When you're going into an island like Iwo, you're looking for any omen you can find to make you feel good. What better one could I have than being backed up like that by the Empire State, my home state. I started believing all that crap I'd heard about it being an easy campaign.

And can you blame me? That first day we'd had a comparatively easy landing and had gone straight across the island. We'd spent a night on the front lines without even knowing we were facing the Japs. Things could sure as hell be a lot worse.

Then came Armageddon. I can't tell you what time of the day it started, but start it did. I'm referring to my first real mortar barrage and it was unbelievable, unlike anything I'd previously experienced. It gave me the most helpless feeling in the world. The artillery shelling was bad enough, but at least you felt you could get a fix on their shells. Not those mortars. It was impossible to figure out where they were coming from or going to, simply impossible.

Do you know the old expression, "There are no atheists in fox-holes"? Generally speaking, that's true. It may be a formal type of God you are praying to, or it may be a rabbit's foot, but you are praying to something. And if you are faced with a heavy mortar attack, you are praying like a madman.

Actually, I can't tell you how many times our company came under heavy mortar fire, but each time we lost Marines.

Anyway, from then on we started to move north, fighting for every inch. The Japanese were well dug in, extremely well disciplined and, above all, everywhere. I can remember Frank Benshadle, the poor kid later killed on his birthday, watching our naval barrage on Iwo before we went in.

"Jeez, Jack," he said, "can there be any Japs left alive on that island?"

Then, shortly before Frank was hit, he changed his tune.

"Christ," he moaned, "did our shelling kill anyone?"

A funny thing occurred during most of the island fighting on Iwo. Normally, while you realized that some Marines would be shot, you were convinced it wouldn't happen to you. After a few days on Iwo, you started to realize the chances of not only your buddy getting hit but of you getting clobbered were extremely high. It became a matter of would you be killed or just wounded? There was little doubt in your mind about your own vulnerability. You would say to yourself, "Please make it a wound when it comes, not my death."

Another thing that occurred on Iwo concerned your natural senses. For instance, you learned to smell Japanese. Perhaps it was their diet and perhaps they could also smell us, but your own sense became so sharp you could tell they were there. You usually couldn't see them, but you knew they were there.

And, come to think of it, I never did actually see too many of the Nips on Iwo, not alive anyway. When you would spot one, he would just be a flash. He'd be down in one of those holes before you could get a bead on him.

There was one time though when we had a field day. We were moving north and were on top of a ridge. One of our men suddenly says, "Sssh, sssh" and points down below.

"Christ," he says, "that guy is going to take a crap!"

Sure enough, a Jap had come out of a cave and moved maybe fifty feet over to this slit trench. If this had happened our first day on the island, we might have laughed too hard to shoot the guy, but we all felt the thing had been too one-sided and we really riddled him.

Then an amazing thing happened. As we sat back and watched that cave entrance, every five or ten minutes another Nip would come out and head for the slit trench, paying no attention to the accumulation of bodies. We knocked off eight or nine of them before they stopped coming.

Back to the senses. You quickly learned to tell the difference between rifle fire and machine gun fire, ours and theirs. The same thing goes for the artillery and you learned to tell how big the shells were from the sound. This was particularly true after dark. I think the improvement of your hearing at night was astounding. One little mistake could easily cost you your life. We had lost men on Iwo who shouldn't have been killed; they just let their guard down for a second and that's when we lost them.

Then there were others who I guess you'd just have to say were doomed. I can think of two guys in my platoon who just didn't have a chance. Their names were Bill Cox and Sy Hart. One was a Mormon Church elder from Utah and the other was a Tennessee hillbilly. I can't remember which was which. The Mormon was the oldest guy in our platoon and the kid from Tennessee was just that, a kid. He couldn't have been over eighteen.

Anyway, these guys were great pals. They'd set up a duet where they'd harmonize together on "Red River Valley." My God, were they good! I mean I was a youngster from New York City. I certainly was no devotee of that kind of music, but I loved their singing; I could listen to them all day.

There was one night when I can't remember a single shell coming at us. I even got a little sleep for a change.

Jeez, do you know the next morning Cox and Hart were dead? They apparently had taken a direct hit from a Jap mortar. They didn't have a chance. That was the type of a thing that made fatalists out of a lot of us.

At any rate we still kept trying to move north even though the resistance seemed to get stronger. I think one of the reasons we were able to move at all was the good mix of our division. Iwo was the only battle the 5th was in, but it was loaded with a lot of men who had fought in earlier campaigns, gone back to the States with wounds or malaria, and were then sent back to the Pacific for a second time.

The best known of this group was probably Gunnery Sergeant John Basilone. "Manila John," as they called him, won the Congressional Medal of Honor on Guadalcanal with the 7th Marines. He was sent home and undoubtedly could have spent the rest of the war in the U.S. That wasn't Basilone's style. He went into Iwo with the 28th Marines of our Division and was killed the first day leading his machine gun platoon forward.

My own platoon also had several men who were on their second Pacific trip. One of our veterans was an American Indian; I think he was Pawnee. He had been a Paramarine and while he never jumped in combat—none of the Paramarines did—he had seen previous action. I think he had been on Gavutu, Guadalcanal and Vella Lavella.

Then there was our platoon sergeant, a man named Jones. He had been a Marine Raider in the Solomons. And, I may add, he was one of several former Raiders who were spread throughout the division. These veterans did a hell of a lot to help stabilize the newer men.

Now, I certainly don't want to leave the impression that we always gained ground. Hell, I can remember one day when we bedded down about thirty yards from where we started.

And there were the hills. There was one of them we went up and down three or four times before we could finally get up and stay.

Generally speaking, Iwo was too small to allow us to bypass most of their fortified positions. Most of them had to be eliminated on the spot. We'd call for artillery, maybe a tank, or else some very gutsy guy would try and flank the position so he could drop a satchel of dynamite into the Nip pillbox, cave or what have you. It was slow work and very costly.

We did have control of the air space over Iwo. There were some kamikaze strikes at our fleet—I remember seeing the *Hornet* or the *Saratoga,* can't remember which, get hit—but I don't remember any Jap planes attacking us on the island.

So we would call for air strikes on some of those strong Jap positions, but our naval pilots didn't fly low enough to really do a job. But, please, that's just my opinion.

I do know some Army P-51s came in after we'd opened up Motoyama I and they were tremendous. Hell, you had to duck when they flew by. They would have taken their planes right into the Jap caves if they could have.

Another thing I can recall are the Jap rockets. I had not seen any of these on Saipan or Tinian. They were weird. They'd rumble through the sky like a huge ash can with this *whoosh* sound. I don't remember that they did much damage even though I guess they knocked the hell out of an ammunition dump.

There is another guy from the 28th Marines I should mention. I didn't personally know him, but the 28th went through us at one point and I did get a chance to see that special machine gun he had. His name was Tony Stein. He'd been a toolmaker from Dayton, Ohio, and he'd cannibalized this .30 caliber machine gun from a fighter plane, probably at Hawaii. I guess it was lighter than the infantry machine gun—he carried it like a rifle. We heard that he had been killed later on, but he did one hell of a job with that gun.

Going up that west beach continued. The 3rd Division was to our right and I think the 4th Division was on their right. I won't say we were going against fortifications every minute, but there was always that damn sniper fire. We suffered a hell of a lot of casualties from their sharpshooters. Not all dead, mind you, far from it. I'd say the wounded outnumbered the dead at least four to one, but most of the wounded men had to leave the island.

But as bad as the sniper fire was, the horror of Iwo to me will always be those mortars I mentioned earlier. You'd never know when they would open up on you, and were they good! I once saw the Nips follow a moving jeep with mortar fire until they got it. This was a truly frightening thing to witness. You know, we're all pulling for the driver to get his jeep out of range, but the poor guy didn't make it.

My turn came on March 9. I guess you might say I got a little careless or maybe I was just plain exhausted. Whatever, I took a sniper's bullet from a Jap I never saw. Thank God my leg bone wasn't destroyed, but it became impossible for me to stand up. They got me over to a hospital on Saipan where I spent as much time sleeping as possible. When it got so I could walk again, I used to watch those Army bombers take off for Japan. I was told by many of the pilots that now that Iwo Jima was in our hands we were saving planes and flyers every day. The planes which had been damaged over Japan or had run into mechanical problems were no longer sitting ducks when they returned to their bases. They could simply stop off at the airfields at Iwo. Another plus was the fact that the Jap planes formerly stationed at Iwo could no longer go after any of these flyers.

Well, I got out of the hospital and returned to the 1st Battalion.

They had moved off Iwo and were back at Camp Tarawa in Hawaii. My God, what a change! It was like going to a brand new outfit. I don't think I recognized five people.

At any rate, we had to start training these new guys for something they called Olympic. For the first time we knew in advance what island we were headed for. It would be Japan, the sacred island of the cherry trees, and as we veterans knew, the island of coming death. The bombing of Hiroshima and Nagasaki may be somewhat controversial now, but, believe me, it wasn't in August '45. To me it meant I would be going home whole and not in a box. My luck must have just about run out.

Well, shortly after the signing on the *U.S.S. Missouri*, the 5th Division followed its original invasion plan and landed at Sasebo in Japan. This is where we had been slated to go in under fire. Hell, there were no landing places. I'm not even sure we would have gotten ashore.

And furthermore, one of our first tasks in Japan was to dismantle the Jap field pieces that were to greet us when we landed. Hell, they had enough artillery to eliminate forty divisions and enough shells to last a year. Any idiot who says the Nips were all through *before* we dropped the big bombs should be committed.

So I came back to the States and was discharged as a sergeant. I'm fifty-seven now, have a grown family and a good job. But every once in a while I'll look at that green blouse with the three stripes on the sleeve and say to myself, "Thompson, you may have ended up a sergeant, but you ain't no Lou Diamond."

The Two Flags Of Iwo Jima

How many people really know that there were two American flags raised on Iwo Jima?

Dick Wheeler, who lives near Reading, Pennsylvania, is one who surely does, because the first one was raised by his platoon.

An author by trade, Dick has written several books and is currently working on a history of the Marine Corps in the Pacific. When I visited with Dick, he not only told me of that flag-raising but talked of the men who first raised "Old Glory" on Mount Suribachi.

"I saw Charlie Lindberg, the flamethrower in our platoon," Wheeler said, "down in Tallahassee, Florida, a year or so ago. The town was putting up a monument to Ernie Thomas, our platoon sergeant. Ernie got the Navy Cross on Iwo. Poor guy was killed on that 'evil, little island.' Our lieutenant, John Wells, was also there. A great guy, John's made a lot of money in oil. He was badly shot up on Iwo."

Then Dick got around to Suribachi.

"Okay. There were five men really involved in the putting up of that first flag: Charlie Lindberg, Jim Michels, Henry Hansen, our Company Executive Officer Harold Schrier and Ernest Thomas. Thomas and Hansen were later killed on Iwo and Lindberg was wounded. Jim Michels was also wounded, but he disregarded it, claiming it was just a scratch. These men were all from the 3rd Platoon, E/21/28th Marines. This was my platoon.

"The flag went up at about 10:30 A.M. the morning of February 23, but since I had been seriously wounded two days before I wasn't with my platoon at the top of Suribachi."

Dick Wheeler may not have been with his outfit at the exact moment they raised the first flag, but several years ago he put together the gripping story of his outfit on Iwo and the flag-raising. It is entitled *The Bloody Battle for Suribachi.* I had read his book and was anxious to ask Dick several questions about that dramatic experience.

For instance, the flag itself was raised with practically no resistance. This in itself was unusual because the caves surrounding the area were loaded with Japanese who could have easily annihilated the platoon. This fact still remains a mystery.

Then there was the question of the flag itself. Where had it come from?

"Our battalion's adjutant had it in his map case," says Dick. "I guess it was just accidental that my platoon was picked. Of course, I like to think we were chosen because we were the best platoon in Easy Company. Of course I'll get an argument there."

And finally, why the second flag?

"Oh, that's an easy one," says Dick. "Our first flag was only fifty-four by twenty-four inches. It just wasn't big enough for distant viewing. So Lieutenant Colonel Johnson, the CO of our battalion, sent out word to an LST to get a bigger one.

"And, by the way, that Johnson was one hell of an officer! First name was Chandler. He was killed a little later on at Iwo.

"And that's really the thing above all I remember about Iwo, the men getting killed and wounded constantly. Of the forty-six original men from my platoon who went ashore on D-Day, forty-two were casualties.

"The second flag came ashore and an AP cameraman, Joe Rosenthal, ended up with one of the truly great war photographs of all time. The new flag was twice the size of the original one and could be seen by all."

As the years have gone by, controversy has arisen concerning these flag-raisings, particularly the second one. Such are the ways of any classic.

The truth is that neither of these raisings was tainted in any way. Their main purpose was to show the troops that the top of Suribachi had been reached. Even the most cynical Marine who witnessed them was touched by the sight of the American flag dominating the high point of bloody Iwo.

Also, most people do not realize that these flag-raisings did *not* signify the end of the battle. In reality, there were three or four weeks of horrendous combat left on Iwo.

Above all, the photos of the flag raisings were not canned pictures. If Rosenthal's camera had not caught that second raising precisely when it did, it would have been just another photograph of the flag going up on a Japanese-held island.

There is one more thing that is questioned. Was it the first or second flag-raising that caused Secretary of the Navy James Forrestal to make his famous remark?

No matter. The important thing is the Secretary did turn to General Holland Smith and say, "Holland, the raising of that flag means a Marine Corps for the next five hundred years!"

Oh yes, a battle-weary Marine is alleged to have viewed the group on top of Suribachi and shaken his head.

"Those guys," he said, "should be getting flight pay."

The Lad from the Deep South

Arliss Franklin

Dick Franklin, known as Frank in the Pacific, was one of the thousands of young southerners in the seventeen-to-eighteen-year-old age bracket who joined the Corps during World War II. He served with the Marines in the Guam and Okinawa campaigns. In the latter fight he was very seriously wounded and for a while it was feared he would never walk again.

After the war ended, Dick resumed his education. After graduating from the University of Alabama, he went to work for the U.S. Science and Education Administration, retiring as a southern regional director in 1980.

In recent years Dick has become very active in the 6th Marine Division association. I visited with him at his division's reunion in New Orleans, where he had this to say about the gathering:

"I feel get-togethers like this are apt to become more precious to you as you grow older. Most of our men no longer have the financial burden of raising their families. They can afford to come here and spend a few days with their buddies with whom they share so many memories, some good, others horrifying. But whatever those memories may be, they sure as hell will never leave us."

At this point Chuck Castle, another veteran of the 6th, joined us.

"Chuck is a perfect example of what I mean," continued Dick. "He was scout for A Company and I was the same for C Company, both of the 22nd Marines. We worked together a lot, particularly down on the southern end of Okinawa, until we got hit. Chuck, you got it the day after I did, right?"

"Yeah, I think so. It was on the outskirts of Naha. Three of us were standing together, which we shouldn't have been doing, when one of their shells came over. It got all three. But none of us was killed, thank God for that."

"The one that got me the day before also hit another Marine, a man named Barnum; I think he was from West Virginia."

And that's the way it goes at a Marine reunion. All six Marine divisions saw very heavy duty. Today, when these men get together, they talk of many things, but eventually they always get around to combat. After all, that's why they went to the Pacific.

PFC ARLISS FRANKLIN
1st Battalion, 22nd Marines

I'll tell you what someone should write a book about—all those rackets, big and small, that various servicemen worked out in the Pacific.

For instance, one night on Guadalcanal one of our men showed up with a gallon of ice cream. We all thought this was great, you know, anything to ease the boredom that was a way of life on an island like the Canal long after organized Japanese resistance had ended.

Then, I began to wonder where the hell it had come from. I did a little nosing around and found out.

It seemed that each day they made ice cream, the cooks would always make an extra gallon or two and put it aside. At night they would go out and sell it at ten dollars or so a gallon. Don't worry, they had plenty of takers. It doesn't sound like much money today, but on a 1944 money scale, those people were turning a tidy little profit— no overhead at all.

Then there were always some officers who would find a way to sell liquor to the enlisted men. Not many would do this, but there were always some.

The big profit, though, went to those Army transport pilots. Planes were always coming in to Guadalcanal from Australia, loaded with supplies, and some of those pilots made a bundle. When you talk about those guys, you're really talking big money.

Here's how they worked it. Apparently, liquor was plentiful in Australia, so they'd pick it up cheaply down there and sell it at a huge profit on the Canal.

On the other hand, American cigarettes were very inexpensive on the island but quite dear back in Australia. So the pilots would load up on cigarettes with a big markup back in Australia. I guess if there's a way to make a buck, someone will always capitalize on it.

Well, let's go back to Moss Point, Mississippi in December 1941. You have probably never heard of the place. It's a Gulf town, very big on football. Eddie Kychuck, who used to coach the Philadelphia Eagles, came from Moss Point. I was a junior in high school at the time.

When the Japs bombed Pearl Harbor, the whole town went into a state of shock. How dare those little yellow people slap America like that! Hell, Uncle Sam was going to whip the hell out of those buck-toothed, four-eyed bastards in no time at all. How wrong we were!

Perhaps one of the reasons we were so far off base was the utter lack of contact our part of the country had with the Japanese. Hell, I'd only seen a half dozen Chinese in my lifetime. I'd never seen a Jap. They just didn't hang around Moss Point very much.

Also, as we had had no contact with them, we had no way of knowing anything about that Bushido thing of theirs. They have been running a television series on kamikaze pilots here in New Orleans recently. I've tried to imagine what type of mind it takes to literally be willing to commit suicide with the certain knowledge that you will be rewarded in the hereafter. It beats the hell out of me.

Anyway, as we greatly underestimated the Japanese, we naturally weren't afraid of them. I can't remember anyone in my hometown who genuinely tried to stay out of the service. I think we all felt it was pre-ordained—if you were young and healthy, you went; that's all there was to it.

My turn came in August '43. I'd just graduated from high school and was about to reach my eighteenth birthday. I wanted to enlist in the Marine Corps, but my parents wanted me to wait until I was drafted, which would probably be during the first part of '44. I finally won them over and they agreed to let me go into the Corps in August '43.

Now, my desire to go into the service is, I think, a perfect example of the difference between my generation of Americans and those of today.

Don't misunderstand me. I can sympathize with today's youngsters. Perhaps they have a better understanding of war's horrors than we did. I'm sure as hell no hawk or war lover. I can't tell you how I'd feel today if I were eighteen again. I can tell you that in '43 I was as eager to become a Marine as anyone you could find.

At any rate, I went in and received the first of many surprises. If you lived in Mississippi, you normally went to Parris Island for boot camp, and of the ten men who went in with me, nine of them did go to PI.

Not me. Somehow my orders read San Diego. This meant a godawful train ride across the country. Hell, I believe I stood up as far as San Antonio, Texas.

I had teamed up with an old man of thirty from Birmingham, Alabama. He was a steel worker who'd been drafted and was one tough guy. After San Antonio, he'd had enough of trying to lean against the seats.

"The hell with this shit!" he said. "I'm a-going to crap out right here on the floor. Let's get all of them newspapers that are ahanging around here and makes us a bed."

My new friend may have been a redneck steel worker, but he sure had brains. We spent the rest of the trip sleeping on those newspapers. It was no great bargain, but it sure beat standing up.

After we reached San Diego, the two of us ended up being the only boots from the Deep South in our platoon, which was numbered 729. Most of the rest of the platoon was from the Midwest, mainly Chicago. And, believe me, it was quite an experience for a boy from Mississippi to be thrown in with these guys.

The first night there, our DI gathered the platoon together.

"All right now," he said, "any of you idiots who have straight razors or switchblades throw them on this bunk. We don't want anyone getting cut up."

So this kid named D'Angelo tossed the first switchblade knife I'd ever seen out on the bunk. I remember saying to myself, "What in the hell have I become associated with?"

But do you know, D'Angelo became one of my best friends at boot camp—as did a fellow named Bob Foss. Another good buddy was a butcher named Bob Nulabonski. They were all from Chicago. I'd dearly like to see them again.

I think one of the reasons I became such good friends with these guys was the difference in the way we talked. I noticed that they kept coming around and starting conversations with me. Finally, I asked one of them why they did this.

"Probably because we love your accent," one of them said. "None of us has heard one like it before."

"Well you know," I answered, "I have never heard people talk the way you do either." From then on we were buddies.

One more shock I received at San Diego was the early morning chill. It may sound funny to a northerner, but remember, I came from the Gulf Coast. Hell, I was about to freeze my butt off standing at attention at 5:30 A.M. in Dago. Even my Chicago friends said it was nippy, and you know how viciously cold their city could become.

Actually though, I can't say boot camp was too tough. Maybe this was because I was so young. I think it was harder on the older boots, men who had been out on their own before going into the Marines. That strict discipline and loss of individuality was probably more rugged for them to stomach than it was for a seventeen-year-old kid.

Anyway, I finished boot camp and was sent to Combat Intelligence School at Camp Elliott. Don't let the term *intelligence* snow you. It had nothing to do with spy work or deciphering codes. We were trained as scouts, which means just what it says. Our job was usually to scout the area that our company was moving into.

And, you know, I was one of the few men who did just what I was trained to do when I got overseas. You know how it was; men schooled in radio work would end up as riflemen, as would Marines trained in motor transport. But other than some miserable duty in a replacement draft on Guadalcanal, I was always a scout in the Pacific, at least until I got hit on Okinawa.

Well, one of the good things that happened while at Combat Intelligence School was teaming up with a great guy named Webb Jessup. He came from the L.A. area. He was also one of the very few men who had an automobile. Every possible weekend we would head up the highway to Webb's family place. It was tremendous.

The thing that struck me the most on that drive was the absolute beauty of the scenery between Elliott and L.A.—my gawd, it was awesome.

I recently had an occasion to drive south of L.A. on that same highway. What a change! The Pacific Ocean is still there, of course, but the way that area has been built up is unreal. You realize things like this must happen, but I still think it's sad as hell.

Well, shortly after I reported to Elliott, the news of the Tarawa invasion broke. While the initial casualty figure turned out to be somewhat exaggerated, the Corps did suffer over three thousand killed and wounded in three days. And the majority of these came from two regiments of the 2nd Division, the 2nd and 8th Marines, even though the 6th Marines caught some hell at the end of the battle.

I think the shock wave that hit the American public at the news of this concentrated butchery was one of the strongest that struck during the war. I know the government didn't want many of the photographs showing the rows of American dead to be published, but one of our generals, I think it was Vandegrift, disagreed with them.

"There is no easy road to Tokyo," he said, "and the American public better realize that right now."

At the same time the 2nd Division hit Tawara, the 3rd Marine Division was fighting on Bougainville and the 1st was getting ready for New Britain. I point this out because I think these battles had a lot to do with the haste with which I was sent over. The Corps needed replacements badly.

I actually left for Guadalcanal the first part of January, 1944, less than three months after I'd finished boot camp. My ensuing stay there on the Canal, the first of two, I may add, turned out to be the low point of my career in the Corps.

This was not due to combat; it was due to an utter lack of identity with anything while I was there.

I'd gone over with the 41st Replacement Draft and I was to spend the next several weeks there on the Canal with that lashup. In reality, you might as well have called us the 41st Work Detail Unit because that's all we did—work. And I mean we turned to, sometimes twelve hours a day.

This back-breaking labor started the minute we landed ashore over near the Tassafaronga area. It was our job to unload the ship and we did, working well into the night. It was raining like the devil, which made the whole deal miserable.

After we were finally finished for the night, the reality of the whole thing hit me. I was not going back to a warm barracks and take a warm shower. I was cold, dirty and hungry and I knew my dungarees were just going to have to dry on my body. I don't think I've ever felt quite so lonely in my life, even later on when I was in some pretty heavy combat.

That first work detail was the beginning of my tour as a stevedore. We were overseas all right but still as a replacement unit, not as part of a regiment.

Now, there is nothing wrong with a job as a stevedore, particularly if you're getting paid well. But, that kind of work is not why I'd joined the Corps. It did, however, give me one of the very few laughs I had during this lousy period.

Here's what happened. We were unloading an ammunition supply when one of our men picked up a San Francisco paper that was lying on the ship's deck.

"Holy Christ!" he yelled out. "Listen to this shit!"

Then he read to us all about the heroic stevedores back in the States who were loading the ammunition onto the ships and how they risked their lives every day handling the explosives. The paper also pointed out how well paid they were due to the hazardous aspects of their job.

And when I say well paid, they could make as much in a day as we could in a month!

Finally, we could stand no more of this baloney. So one of our men threw in a perfect squelch:

"Who in the hell do they think is unloading *this* goddamn ammunition, coolies?"

To make matters worse, about ninety percent of the gear we unloaded was either marked U.S. Army or U.S. Navy, which did not sit well with a group of bitching Marines.

You know, it might not have been so bad if we could have gone into a bar somewhere and maybe run into some young ladies. But, hell, our off-duty recreation was watching the trees grow. That is, of course, unless we could steal some Army beer—that became our on-duty fun and games, walking away with the beer slated for the dogfaces. The Army would always have an armed guard on their brew, but one way or another, we'd always manage to get a case or two. I always felt the guard would look the other way as long as we didn't get greedy. He knew how miserable we were.

Then, I think it was May or so, they loaded our 41st Replacement Draft aboard ships and we headed for Guam. We knew this meant combat, but anything was better than that crummy work detail duty. The bickering and discontent had really become intolerable. I think the last day we unloaded a ship, two Marines, good friends, got into a fist fight over a lousy candy bar. That's how bad it was. You could always count on a fist fight at just about every chow line.

Well, we went into Guam, about ten days after the invasion. Here most of us joined the 22nd Marines, which was then part of the 1st Provisional Brigade and, my gawd, how things changed. Now I had a feeling of permanence—a sense of belonging. The 22nd was a fine regiment that had fought on Eniwetok and had hit Guam on the first day of the attack. Serving in an outfit like the 22nd made all the difference in the world to me—this was the real Marine Corps.

Once in the 22nd, I was attached to an intelligence unit. Our job was to try and locate many of the Chamorros who had taken off for the bush when the battle started. Remember, they were American citizens and they were in terrible condition. They'd had very little to eat for days and were really just wandering around. They were scared to death of the Japanese, who did kill several of them. I guess the Nips were so damn angry over the fact they knew they were beaten, they'd shoot just about anything that moved that wasn't Japanese.

The area my unit was operating in was called Talofofo. There were several Jap soldiers there, but the rounding up of them was supposed to be the job of our rifle companies. Our unit's job was to find the Chamorros not the Japs, but it wasn't always easy to stay away from those Nips. They'd pop up everywhere. It wouldn't surprise me if a couple of those guys came out of the bush tomorrow.

The thing above all that I recall about this duty is the feeling of belonging. I can't overemphasize what this meant to me. Now I felt I was a part of a team really accomplishing something. It sure beat the hell out of unloading cases of beer from an AKA.

This tremendous change for the better also allowed me to realize what a great bunch of men we had, including the officers. Hell, we rarely saw our officers when I was on those horseshit work details. It wasn't like that on Guam.

One of our lieutenants was a man named Jack Vaughan, the epitome of what an officer should be. The last time I heard about him, he was in the Peace Corps. As a matter of fact, I think he was originally the number one guy in the whole thing. If this is so, he would have been a great Peace Corps leader—Jack cared about people.

Another Marine I served with there is my very good friend Kenny Schwartz, who, incidentally, is one of the many enlisted men I know who has done very well in later life. Kenny is now quite a successful real estate operator in Florida.

My long-lasting friendship with Ken is a very good example of what I mean when I say the Marine Corps is great for getting people together who are on opposite ends of the pole.

Kenny, you see, is a Jewish guy from Boston, while I'm a Protestant from the Deep South. How different can you get?

Actually, I learned about something from Kenny that I knew nothing about. You don't see much of it any more, and thank God for that. It's called anti-Semitism.

This was new to me; believe it or not, there was no anti-Jewish feeling in my home town of Moss Point. I don't say we had many Jewish families there when I was growing up, but we did have some. One of my favorite high school dates was a Jewish girl. My family and everyone I knew just didn't look at them as being any different from anyone else. I'm not being patronizing in any way—that's the way it was.

Apparently things weren't that way in pre-World War II Boston, not according to Kenny. He said anti-Semitism did exist in Massachusetts forty years ago and quite a bit of it. I'm sure it's long gone by now, but I guess it was there back in the Thirties and early Forties.

Now, before anyone jumps up and down yelling about a Mississippi boy talking about that kind of thing—yes, we did have *racial* problems, plenty of them. However, the change in that situation has been huge since the end of World War II—all for the better. The situation is still not perfect, but I'll surely match it up with any other section of the country.

Well, back to the Corps. We left Guam sometime around the end of '44 and headed back to Guadalcanal, and it was there we formed the 6th Division, the three infantry regiments being the 4th, 22nd and 29th Marines—all being regiments that had already seen a goodly amount of combat. I think the 6th was the only Marine division that never served in the United States.

What a difference on the Canal this second tour was from my first. Now I was a member of the 22nd, not a stevedore. I was scout for C Company of the First Battalion, and when we did our training, you knew it could possibly save your life later on.

This training was really rugged. None of us knew what island we'd be assaulting, but we did realize it would have to be a lot closer to Japan than Guam. Most of us expected it to be a major operation and we weren't to be disappointed.

Then the word came through that the 3rd, 4th and 5th Divisions had hit the island of Iwo Jima. Wow! That place is only about six or seven hundred miles from Japan. We had heard our invasion force was going to consist of more than one Marine division and it didn't take much imagination to figure out we'd be going in with the 1st or 2nd Division, maybe both.

There is one more thing about that training on the Canal that I'd like to mention because it turned out to be a mystery that has never been solved. Here's what happened.

As company scout, I was out in front of our unit on a training exercise. The jungle we were going through was thick as hell. Out of nowhere I stumbled on a Nambu machine gun. This in itself was no big deal. After all, there had been plenty of fighting where we were training just a year or two before. But here's the rub. The Nambu was not only in perfect working order, but it had been oiled very recently. Hell, if it had been left unattended, the jungle climate would have corroded the hell out of it in no time at all. There can be no question—someone had it hidden there and for a reason.

Who knows? Perhaps a few diehard Nips were planning one last ambush on some unsuspecting Marines. There were definitely Japs still in the jungle. You were always hearing rumors of their sneaking into our area at night, trying to get food. The classic tale was of the Nip whom they caught dressed in Marine dungarees, standing in a chow line. Someone said they let him have his dinner, then gave him a kick in the ass.

Whatever, we never did find out why the Nambu was set up the way it was or who was taking care of it. But damn it, I've never stopped wondering about it.

At any rate, the time came for us to move on for what was to be the bloody showdown on Okinawa, and this brings up my old buddy, Ben Masselink, one of ten thousand guys who claimed they were going to write the great American book about the war after it was over. I don't know if he did write the book, but I do know he became an author because I've seen his name listed many times for screen credits. I've also seen several magazine articles with his name down as the author—at least I think it's the same Ben Masselink.

Anyway, just before we left for Okinawa, Ben came over to me.

"Frank," he said, "I got me a chance to get ahold of a bottle of bourbon, but I'm real short of cash. Could you lend me twenty? You're sure to get it back after the campaign unless I get killed. Then you'll just have to eat the twenty. Of course, you could get killed too.

Then, what the hell, you won't need the twenty anyway."

"Oh, that's a nice thought, Ben," I answered. "But I guess you're right. There has to be a good chance we won't both come back. Here, take the twenty and live it up!"

I lost track of Ben after the landing—we weren't in the same company—and I never heard from him again. But, damn it, I'd surely like to run into him. We could take the twenty I gave him, double it, then sit down and drink some good bourbon to our hearts' content.

Well, our first stop after we left the Canal was the island of Ulithi, where Uncle Sam was putting together a huge fleet for the Okinawa invasion. There, much to our surprise, they put our whole regiment ashore for a beer party, and what a blast it turned into. They seemed to have an endless supply of the stuff. Christ, our whole battalion got bombed.

Then someone came up with a stupid idea.

"Let's have a touch football game!" this clown yells.

What a disaster! Everyone is laughing and falling all over the place. Hell, that coral these guys were scraping their hands and knees on was living organic matter—it made the cuts extremely infection-prone. Our corpsmen ended up having a field day. Half of my company could hardly walk for a few days after that football game, if you want to call it that.

When the time did come to shove off from Ulithi, we moved from the transport we had been on over to an LST and now it was the Navy's turn to be stupid. As I look back over thirty-six years on their crassness, I still find it difficult to see how they could have shown such a lack of feeling for the troops they were to carry.

Here is what they did. After we were all aboard, crowded as hell, they brought the final piece of cargo aboard and laid it down right next to us. Can you guess what this cargo was—white crosses and stretchers, that's what! How would you like to be aboard a ship, headed for a big battle, and staring at those things? How ghoulish can you get?

So be it. When the 6th Division did make its landing, I think we were in great shape. Two of its regiments, my 22nd and the 4th, had served under divisional commander Lem Shepherd on Guam. Shepherd was then in command of the 1st Provisional Brigade. We knew he was as good a man as you could find. You know what I mean, the kind of general who knows what he's doing and isn't in a big hurry to lose lives needlessly. Naturally, you're thinking first of your own hide, but you're also thinking of the men serving with you. You like to feel the guy making the big decisions is also thinking of the men under him. We believed Shepherd fit the bill in this department.

Well, we went into Okinawa on April Fools' Day, 1945. I don't know who was fooled, the Americans or the Japs. All I know is the landing met no resistance whatsoever. In a way it was a letdown. Here you've set yourself up for a dreadful ordeal getting ashore and it turns into a cakewalk. However, it was the most pleasant letdown I've ever had. You can't imagine what a feeling of relief you get when you realize you are safely ashore and so are all your friends.

Shortly after our landing we started to move across the island. We had come ashore near the narrowest part of Okinawa and as resistance here was very slight, we moved quite fast. While there would be occasions when our division would run into some rather nasty Jap positions, the early stages of the Okinawa fight were nothing compared to what we'd later run into. I don't have the statistical data, but generally speaking, you can divide the campaign into two operations. First, the landing and the drive north. Compared to the other island campaigns in the Pacific, this was a snap.

The second phase, our move south, is as different as night and day from the first one. I think it would be impossible for any outfit to have a more brutal time than we had down at the southern end of Okinawa.

This brings up a point that I've always maintained. U.S. ground forces suffered about 40,000 battle casualties on Okinawa. The 6th Marine Division had the dubious honor of heading this list with 8,326 of these casualties, which is a devastatingly high figure for one divison in one battle.

The 1st Marine Division was a close second, suffering 7,901 battle casualties, and the four Army divisions were sure as hell in the fight —their dead and wounded round out at over 22,000. I just checked these figures last night in *Okinawa, The Last Battle,* published by the Department of the Army, and they are official.

Now, the very large percentage of our casualties occurred down at the southern end of the island. After we had immediately captured the Yontan Airfield and then moved north to gain complete control of about two-thirds of the island, why did we have go go south at all? Why couldn't we have taken the four Army divisions and our three Marine divisions—the 2nd Marine Division was in reserve when we landed—and set up a defensive line across the island, perhaps on the northern bank of the Asa River? All you had to do was look out onto the ocean to see how completely we dominated the sea. I think it would only have been a matter of time before the Japs would have broken their backs trying to get at us.

Hell's bells, our blockade of Naha and that whole southern area could have been complete. We would have just sat back and watched them squirm. If they came at us, we could have shot them to kingdom come. Sure, we would have suffered casualties; you always do, but nowhere near as many as we did by going after them.

Well, I guess hindsight is always better than foresight. The point is we did go south and it wasn't long before we had to capture every hill and cave in that part of the island.

It seems that each company in our regiment, or in the whole division, ran into at least one butchery. I guess ours was a spot about a half mile south of the Asa River, not far from Naha. Maybe that's why I've always felt that *north* of the Asa would have been a great place to set up that defensive line I was talking about.

Anyway, my Company C ended up taking the goddamned hill—they even started calling it Charlie Hill after we took it—but there were only eighty of us standing when it was over. I guess I should say lying, not standing, because we had to beat off one hell of a counter-attack to keep it. And you didn't fight that war standing up. I was going to find that out the hard way a few days later on the outskirts of Naha when it was my turn to get clobbered—which came about on May 16.

That morning our Captain Lloyd decided he'd take a reconnaissance patrol into Naha—I think this was to be the first patrol we sent into the town. We had gone about halfway when the Japs started to throw mortar shells at us. I was on the point looking around at this huge hunk of rubble that had been Naha. I was in the prescribed kneeling position, trying to make myself as small a target as possible, when Lloyd yelled over to me.

"Let's get the hell out of here before we get blown apart! I've found out what I wanted to know—this joint is still crawling with the bastards."

So I straightened up and started to turn around. As I did, fragments from an exploding shell hit me in the back. Naturally I went down, stunned by the shock. Then I tried to get up, but I found I couldn't move my leg. "My God," I thought to myself, "I'm paralyzed." Then I yelled to my buddies.

"My legs won't work; my legs won't work!" I was scared out of my wits.

Two of my friends from Company C dragged me over next to this tank that had just come up to our position. I guess they figured if they put me on the back of the tank, I'd get some protection. But as I was pure dead weight, they couldn't lift me up.

Then one of our corpsmen, a man named Okel, who had been weightlifting champion of California, came over. Christ, he picked me up like a sack of wheat and slung me onto the tank—a move that sounded great at first but ended up almost getting me killed.

You see, nothing draws Jap fire more than a tank. I don't think the Nips even noticed me, but they sure spotted the tank and they were trying to hit it with everything they had. One of their machine gun bullets caught me in my right leg. It wasn't a bad wound, didn't crack the bone, but I knew it was only a matter of time before I'd be killed.

So I grabbed the side of the tank and dragged myself down into a ditch. By this time I'm fully aware of what's going on. I figured the only hope I have of ever walking again is to get to an aid station as soon as possible. I lay in the ditch, trying to figure what the hell to do, when a short lieutenant—he couldn't have been more than 5'6"—showed up.

"What's the matter, buddy?" he asked.

"I've been hit in the back," I told him, "and I can't walk."

He said, "Pardner, I can't lift you, but I sure as hell can drag you."

Well, that little lieutenant dragged me close to half a mile, until we ran into some stretcher bearers. They took me back to a field hospital, you know, like the place they have on the television show *M*A*S*H*.

Now here's a funny one. As company scout, I could at least recognize the faces of all the officers in our battalion. I had never seen this lieutenant before—nor have I seen him since. We had taken a lot of casualties, particularly on Charlie Hill, and he might have been a replacement. Anyway, that's one guy I'd really like to thank. I hope he made it through the campaign.

I spent several days at the field hospital where they took the shrapnel out of my back, relieving the pressure on my spine. I was heavily drugged with morphine, but I can still remember the first time I could once again move my legs. I just can't describe the joy that I experienced when this happened, but I'm sure you can understand what I'm saying.

My next stop was an underground hospital that had been built by the Japs at the Yontan Airfield. From there I was flown to a base hospital on Guam, where I had the great joy of actually walking for the first time since that shrapnel had gone into my back on the outskirts of Naha.

My next stop was Pearl Harbor and some further treatment after which they flew me to the Oak Knoll Naval Hospital in Oakland, California. I ended up being discharged from the Corps about a month after the Japanese surrender.

Then, like so many thousands of other veterans, I took advantage of the GI Bill of Rights and enrolled at the University of Alabama. We didn't have Bear Bryant as head football coach in those days, but we surely had a great university.

But, you know, I never did get all that excited about the school. Oh, I worked hard and graduated all right, but something was missing and my mother noticed it.

"Dick," she asked me, "your daddy is so wrapped up in his school, Ole Miss, but you just don't seem to feel that way about the University of Alabama. Why is that?"

"Mom," I told her, "I guess those kind of feelings are the exclusive property of the 22nd Marines of the 6th Division."

Two Americans Die

"The Marines are okay for my money, in battle or out."
—From one of Ernie Pyle's last battle reports

Two of the most illustrious Americans killed in World War II died during the Okinawa campaign. And neither one of them died in the heat of the battle.

Ernie Pyle, the GI's correspondent who had survived some of the roughest fighting in the ETO, was killed by a sniper in a minor campaign on the island of Ie Shima. He was with the 77th Army Division at the time of his death, having just left the 1st Marine Division on Okinawa.

The second tragic death was that of Lieutenant General Simon Bolivar Buckner, who was killed on June 18 on Okinawa. Joe Fater of the 8th Marines was in the area where Buckner was killed. He was one of the many young V-12 officers who made their combat appearance in the Okinawa campaign.

"Push, push," recalls Joe, "maybe push the Nips into the water down at the southern end. That's what we were trying to do.

"The 11th Marines, the artillery regiment of the 1st Division who had been on the island since the first of April, were under the command of a real Marine Corps legend, Wilbutt Brown. He was known as 'Big Foot.'

"Jeez, I remember the first time I saw Brown all I could see were his feet. He was a big guy anyway, but he looked like his dogs were size fifteen triple E.

"Well, this Brown was a real pioneer in coordinating artillery, aerial and naval shelling. He was a master at it.

"Our shellfire was knocking the shit out of the Japs. Their resistance was ebbing, but they still managed to keep some artillery on the reverse side of the hills. This made the Jap guns hard as hell to get at.

"But the fire from the ships was coordinating perfectly with Brown's artillery. We were slowly reducing what was left of that damn Nip artillery and we were getting less and less shelling from the Japs.

"Well, General Buckner was with the Marines. I think it was June 18 or thereabouts. The Japs were still fighting, but their organized resistance was coming to a close. I guess Buckner wanted to get a close look at the end of the battle that had cost so many American lives.

"The Nips sent over a small barrage—it couldn't have been more than five or six rounds. One of these rounds hit a rock and sent hundreds of splinters in all directions.

"Jesus, one or more, I don't know how many, of these splinters hit Buckner. The battalion surgeon was right there and he put his hands into the general's guts, trying to hold him together, but you couldn't do anything for him.

"You see, this wasn't at the command post; it was at the observation post. When Buckner had come to the front, Colonel Bill Wallace of my 8th Marines had taken the general up to the lines. If you ask me, a guy who is the commander of a whole army just shouldn't have been at the front like that.

"You know, his father was the Confederate general who surrendered Fort Danielson to Ulysses S. Grant in the Civil War. Buckner was about sixty years of age. If he hadn't come to the front that way, he would have gone back to the States one of the real leading generals of the U.S. Army."

Buckner was the highest ranking officer killed in the Pacific War. After his death Lieutenant General Roy Geiger (USMC) took over the command of the 10th Army. He was the only Marine in history to command an army.

The 2nd Battalion at Sugar Loaf— The Hill of Death

"Hey, what platoon are you guys?"
"Platoon? Hell, we're the 2nd Battalion, 22nd Marines, what's left of us anyway."
—2/22nd, coming off Sugar Loaf Hill

Sugar Loaf is the name of what was originally called a "prominent hill." It is located about half a mile from Naha, a seaport on the island of Okinawa. It is not a high mount such as other Marine battlegrounds like Suribachi or Tapotchau. Rather, it is a large, domineering hill surrounded by other hills and ridges. This entire area had been very heavily fortified by the Japanese in 1945, especially Sugar Loaf and its neighboring hills, Horseshoe and Half Moon.

Blocking the entrance to Naha and impossible to outflank, the area had to be reduced by brute force. The result was one of the most horrendous bloodlettings in the history of American combat. The author does not care to pit the number of dead Marines at one place against those at another battleground. Suffice it to say that the losses suffered by the 6th Division in the Sugar Loaf to the Naha area can stand alongside such other Marine Corps charnel houses as Belleau Wood, Mont Blanc, Tarawa, Saipan and Peleliu. The valor that was so conspicious on Iwo Jima was displayed at Sugar Loaf. And uncommon valor also prevailed at a place called Shuri Castle, near Naha, where the 1st Marine Division fought. In actuality, the entire fighting south of the Asa River on Okinawa was a bloody nightmare.

As for Sugar Loaf itself, the first Marine assault occurred late in the afternoon of May 12 when a handful of survivors from George Company, 2nd Battalion, 22nd Marines reached the summit. These Marines quickly realized they were out of their league and the remnant of George Company then exercised the maneuver the Corps calls "an advance to the rear." During the following two days the other companies of the 2nd Battalion, Easy and Fox, were to share the fate of George: they would be shot to pieces.

In retrospect, some of the assaults on Sugar Loaf (and there would be as many as fifteen) seem to have been sheer madness. It is easy to criticize the course of a battle close to forty years after the struggle, when the confusion and the concurrent tensions of battle are no longer present. The fact remains that a key area was taken from the Japanese after a week of hell that saw, among other things, the 6th Division Artillery fire 92,560 shells. There is no record of how many were fired by the Japanese, but as one veteran put it, "I don't remember them Nips running out of anything!"

At a reunion of the 6th Marine Division in New Orleans three former members of Fox Company of the 22nd agreed to share their memories with me. They were Bill Woolman, a Nebraskan who is now a California cabinet maker; Joe Horgan, a construction man from Philadelphia; and John Nuyianes, also from Philadelphia. One of the many Marines to carry the sobriquet of Bull, John is a retired sheet metal foreman who lives in Feasterville, Pennsylvania. Woolman and Nuyianes were in a mortar squad, while Horgan was a rifleman. All three were PFCs on Sugar Loaf.

In such a sitdown one man usually carries the conversation and the others frequently pitch in with additional information. In this case the leader was Nuyianes. Bull has a simple explanation for this.

"For many years after the war," he says, "I couldn't talk about the horrors at all. Why, I couldn't even enjoy cooked meat because the smell reminded me of the Japanese we'd burned with flamethrowers. A psychologist told me one of my problems was keeping it all bottled up. Instead, he said I should let it all go. Now when I get going about Okinawa, I can't stop. At least this way I don't have the bad dreams anymore."

After twenty minutes chatting with the three men from Company F, I received a bonus. Bill Woolman spotted another Sugar Loaf veteran sitting nearby.

"Wait a minute," he said, "there's Ed DeMar from George Company. He was with Lieutenant Bair and that first group to go up Sugar Loaf." He then asked Ed to join us.

Ed DeMar, it turned out, was First Sergeant Edmund DeMar, USMC (ret.), a thirty-year man. Born in Brooklyn, he was raised in Madison, Connecticut, and joined the corps in 1940. He stayed on active duty until 1963 when he transferred into the Reserves. He retired in 1970. He now lives in Kittery, Maine, where he is an instructor at a maritime school.

As with most career men, a good deal of the Corps has stayed with Ed. When you call him on the phone and say, "Is this Mr. DeMar?", he answers, "Affirmative"—you know immediately that he was an excellent "top soldier."

Ed jumped into the interview with both feet, carefully relating the May 12th move up Sugar Loaf as if it had happened only yesterday. After he finished, the men of Fox Company continued their own recollections of those grim days of May 1945.

As in the section on "Company K at The Point," it is not important to identify each speaker. What is being said is what is important.

PFC JOHN (BULL) NUYIANES
PFC JOSEPH HORGAN
PFC BILLY A. WOOLMAN
F/2/22nd Marines
          and
PLT. SGT. EDMUND DEMAR
G/2/22nd Marines

That's a good question, who in the hell did name it Sugar Loaf Hill?

It was Woodhouse, the lieutenant colonel in command of our battalion. Remember he said it looked like a loaf of bread with all those honey-combed caves loaded with the Nips.

Yeah, I'd say it was three hundred, maybe four hundred feet wide, somewhat larger than a football field.

That's about right. And the whole place had been built like a huge fortress. Caves and tunnels all over the place. But, damn it, there was no way around it.

You see, it was the key to that whole Naha-Shuri-Yonabaru line—don't ask me to spell it. You couldn't possibly take Naha without knocking off Sugar Loaf.

But, Jeez, it was tough. They had these guns that would fire, then disappear. I recall a 20 millimeter that would fire several rounds then just evaporate.

Oh, that stinker! I'd tried to catch those guys with a BAR but no soap. Then one of our planes came over and doused the area with napalm. All of us who saw that fire gave out a big cheer—you'd think it was a high school football game.

Christ, a few minutes later there it is, back in action. It hadn't been touched. I don't know how the hell we ever did get it.

I sometimes wonder how we took anything at that place, it was so rough; I mean the whole area around Sugar Loaf.

And we weren't all heroes, not by a long shot. I don't want to mention no names, but after we'd been shot up so badly, I ended up acting gunnery sergeant; I was still officially a PFC.

Well, we were told to move out one night, heading into what was sure to be heavy duty. And if there was one thing we hated, it was going after those Nips after dark.

Our left flank was supposed to be covered by a couple of machine gunners. I told them what the scoop was, but they wanted no part of it.

"Hell," they told me, "if we go out there, we're crazy! You know damn well all of us have orders to shoot everything that moves tonight. Christ, if the Japs don't get us, we'll be shot by Marines!"

So they stayed put, which put us in a hell of a lousy spot, you know, with our left flank open like that.

Now, you may say, did we have them court-martialed? The answer is hell, no! We'd been fighting almost constantly for two or three weeks. Those guys were lucky they were in one piece as it was. What the hell, they may have been hit later on anyway—most of us were —I don't know. But I do know if they made it through Okinawa and are still alive, they've had to live through that night all these years. They know we took casualties that night we might not have if they had been with us. That's the way it was.

That's right, but you forgot to say that it was raining like hell that night and was pitch dark. We were lucky we didn't catch any fire from our own men.

Okay. Now, that happened a few days after Sugar Loaf, in Naha, which I guess was between a half mile and a mile from the hill.

As for Sugar Loaf itself, we tried to capture it, over on its right side, on May 13. The first Marines who tried to take it, to the left of us, were from George Company, also of our battalion. Only a handful of 'em got to the top and they couldn't stay, they were just shot to pieces.

That's right, and there's Ed DeMar over at the other table. He's one of the few men who did get to the top that first day.

"Hey, Ed, this guy wants to know about our battalion at Sugar Loaf. I've told him you won the battle single-handed. Come over and set him straight."

Okay, you want to talk about Sugar Loaf. Well, I was in charge of the 3rd Platoon, George Company, 2nd Battalion, 22nd Marines. If I'm not mistaken, we were the first company to go up that damn hill. We jumped off 1600 hours on May 12, 1945. We didn't know at the time the place would be named Sugar Loaf. It was just known as "prominent hill," target some damn number, whatever it was. I was in charge of the platoon because our second lieutenant, Joe Carrigan, from Pittsburgh, Pennsylvania, had been wounded a few days before the 12th.

Anyway, we had been already seeing a lot of combat for a week or two before the 12th. First Lieutenant Bair, Fox Company's executive officer, had taken the company over from Captain Stebbins who had been riddled in the leg by machine gun fire. Bair called me and the tank commander over—I think it was around noon on the 12th —to tell us what end was up.

"Okay," he said, "Ed Reuss's first platoon has nineteen men left. The others are just as badly off. DeMar, how many men do you have left?"

"Twenty-eight."

"Well, we've got to take the hill. No one knows what we'll find up there, but we've got to go up. Easy Company is pinned down and taking a lot of KIA's and WIA's. Can't do a thing. It's up to us. We will have these four tanks with us. Synchronize your watches for 1600."

So I gave the word to the platoon there. Hell, it's like those AEF veterans used to tell me when I was a kid. You know, "over the top" and all that stuff. This means one thing. If the Nips have strength in the area, and it sure as hell looks like they do there, we're bound to catch hell. I'm concerned for my own butt, but also for a reputation I had gained that I was rather proud of. Here's what I mean:

A few months ago I got a letter from Jerry "Zimmy" Zimmermann, a nineteen-year-old BAR man in Dick Rupe's squad of my platoon.

"Sarge," he wrote, "I don't think any of us knew your name was Edmund because we all called you 'Mommy' Demar."

Okay, the nickname may be corny, but the reason I got it was pretty important to me. You see, I was twenty-six and here I am in charge of a platoon of Marines whose average age is probably between eighteen and nineteen; some of them had not even reached their eighteenth birthday. You start seeing Marines like that get their heads knocked off and it gets to you. I honestly think I did my best to look after those kids. After all, what the hell is a leader good for if he doesn't look after the troops?

And, by the way, Zimmermann did not go up the hill with us because the same machine gun that got Captain Stebbins also hit Zimmy.

Okay. The men are all getting ready, but believe me, no one is looking forward to it. Then the tank commander comes over to me. I can see he has a worried look on his face.

"Look," I said to him, "I know what you're going to say. You're going to tell me to stick close, not to leave you high and dry so in case any of the Nips come out of their holes with satchel charges, we can take care of 'em. Well, tank commander, we're going to stick to you like flies on horseshit. Don't worry about a thing there."

So he goes back to his tanks and brings them up to the line. He's looking out of his turret in the center. Bair is on his right and I'm on the tank's left. Bair was about 6'2″ and weighed 225 pounds. Hard as a rock. He was our old machine gun man who had picked up the Silver Star on Guam.

Okay, so we started out. I would have rather gone in the other direction, but what can you do. The first hundred yards are not too bad, but then the crap started. Small arms fire, mortars, artillery— I expected to see the kitchen stove coming at us any minute. Now some of our men are starting to get hit. The Nips have their artillery set up on the other side of the hill, placed in such a way that they're hard as the devil for our artillery to hit.

So our tanks are also starting to catch it. The small arms fire doesn't do too much to them, but the artillery does. I know one of them was hit and another was stuck in a large shell hole. A third one was still moving, over on my left flank, and I don't know where the g.d. fourth one was.

But you know, this was nothing new. Those tankers always did get into trouble. There were fifteen of them in those tanks that started up the hill with us. Before the attack was over, thirteen of these men were either WIA or KIA. They weren't all hit while in their tanks; some caught it after they'd left them, but they sure got hit! My point is that when you go up a hill like Sugar Loaf, everyone is vulnerable to Jap fire.

Anyway, just as we're getting close to the top of the hill, the third tank went on the fritz. I don't know if it'd been hit or what have you; all I could see was it wasn't moving.

Being stalled there made it a real sitting duck. This squad leader of mine, his name was Dick Rupe, could see that those tankers had to haul ass out of that tank because it would be only a matter of time, and not much of that, before the Nips started zeroing in on it. So he jumps up on the tank and starts banging the escape hatch with the butt of his M-1.

"Get your ass outa there, get your ass outa there, quick!" he's yelling at the top of his lungs.

Wham, that hatch opened and those guys started piling out, looking for any cover they could find. We were all exposed to the Jap fire no matter where we were, but you'd try and protect yourself one way or another.

Now every man at Sugar Loaf could have been given a medal. But to get a Bronze Star, a Silver Star or a Navy Cross, you had to not only have guts, but you had to also have luck, particularly if you were an enlisted man.

You see, let's say you do something real ballsy, and Lieutenant Ninety-day Wonder says, "Wow, Ski, or whatever your name is, I'm going to put you up for a citation."

Then an hour or two later the lieutenant catches one in the head. There goes the medal out the window!

Here's what I'm driving at: I wish I knew the whereabouts of Rupe, Richard M. Rupe, that is. I ended up being a thirty-year man, retiring in 1970. I did some duty in Washington, D.C., before I retired and I know my way around. I might still be able to get Dick a medal. I don't know, maybe he doesn't give a damn, but he sure earned a medal.

Well, shortly before Rupe had jumped up on the tank, Bair had picked up a machine gun minus the tripod from two of our gunners who had been killed on their way up the hill. He had cuddled it in his arm with the ammunition belt slung over his shoulder. The darn thing must have weighed forty pounds. He was firing the gun from his hip like Victor McLaglen in one of those movies from the Thirties. And what a sight he was, standing there, all alone, at the top of Sugar Loaf! Jesus, he looked like that Marine Corps statue we have at Parris Island. It might have taken us some nine or ten more days, and thousands of Marines, to permanently secure the hill, but on that twelfth day of May, late in the afternoon, for a short time, it was under the command of one First Lieutenant. Dale Bair and his machine gun.

I wish to hell I could have taken a photograph of him, but when I reached the top of that hill myself, the last thing in my mind was to snap a picture.

Of course he eventually got hit. I think it was in his right leg. He spun around from it, but he didn't go down there. It did look as if it had taken some of his flesh away, but he still kept firing.

Anyway, he's motioning to me for something. I'm trying to find out what he's up to when I caught a load of shrapnel in my left thigh and go down. I know this is no joke because I can't move my left leg.

Then Bair gets hit again, this time in his buttocks. Remember, where we're now located there's Japs all around us. We seem to be firing in all directions, and also getting it from every direction.

Bair does go down this time, ass over tea kettle, but damn it, he's soon trying to fire that damn machine gun again. I'm trying to patch up my thigh which is now bleeding like hell. I know I've got to get some bottle blood, but I don't know where the hell I'm going to get it. All I know is that everywhere I look there is nothing but a screwed-up mess. Years later I did get a valued opinion from someone who had an overall view of what was going on. This happened at our divisional reunion at Orlando, Florida, in 1980 when I ran into Dick Pfuhl. He was an Easy Company officer at Sugar Loaf. We were enjoying a few cool ones when I gave him a gentle needle.

"Dick," I said, "it was your Company E that was pinned down so badly that George Company had to step in and go up that lousy hill there."

"That's right, it was, but I had my binoculars on your company at the top of the ridge. My God, you men were all fighting like the devil, what was left of you anyway. What a job you did with nothing!"

And that same Dick Pfuhl was one hell of a Marine! He picked up three Purple Hearts and a Bronze and Silver Star. He died a few months ago of a heart attack.

Okay, back to Sugar Loaf. All of a sudden, I don't know why, there seemed to be a lull in the firing. I looked around and all I could see was dead and wounded Marines. I looked over on my left and I can see a great little guy named Jim Davis—we called him "Little Bit" —who had been hit badly, oh Christ, real badly. He must have been out of his head. You could just sense he didn't know what was going on.

"Mother, mother," he's yelling and "dad, dad, please help me!" Then after a while his yelling stops and he's just moaning.

In the meantime, I'm trying to figure out what the hell I was going to do. We had made it to the top of the hill, but there was no way we could hold it. Hell, I can't remember but four of us who were actually up there. Rupe, Bair, DeMar and one other—I think it was Chaisson, but I'm not sure—were there at the top, I know that. Then there were those tankers real close, but that was about it, as far as I can recall anyway.

There is one thing I did know for sure: if we don't get off of there quick, they'll be only dead Marines on top.

Then, and to this day I don't know who was doing the yelling, I heard a voice:

"DeMar," it says, "can you crawl?"

"Buddy," I answered, "I'll crawl all the way to Madison, Connecticut, if I have to!"

"We've requested some smoke so those of you still alive on the top can get the hell down."

"Okay. I'm not going to move until that smoke comes.

Well, the smoke came and I started to crawl. Pretty soon I bumped smack into another Marine. It was Stoney Craig. I told him to get moving, but when I got a good look at him I could see that Stoney was never going anywhere again. There wasn't nothing anyone could do for Stoney so I kept crawling.

By this time I'm really feeling quite lousy. I'm keeping my senses though and I know I have to get my goddamn pack off, because it's full of antitank grenades. If they ever go up, I'll be blown to pieces. I know there's a Marine crawling behind me because he's asking if there's anything he can do for me.

"You bet," I finally said to him, "Can you cut this goddamn pack off? With this leg of mine the way it is, there is no way I can maneuver."

So he cuts off my pack, which is a damn good thing, because at this time heavy small arms fire started again from the Nips.

Another one of our tanks had moved up. The driver of the tank that was there first was crouched over near the second tank. He carried me over to the new tank and then lifted me on top of it. Then he stuck a bandage on my thigh.

Oh my God, the next thing I knew he takes a slug and goes down. Gerald Bunting, the commander of the driver's tank, then picks him up and puts him next to me on the new tank. The driver is bleeding all over me. I figure that since he had patched me up, I ought to return the favor, but one look at his neck, where the bullet had gone in, was enough for me to know I couldn't do nothing for him.

Then Bair comes over, still lugging his machine gun even though he had been hit a third time. I threw him my .45, figuring he could use it more than I could. I thought I still had a couple of grenades on my cartridge belt I could use if any Nips charged the tank on its way down the hill. What I didn't realize was the straps those two grenades were hanging from had been shot off and were in shreds.

Oh, and let me add that just before we went down the hill, someone, probably Rupe or Chaisson, had also stuck "Little Bit" Davis on the tank.

So, you know, we go down the hill riding on the tank. I'm trying to make sure the tanker and "Little Bit" don't fall off the tank. While I'm disabled, those two other guys are a hell of a lot worse off than I am.

What a ride! I was covered with blood, a lot from my arm wound and a tremendous amount from the tanker. We must have looked like something out of a horror movie.

Anyway, we got down the hill and were taken over to Fox Company's command post. It really didn't make any difference which CP it was. It wasn't going to be long before all three companies (E,F,G) of our battalion were going to be merged into one company. Even then you had only a handful.

Well, one of the men at the CP came running over to help me off the tank.

"No," I said, "help those other two; they need it more than I do."

He took a look at the others but just shook his head.

"Not a chance for either of 'em. The big fellow (the driver) might already be dead."

Then he took me down and stuck me on an amtrac that took me to the battalion where either Doc Flick or Goldin, can't remember which, went to work on me. It was no more Okinawa for Ed DeMar.

As for the others, both "Little Bit" and the tank driver, I wish I could remember his name, were gone. Gerald Bunting went on to have two more tanks shot from under him on Okinawa. He was awarded a Purple Heart and a Silver Star.

Ed Reuss's platoon that had tried to go up on our right with eighteen men ended up with just a few survivors—Ed wasn't one of them. He was fatally wounded trying to direct his platoon's fire against the Nips.

Lieutenant Bair got down off the hill but was a long time recuperating. He was awarded the Navy Cross as was Chaisson, who was later hit in the arm by a sniper. My squad leader, Dick Rupe, got hit on May 13th. Along with Chaisson, he played a very important role in getting the wounded out of there. Like Chaisson, he deserves a medal.

One more thing about my treatment. I was stuck on a truck at the battalion aid station to be sent to the regimental station. Just before I left, Doc Goldin gave me a bottle of whiskey. I thought I was supposed to take a nip or two and then give it back to him. I'll be darned if the truck didn't take off while I still had the bottle.

Well, when I got to regimental, this chaplain came over and asked me what religion I was. I told him Protestant. Then he started looking at my dungarees.

"Good grief, sergeant," he said, "is that all your blood?"

"No, sir," I said, "some of it is, but most of it belonged to a tanker who had just tried to patch me up when he took a fatal round in the neck."

Then the chaplain reached down in his bag and broke out a bottle of brandy. "Here, sergeant, take a couple of tumblers of this. It'll make you feel better."

Between the brandy and the whiskey, it was more liquor than I'd seen in weeks. [Now, back to Fox Company.]

Ed, that's more liquor than I saw until I got back to the States. But, you're right about your company on the 12th. And on the next day, it seems to me, what was left of George and Easy and our Fox Company tried to go up the darn hill from another angle.

Yeah, that's when Rusty Golar gave me the needle. I'm trying to move up with the mortars when I see Rusty and the machine gunners. They were trying to fix a firing pin on one of their guns. I started to walk over when Rusty spotted me. He starts to laugh.

"Oh, Christ," he says, "here comes the dumb Polack—he can't help us."

You gotta remember that's just a way we had of horsing around, you know, saying things like that. The poor guy was killed a short time later, but what a job he did.

For calling you a dumb Polack?

Of course not, you remember what he did, the crazy redhead. His group finally got to the crest of the hill where they set up their machine guns. Wow, Rusty kept his gun going until he ran out of ammunition. Then he picked up a rifle and kept firing with that until he had nothing left. Finally, he picked up one of the wounded men and started going down the hill.

Yeah, I didn't seen him, but I heard about it. That's when the sniper got him.

Rusty was always like that, he got the Bronze Star on Guam.

Yeah, and I think he got the Silver Star, posthumously, for Sugar Loaf. Courage is a word you don't normally use during a screwed-up fight like Sugar Loaf, but I guess Rusty had it.

So did the Beast, you know, Harry Zigirian. I hear he's now working for the post office in Providence, Rhode Island, supposed to have a good job.

Oh Jeez, the Beast! How many times did he get hit on Sugar Loaf?

I think it was three. But he wouldn't let them evacuate him, kept going back for wounded Marines. What a guy! He got the Navy Cross.

Don't forget Courtney, Major Henry Courtney, our battalion's executive officer. I can't remember if it was the night of the 13th or 14th, but he led everyone he could get ahold of up that hellhole.

Hey, I know that; I remember his exact words. He was a mild kinda guy, but you know, we'd already been driven off the place three or four times. He was just disgusted—pissed off beyond belief, if you follow me. So he goes around trying to get everyone he can get to follow him.

"I'm going up," he told 'em, "anyone who wants to come with me, come ahead. We've got to finish this thing."

He ended up with forty or fifty men, about half of them from the rear echelon. He made sure they were loaded down with hand grenades and they took off, throwing those grenades every time they felt they had a target.

I know they got to the top because they held it all night. Every time the Japs tried to drive 'em off, they'd let go with a bunch of grenades. The major was killed, knocked down while throwing some of those grenades. They were pulled off the hill the next morning but only a handful were left. Courtney got the Medal of Honor, at least his widow did.

Oh, I think he might have gone a little wacky but, you know, that happens. It seems like you'd spend an eternity trying to take a place like Sugar Loaf, watching so many of your buddies getting shot up so badly. Then you think the hell with it and you do something you wouldn't normally do.

Yeah, well the angle he first started up on was fairly secure but he soon had to expose himself to the fire from Horseshoe and Half Moon ridges on either side of Sugar Loaf.

Don't forget that fifty-foot slit trench they had somewhere going up the hill. You know, I didn't even know it was there until some ten or so years later. I guess the Nips were in one of those caves.

Anyway, they'd shoot the hell out of us and go back to where they were before.

Oh, those caves were a bitch, nasty as hell. I can remember jumping over the trench I think you're talking about, but it was empty. I guess the Japs were back in their holes at the time.

At any rate, that's when I spotted the Jap 75. It was in a well-camouflaged spot. Nothing could get at it. It was the bastard knocking off all our tanks. It was zeroed in on the route they would take and when the tanks would reach a certain spot, the 75 would open up. It was also knocking the hell out of the riflemen because you'd always have a squad or so behind each tank.

We sure did lose a lot of tanks there, no doubt about that. Well, we got about three-quarters of the way up the hill when we set up our 60 millimeter mortars and started firing and kept it up as best we could. I moved forward a ways to try and get a better idea of just where we should be firing. Here I had a perfect view of the top of Sugar Loaf. I could see only one Marine there at the top. It was Don O'Kelly, one of Fox Company's radio men. I don't believe Don could have been eighteen—heck, he could have been one of the Marines who somehow got in the Corps even before he was seventeen. It happened. Don was just sitting there. I know there were no Japs on the top.

That's probably right. I don't remember seeing any Nips on the top at any time. They just seemed to wait until we tried to get to the top and then they'd open up on us.

You know, come to think of it, I don't remember seeing any Japs there either. I guess they used the place as a come-on for us.

At any rate, after seeing O'Kelly up there, I looked in one of the caves that was near where we had the mortars. Oh, my God, what a sight! Dead Marines, dead Japs, dead Marines, dead Japs—everywhere. I recognized one of our corpsmen, a nice guy named Webb, but it wasn't easy. The poor guy had been blown apart. What a sight!

So we ended up spending most of that night firing the 60s. One of our gunners—a guy called Frenchy—kept going so fast he scorched the hell out of his hands.

Then, the next morning, who shows up but Father Kelly, right on the lines. He's up there giving Holy Communion to anyone who wants it. I was in a hole with a guy named Tony Cristani. We're both Catholics.

"Tony," I said to him, "why don't you go over and take Communion? I'll stay by the gun while you go."

"No, John, you go. I'm just too tired right now."

So I went over to see the Father who was holding forth a short ways from our hole. I took Communion and had taken about two steps on my way back to Tony when I heard one of their shells, probably from a knee mortar, come whistling in. I hit the deck as fast and as hard as I could. Wham, it sounded right next door. I ran over to see if Tony was all right. Oh, my God, what a sight he was! He looked as if his whole jaw had been blown off.

I also saw that shell coming in. You could tell how close it was going to be so I tried to burrow into the ground. I can't remember which one, but one of us grabbed a poncho to carry Tony in. Bull, I know you helped carry him and there were two other guys who lent a hand. Can you remember 'em?

I think they were Parkay and Ward.

That's right. Anyway, we got Tony back to the aid station. I don't think we felt he was going to make it but we wanted to do the best we could for him.

The great thing about it is not only did he pull through but back in the States they did a great job on his jaw. He runs a bar over in Chester, Pennsylvania. I was just there a couple of months ago. Tony is in great shape.

Well, while I was at the aid station, there was a second lieutenant who started to talk with me.

"Bull," he asks me, "what shape are your 60s in?" Actually, I think he was the officer in charge of the 81 mortars.

"Very bad," I told him, "useless. One or two of 'em have been blown up and the other two or three have burned out tubes."

"How about the rest of Fox Company?"

"Shot to pieces. So are Easy and George. Our captain, Mike Ahearn, is down. I think he was evacuated, but you know the captain, it took a direct order to get him to leave, and even then he fought against it."

"Are any of Fox Company's officers standing?"

"Yeah, Mike Flynn is and I think Lieutenant Hutchinson is still on his feet."

"Then you have to go back."

So we went back to our 60s but we really didn't know what to do. The mortars were just no damn good.

That's right, we went back but all the guys who'd brought in wounded buddies didn't. I don't want to mention no names, but those guys who snuck into a rest area had seen enough during the recent weeks to last a lifetime. They were really out of it so they took off. They showed up a little later on. You know, there's just so much a human being can take.

You're so right, I don't blame anyone who took off for a while.

Anyway, we're in our position but don't have any guns set up. Then Colonel Woodhouse showed up.

Hey, wasn't Woodhouse killed by then?

No, he got it from a sniper a day or two later.

Anyway, Woodhouse can see the 6os ain't set up.

"What's happened to this gun position?" he asks.

"No mortars, sir, not that work anyway. And you better get down; those Jap knee mortars are coming over here pretty good."

"Okay, I'll get you some BARs. We haven't got this damn hill yet, not by a long shot. The Japanese are bound to try a counterattack to take away what we do have. We want to be ready for them."

Yeah, that sounds like Woodhouse. He wanted to be sure everyone was doing something.

But a little later a corpsman came by and started pinning those little R&R cards on the men he'd thought were all through, who just had to go back for a rest. He pinned one of 'em on me which I thought was great. I was beat all right.

So I'm all set to get the heck out of there when Mike Flynn and Hutchinson come over to me.

"Look, Bull," Lieutenant Flynn said, "you know what Fox Company is down to, hell, we can barely raise a corporal's guard. The whole 2nd Battalion is in the same shape. We're going to get replacements in a few days, most of 'em will be from a replacement draft, but several will come from our own rear echelon troops.

"My point is, none of 'em are going to know much about real line company combat. We're going to need a gunnery sergeant who knows what the hell is going on. If you stay, I'll make you acting gunny. When things quiet down, the rank will be made permanent. I know a jump from PFC to gunny is a hell of a big one, but what do we have left?"

So, what the heck! I stayed. We didn't get the replacements for a couple of days—I think it was after we were relieved—but I remained acting gunnery sergeant until I got hit on June 17th, down on the Oroku Peninsula.

Yeah, and you did a good job. But you know, you corrected me on when Woodhouse was killed, and you were right. You see, I'd heard that he had got it on Sugar Loaf and I never forgot it. You remember how punchy we all were. You're trying to stay alive and you keep hearing about other guys getting hit.

Yeah, you'd hear something like:

"Brown just took a mortar full blast." Or:

"Smith just got one in the leg; it looks like a Hollywood wound; the SOB will be heading for the States, more power to him."

And all the time you're wondering when it'll be you. Will it be a Hollywood wound, a burial bag or what have you—who knows?

Of course, that's why those days around Sugar Loaf all seem to run together. The constant threat to your own life and the sight of so many friends getting hit just turns those memories into a constant nightmare.

Sure, I can remember one man writing a letter home on Mother's Day, then he got killed a few days later; he couldn't have mailed the letter. I hope the burial detail saw that his mother got it.

Yeah, we spent Mother's Day in that area. I can remember what one of my buddies said he would like to be doing with his girl friend on that same day—it wasn't very motherly.

Well, the 29th Marines, one of the other regiments in the 6th Division, relieved what was left of our battalion. I don't recall the exact date, but I think it was around the 15th of May. The 29th had probably been in the area the whole time, but up until May 15th or so, most of the fighting had been done by the 22nd.

Okay. The 29th Marines did relieve us and they did a great job. What the hell, we were really the same kind of guys, just in a different regiment, that's all. But in his book (*Goodbye, Darkness*) Bill Manchester makes it sound like the 29th did the whole job. They had a lot of ghosts from the 22nd right there with them.

Oh, I read Manchester's book. It's great! Hell, I had to have a dictionary with me to understand some of the words. But it was the Major Courtney part that annoyed me. He makes it sound as if Courtney was in the 29th. Hell, he was our major, 2nd Battalion.

Anyway, there was a lot of war left after Sugar Loaf but Fox Company really wasn't the same—so many new guys.

Right, you didn't get to know most of 'em. We lost men at a place south of Naha they called Hill 59—or something like that—that I never got to know at all.

But they were Marines all right. I remember one of 'em going into a farmhouse that had three Nip soldiers in it. He got them all. He was hit a little later himself over on the Oroku Peninsula, and you know, I can't even remember his name. You just didn't get to know the new guys like you knew your buddies who had gone into Sugar Loaf with you.

The Oroku Peninsula, that's where I was almost killed. I'd been getting ammunition and was caught out in the open by sniper fire. One of those little bastards hit me in the right arm with a dum-dum bullet. Of course, they were against the Geneva Convention but that didn't seem to bother the Nips. You know what those bullets are like; they have a soft nose that expands when it hits you. It shattered the hell out of my arm.

Anyway, I'm in a hell of a fix. I jumped in a hole where their small arms fire can't get me because there's now more than one of 'em shooting at me.

Then luck, and a good officer, came to my aid. It seems that Mike Flynn had been watching with binoculars. He called for a tank to come and get me.

So the first thing I know I hear this tank coming; don't know if it's ours or theirs. It comes right up to my hole and, thank God, I hear a friendly voice.

"Hey, buddy, Mike Flynn says we better come and get you out of there. Get in here fast, before their artillery opens up."

What a relief! I can now only use one arm, but with the tanker's help, I got in his vehicle and we got the hell out of there. I'd been saved all right, but my arm was bad news. I was scared to death they would cut it off.

And that's just what they tried to do, but I wouldn't budge. Maybe I was taking a big gamble, but I guess I was just so beat at the time I was willing to take a chance. As you can see, it's no bargain [it's easy to see where a good deal of muscle has been sliced off his arm], but at least it's there and it works most of the time.

Then while I was in the hospital on Guam, I got some real bad news. Mike Flynn had been hit by a sniper the day after I was hit, only this Jap was a better shot than the one who hit me. The lieutenant took it in the head and never knew what hit him. This really broke me up. Lieutenant Flynn was one hell of a guy!

There is something else I should say. After I got out of the hospital, I knew I would be getting a discharge and I began to think of what the lieutenant said about my being a gunnery sergeant and that he would make it official after things quieted down. So, I decided to write Marine Corps Headquarters and tell them what Mike had done. I pointed out that while Lieutenant Flynn was dead, I would not have any trouble verifying that he had advanced me to gunnery sergeant. Besides, Lieutenant Hutchinson, another great guy, was still alive. I knew he'd back me up.

My letter was answered all right. Nobody was questioning me. But, as I was now in a casual company, nothing could be done about it. I did get a Purple Heart and a Bronze Star, but I would have been happier if they'd paid me as a gunnery sergeant from the middle of

May until I was discharged. Wouldn't you feel the same way?

Bull, things like that happened to a lot of guys. The Corps is a great outfit, best of its kind in the world, but it's not known for throwing its money around.

You can say that again!

"HEAVY"

Whenever Americans go to war, one of the toughest transitions that must be made is to accept the difference between officers and enlisted men. The Marines are no different from any other service. It can be maddening for an eighteen-year-old Marine to realize that one of the first things set up in a new camp is the officers' head.

"Jeez," George Bailey, a member of the 21st Marines, told me, "it seems on Bougainville our rifles were still hot when we were told to build an outhouse for the officers."

Situations like this were commonplace and they fostered a resentment toward many officers that will always be with us.

Perhaps the fact that the military caste system, especially the social part, is so repulsive to most Americans explains why, when a real great officer does turn up, his men never forget him. Such a man, according to Ed DeMar, G/2/22, was Dick "Heavy" Pfuhl.

"Here's the kind of a guy Heavy was," DeMar told me. "One of those flyboys, who used to make a killing bringing whiskey from Australia to Guadalcanal, had sold a bottle of Scotch to a guy in Heavy's company for seventy-five dollars. When the put-upon Marine told this to Pfuhl, he blew his top. First he took a big swig from the bottle, then he collared the men from his company and they took off after the profiteer.

" 'Buddy,' Heavy said to the pilot, 'that was great booze you sold to my man here, but you forgot to give him his change. Including handling charges, I figure you owe him about sixty-five dollars.'

" 'Baloney,' " or some such word, was the reply.

"I should point out that Pfuhl, who had been a football star at St. Louis University, was 6'2" and weighed in at about 225 when he was in shape, with a good many of those pounds in his shoulders and chest. And he was in shape when the 22nd Marines were on Guadalcanal.

" 'I said,' repeated Heavy, " 'you owe my man here sixty-five dollars.'

"The pilot did not have a chance and he knew it. He realized he was very close to a fast five in the chops from Lieutenant Pfuhl. He also knew that a scrap would blow his little racket sky high. He would not only lose a good thing but probably a couple of molars in the bargain.

" 'I guess you're right,' the pilot said and paid the Marine his sixty-five dollars.

"Actually," DeMar continued, "Heavy was not an officer in my Company (G); he was in Easy Company. We were, however, in the same battalion and when guys tell you how good an officer is and he isn't even in your company, the man has to be the real goods."

Richard M. Pfuhl was one of the few original 22nd Marines who served from Linda Vista, California, up to and including Okinawa.

Heavy started as a private, received a commission overseas and ended up a captain by the end of the war.

A few years back, some of Pfuhl's friends persuaded Heavy to write a book, *Chasing the Sun* (Ten Square Books, 1979). The book is a gem, full of such recollections as Heavy's visit to a Navy doctor on Guadalcanal where the conversation went like this:

"Doc, I've got an indentation on my shinbone about an inch deep."

"That's a pitted edema."

"What do I do about it?"

"Live with it."

"And I have a ringing in my ears."

"That's tinnitus."

"What do I do about it?"

"Live with it."

As Heavy points out, it wasn't only the enlisted men who got the fast shuffle. I'm surprised the doctor didn't give Pfuhl some pills; maybe he did.

Dick Pfuhl died of a heart attack last fall, but his memory is treasured by the men of the 2nd Battalion, 22nd Marines. It was Herb Milke, G/2/22nd, who loaned me his autographed copy of *Chasing the Sun*. Before he gave the book to me, he issued a warning.

"Henry," he said, "with Heavy gone now, that book is irreplaceable. If you lose it, you'll get a K-bar up the gazzoo!"

I didn't lose the book.

Five Marines

**Frank (Gus) Cooper
Norris Byron
Stan Oblachinski
Herb Milke
A. W. (Mog-Mog) Martin**

The above gentlemen represent three different interviews.

My visit with Gus Cooper was in New York City, while the pair of 11th Marine artillerymen, Byron and Oblachinski, were seen in Kansas City, Missouri. The two 6th Division men, Milke and Martin, my final interview, occurred at a slop chute—where else?—called "Don's 21" in Newark, New Jersey.

Sitting down with Cooper turned into a particularly pleasant meeting as Gus is one of the few men I interviewed whom I knew before starting *Semper Fi, Mac.* Along with the Marine Corps, the two of us share an ardent love of golf and the Boston Red Sox.

Gus was born and raised in Minneapolis, Minnesota. After the war he joined the New York Life Insurance Company. He retired from this firm in 1979 and now lives in Dundee, Florida. Cooper opted to stay in the Marine Reserve after World War II and retired a few years ago as a colonel.

Norris Byron was raised in New Jersey and entered the Corps shortly before the Pearl Harbor attack. Like almost all Guadalcanal men, Norris suffered from malaria but feels it is now pretty much out of his system.

He runs a successful business in industrial sterilization in Budd Lake, New Jersey. As he puts it, "It's great to go down the road of middle age, make a pretty good living and, above all, not take any guff from anyone."

His buddy from the 11th Marines, Stan Oblachinski, spent eight years on active duty, retiring with that most envied of ranks, chief warrant officer.

Today Stan is the chief executive chef at MIT. When the XYZ Company sends a group of its top people to MIT for a brush-up course in business management, the food they get is a hell of a lot better than the fish heads and rice (plus maggots) that their chef was eating in the fall of '42.

As for my interview with Herbie Milke and Warren Martin, it is only fitting that it should be the final meeting of my two-year project, for the three of us were all on Guam when the whole thing ended on the decks of the *U.S.S. Missouri* in Tokyo Bay thirty-seven years ago. And we three went to China in the 6th Division where we witnessed a rather nattily dressed Japanese general hand his sword over to our Major General Lemuel Shepherd at a race track in Tsingtao. It was a beautiful sight to see.

Both Milke and Martin, one a retired production manager and the other a retired police detective, live in North Arlington, New Jersey. And with these two men I ended my attempt to project the World War II Marine into history by reliving his personal memories.

CAPTAIN FRANK COOPER
1st Engineer Battalion, 1st Division

I saw a picture of Gerry Thomas in the *Leatherneck* the other day and he's still got that square jaw. But, my God, does he look old! How did he get that old?

But wait a minute, I think Gerry was in World War I. He has to be in his mid-eighties. Hell, I'm sixty-three, I'm no spring chicken. I guess everyone who was on Guadalcanal has to be getting up there.

Whatever, Gerry is one hell of a bright man; did a great job there on the Island for Vandegrift.

And, you know, we had a lot of old-line regular officers with us out in the Pacific in the summer of '42. Hard-Hearted Hanneken was another [I pointed out that Herman H. Hanneken was also known as Hot-Headed Hanneken—Cooper laughed]. Herman must have campaigned all over Latin America before World War II. Then when war did come, he served on the Canal and New Britain. He even made it to Peleliu, but I guess he was pretty well used up by then. Herman just had seen too much, that's all.

Then there was that old Mustang, Harold E. Rosencrans. He was also a World War I man. Hell, he was blown about forty feet up in the air at Tulagi, had the 2nd Battalion of the 5th Marines then. Of course, a lot of us felt he never really came down, but things are sometimes like that.

In May 1941 I was finishing up my senior year at the University of Minnesota. I applied for and was accepted by the Marine Corps for OCS. They told me I would be called up shortly after graduation.

Well, I graduated and waited by the phone, so to speak, for my orders. Damn it, I waited and waited and still no orders. Finally I took a job selling men's winter underwear at Donaldson's in Minneapolis. Still no orders and I continued to wait. After all, winter underwear used to be a big item in Minneapolis; we moved a lot of those long johns.

Then came December 7th. I was playing cribbage (quite a popular Marine Corps game, particularly among the old-timers in those days) when we heard about the attack on the radio.

That was that. I walked over to the telephone, called Western Union and sent a telegram directly to Tom Holcomb, the Marine commandant, requesting an immediate call-up. Five or six weeks later I was on my way to OCS in Quantico. I noticed when I left Minneapolis that the thermometer registered twenty-five below. In other words, it was a pretty good time to head for Virginia. Donaldson's was probably selling a hell of a lot of winter drawers, but someone else would have to peddle them.

My company commander at Quantico was one Captain Lewis W. Walt and he was a picture-book Marine. You know the type, always turned out like someone on a recruiting poster, always in a hurry and always enthusiastic as the devil.

Walt volunteered for Red Mike Edson's Raiders before we graduated and the next time I saw him he had just moved from Tulagi to Guadalcanal. This was September of '42. At this time I was a member of the 1st Engineering Battalion, a first lieutenant with a college degree in journalism, if you can figure that one out. When I spotted Lew, my unit was laying what I believed was the first antitank mines ever used in the Pacific. We put in some 1,500 mines, which enabled us to cover partially a stretch of beach that Vandegrift didn't have enough men to cover. These mines were about eight inches in diameter.

At any rate we'd buried these mines just a little under the surface, charted them and sent copies of their locations to headquarters.

Then along came Red Mike Edson. He didn't like where we'd put those mines so he told us to take up every one of them. We located all but two, which took some *very* delicate work with a bayonet to find.

Well, we finally found the missing ones and this goddamn fool, forget his name, thank God, picked up these two mines and slung them over onto the pile we'd carefully been setting up.

Oh God, what an explosion! Surprisingly enough, my unit took only eight casualties, six wounded and two killed. But these were the first men I'd seen badly hurt and, of course, the first men under my command who were killed.

So I steeled myself and kept my cool until the ambulance came and took all my wounded to the hospital. Then I went into the jungle and cried like a baby.

Okay, back to my days in the States. After I finished up at Quantico, I was sent to San Diego where, much to my surprise, I became an engineering officer in the 22nd Marines reinforced, a new regiment that was being formed. It seemed to be common knowledge that the brass wanted to put the regiment together as fast as possible so it could move overseas. As I was to find out, when people used the word "fast" in the Corps, they weren't kidding.

Now going overseas in mid-'42 was a much more serious movement than it would get to be later on. The Jap fleet was still very powerful then and all American movements were supposed to be top secret. However, someone found out our destination, don't know how, but they did. They even had a naughty little ditty out on what the boys were going to do to Samoa of Samoa when they got there.

All right. One morning I got the word to go somewhere, can't remember where, but it was quite a jaunt, with most of my platoon, and pick up a pontoon bridge.

Well, we went to get the bridge and didn't return to camp until late that afternoon.

Oh, what a shock I got! The whole goddamn camp was gone. I ran back to my quarters where there was a big sign that read:

"COOPER, GET YOUR ASS TO SAN DIEGO AT ONCE! WE ARE SHOVING OFF."

That was it. In a matter of hours we were on our way. And guess where we ended up? Why, Samoa, of course. We were to relieve the 7th Marines, who were on their way to Guadalcanal. The whole thing happened so fast I hardly had time to take a quick breath. But, as Al Jolson used to say, "You ain't seen nothin' yet!"

When we arrived at Samoa, we were told to transfer a lot of our men to Company B, 1st Engineer Battalion that was going to the Canal with the 7th.

So following the time-honored custom of the military, we gave up all our meatballs. Actually, I should say what we thought were meatballs; most of them did a great job later on.

Then the officer from Company B, who was to take over our men, had an accident and couldn't make the trip. Guess who was ordered to take his place? Why, Gus Cooper, that's who! And that's how I made a very quick trip to the Canal in the late summer of '42.

I reported to one Captain Johnny Brewer of Company B. He was laughing like hell.

"I've got great news for you, Cooper," he said. "I realize you know all the men that have transferred out of your old outfit into our company. You'll be glad to know they're all under your command."

That SOB knew we'd given him our lemons and he was giving them back to me.

Anyway, I reached the Canal on September 18th; so a very short time after I'd picked up that pontoon bridge back in San Diego, I was at war.

Well, you know what engineers are supposed to do—build bridges, build roads, provide water, fix demolitions, all those good things. And that's what we did during the day. At night we'd turn into riflemen and man the defense line.

As for my new captain, I soon found out he was a great guy but a bit of a nut. He'd just lie there behind the coconut logs and the sand bags and watch the shells, ours and the Japs.

"Beautiful, beautiful, aren't they beautiful?" he'd say.

Jeez, they sure as hell weren't beautiful to me.

All right, sometime in October the 164th U.S. Infantry came into the Canal. They were big raw-boned kids, looked like great soldiers, and as it turned out, they were great soldiers. But just about the time they landed—I think it was their first night ashore—what seemed like the whole damn Nip navy came in and gave us hell.

The next morning an officer of the 164th came over to me. He looked distraught as hell, looked as if he might have been crying. I saluted him and asked what I could do for him.

"Can you show me where I can bury a lot of swell kids from the Dakotas? he said.

I've never forgotten the look on that man's face.

Okay, I think sometime late in October our Company B was rushed into the lines with the 7th Marines. I think that Army outfit, the 164th, went in also. Christ, what a debacle, but I think our outfit held its own.

You see, the infantry was usually delighted to have the engineers go into the lines with them because we have such firepower. We had machine guns up the ass. We needed them for each truck and when we went in as infantry, we'd just take them off the trucks.

Anyway, that fighting in late October was probably as important as any combat held on the Canal. Once again we showed the Japanese that with all their Bushido beliefs they couldn't break the Marines, and in the long run that was the key on the Canal.

Now I've often tried to figure out why a people like the Americans with probably the highest standard of living in the world can revert to somewhat of a primitive nature—and that's what close combat is —and defeat a people who placed the emphasis on a military way of life as the Japanese did. I think one of the answers is our sense of humor.

For instance, did you ever hear of the George Medal? I don't know who originated this medal, but the citation reads something like this: "To one who was on Guadalcanal when the shit hit the fan."

The medal, showing a cow with a turd hanging out of its rear end, was quite popular. I lost mine years ago, but I'd love to get another one.

I had a couple of men in my outfit who should have got that medal. One was a redheaded sergeant from Brooklyn named Pat Quigley and the other was Lawrence Adams from Virginia. They were great pals.

One night when we were getting a real tough shelling, Quigley yelled over to me.

"Gus (we never mentioned rank at night), did you hear what that shell said?" I thought he was off his bonnet, but I yelled back, "No, what did it say?"

Then it was Adams turn to answer.

"It said, pardon me, sir, but have you seen Cooper?"

Of course it wasn't always fun and games. Over there by the Matanikau with the 7th Marines one of our men who had been a great young athlete had one of his legs smashed. Hell, it was hanging by a thread. Anyone could see it couldn't be saved. He pleaded with me to shoot him, but, of course, I wouldn't do it; couldn't have if I had wanted to.

Well, about six months later I receive a letter from this lad. He talked about a new leg and a new life, how he'd done pretty well readjusting. But you know something? Damn it, he missed the outfit. I'm certain that no matter what, you find camaraderie in combat that can't be beat. Don't take this to mean I favor war; it's a bag of garbage. I'm just stating a fact, that's all.

We finally left the Canal and headed for Australia. This is where the 17th Marines were formed by uniting our Engineer battalion, the Pioneer and the attached Seabee battalion into a regiment. The Seabees were still Navy but were attached to our new regiment and for all intents and purposes were part of the 17th Marines.

We spent about nine great months in Australia. I'll just mention one occasion and that was the Fourth of July, 1943. A bunch of Australians gave a party for our officers. Jeez, what a blast! We toasted the king and queen, Franklin and Eleanor; hell, I think someone even toasted Ted Williams. It was tremendous!

We left that dear land in September and went to Goodenough Island off New Guinea. And by the way, we're the ones who built that famous home MacArthur had made there on Goodenough. I think he spent thirty-six total hours there.

Then it was Cape Gloucester and the great beer hoist. One of my sergeants took a detail over to this Army depot and they started to load their truck with beer. Then an Army sergeant came over.

"Hey," he said, "what outfit are you guys?"

"First Engineer Battalion."

"Christ, that's a Marine outfit; you can't have that beer."

"But the colonel said we could."

"Izzat so? I'll find out about that."

So he goes into this hut where they had a field telephone to check with his colonel. My boys could never say when he came back because they were long gone by that time. And so was the beer.

Oh, there was somewhat of a stink for a while, but I never heard of anyone giving back any beer.

Our job on Gloucester was just about the same as it was on the Canal, building and occasionally fighting. I think it rained almost every day there, so we had plenty to do.

Our next stop was Pavuvu, in the Russell Islands. We were sent there ahead of the rest of the division as we were to lay out a camp for the whole 1st Division. It was here that we saw the end of the 17th Marines as a regiment. The three components, Engineers, Pioneers and Seabees, went back to being separate battalions, which didn't really change matters much.

Well, setting up that camp was a real ball-breaker. Our colonel, a great guy named Ike Fenton, could see that the men were really pissed off. So he called the officers together.

"All right," he said to us, "I know the men are really teed off about setting up these quarters for everyone but themselves. Tomorrow they start working on their own place.

"And to start things off right we're going to have a rat hunt. The more rats they can kill, the more beer I'll see they get."

Goddamn it, you should have seen those men knock off those rats. I guess things are pretty bad when the big social occasion is a rat hunt. But I think our men would have attacked Japan for some beer.

Anyway, the whole division finally arrived on Pavuvu, where they licked their wounds and got ready for Peleliu.

Our divisional commander by then was a man named William Rupertus and, if you ask my opinion, I think he was a little punchy by then. We used to call him "Rupe the Stupe."

Now, you never know for sure what is scuttlebutt and what is the straight poop, but I heard that Rupertus was dead set on taking

Peleliu with just the 1st Marine Division and in taking the place in a hurry.

Damn it, all you had to do was be on that island for one hour and you knew this was impossible. I went in early and things were just SNAFU every day I was there.

Hell, we had most of a damn good Army division in reserve. He could have called it in long before he did. Cost us a lot of Marine lives by not doing this. As a matter of fact, it was Roy Geiger, the Corps commander, who finally ordered in the 81st. That's the scoop we got, anyway.

One of the big problems on that hellhole was fresh water; we'd been told there was none of it on the island. We had a Marine gunner who just wouldn't believe this. His name was Joseph J. Agresto. He managed to get some purification equipment ashore and I'll be damned if he didn't find water. That island was just about as hot, both in heat and in bullets, as any place on earth. Water was pure gold.

The big bottleneck was a place called Bloody Nose Ridge. I think its real name was Umurbrogo, so naturally the men had to call it something else.

Our command finally figured out that the thing to do was first bypass Bloody Nose and then come back and reduce it. I can't tell you how much work our outfit did to try and help the rifle companies here, but it was constant. Along with the Seabees and the Pioneers, we got an airstrip going, and our airplanes ended up bombing Bloody Nose from a runway about a half mile from that hellish place. They called it the shortest bombing run in history.

At any rate, I'd actually volunteered for Peleliu. I could have gone home from Pavuvu, but I asked to stay. But I'd finally reached a point where I just didn't want to take any more. I ended up in sick bay with complete dehydration. Colonel Fenton came to visit me and to tell me he was going home. Like me, Ike had been in the Pacific since the Canal and he was also beat down to his socks.

"Ike," I said to him, "there's no way you're going home without me." Fenton laughed.

"Okay, Gus," he said, "pack your sea bag."

Shortly after that we headed for the States, first stopping at Guadalcanal and while there I spent an hour or so standing on a ridge looking down on the beach. I could see rusting Japanese hulks at the water's edge.

Okay. About two years before, those Nip ships had been unloading Jap troops. It was real touch and go if we could survive on that tiny perimeter we had, but how things had changed. It was now November of 1944 and the Japanese Imperial Navy was on its last leg and, over in Europe, so was the Nazi war machine. Douglas MacArthur had returned to the Philippines and we all knew the next island the Marines would hit would be on Japan's doorstep. I guess you can say we accomplished something. But then again, wasn't that why I went to the Pacific, I mean, to help turn the tide?

PFC NORRIS BYRON
CWO STANLEY OBLACHINSKI
11th Marines

Norris: I think Guadalcanal was just about the only place where the Marines were constantly under shell fire from the Japanese Navy, at least other than places like Wake Island at the very beginning of the war. And let me tell you, it was pure horseshit. Torture. A guy could lose his marbles.

The first time I went through this shelling was murder. You know, in the World War I movies you see guys in shell holes, smoking cigarettes and someone like George Brent or Jimmy Cagney is talking to the men and no one is really going up the wall.

Well, it don't happen that way. Some of that shrapnel was this big [Norris indicates a foot or so long]. That crap could go through a man, cut him in half. And if the poor bastard took a direct hit, it was Goodbye Columbus. I mean it would take you hours to try and put the guy back together again so you could bury him. I knew guys who were actually hurt by being hit by parts of their buddies' bodies.

Stan: The morning after the first night we were really shelled. I knew something was wrong. I knew I shouldn't have been there. One of our guys must have taken a direct hit because I mean it was sickening. Half of the guy must have blown over to Tulagi.

Norris: Those airplanes were no bargain either, but that was normal. At the beginning there, before any of our planes had come in, the goddamn Japanese were sending in fifty or sixty bombs at a clip. Our antiaircraft would fire up at them, but I don't think they hit shit. Maybe they kept the bombers up high, but they didn't seem to hit nothin'.

Stan: It was the naval shelling that was brutal though, usually at night. They'd send over a little plane and out of it would come a parachute with a flare. We'd be yelling, "Come down, you little bastard, come down." You see, the flare would be lighting up the whole area. Then the Nip guns would open up. Holy Christ!

Norris: Oh yeah. That plane would buzz around like an angry bee. And that flare would just seem to hang there. You'd think the fuckin' thing would never come down.

Stan: The Corps Artillery would also open up at those planes. What did they have? Oh, I think they had 155 rifles and 90 millimeters. One of those two had Long Toms, can't remember which. But I don't think they hit many Jap bombers, none of them.

Norris: One thing we became experts at was digging those foxholes. Christ, I think mine was as big as this room. I think most of their navy shells were antipersonnel types. Some of them had delayed fuses. That way they seemed to scatter that shrapnel in every direction. You might get hit by shrapnel from a shell that was in the ground ten or twenty yards away. So, you had to have your ass down deep in the earth or you were apt to get hit.

Stan: Okay. I went into the Corps at Boston, Massachusetts, in 1939. At that time they'd send you down to New York City on the old Fall River Line. And from there you went to Yemasse, South Carolina.

Hell, I'd never been out of New England before in my life. I can still remember that guy yelling, "YEMASSEE, SOUTH CARO-LINA."

Well, after boot camp I joined the 1st Marine Brigade at Guantanamo Bay. There was no 1st Marine Division then. Hell, the Corps had never had a division at this time.

Christ, all we did down there was soldier. No liberty port at all. There was a town across the bay. The Navy could go there but not the Marines. They claimed we'd always have fights with the sailors, so of course it was the Marines who got dumped on. No matter what they say, the Navy brass was not exactly always pleasant to Marines in those days.

We did have our own slop chute where you'd get this Cuban beer. And when I say slop chute, what I mean is this big tent. You could sit there and drink this beer until you were in a stupor. Then you'd go back to your own tent and cork off. The next morning you'd soldier again.

Naturally, the enlisted men were always trying to sneak out. But they had these Horse Marines patrolling the area. If they'd spot you, they'd let go with their .45s. I don't remember that they ever hit anyone. Hell, I can't believe they'd shoot a guy just for trying to get a broad, but they scared the hell out of you.

Now, I'm not saying the Corps did this on purpose, but we did have one hell of a lot of big Polacks like myself in my outfit, which was the 11th Marines, the artillery. You had to be big to try and maneuver our guns and all that equipment the way it was set up then. Believe me, it was work.

Norris: Yeah, and tell him you had the wooden wheels, not the rubber tires, which made it twice as hard to push those guns around.

Stan: Right. And we didn't have Higgins boats then either. We had what I guess you'd call a twenty-six-foot launch, something like a whale boat. When we'd try to practice landing, they didn't dare beach the boats because they were afraid of damaging them. Hell, the Navy didn't have any money then and the Marine Corps had even less.

Anyway, we'd have to wade in a good deal of the way. And when we got ashore, these people would appear out of nowhere selling rum. We'd usually bivouac up in the hills and frequently we'd all get drunk. Guys would be singing up a storm.

Then, the next morning the company commander would come into the camp and give us the word.

"All right, you shitheads, you had a great time last night. Full marching order, get those packs on. We're going on a forced march." I'll tell you that peacetime soldiering wasn't all fun and games.

At any rate, I think it was November of '41, we came back to the States. We ended up in New River with nothing but tropical gear and real thin blood from all that time in Cuba. Christ, it was like going to Alaska for us. The Marine Corps didn't even have any sweaters for us. We had to get them from the Red Cross.

Norris: November of '41. That's when I joined up. I was living in New York City, which meant I went to 90 Church Street to enlist. Actually, I went there to join the Navy, believe it or not; it was only by chance that I got in the Corps.

You see, they had a huge line waiting to join the Navy. So I asked this CPO (chief petty officer) if there was any place that don't have a big line. He laughed.

"Try the eleventh floor. They probably don't have a line. That's the Marine Corps. Of course, you might get your ass shot off." Then he laughed again.

Well, the hell with him. I joined the Corps and quickly got shipped down to Parris Island. From there I went to Verona in North Carolina, where I was put in the 11th Marines with Stan here. We were both in the 1st Battalion which meant pack howitzers. My God, what a dump that place was. We had a guy in our outfit named Mike Santaro; he was from New Jersey. His uncle came to see him and he couldn't believe it.

"Mike," he said to his nephew, "I won't tell your dad, but what the hell did you do to get sentenced to his place?"

Stan: Oh, I remember that; his uncle thought Mike was in the brig. If you see that movie, *Stalag 17*, you'll see what I mean.

Okay. In the spring of '42, I think it was, our 1st Battalion headed overseas in support of the 7th Marines. We went to Samoa as part of BLT-7 (Battalion Landing Team) whose commanding officer was Chesty Puller. Our artillery battalion was under the command of a light colonel named Joe Nolan.

Norris: Yeah. Well, there on Samoa we did something unusual. We formed a fourth battery. An artillery regiment would usually have three companies, but we ended up with A, B, C and D.

Stan: Right. As for Samoa, it was one island that wasn't overrated by the travel agents. It was beautiful, tremendous people. The only thing bad there was the *mu-mu* but other than that, it was really a tropical paradise.

And let me tell you a story about those beautiful people.

All the top chiefs on the island wore a leather belt and, of course, all Marines had leather belts, so many of the native girls thought we were chiefs.

So a buddy of mine named Vulockich and me ended up with a couple of real nice native girls and we go up into the hills for a little party. We'd been sitting around, drinking a native concoction called *cavacava*. It was alcoholic but not very strong. It was good though.

Anyway, we had a 2200 curfew and, oh, I'd say it must have been at least one in the morning, who walked into this little camp we had but Chesty Puller. Oh, we were scared shitless! I was a sergeant then and I figured I'd get busted for sure. But old Chesty just came over and sat by this little fire we had for a while, told us how we had some real tough times ahead, then took off. He didn't even ask for our names.

But the big question in my mind has always been, what the hell was Puller doing wandering around those hills at night like that? Who knows?

Well, everything went great until we got the big shock. The 1st Marine Division hit Guadalcanal on August 7th without us, without the 7th Marines and the 1st Battalion of the 11th Marines. It seemed a little funny to say now, but August of '42 was different. We had never been in combat. All we knew was our outfit was going against the Japs without us.

Norris: Oh, we all felt that way. And, of course, Vandegrift most of all. He wanted his whole division together.

Stan: Then the 22nd Marines came to Samoa, which meant the 7th Marines could take off for the Canal and they weren't going anywhere without the 1st Battalion of the 11th.

Norris: Yeah, but for a while it didn't look like we would make it. On the way from Samoa to the Canal we got the word one of our carriers went down. I think it was the *Wasp*. So we turned around and headed back to Samoa. I don't know what happened next, but I do know we changed course and headed for Guadalcanal again. We reached there on September 18th. There was one hell of a lot of war left there on the Island.

Stan: Yeah, and from then on we supported the 7th Marines. Chesty Puller had a battalion in the 7th then and you know wherever he was, there was going to be action. We fired one hell of a lot in support of the 7th at The Canal; it seems to me the Nips were always hitting them.

[At this point Norris had to leave and Stan started on Peleliu.]

I was a Marine gunner by then and because by 1944 I was considered a real old-timer, I was given a special group to take in. Christ, they gave me every misfit in the 11th Marines. I don't think any of them had been in combat.

Okay, we're going in without our artillery; that will come in later. Of course we have our side arms; couldn't go in without them.

So, just before the assault I get my group together.

"Listen," I told them, "you're going to see something the likes of which you've never seen before. Just try and stay alive and try and concentrate on what is in front of you. And, above all, try and do what I do."

Anyway, we go in and just as we hit shore, the ramp goes down. I start to run because I can see these Japs are hitting the whole area with mortar fire. Christ, there's fire all over the place!

As I'm running, I spotted this good-sized shell hole and I got my ass in it as quick as I could.

Well, remember, I just told you I'd told the kids, and by '44 that's what they were, kids, to do what I did. Well, they did, all right; at least twenty of those kids jumped in on top of me. Christ, my head is driven right into the sand; I think I'm going to suffocate. Of course I'm cussing all these guys like mad, but, you know, they just didn't know what end was up. This is one case when untrained Marines were sent into a fierce battle and they should not have been.

Well, we finally get out of the hole and start moving. The first thing I knew we were on the edge of an airstrip where I spotted three or four tanks. I thought it was great that we had gotten these things ashore this early; then I got a better look at them. Hell, they were Japanese and they were headed right for us.

"Men," I yelled, "split up. We'd better get out of here."

Jeez, these kids go in every direction. If it hadn't been so serious, I would have laughed at one of them. He actually climbed up a tree. I guess he thought a bear was chasing him.

Anyway, thank God some of our planes came over and knocked the hell out of those Nip tanks. Our pilots had to fly real low to do it, but they didn't care.

I then told the kid who'd climbed up the tree to come down. He had this sheepish grin on, but he climbed down.

Later on I saw something on Peleliu that I still have trouble believing. A tractor of some kind, maybe it was a bulldozer, hit a mine. I swear that tractor went up in the air and it took a tremendous force to drive that baby up like that. The driver also soared and it was almost as if he'd never come down. He was killed.

Well, our guns, 105s, did get in and we went to work. This time we were backing up the 1st Marines, which were under the command of my old friend, Chesty Puller. The pounding the 1st Marines took there was so bad it's hard to imagine.

The worst thing was probably Bloody Nose Ridge. We never did take that area, not while I was on the island anyway. As I remember the place, it was more a series of ridges than one ridge and it seems they all had layers and tunnels and different kinds of those damn fortifications.

The 1st Marines were taken off Peleliu somewhere around the 23rd or 24th of September. They'd gone in on September 15th. And this was one case where a Marine regiment did not really accomplish what it wanted to, simply because it was just shot to pieces. You can say all you want about bravery, but dead men and badly wounded men can't advance. If ever a Marine regiment was put out of action by the simple arithmetic of casualties, it was the 1st Marines on Peleliu.

Well, after Peleliu I finally went home and had a very long furlough. Then I was sent to Ordinance School at Quantico, where I ran into a real half-ass colonel.

Now, don't kid yourself. We had some great officers in the Corps, but we had our share of lemons. This colonel I'm talking about got it into his head that his unit was going to win a war bond drive.

Well, what the hell, I'd spent about two and a half years in the Pacific. I already had a war bond coming out of my pay every month. I wasn't about to go for another one. Do you know that SOB told me if I didn't take an extra bond every month, I'd regret it. Well, "Semper Fi, Mac," take care of your own war bond drive.

Oh, my God, that colonel wasn't kidding. When I graduated from the school, I ended up with my certificate in one hand and my overseas orders in the other.

So, back overseas I go. I was on Guam when the war ended, but they weren't going to let a Marine warrant officer go home who just had a few months overseas even if it was his second trip over.

Now this takes the cake. I got sent to China around Christmas, 1945, and I arrived there with only my khakis. So, there I am freezing my butt off and all because I wouldn't buy an extra war bond from a chicken shit colonel.

I will tell you one thing about that duty in Tientsin, China, in 1946. There *were* fire fights with the Chinese Communist troops and Marines *were* killed. Not many, but one was too many as far as I'm concerned.

As I look back, though, I have no regrets. I was at Guadalcanal, New Britain and Peleliu. The only time I was hit was caused by some shrapnel in the right cheek of my butt. I was so embarrassed I just had the corpsman patch it up, never did report it. So, as long as the only thing that happened to me was a temporary sore ass, I guess I have no complaints.

PFC HERBERT MILKE
22nd Marines
CPL. A. W. (MOG-MOG) MARTIN
29th Marines

Herb: I had a first cousin at Pearl Harbor, name of Everett McCarthy. He was in the 1st Defense Battalion and he got pretty well racked up by the Japs that Sunday morning. They thought he was a goner, even had him laid out alongside some sailors and marines who were dead. He used to get a kick out of telling us how astounded everyone was when he started to cry for water, you know, lying there in the middle of a pile of bodies.

Mog-Mog: Jeez, Herb, he should have asked for a cold beer; that would have really shook the other group up.

Herb: Yeah. Anyway, as it turns out, Mac was a long way from being dead. As a matter of fact, after I got hit on Okinawa, who shows up but McCarthy. I'm lying in a sack at the battalion hospital and I hear this, "Hey, forget to duck?"

Christ, it was Everett. He was with the 1st Division at the time. But I'll tell you, I was feeling crummy and it was great to see someone from home.

Mog-Mog: Okay. I was in the Marine Corps Reserves when the war started. My serial number is 270,405, which makes me salty as hell.

Herb: Yeah, you're saltier than Smedley Butler.

Mog-Mog: Knock it off.

Well, the Corps didn't waste any time after the Pearl Harbor attack. I got a phone call the next day telling me to get my butt over to the Brooklyn Navy Yard. So the next day I grabbed that ferry that used to go from Newark to Brooklyn for a nickel and wham, I'm on active duty.

After about a month there at Sands Street—and what great duty you had there in December of '41—I was shipped to the Charlestown Navy Yard near Boston. More good duty.

Next, I go out to Woods Hole, right at the beginning of Cape Cod. We had a Naval Sections Base there at the same spot that Jacques Cousteau now does shows for the Oceanographic Institute.

Then, I went down to New River where they made me a rifle coach.

Yeah, those first two years of the war I had some great duty and some great liberties. I can't tell you much about those things; my wife might read the book and she'll shoot me. Of course, I'd be just lying anyway.

All right. They finally shipped me to California where I went into something called the 2nd Special Battalion, an outfit that ended up going into Saipan with the 2nd Division. I was a rifleman, of course.

Now, I've heard people say there was a battalion of the 29th Marines there on Saipan, but, damn it, I think they mean our 2nd Special Battalion. A lot of our guys later became part of the 29th, but I don't think we actually were the 29th on Saipan.

Then again, what the hell difference does it make? After Saipan I was shifted in a hurry to the 4th Marines of the 1st Provisional Brigade and went into Guam. Picked up my first wound there. I moved into the 29th over on Guadalcanal after we left Guam.

Herb: Well, while Martin was on Saipan, I was in the brigade's signal company. We were the floating reserve for Guam and what a drag that was. Day after day on an LST, just screwing around. We were about to go bananas.

Then, when we finally did hit Guam, I ended up only a quarter of a mile or so away from Martin, but we didn't find this out until thirty years later.

After Guam, the brigade (4th and 22nd Marines) went to Guadalcanal where, along with the 29th, we became the 6th Division. Lem Shepherd, who had been in command of the brigade, took over the 6th.

I ended up in the divisional signal company, which was real good duty. But you know the Corps, they sent you where you were needed.

And when the stuff really hit the fan on Sugar Loaf, they were grabbing everyone they could find. I ended up with a rifle in my hands as a part of Company G of the 22nd on May 16th.

Mog–Mog: Sugar Loaf. What a mess! You know it kinda annoys me when different outfits argue who the hell took the place. Hell, we all took that dump; outfits were relieving outfits all over the place. Companies and even battalions were getting mixed up everywhere.

Herb: Yeah, when I joined George Company, I don't think a lot of the replacements even knew what company they were in, especially the guys who had come directly from the replacement drafts.

Mog–Mog: That's right; I'll betcha replacements got hit and even killed without knowing who they were with.

Oh, by the way, for my name put down "Mog-Mog." Everyone in my outfit will know my name.

You see, on the way to Okinawa we stopped at Ulithi. We all had a chance to go ashore. I guess the different outfits went to separate little islands. My group went to this shitty little place called Mog-Mog. Christ, there was nothing there at all. We were all given the magnificent sum of two cans of beer. Big deal!

Anyway, for days afterward I used to just shake my head and say, "Mog-Mog."

Jeez, even now it upsets me! No hamburgers, no hot dogs, no nothing. The only thing I saw was two Doberman pinschers. Even those dogs were bored silly. When I see my old buddy, Sam Lenardi —he also became a police officer—he still calls me Mog-Mog.

Herb: I'll tell you something we all saw at Ulithi, the *U.S.S. Franklin*. What a pasting they took!

Mog–Mog: Christ, how they even kept that afloat I'll never know.

Herb: Okay. Well, after the war our division went to China. It was the best duty I had in the Corps. Can you imagine what it was like to sit down in a restaurant and order a steak?

Mog–Mog: Oh, I had a great dinner at one of those Chinese joints and the next day the divisional health officer condemned the place. But I didn't care. I'm not saying the steak I had was great, but what a delight to sit down and order it!

Herb: Well, five of us went into another restaurant and ordered chicken. So this Chinaman comes out with one chicken.

Christ, can you imagine five hungry young Marines and one chicken? We told that guy he had to do better than that. So he goes around jabbering a mile a minute in Chinese about the crazy Marines, but he brought us another bird.

Then we made a big discovery. These nuts hadn't even cut the heads off those birds. There they were, the heads and the necks, tucked underneath the wing. I guess those Chinks even eat the beak.

Mog–Mog: If you remember that first night we pulled into Tsingtao we couldn't go ashore. But, remember, a lot of these guys hadn't even talked to a woman for two years.

Jeez, you had guys climbing down the lines to get ashore. I don't know how they found the cathouses, but they did.

Herb: Do you remember how our doctors scared us? They told us if we didn't watch out, we'd catch some Oriental VD and the damn thing would fall off. Of course, I never went to any of those cathouses, but a hell of a lot of our men did.

Mog–Mog: A guy in another outfit told me their doctor was a nut about short arm inspection. He said that everyone would needle each guy when it became his turn.

I guess they had one guy in his outfit who went to the cathouses every chance he could; you know, one of those guys who could never get enough. They all gave that guy a big cheer whenever he'd pass the short arm.

Herb: How about that crazy money? You'd be getting 2,700 Chinese dollars for each American one on Monday, 3,400 on Tuesday, 2,600 on Wednesday and so on. Someone was making a killing on that crap.

Then there was the Japanese surrender. The whole division (minus the 4th Marines that had gone to Japan) lined up so the Japanese officers could give up their swords. I remember that they played "The Star Spangled Banner" and "God Save the King."

Then they broke into the Chinese national anthem, whatever the hell that was. It sounded like a bunch of cats fighting in an alley. Half the Marines were laughing like hell.

Mog–Mog: Yeah, but you know, there were plenty of the guys who were still having nightmares from Okinawa when we were in China. I don't know, maybe they still do.

Herb: And if they do, can you blame them? It was almost impossible to be in a rifle company and not get hit. And so many of them got killed.

Mog–Mog: That's sure right. And you know, one of the closest brushes with death I had came from one of our tanks. A bunch of us had crapped out for the night in one of those tombs they had on Okinawa. When the dawn came up, one of us looked out and, Christ, there's an American tank, I think it was a Sherman, pointing that big gun of theirs right at the center of the tomb.

Oh Christ, someone runs out yelling, "Americans, Americans, we're American Marines!"

Well, a few minutes later that tanker gave us the word.

"You guys are the luckiest sons of bitches on this lousy island," he told us. "I figured that tomb was an ideal spot for some Nips to be holed up. So I lined up on it and, honest to God, ten seconds later and it would have been 'Katie, bar the door.'"

Then the tanker stopped for a minute.

"Come to think of it," he said, "I was pretty lucky myself. I don't know if I could have lived with it if I had let one go at you."

Now, as I look back on that, I think there were six of us in that tomb. At least two, maybe three, of them were killed during the next week or two.

One of these guys who bought it had a wife and a young son. He'd come from southern New Jersey.

Well, a year or so after the war, his widow brought his body back home. She called to tell me about the coming funeral and, naturally, I attended.

Well, my God, it all came back. It never really leaves you.

Herb: Well, I told you I got hit on Okinawa. Actually, I got hit twice, both times on May 31, 1945.

We started off at 0600 on that last day of May. We were going up this hill. I can't even remember if the place had a name, but it was over by the railroad yard.

Then, wham, we walked smack into a mortar attack. I got hit in the face and the blast blew me into a ditch. The other two guys in my fire team also were hit. A man named McGee got it in the eyes, badly, and the other guy, he was a redhead—can't remember his name—was hit in the throat.

I went back to work trying to help those two buddies of mine because they were worse off than I was. Always remember, we do take care of our own. I saw plenty of men leave cozy foxholes to go out and bring a wounded guy in. It takes four men to a stretcher if you're going to do a good job of it.

Next, I started to move again with my platoon. We got to the top of the hill and started down the other side.

Then, a Japanese machine gun that was on the reverse side of the hill opened up on us. Jeez, it knocked out eighteen Marines at one clip. I was hit in the shoulder and neck so they carried me out. That was the end of Okie as far as I was concerned.

Mog–Mog: I got hit on Okinawa also, in the side, over near Sugar Loaf. And you know what? They made me a corporal. How about that; could they spare it?

Herb: I'll tell you something. I didn't get a Purple Heart for the wound from the mortar because I didn't go back to the battalion field hospital until after I was hit by the machine gun fire. I spent three months in the hospital from that second wound and I guess they felt they had to give me a Purple Heart.

Mog–Mog: Here's a name to remember, Mayhew. This guy took a bullet through his chest; went right in the front and came back out the other side. But it didn't hit nothing vital. They flew the guy over to Guam, patched him up and stuck him on an LST, heading back for Okinawa. We were so hard up for men on the lines that poor Mayhew was back in action three weeks after a wound that frequently sent a guy back to the States.

And here's another one. A second lieutenant named Herskella actually had a heart attack during the fighting on the southern end of Okinawa. But they weren't going to evacuate him because he hadn't been wounded. I think he's still alive, even though he's had three or four attacks since. That was the story going around anyway. He was a good officer. You sure as hell can't blame a guy for having a heart attack.

Herb: Oh, we had a lot of good officers in the 22nd, but we had some dogs also. Like everyone else, you had good ones and bad ones.

One of our good ones was Angelo Bertelli, the great football star. He has a liquor store now over in Clifton. It seems to me we had plenty of football players in the 22nd.

Mog–Mog: We had them in the 29th also. Irish George Murphy played end for Notre Dame; he was killed on Sugar Loaf, trying to rescue another Marine.

I'll tell you someone else I saw on Okinawa. Tyrone Power, he's dead now, used to be a headline movie star. He was a Marine transport pilot.

Herb: That's right. Andy Sinatra, once a president of the 6th Division association, was shot up real badly on Okinawa. And who flies him to the hospital on Guam but Tyrone Power. He talked to Andy a lot about those Hollywood beauties he knew.

Mog–Mog: Jeez, Power must have known them all.

Well, there's one thing I do want to tell you, but no names. Okay? It's something that happened at a 6th Division reunion in Boston. You know what I'm going to say, don't you, Herbie?

Herb: About the medals?

Mog–Mog: That's right. Well, we're all having a good time up there. There's this small group of us; everyone had seen a lot of combat and we've all got half a bag on, you know what I mean.

So, there's a guy there who belongs to a well-known law enforcement agency. We'll call him Lieutenant X and, by the way, he's a hell of a good guy.

Anyway, we started to talk about decorations and this guy throws in a shocker.

"I hate to tell you guys this, but after the battle of Okinawa all the officers got together and we decided who should get the medals. Believe me, the officers got first consideration. I mean, that's the name of the game. You know, Semper Fi."

Oh hell, I guess we all really knew that, but we didn't like to think about it.

Herb: I'll tell you though, I met one guy at a Marine banquet in Indiana. He had more medals than anyone I'd ever seen. I asked him how the hell he'd gotten them all.

"You know," he said, "the secret is to be near a colonel when you do anything special. It ain't what you do—Christ, half the guys in combat deserve medals—it's who sees you do it."

Anyway, he's also got five Purple Hearts. So I just smiled at him.

"Look," I said, "you're probably right, but the colonel didn't shoot you five times, did he?"

Mog–Mog: You know, you get going like this and you can go on forever. I remember being on Okinawa one night and it was raining; oh Christ, it was raining and there was mud and crap everywhere.

I was there with my buddy, Sam Lenardi, and the time dragged and dragged. Who knows what time it was. In the movies Clark Gable would look at his watch, but we didn't have a watch.

So, sometime in the night we heard a swish but nothing else.

Christ, in the morning we looked over and there's an 81 millimeter —no, it was a 90 millimeter, we had the 81s—sticking in the mud. Well, I figured there was nothing going to happen to us that day and it didn't.

But Jeez, if that thing went off, it was all over!

Herb: Oh, you can talk all night all right. I wonder, do people really know that heavy combat really means just the area near each guy? Sure the officers, some of them at least, were concerned with a bigger picture, but if they were junior officers, they were pretty much thinking about their own ass like everyone else.

Now, this doesn't mean you weren't thinking about the guy next to you—you were. The chances were that one Marine would nearly always help another one.

Mog–Mog: Yeah, time and time again I saw a Marine risk his skin to save a buddy. That's no bullshit. Maybe the guy didn't want to break his balls and he sure didn't want a hide full of lead, but when everything was on the line, you could usually count on the guy next to you, not always, but most of the time. It happened that way, that's all.

Taps At The Slop Chute

There had never been anything like the Pacific war and there can never be anything quite like it again. The massive area called the Pacific covers a staggering number of miles. The island-to-island maneuvering by both the Army and the Marine Corps was an epic that can never be repeated. Advances in technology and man's ability to wage war have made the military tactics of the mid-1940s as obsolete as the World War I Spad.

But this book is not about advanced technology or military tactics. These factors enter the story only as they relate to the men. The men were the ones who had to go ashore on the islands.

An admiral once told a Marine general that his landing craft could only go in so far—

"If we go any further, we'll lose our coverage," the general was told.

"Is that so, admiral?" replied the general. "Well, this is the only coverage my Marines have." And he fingered his dungaree blouse.

The Japanese soldier who fired at these dungaree blouses was either a fanatical nut or an extremely brave man. Take your pick, it makes no difference in the long run. When all the bombing and shelling was over, the Marines, with bayonets on the ends of their rifles, had to go in and kill just about every one of those Japanese soldiers. The Marine Corps, which had numbered 17,000 in 1939, suffered over 80,000 casualties playing their part in subduing the Japanese forces.

These are the men remembered in this book. They came from a generation that was raised in the Great Depression. If the old man was not doing well, they went into the 3 Cs (Civil Conservation Corps), but if things were good at home, they sat down to a large Sunday dinner between 1:00 and 2:00 P.M.

At night the family would enjoy a supper of sandwiches from the roast and sit around the radio and listen to Jack Benny. It was that kind of an age.

Then came Pearl Harbor. During the next three or four years, over half a million of these Americans joined an organization most of them knew very little about—the Marines.

From then on they did a job they felt had to be done. And now, four decades later, most of them will sit down, especially if you are yourself a Marine, and talk to you about it.

It is true that these men know what a job they did and they are not always modest about letting you know it. But in the long run, they really don't take themselves too seriously. After a couple of drinks one of them is sure to sing for you:

> *When this bloody war is over*
> *Oh, how happy I will be*
> *Just to be a plain civilian,*
> *No more soldiering for me.*
> *No more Dress Parade on Sunday,*
> *No more asking for a pass.*
> *You can tell the Sergeant Major,*
> *Stick the Marine Corps up his ass.*

But they'll only sing that to a Marine.

Index